W9-BSY-453

HOTEL

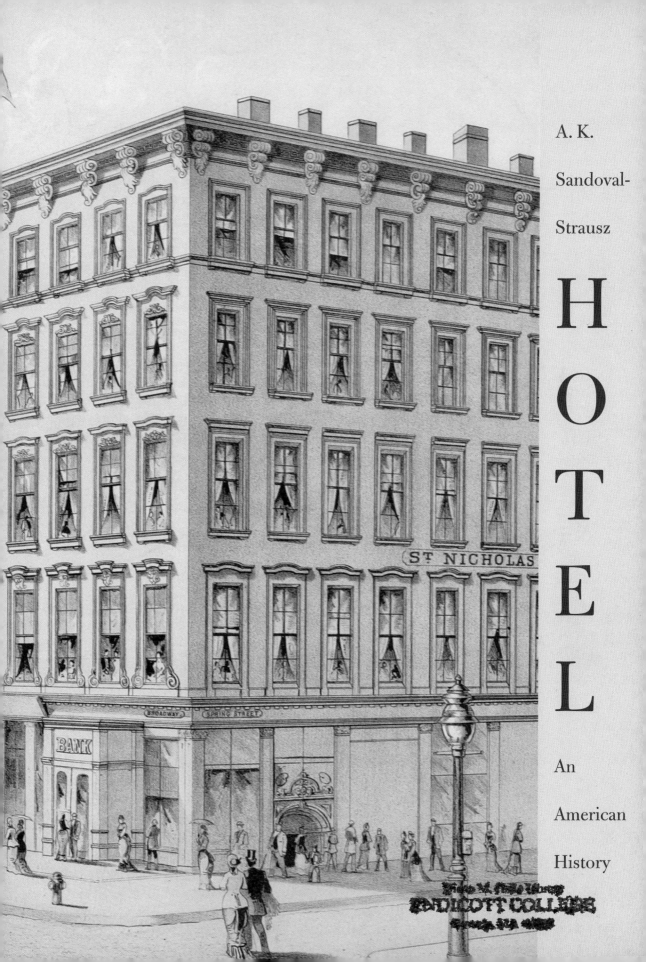

A. K.

Sandoval-

Strausz

HOTEL

An

American

History

Frontispiece: The St. Nicholas Hotel, which opened for business
in 1853 on Broadway, in the middle of New York City's leading
hotel district (Collection of the New-York Historical Society)

Parts of Chapters 1, 5, 6, 9, and 10 appeared in different form as "Why the
Hotel? Liberal Visions, Merchant Capital, Public Space, and the Creation
of an American Institution," *Business and Economic History* 28 (1999), 255–
265; "A Public House for a New Republic: The Architecture of Accommodation and the American State, 1789–1809," *Perspectives in Vernacular
Architecture* 9 (2003), 54–70; "Travelers, Strangers, and Jim Crow: Law,
Public Accommodations, and Civil Rights in America," *Law and History
Review* 23 (2005), 53–94; "Princes and Maids of the City Hotel: The Cultural Politics of Commercial Hospitality in America," *Journal of Decorative and Propaganda Arts* 25 (2005), 160–185; and "Homes for a World of
Strangers: Hospitality and the Origins of Multiple Dwellings in Urban
America," *Journal of Urban History* 33 (2007). Permission to use this
material is gratefully acknowledged.

Designed by Sonia Shannon.
Set in Monotype Bulmer type by Duke & Company, Devon, Pa.
Printed in Italy by L.E.G.O. SpA.

Library of Congress Cataloging-in-Publication Data

Sandoval-Strausz, A. K.
Hotel : an American History / A. K. Sandoval-Strausz.
    p.   cm.
Includes bibliographical references and index.
ISBN 978-0-300-10616-9 (cloth : alk. paper) 1. Hotels—United States—
History. 2. Hotels—Social aspects—United States. I. Title.
TX909.S25 2007
917.306—dc22

                    2007010239

A catalogue record for this book is available from the British Library.

The paper in this book meets the guidelines for permanence and durabil-
ity of the Committee on Production Guidelines for Book Longevity of the
Council on Library Resources.

10 9 8 7 6 5 4 3 2 1

For my parents,
Cecilia Sandoval Londoño &
Iván Károly Strausz,
who traveled a long way.

CONTENTS

Introduction

THE HOTEL IS EVERYWHERE in the modern world. Hotels line downtown streets, surround airports, anchor convention centers, house casinos (fig. 1), and shelter vacationers on tropical beaches and in mountain resorts. In the popular imagination, the word itself conjures up a series of often contradictory associations: traveler's haven and criminal hideout, wedding location and trysting ground, ritzy cocktail lounge and skid-row residence. The ready recognizability and broad familiarity of the hotel setting have made it a common icon in world culture: hotels appear regularly in media as diverse as Latin American *telenovelas,* German prose, Indian cinema, British situation comedy, Japanese novels, and American popular music. Throughout the world, the hotel represents a complex set of possibilities and tensions that mark it as an archetypal kind of space. All wayfaring cultures have created their own forms of institutionalized hospitality: the *pandocheion* of the ancient Mediterranean, the *caravanserai* of the medieval Islamic world, the German *Gasthof,* and the *posada* of Spain and Latin America, to name only a few examples. But by the age of global mass tourism in the late twentieth century, and one hundred years earlier in the Atlantic world, it was the hotel that had become the dominant form of travel accommodation.[1]

Despite the international ubiquity of the hotel, we know relatively little about its history. Perhaps because hotels are so common in today's world, their presence is taken for granted and their significance left unexamined. But the existence of the hotel as an institutional type is not self-explanatory—it needs to be accounted for, as do its distinctive architectural form and social character. The hotel as we know it today did not evolve randomly or naturally, nor did it develop as some sort of automatic response to structural needs. Rather, it was the deliberate creation of an identifiable group of people who lived in a specific place and time: the cities of the United States in the early decades of the republic.

In *Hotel: An American History* I approach the hotel as a historical artifact, one that can help us understand the people,

1 An architectural model of Antoine Predock's Atlantis Hotel, commissioned in 1995 and intended for Las Vegas. (Photo by Robert Reck)

the nation, and the world that created it. The hotel was (and is) an artifact of an epochal shift in which people were gradually dissociated from place. For more than a millennium, most people in Europe and much of the Atlantic world had been fixed in place by work, kin, custom, and political power. While the early modern period produced a number of exceptions to this rule, it was not until the eighteenth century that the rise of capitalism, the decline of feudalism, and the emergence of new notions of personal liberty combined to give birth to an age of unprecedented human mobility. This did not mean that people were completely severed from place, separated from one another, and left wandering the earth; but it certainly did mean that their relationship to geographic locations was becoming more tentative and temporary than ever before.[2]

The hotel was part of this epochal shift, but it was also a decidedly American creation. Its origins were inextricably bound up with the politics and culture of the early United States, and its development reflected persistent tensions in the nation's institutions and ideals. The hotel bore the marks not only of American beliefs about democracy, commerce, and equality but also of a crucial underlying fact of the nation's human geography:

its people were among the most mobile in the world. It is thus in some sense logical that Americans were the ones to invent an architectural and social form that became the international standard for sheltering travelers.[3]

The separation of people from place had many effects. Among the most important was the way it altered everyday life in cities and towns. Urban areas were the most frequent destinations of those on the move, and the rapid urbanization of the eighteenth, nineteenth, and twentieth centuries depended fundamentally upon people's ability to move about. The growth of cities in both size and number and the exceptional transience of urban populations meant that city dwellers increasingly found themselves surrounded by people whom they did not know. This was an unaccustomed and discomfiting condition for those used to life in small, close-knit communities, and the figure of the stranger, whether in the singular form of the unknown individual or the plural form of the anonymous crowd, became a major preoccupation. It was no coincidence that the sociologists, urbanists, psychologists, and other theorists who sought to define modernity invariably included the interrelated conditions of mobility, transience, and anonymity as essential aspects of modern life.[4]

These conditions made hotels an indispensable part of the urban fabric of every American city. Hotels facilitated human mobility by serving travelers and strangers who were away from home and needed shelter, food, drink, and other services and goods usually obtained within the household. Hotels also provided an important service to the settlements in which they were located: they helped integrate them into expanding networks of commodities, capital, and information that were vital to community prosperity in the formative decades of national and international capitalism.

But the rise of the hotel also connoted something that went beyond its basic function and indicated a change in the way people understood their world: the hotel made hospitality into an important model for other human relationships and institutions. When a city or town opened a hotel, it was demonstrating its willingness to welcome outsiders. From the perspective of the present this seems natural, but it was far from that in an age when most communities viewed strangers with suspicion and regularly ordered them to depart. Hotel construction was thus a material manifestation of cultural tolerance, a significant episode in the development of the modern idea of a pluralistic, cosmopolitan society. The hotel became a patterning device that shaped specific aspects of American life, including sociability and politics, residential architecture, and the rise and fall of racial segregation. Ultimately, the influence of the hotel derived from the fact that in a mobile, transient world of strangers, it made sense to apply the logic of hospitality not just to travelers but to everyone.

WHY THE HOTEL?

Studying hotels offers a new way to look at people's responses to modern life because the hotel was a microcosm of some of the key challenges of modernity. Hotels were points of contact between local communities and the larger society beyond—spaces that simultaneously emphasized and blurred the distinctions between insider and outsider, self and other. Because hotels were by their very nature centers of mobility, transience, and anonymity, they were places where traditional forms of community-based social control broke down. Yet at the same time, they also functioned as important community gathering places, locations where local people came together to meet, mingle, confer, and celebrate (fig. 2). Hotels thus exemplified the problems of disruption and disorder that came with any influx of strangers into communities. As focal points of the heightened mobility and transience that characterized the modern world, hotels confronted Americans with dilemmas of inclusion, exclusion, freedom, and control.[5]

These dilemmas find their most basic expression in the idea of hospitality, which serves as an essential organizing concept for this book. Hospitality involves more than just providing shelter and food to travelers; it is also a sacred responsibility, one with religious roots in the ancient world and continuing ethical relevance in the modern era. Hospitality thus partakes of a cultural significance that transcends its quotidian operation: it both expresses the values of the culture that creates it and registers changes in those values, making it a sensitive and revealing indicator of the timing and causes of historical change and the nuances of human experience. The period covered in this book was one of radical transformations in both the practice and theory of hospitality. In the mid-1790s urban entrepreneurs invented a new building type to replace the inns and taverns that had served wayfarers in North America for nearly two centuries. In 1795 Immanuel Kant, the father of the modern philosophy of international law and human rights, published *Toward Perpetual Peace,* in which he proposed that international conflict could be ended only under "conditions of universal *hospitality*" in which all people had the right not to be attacked or otherwise mistreated while traveling abroad. In Kant's view, only when a "*right to visit* . . . belong[ed] to all human beings" could "distant parts of the world . . . enter peaceably into relations with one another."[6] As we shall see, it was no mere coincidence that these Americans' construction efforts and Kant's intellectual project took shape at precisely the same time: both were expressions of a significant turning point in the history of the Atlantic world.

In the broadest sense, I address one of the basic concerns of the humanities and social sciences: understanding the operation, effects, and implications of markets and capitalism.[7] It is my belief that the development of the hotel was a revealing episode in the rise of capitalism, one that demonstrates key aspects of its functioning and influence. In writing the history of the hotel, I seek to advance one of the basic goals of social history by describing a largely unexamined means through which large-scale, long-term structural change was manifested in everyday life.[8] Historians have traditionally seen industrialization as the dominant socioeconomic influence on the development of modern America.[9] More recently, they have also discovered other mechanisms by which capitalism generated change, including the restructuring of home and family, the emergence of the middle class, and the development of consumer culture.[10] Scholars using any of these interpretive frameworks share a fundamental concern with the rise of markets and capitalism; where

2 Hotels were favored venues for elite sociability, like this 1912 white-tie Sunday dinner at the Plaza Hotel in New York. (National Museum of American History)

they differ is in what they think are the points of articulation between economic change and lived experience. One of my principal arguments in this book is that alongside other economic processes that influenced people's lives, we need to consider the human geography of capitalism: the ways in which the development of markets shaped relationships between people and places.[11]

In pursuit of these descriptive and interpretive goals, I approach space—whether architecturally, geographically, socially, or legally defined—as an essential category of analysis.[12] I seek to demonstrate how the shifting relationship between people and places not only reflected historical conditions but also generated historical change.[13] This requires special methods and interpretive strategies derived from social history, cultural landscape studies, and architecture. Scholars have for several decades recognized that accounts based on traditional written sources tend to exclude most of the population, and that any accurate description of the past or present requires a much broader range of evidence. In this book, I turn to the built environment as a major source, which means interpreting the past as much by analyzing landscapes as by reading texts.[14] This approach is particularly important to the study of urbanism because of all the features specific to cities, it is their spatial-structural character that most clearly sets them apart. Using landscape to write history presents particular challenges and opportunities. The built environment expresses values and preferences in a different way than written statements do. A building is typically not as explicit as a book or a speech, and it requires more interpretation. Landscape evidence, however, has the advantage of presumptive sincerity. It is extremely easy for people to say one thing and do another, and we expect a certain amount of dishonesty and hypocrisy. But when they construct a building—especially a large and complex one like a hotel—it is harder to argue that they didn't really mean it.

In short: talk is cheap; buildings are expensive. If we want to do scholarship "from the bottom up," we must take what people built as seriously as what they wrote down.

A WORD AND ITS CONTEXT

Defining the term *hotel* is the first task at hand. While the usage of the word in this book generally conforms to the current commonly understood meaning, parts of the argument depend on fine linguistic and typological distinctions that require more extended explanation.

The word *hotel* entered the English language in the 1760s as a borrowing of the French term *hôtel,* which referred not to a travel accommodation but rather to the residence of a nobleman, a town hall, or any other large official building. In English, the term signified a guest house of particularly high quality, though such pretensions were contested: one wag wrote of "those taverns called hotels, where, under a false idea of furnishing better accommodation than is to be met with at inns, they contrive to pick the pockets of their guests." The term gained currency quickly, and within a decade of its introduction, the London playwright Thomas Vaughan could use *The Hotel* as the title for his 1776 comedy (which was set in an establishment containing "good beds, handsome furniture, a man-cook, and civil waiters; lodging fit for an Ambassador at least") and be confident that his audience would be familiar with such a place.[15]

By the time of Vaughan's play, the word had crossed the Atlantic and was in use in North America. On the eve of Independence, a twenty-year-old future United States senator named Rufus King wrote to his brother-in-law that the bread makers of Boston were "constantly employed in baking for their hotels." Several years later, the word was used in a congressional resolution prohibiting the use of federal funds to build accommodations for politicians in the new capital at Washington. American usage was similar to that in England, though it also served as an alternative to more formal nomenclature: broadsides announcing events at a city's leading public house often employed the word, as in a 1792 posting for a "meeting of a respectable number of freeholders from various parts of the state, at Corre's Hotel" in New York City. This appears to have been a colloquial usage, since this and other establishments referred to as hotels in newspapers were listed in city directories and other formal documents as "taverns" or "inns."[16]

In early usage, then, the word *hotel* attached to a function rather than a particular building type. The first structures to which the word was applied in English were the portico houses of the Covent Garden district in London. These houses had originally been built in the 1630s and were used by members of the House of Lords for their urban residences. The parliamentarians were followed after 1650 by shopkeepers, artists, and writers, whose presence led to the opening of the Theatre Royal in 1663 and the official establishment of a produce and flower market in 1670. These developments gradually convinced local aristocrats that their old neighborhood was in decline, and they began to decamp for more fashionable parts of the city. The portico houses thus fell out of use as private residences between 1730 and 1760. They were soon adapted to new purposes, however. Thanks to its theaters, Covent Garden had become popular as an entertainment district; it was also home to a large community of immigrants from France. The neighborhood thus provided an ample visiting clientele for the keepers of inns, coffeehouses, and similar institutions, and as the titled elite moved out of their portico houses, publicans moved in and reopened them as guest accommodations. It may have been merely coincidental that French émigrés would have referred to these converted noblemen's residences using their word *hôtel*.[17]

It was only at the end of the eighteenth century and over the course of the nineteenth that *hotel* became a specific architectural category. The connection of the word with a building type occurred in the same years in both England and the United States. Earlier in the century, the thriving British economy had generated increasing prosperity and fueled the rapid growth of provincial spa towns like Bath and Tunbridge Wells. These had originally been intended as resorts for an urban aristocracy eager to separate itself from untitled yet wealthy merchants. Before long, however, members of the rising commercial class also sought entrée to venues where they could aspire to higher social status through displays of their smartly attired bodies and carefully cultivated manners. It was here, beginning around 1790, that Englishmen first constructed architecturally distinct hotels. These towns, like other settlements across Britain, had long been served by alehouses and inns, relatively small establishments built on the same scale as dwellings. Hotels were much grander structures that included not only bedchambers and dining areas but also ballrooms, dancing halls, and assembly rooms. The first purpose-built English hotels, then, were intended not to facilitate mobility but to foster exclusivity; indeed, a dedicatory plaque on one of the first specified that it was intended mainly for the use of the king and the nobility. The extent to which these establishments can be considered predecessors of American hotels is thus somewhat limited.[18]

There were also related building forms existing outside the English-speaking world and therefore not encompassed by the word *hotel*. The design context for the American hotel is to be found primarily in England, but travel accommodations underwent significant changes throughout the North Atlantic region toward the end of the eighteenth century. In France an establishment at Calais accommodated large numbers of travelers in the 1780s, though its precise size and social character remain unclear. Likewise, German sources suggest that Frankfurt, a politically important city that was also home to a semiannual fair, boasted establishments with more than one hundred beds by about 1800. If these accounts are reliable and representative, they may indicate that the rise of the hotel was part of a more generalized transformation of travel accommodations, and that there were alternate

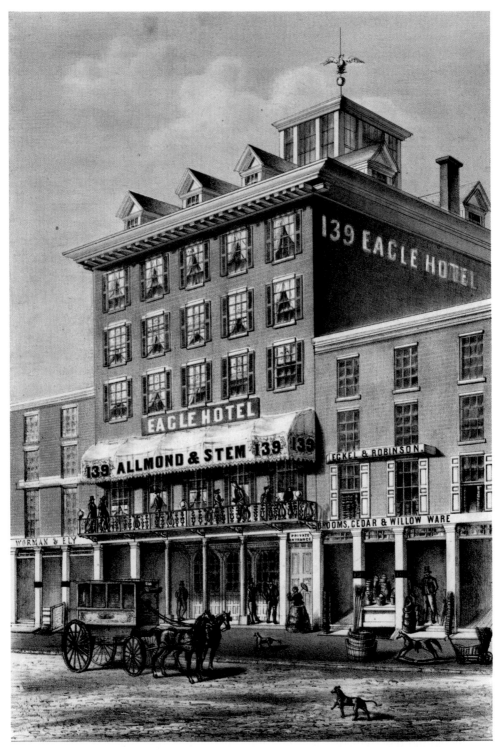

3   Hotels took a variety of forms, and while large and luxurious establishments attracted the most attention, smaller hostelries like this one in Philadelphia in the 1850s were far more representative of the type. (The Library Company of Philadelphia)

building types that either came to be known by the term *hotel* in their own languages or lost out to the Anglo-American form.[19]

What is certain, however, is that by the middle of the nineteenth century, travelers from Europe, the United States, and Latin America were all in agreement not only that American hotels were fundamentally different from similar institutions elsewhere in the world, but also that they were setting the standard for hotels everywhere. As we shall see, some observers focused on the quantitative distinctiveness of American hotels, noting their size and number; others concentrated on more qualitative factors, citing a different mode of service and a public culture that was absent from similar establishments elsewhere. These and other accounts corroborate American preeminence in hotel construction and management and indicate that sustained hotel building came to the rest of the world only later—a sequence evidenced by the international adoption of the word *hotel.*

I will focus on the hotel as it developed in the United States (fig. 3), in terms both of how it differed from the establishments it replaced and of how it contrasted with similar ones abroad. While I do not embrace American exceptionalism, I do agree with historical observers that the hotel as it was invented and developed in the United States was a unique institution. Complex cultural artifacts like hotels are more than just building types that exist in the physical world—they are also expressions of human relationships, exemplars of ideologies, and scenes of social conflict. I argue that the hotel was the physical manifestation of a distinctly American vision of mobility, civil society, democracy, and, ultimately, space—a vision which, if the subsequent propagation of hotels in virtually every nation and culture on earth is any indication, has shown itself to be quite compelling.

Part One Buildings and Systems

IN EARLY AMERICA, public authority was deeply invested in policing people's comings and goings. Colonial communities generally discouraged visits from strangers and kept a close watch on those who made their way into town. Certain approved travelers, such as circuit-riding judges and other officials, were of course welcomed, but most others, including itinerant peddlers and preachers, fortune-tellers, and especially people without work, were viewed with suspicion. Towns often passed laws according to which all outsiders were immediately scrutinized upon arrival; those who might accommodate them were in turn charged with particular duties. Innkeepers were assigned the role of both guardian and sentry: they not only were responsible for sheltering visitors and their possessions but were also expected to notify authorities of the arrival of any and all outsiders; if they failed to do so, they could incur fines or other penalties. Related measures obliged visitors to present themselves before magistrates and secure permission to remain.[1]

There were two primary reasons for this close surveillance of travelers. The first and more general was that outsiders might disturb the stability and order that were so much valued in colonial America and that most people consciously or subconsciously associated with fixed residence. In early New England, for example, many Puritans felt anxious about the threat posed to their shared religious project. In 1654 Edward Johnson, an early settler and the first historian of the region, exhorted his fellow colonists: "Let not any Merchants, Innkeepers, Taverners and men of Trade in hope of gaine, fling open the gates so wide, as that by letting in all sorts you mar the work of Christ intended." Notably, this pronouncement was directed at merchants and keepers of public houses, two easily identifiable groups whose livelihood depended upon making journeys and providing hospitality to outsiders. Such uneasiness about the destabilizing effects of mobility was not limited to New England. While that region was the most wary of newcomers, colonial laws in New York, Delaware, and North Carolina also included provisions aimed at "the prevention and discouraging of Vagabonds" and "the Restraint of Vagrants."[2]

Existing alongside this generalized cultural insularity were other, more specific imperatives. Chief among these was a desire on the part of communities to avoid having to support outsiders. The great majority of European Americans lived in small farming villages with strong traditions of communal self-government, including the widespread practice of providing for those who could not do so for themselves, whether due to illness, injury, or other causes. Under such circumstances, these communities guarded their boundaries and policed their environs in order to prevent outsiders from becoming public charges. In legislation that grew increasingly harsh and restrictive with the passage of time, colonies took such measures as obliging ship captains to hand over lists of their passengers and to return those without crafts or personal wealth to the ports where they had embarked. Similar laws specified that people who managed to enter a community but were later found to be unable to support themselves could be transported back to their towns of origin; if they defied this law by coming back, they could be whipped. Later enactments went so far as to dispense with specific requirements, giving town magistrates plenary authority to order anyone to leave. That such laws were indeed enforced is demonstrated by the diary of Robert Love, who in 1765 was charged by the selectmen of Boston with the responsibility of finding unauthorized visitors and ordering them to depart; over the following nineteen months, he kept a record of the hundreds of people he commanded "in his magisty's name" to depart the city. Laws of this kind sometimes went beyond banishment to imprisonment, attempting to dissuade needy visitors by threatening them with confinement and hard labor at a workhouse or almshouse. To the extent that public houses extended any sort of welcome, then, they did so under the supervision of local authorities and in a generalized atmosphere of antipathy toward travelers and strangers.[3]

Suspicion toward outsiders and restrictions on movement had come under pressure from economic development starting in the mid-seventeenth century, and travel—for commercial, administrative, and religious reasons, among others—was on the rise throughout the late colonial period. It was not until after the Revolution that things truly began to change; but when they did, it happened quickly. The early national period saw the emergence of new political and economic beliefs and practices that carried with them a new understanding of the nation's geography, and in time, older restrictions on travel fell into disuse. But even before this process took hold, the clearest evidence of a new understanding of space in America was a new architectural form that multiplied across the national landscape.[4]

One *A Public House for a New Republic*

Inventing the American Hotel, 1789–1815

GEORGE WASHINGTON began his journey on an overcast October morning in 1789. The president and a small retinue of officials and servants mounted their horses at nine o'clock and rode northward out of the national capital at New York City. It was slow going. "The Road for the greater part, indeed the whole way," Washington wrote in his diary, "was very rough and Stoney," and a steady morning rain and "frequent light Showers" that lasted through the afternoon left the riders wet in their saddles. Yet on the whole the transplanted Virginian was pleased with what he saw that day. He noted that the "Land [was] strong, well covered with grass and a luxurient Crop of Indian Corn intermixed with Pompions [pumpkins]," and farmers informed him that "their Crops of Wheat and Rye have been abundant." The party also passed "four droves of Beef Cattle" and "a flock of Sheep" being driven south to the city markets. Washington observed that the local livestock "seemed to be of a good quality," but hedged somewhat on the hogs, which he deemed "large but rather long legged." As daylight began to fade, the president and his entourage stopped for the night at the Square House Inn in the town of Rye, New York, thirty-two miles from where they had set out.[1]

Thus began Washington's presidential tours of 1789–1791, the most important travels in American political history. Shortly after taking office, the president had begun planning an official journey through the thirteen United States so that he could "acquire knowledge of the face of the Country the growth and Agriculture there and of the temper and disposition of the Inhabitants towards the new government." While his interest in geography and agriculture were doubtless sincere, the primary purpose of the tours was political. Washington had assumed the presidency of a nation that had spent almost its entire thirteen-year existence on the brink of collapse. The external threat posed by the British Army was laid to rest by the Treaty of Paris in 1783, only to be replaced by internal factionalism and instability under the feeble Articles of Confederation. The Constitutional Convention of 1787 barely managed to agree on a new governing framework, and the Constitution itself met with considerable opposition and was ratified by unexpectedly narrow margins. It was with good reason that many contemporary observers expected the infant republic to die in its cradle.[2]

Washington envisioned a grand national tour on which he would make personal visits to cities and towns, using his extraordinary popularity to solidify public support for the fragile new federal government. There was no doubt about the president's standing among the citizenry: he had led the Continental Army to victory against the world's greatest military power, and his resultant status as America's first national hero had allowed him to win every single electoral vote in the election of 1788, a feat never to be equaled. Still, Washington had concerns about the proper execution of the tours. He understood that their success—and perhaps the fate of the nation—depended heavily upon his performance as a unifying national icon; and his keen political instincts and preoccupation with personal comportment told him that his every action would be freighted with symbolic significance.[3]

It was for this reason that Washington decided to refuse private hospitality and stay only at public houses. When it had become known that the president would be making a national tour, he had begun to receive letters from local officials, former comrades, family members, and other acquaintances inviting him to stay at their homes when he made his appearance in their communities. Washington was grateful for the generosity of his aspiring hosts, but he believed that accepting such offers risked the appearance of favoritism. The act of showing special consideration by lodging with private individuals, even members of his own family, would set a bad example that might undermine Washington's public image as a man above politics and compromise the proper impartiality of the presidency. He therefore declined such invitations and instead resolved to put up at the same inns and taverns where other travelers sought shelter.[4]

Washington held to his principles, but at the cost of considerable personal discomfort. Over the course of more than two thousand miles of travel that took him from the northernmost state of New Hampshire to Georgia in the far South, he made regular notations in his diary regarding the quality of America's public houses. While the president was sometimes pleased with the inns and taverns at which he stayed, during the last third of his northern tour he became increasingly dissatisfied with them, noting that several were "indifferent" and observing on other occasions that the previous night's tavern was "not a good house," though he was gracious enough to recognize when "the People of it were disposed to do all they cou'd to accommodate me." Travel conditions on Washington's southern tour of 1791 were even less satisfactory. In addition to the usual uneven quality of public houses, there were many instances in which none was available at all. Traveling in North Carolina, the president complained that though he wished to get out of the rain, "the only Inn short of Hallifax having . . . no Rooms or beds which appeared tolerable, & everything else having a dirty appearance, I was compelled to keep on." Farther into the journey, Washington grumbled that "the accomadations on the whole Road [to Savannah] we found extremely indifferent—the houses being small and badly provided either for man or horse."[5]

Uncomfortable lodgings notwithstanding, Washington's presidential tours were a tremendous success. They increased the prestige of the presidency, fostered popular faith in the federal government, and helped bind the states into a nation by cultivating a collective sense of identity.[6]

The tours may also have led to the creation of the American hotel.

When President Washington first took office in 1789, the finest public house in the United States was a three-story building about fifty feet long on a side, containing perhaps twenty rooms, and valued at roughly fifteen thousand dollars. Two decades later, in 1809, the nation's leading public accommodation occupied an enormous seven-story edifice which covered nearly an acre of land, comprised more than two hundred rooms, and cost more than half a million dollars. But the invention of the hotel was more than just a milestone in the history of public houses. It also reflected important changes in the way Americans defined their communities, engaged in politics, organized their economic activities, and socialized with one another. The transformation of public houses not only reveals the origins of one of the most familiar building types in the modern world, it also shows how the ideals of the Revolution and the conflicts of the early republic were manifested on the American landscape.[7]

PUBLIC HOUSES IN EARLY AMERICA

Public house was the formal name for an establishment that sold alcoholic drinks and rented lodgings to travelers. Public houses were more commonly called taverns, inns, and sometimes ordinaries, terms that were used interchangeably: Washington, for example, wrote of "the Tavern of a Mrs. Haviland at Rye; who keeps a very neat and decent Inn."

What made a public house public was its having been licensed by state or local officials. A tavern license involved a fairly simple quid pro quo: the innkeeper was given the privilege of entering the highly profitable business of retailing alcoholic drinks in exchange for a promise to offer overnight accommodations to the public. Because strong drink posed a potential threat to public order, licenses were granted only to people who could be relied upon to keep an orderly premises where drunkenness, gambling, and other forms of vice would be prohibited. Selling alcohol without a license was a serious crime, and an unlicensed tavern could be closed down and its keeper subject to fines or imprisonment. In this way, colonial governments killed three birds with one stone: they established control over the sale and consumption of alcohol, provided wayfarers with shelter, and established a source of revenue in the form of licensing fees. Virtually every community in British North America was home to one or more public houses, thousands of which served drinkers and travelers in the colonies.[8]

Eighteenth-century Americans expected little of their public houses architecturally. George Washington suggested as much by the decidedly backhanded compliment he paid a Connecticut establishment, which he described as having "a good external appearance (for a Tavern)." The great majority of taverns in British North America were dwelling houses or other structures that had been constructed for a different function but were subsequently adapted to a new use. Because they were not purpose built, early American public houses did not share any distinctive architectural features or have an identifiable form. Their appearance instead followed from the vernacular building styles common to the region in which they were located (figs. 1.1, 1.2). In order to identify public houses that were visually indistinguishable from private homes or shops, most publicans put up hanging tavern signs emblazoned with memorable names and symbols. In some cases, even these visual cues failed to compensate for the tavern's architectural anonymity, leaving travelers unable to find shelter without the assistance of local residents.[9]

The humble character of eighteenth-century public houses was also discernible in their valuations: most taverns were assessed at between several hundred and a few thousand dollars. A few socially eminent inns averaged well under ten thousand dollars, and even purpose-built establishments in the first rank of prestige and elegance never exceeded fifteen thousand. In cost, as in external appearance, taverns rarely stood out.[10]

The internal arrangement of American taverns was correspondingly unprepossessing. A 1973 archaeological study commissioned by the Colonial Williamsburg Foundation determined that taverns in eighteenth-century Virginia generally comprised only six to ten rooms, a size that recent studies of public houses in Massachusetts and Philadelphia suggest was close to the norm in the period. All of a tavern's functional spaces—its kitchen, bar, public rooms, bedchambers, and the quarters of the innkeeper's family—thus had to be crowded into a small number of available rooms. As a result, a tavern's interior spaces tended to be unspecialized: drinks might be served from an enclosed cage in a front room where food was also prepared (fig. 1.3), and the space around the hearth could double as a sleeping area. Because even the main room of a tavern could be relatively small, it

1.1   Early American inns and taverns followed the vernacular architectural styles of their regions and were difficult to distinguish from dwellings. Like most other public houses, the Spread Eagle Tavern in Strafford, Pennsylvania, was marked with a distinctive hanging sign. (The Library Company of Philadelphia)

could easily become overcrowded. Patrons were consequently accustomed to drinking and talking cheek by jowl with other customers.[11]

The close quarters of the tavern also dictated particular sleeping arrangements. The small number of rooms in taverns made it impossible for guests to have their own bedchambers. Eighteenth-century travelogues regularly mentioned shared rooms, and colonial-era inventories recorded the presence of multiple bedsteads in individual chambers. When public houses were crowded, guests were often squeezed into even closer contact with one another: the sharing of beds was not uncommon. While most travelers simply accepted this custom as a necessity, it was resented by respectable wayfarers, who complained constantly about being forced into such close encounters with the unclean bodies and rude manners of tradesmen and laborers. One traveler complained that "after you have been some time in bed, a stranger of any condition (for there is little distinction), comes into the room, pulls off his clothes, and places himself, without ceremony, between your sheets." (This practice persisted for decades in some public houses: in *Moby-Dick*, Ishmael and Queequeg share a bed at the Spouter-Inn.)[12] Another confided to his diary that because other tavern patrons were drunk and staggering, and "kept up

GREEN DRAGON TAVERN

When we met to Plan the Consignment of few Shiploads of Tea. Dec 16 1773

John Johnson Water Street Boston Mass 1773

1.2   On well-traveled roads near cities, colonial-era public houses were often of more substantial construction. The Green Dragon Tavern outside Boston was built of brick and resembled a large urban residence but for the sign over the front door. (American Antiquarian Society)

the Roar-Rororum till morning," he had "watched carefully all night, to keep them from falling over and spewing upon me."

These were by no means the only criticisms leveled at American public houses. The nation's inns and taverns elicited torrents of invective from diarists and travel writers. The most common complaints involved tavern beds, which were described as dirty, uncomfortable, and insect ridden. An Englishman traveling through the United States in 1794 griped regularly about such infestations but apparently became so accustomed to them that even at an establishment which he described as "a good inn," he found that "at bed time, I was sadly tormented with bugs." Indeed, such complaints were so common that by the turn of the century they had become something of a cliché in travel writing. One diarist notified readers of his 1798 travelogue that he would dispense with such material: "I never complain of my bed," he advised, "nor fill the imagination of the reader with mosquitoes, fleas, bugs, and other nocturnal pests." Other travelers were less forbearing. An American army officer arriving at a Massachusetts tavern in 1789 was pushed beyond the limits of his patience by the "wretched bed" that awaited him. "Why," he ranted, "cannot the people of this country treat themselves at least as well as they do their brutes, & live a little more like rational beings?"[13]

1.3 John Lewis Krimmel's painting of a tavern interior shows the small size of the barroom and displays a common feature of early public houses: a built-in cage from which the tavernkeeper dispensed drinks to patrons. (Toledo Museum of Art)

Other complaints about taverns centered on various aspects of their service, such as food quality and expense. At a time and place in which most food was locally produced, innkeepers' offerings could be limited. One wayfarer who had been served only bacon or chicken at every meal joked, "If I still continue in this way [I] shall be grown over with Bristles or Feathers." Another, echoing a frequent complaint about cleanliness, observed of his stew that "everything was so nasty that One might have picked the Dirt off." Also galling to many travelers were publicans' high prices. One man on a journey from Charleston to Philadelphia found that even at "by far the worst House we visited . . . in the morning our greasy landlord . . . charged us an enormous Price for the worst of Accommodations."[14]

This is not to say that all early American public houses were of low quality. The colonies were also home to a few taverns whose keepers aspired to a higher level of refinement. In a few cases, innkeepers plied their trade in the converted mansions of the colonial elite. The most famous of these was Fraunces Tavern in New York City, which had been the residence of the merchant and politician Stephen De Lancey before Samuel Fraunces reopened it as a public accommodation. Establishments like Fraunces Tavern and the Raleigh Tavern in Williamsburg distinguished themselves by having more meeting rooms and offering some private quarters, but even the best of these had only a few public rooms and contained no more than fifteen or so guest chambers. A few purpose-built public houses appeared around 1770, when merchants in the largest cities financed a few more substantial establishments typified by Philadelphia's City Tavern (fig. 1.4). None of these, however, departed significantly from the basic architectural continuity of the American tavern. Publicans had clearly come to recognize the appeal of more elegant interiors, but the disruptions of the Revolutionary War and the hard times that followed limited the possibilities of the American public house for nearly a decade after the withdrawal of British forces.[15]

THE FIRST HOTELS

In the first decade of the republic, Americans began to design and build a new generation of public houses. Hotels were very different from the public accommodations that had been in use since the beginnings of European settlement nearly two centuries before. Their size alone demonstrated that they were intended as dramatic gestures on the landscape in the same way that a mile-high skyscraper or million-seat stadium would be today. But the hotel's revolutionary character went far beyond size because hotels were also functionally and symbolically distinct from inns and taverns. The hotel was itself a project—a deliberate effort by a small commercial elite to shape the nation's future by exerting control over architectural and geographic space.

The first American hotel was the brainchild of Samuel Blodget, Jr., a merchant and financier who devoted tireless effort and his entire fortune to the project. Blodget was born in 1757 into a family of successful New England entrepreneurs. He served as an officer in the New Hampshire militia during the Revolutionary War before entering the mercantile trade. Blodget was a pioneer in the nation's early insurance industry and eventually founded the Insurance Company of North America, the nation's first fully capitalized underwriter. Two extended trips to Europe in 1784 and 1790 inspired him to study architecture, and he later conferred with Thomas Jefferson over the building plans for the Capitol and designed the first headquarters of the Bank of the United States. When the decision was made to move the national capital from Philadelphia to the new Federal City at Washington, Blodget saw an opportunity to combine his work experience with his artistic pursuits. Taking advantage of a wartime acquaintance with George Washington (who described him as "a projecting Genius"), Blodget lobbied to have himself appointed as supervisor of buildings and improvements in the capital, and was named to the post in early 1793.[16]

With the presidential residence and the houses of Congress already under construction, Blodget decided that the next highest priority was to provide the Federal City with a worthy public house. It soon became clear, however, that the nation's budget could not support another major project, and Blodget was compelled to find an alternate means of funding the undertaking. Drawing upon his considerable experience in raising capital

1.4 Philadelphia's City Tavern (1772) was widely considered the finest in the colonies. It was a purpose-built structure but was modeled on the residence of one of its subscribers rather than representing any identifiable public-house architecture. (The Library Company of Philadelphia)

for other kinds of ventures, he resolved to finance the building with a national lottery. Blodget quickly obtained the necessary legal authorization from the city commissioners and immediately set about publicizing the lottery with advertisements placed in various mercantile newspapers across the nation. The notices announced "A LOTTERY FOR THE IMPROVEMENT OF THE FEDERAL CITY" and set forth the rules of the game: fifty thousand chances would be sold for seven dollars each; the grand prize would be a "Superb Hotel, with baths, out houses, &c. &c. to cost 50,000 Dollars." (The remaining monies were to be paid out for the other prizes.) The drawing was set for that September, at which time, it was promised, "The keys of the Hotel will be delivered to the fortunate possessor of the ticket drawn against its number." The advertisement also announced a competition for the best architectural plan for the hotel, with the winner to be awarded one hundred dollars and "preference . . . for a Contract, provided he be duly qualified to compleat his plan." With a nationwide network of ticket agents sending in receipts from sales, Blodget began to hire stonemasons, carpenters, and other craftsmen to build his dream.[17]

The cornerstone of the Union Public Hotel (fig. 1.5) was laid on the Fourth of July of 1793 in a public ceremony that reportedly drew fifteen hundred onlookers to the largely unbuilt Federal City. A journalist who excitedly wrote that the new hotel would "form the most magnificent building in America, perhaps in any other country" had clearly allowed

1.5 The Union Public Hotel in Washington, D.C., was many times larger than any inn or tavern that had ever been built in North America. (The Historical Society of Washington, D.C.)

his enthusiasm to get the better of him, but the structure was indeed impressive. The plans, which had been drafted by James Hoban, the Irish architect who had also designed the White House, called for an edifice constructed of brick and stone in a Georgian style that conveyed both elegance and establishmentarian respectability. The hotel, which was ornamented with classical columns and a pediment, measured 120 feet wide by 60 feet deep, its pitched roof rising to a height of about 70 feet. The hotel's internal arrangement went far beyond that of any public house in the nation. The main floor consisted of several public meeting rooms, the largest of which was a quite substantial 57 by 37 feet. Its upper stories contained dozens of bedchambers, and the basement added forty more rooms. The Union Public Hotel would have been an impressive sight in any American city at that time; it was all the more so in a still-developing community like Washington, where it was the largest privately owned building and was rivaled only by two structures of national importance—the White House and the Capitol.[18]

Practically from its inception, however, the hotel was beset with financial difficulties. The Washington city commissioners had allowed the lottery to begin only on the condition that Blodget exempt them from any liability, and he had personally indemnified the venture by putting up as collateral all the real estate he owned in the city. Meanwhile, construction was running behind schedule, and the funds raised from the lottery were proving insufficient to complete the hotel. When in the fall of 1793 the holder of the winning ticket came forward to claim his prize, he was disappointed to find it unfinished. News of the debacle soon reached the city commissioners, whose inquiries revealed that Blodget had been engaged in land speculation in and around the Federal City, raising questions about the propriety of his conduct. President Washington concluded that Blodget was not at all the kind of person he had wanted as building supervisor, and the city commissioners promptly fired him. Blodget's troubles were by no means at an end, however. The hotel project moved toward completion so slowly that the lottery winner sued Blodget for the extant parts of the hotel and enough money to have it finished. The court ruled in favor of the plaintiff, and when Blodget's forfeited land sold for too little to pay for the remaining construction, the father of the first American hotel found himself in debtors' prison.[19]

While the Union Public Hotel project ended badly for Blodget, the building itself turned out to be of considerable importance in the early days of the United States government. Because the structure was not ready for the removal of the federal government to Washington in 1800, a number of private boardinghouses opened to accommodate members of Congress and other federal officials. While the hotel's basic function had been rendered unnecessary, the federal government nonetheless found the funds to purchase it and renovate it for use as the first headquarters of the Postal Service and the Patent Office. It was soon to fulfill an even greater purpose, however. During the War of 1812, British forces sacked Washington and set fire to the Capitol, rendering it unusable. When the invaders were finally driven from the city, the Madison administration decided that the hotel's public rooms offered the best available facilities for the accommodation of Congress, which held session there for fourteen months in 1814–1815.[20]

The Union Public Hotel failed financially, but the structure also had a hopeful legacy. Even before it was finished, the hotel inspired a host of local imitators who, though lacking the funds needed to build on a comparable scale, nonetheless provided Washington with a number of well-appointed public accommodations. More important was the Union Public's influence as a bold new departure in American public architecture. As the exemplar of new possibilities, the hotel soon made its influence felt.[21]

Early in the spring of 1793, soon after the announcement of Blodget's hotel lottery, ten of New York City's leading entrepreneurs formed a committee to purchase the City Tavern, the finest and most prestigious public house in the city; and having paid the owner a consideration of six thousand pounds, they promptly demolished it.[22]

At the time, this must have seemed like an odd thing to do. The City Tavern was one of the most prominent institutions in the city, the place where New Yorkers welcomed their heroes: George Washington had stayed there the night before his inauguration, and the marquis de Lafayette, the French general whose cornering of British forces at Yorktown had secured the triumph of the American Revolution, had been fêted there. It was also the favorite public house of the very men who had destroyed it. The members of the committee came from a wealthy, well-organized merchant class. All were involved in transatlantic trade, most were members of the Chamber of Commerce, half were scions of the city's leading mercantile clans, four were directors of the Bank of the United States, and several sat on the boards of other banks and insurance companies. Each of the ten had surely visited the City Tavern on numerous occasions to organize companies, negotiate contracts, settle accounts, or simply drink and talk.[23]

Their motives became clear that autumn, when the New York Tontine Hotel and Assembly Rooms Association, as the committee became known, announced a prize of twenty guineas for the best design for a hotel to be built on the site of the old tavern. Construction began in early 1794. The City Hotel (fig. 1.6) was a brick structure fronting 80 feet on Broadway and extending 120 feet back toward Temple Street to the west. The hotel's architect applied the modish Federal building style, marked by stone embellishments above and between the windows and by roof dormers. The interior of the City Hotel was designed to incorporate many different functions. Its exceptionally tall main and second stories were to house a ballroom, public parlors, bar, stores, offices, and a circulating library that was the largest in the United States at the time. The hotel also offered numerous private bedchambers, with most of the building's 137 rooms devoted to lodgings for overnight guests. Like its counterpart in Washington, the City Hotel surpassed practically all the other buildings in New York. It stood taller than all but the spires of the metropolis's largest churches, and its cost of more than one hundred thousand dollars meant that the only building in the city that was more expensive was the newly built headquarters of the New York Stock Exchange on Wall Street.[24]

From the day it opened its doors and for nearly forty years thereafter, the City Hotel was the grandest and most important public house in New York City. It continued to serve as a business meeting place for Gotham's power elite, who went so far as to relocate the New York Customs House to the hotel the year after it opened. The City Hotel's ballrooms and parlors were sought-after venues for private cotillions, concerts, and at least one finishing school, and the tony clientele attracted small entrepreneurs, who opened pleasure gardens and ice cream shops nearby. The hotel became an important political space, hosting rallies, party caucuses, and similar meetings; it was also used in a nonpartisan civic capacity to welcome public figures, from a 1797 reception for recently elected President John Adams to a party given in honor of Andrew Jackson in 1817 to a grand ball for the returning General Lafayette in 1824. Indeed, the City Hotel's prestige was so enduring that as late as 1835 it was the first establishment mentioned in a popular song about New York hotels. Its success proved that despite the debacle of the Union Public, a hotel could succeed given the right location and financial support.[25]

The influence of the Union Public Hotel and the City Hotel was not limited to the cities in which they were built. Their combined example prompted people elsewhere in the United States to try to reinvent public houses in their own communities. While the hotel projects of the second half of the 1790s did not result in actual buildings, the attempts reflected a continuity of method and purpose that bound early hotels together as an architectural cohort. Moreover, they prefigured successful hotel construction in the decade that followed.

1.6 The City Hotel (1794), located on lower Broadway in Manhattan, was the nation's first functioning hotel. (Collection of the author)

The first of these hotel projects was the work of a consortium of merchants in Newport, Rhode Island. Newport was the seventh-largest city in the United States, a position it had attained by aggressively pursuing trade with England, France, Russia, and China. But the Revolution was not kind to the seaport. During the war, the British Navy disrupted its commerce, and afterward it lost its status as a favored imperial seaport. To make matters worse, a series of storms had left the city's waterfront a shambles. In January 1795 a group of thirty-six Newport merchants applied to the state legislature for permission to conduct a lottery. (They certainly knew of the Union Public Hotel lottery, since their local mercantile newspaper had carried Blodget's advertisements and subsequent reports of the prize drawing.) The petitioners made up Newport's commercial elite, counting among them the state's leading maritime entrepreneurs, its most senior judge, the founder of the Bank of Rhode Island, and the son of a signer of the Declaration of Independence. The merchants presently received an act of incorporation to conduct a lottery "for rebuilding the Wharf in *Newport,* commonly called the Long-Wharf, and for building a Hotel in the said Town." The act specified that the proceeds were not to exceed twenty-five thousand dollars, which meant that the face value of the prizes would total a quarter of a million dollars, a sum ten times larger than that of most lotteries conducted at that time. Beginning that spring, the merchants advertised the lottery in publicly posted broadsides and in Newport's leading commercial newspaper; after assorted delays, they held the drawing and distributed the prizes the following May. The hotel, however, apparently went unbuilt.[26]

The fourth and fifth hotel projects were proposed by the two most important architects in the early American republic. Charles Bulfinch, the first professional architect born in the United States, drew the plans for numerous homes, churches, hospitals, university buildings, and state capitols, and was later appointed by President Monroe to redesign the Capitol building in Washington. Bulfinch's career was made possible by his family's wealth and transatlantic connections. His grandfather Charles Apthorp, who in the 1750s was reputed to be the wealthiest man in Boston, had a remarkable private library which afforded the young Bulfinch access to the leading works on European architecture, from Vitruvius and Palladio to their English interpreters Isaac Ware and William Kent. Apthorp also arranged a tour of England, France, and Italy that allowed his grandson a firsthand look at the finest public architecture in Europe. Upon his return in 1787, Bulfinch decided on a career in architecture.[27]

In 1796 Bulfinch sought backers for a hotel project. The notice that appeared in the *Columbian Centinel*—Boston's leading mercantile newspaper, the same one that three years earlier had run advertisements for the Union Public Hotel lottery—read simply: "A subscription is filling for building a large and elegant Public HOTEL, for the accommodation of strangers, from a plan lately presented by CHARLES BULFINCH, Esq. Its cost is estimated at £21,000 divided into 200 shares." Bulfinch never was able to attract investors, probably because his previous project, the architecturally superb but financially disastrous Tontine Crescent townhouses, had very publicly bankrupted him and inflicted heavy losses on many of his investors. The advertisement is, in fact, the sole remnant of the planned hotel; yet its brevity belies its usefulness as a testament to Bulfinch's vision for a hotel for Boston. The key item is the estimated cost of the structure. The twenty-one thousand pounds (about seventy thousand dollars) that Bulfinch budgeted for the hotel was far more than had ever been spent for a public house in the city. Moreover, the cost of the planned hotel was far more than that for Bulfinch's next project: the Massachusetts State House, for which the state legislature had initially allocated only eight thousand pounds. Bulfinch's vision of a hotel for the city of Boston, much like Blodget's for Washington, dictated that it would be one of the most magnificent buildings in the city.[28]

Benjamin Henry Latrobe, the man who twenty years later would design the new United States Capitol, started his career in American public architecture with a hotel project. Born in the north of England, Latrobe was sent abroad to be educated in 1776 at age twelve, and he spent the next eight years in Prussia, France, and Italy. Convinced that he had a vocation in architecture, Latrobe returned to England to commence his studies, and by 1789 he had become chief draftsman at a London design office. Ever on the move, he emigrated to the United States in 1796. Latrobe's genteel upbringing allowed him to become friendly with the most prominent families in Virginia, and he spent twenty months in their employ, first as an engineer on swamp-drainage and canal projects and then as a designer of private homes.[29]

In late 1797, however, Latrobe turned his energies toward designing a grand public building for Richmond, the eleventh-largest city in the United States. He drafted a full set of architectural plans for an integrated hotel and theater complex, with the hotel's bedchambers, parlors, and assembly rooms making up two sections on either side of a central performance space. The exterior drawings show a three-story structure whose largely undivided mass was to be decorated with classical detailing. But the most revealing aspect of the drawings was how they detailed the hotel's interior. Latrobe intended not only that the internal spaces of the hotel be numerous but that each was to have a specialized function for which it would be designed. The plan of the ground floor (fig. 1.7) included a "supper room," "liquor bar," "coffee bar," and "private dining room." The upper floors contained a "servants lobby," "ladies dressing room," a place for "private card parties," and numerous rooms marked "chamber." The elaborately subdivided space in Latrobe's hotel contrasted sharply with the small, undifferentiated interiors of American taverns. As it turned out, however, Latrobe's plan was too ambitious for a city of the size and fortunes of Richmond, and the structure, like others before it, went unbuilt. The third consecutive failure of a hotel project to get farther than the draftsman's table portended something of a hiatus in the planning of hotels; for several years thereafter, the historical record shows scant evidence of further attempts to build large public houses.[30]

Or so it seemed until 1806, when Boston's mercantile elite moved to create a grand new hotel which would surpass, if not outright dwarf, any public house ever built in America. The leading figures behind the project were Crowell Hatch, Andrew Dexter, Jr., and Samuel Brown. Hatch was an enormously successful entrepreneur who had been one of the founders of the Massachusetts Fire and Marine Insurance Company. His operations were primarily transatlantic, but his ambitions were global: in the late 1780s and early 1790s he had led an effort to establish trade with China by way of the Hawaiian Islands. Dexter was the scion of a prominent merchant family that included a Land Bank commissioner and a United States congressman. He was active in oceangoing trade, and for good measure had married the daughter of the Boston shipping magnate Perez Morton. Brown, for his part, was a trader who had held the coveted post of purchasing agent for the U.S. Navy in Boston and had been involved with Hatch in pursuing markets in the Pacific. After more than a year spent obtaining an act of incorporation, attracting investors, and hiring Asher Benjamin, a student of Bulfinch's who went on to write some of the most influential architectural treatises of the early nineteenth century, construction on the project began, and it was completed three years later in 1809.[31]

The result was the Boston Exchange Coffee House and Hotel (fig. 1.8). The edifice was positively enormous. A contemporary account, which referred to it as "an immense pile of building," described its dimensions: it was "seven stories in height, with a cellar under the whole, and covering 17,753 square feet of ground. Its shape is an irregular square . . . measuring 132 feet in its broadest front, and only 94 feet on its narrowest, from which the line of the sides diverge nearly equally." The front of the hotel was ornamented with six Ionic columns supporting a marble architrave, cornice, and pediment. The interior was equally impressive. It consisted of a five-story atrium ringed by balconies, each level supported by twenty columns, and surmounted by a dome whose apex was suspended

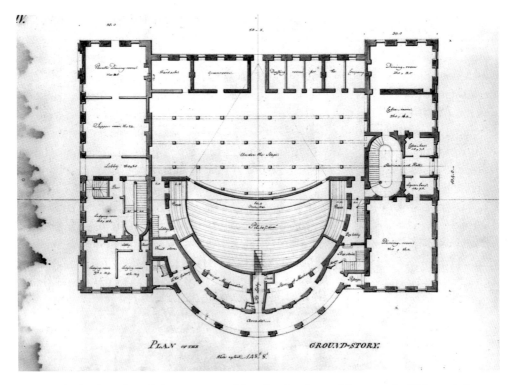

1.7 Benjamin Henry Latrobe's 1797 proposal for a hotel and assembly rooms for Richmond shows the complex subdivision and purpose-specific assignment of space that characterized hotel interiors. (Library of Congress)

eighty-three feet over the floor. The top of the dome was paneled in glass and crowned by a cupola with an elaborate housing for a great telescope. The Exchange Coffee House contained more than two hundred rooms, including a basement kitchen, larder, and cellars, a dining hall, a ballroom, a bar, a coffee room, various shops, a public reading room, an observatory, a newspaper reading room, offices, a Masonic lodge, and numerous apartments that opened onto the five galleries of the central atrium. Little wonder, then, that a traveler commented in 1818 that the incredibly elaborate rooms and the whirl of activity within the hotel "give it the appearance of a small city." The cost of the hotel exceeded the staggering sum of five hundred thousand dollars.[32]

A building of such magnitude—it is said to have been the largest in the United States at the time of its completion—attracted an enormous amount of attention. Travel diarists remarked upon it as they recorded their impressions of the city, it garnered lengthy descriptive accounts in newspapers and magazines, and one admirer was even inspired to write a long ode to the edifice. People flocked to the hotel. As had been the case with the City Hotel, the Exchange Coffee House became the preeminent place to see and be seen: newspaper advertisements and articles reveal that the establishment was in constant use

1.8   The Boston Exchange Coffee House and Hotel required an investment of more than half a million dollars and was one of the largest buildings in the United States when it was completed in 1809. (University of Chicago Libraries)

for balls, concerts, and other fancy occasions. The hotel was also a center of finance, with numerous insurance agents and brokers establishing their headquarters in the many offices available for rent. Indeed, the grand pretensions and high public profile of the Exchange Coffee House were such that the building's demise takes on the quality of a Greek tragedy of hubris punished. The hotel's enormous height turned out to be its downfall: when a fire broke out in the attic in 1818, there were no ladders in the entire city of Boston long enough to reach the flames, and the building was destroyed.[33]

The Exchange Coffee House marked the zenith of the first generation of American hotels. Its grand scale and enormous cost were emblematic of how dramatically public houses had changed in the previous twenty years. A small number of hotels were built subsequently, most notably Washington Hall and Tammany Hall, New York City's hotels–cum–political headquarters, but these paled by comparison with the behemoth in Boston. Meanwhile, rising tensions between the United States and Britain over trade rights and the kidnapping of sailors led to a series of embargoes that severely curtailed trade and damaged the American economy. Large-scale building projects, risky ventures even in prosperous times, seemed ill-advised in the treacherous commercial and diplomatic situation that culminated in the War of 1812. The first generation of American hotel building came to an end as construction entered a decadelong period of stagnation.[34]

The earliest hotel projects involved a deliberate attempt to create a new class of public houses that would stand unmistakably apart from their predecessors. Their sheer magnitude and refined aesthetics suggest, moreover, an effort to make the hotels into important public monuments. When we consider this first generation of hotels—initiated by elite merchants willing to spend unprecedented sums of money, designed by the most important architects in the United States, and sited in the most prominent urban locations possible—we are faced with a very basic question: why?

Hotels did not arise naturally or automatically out of the structural background of their times. The very suddenness of the first hotel projects, with five of them initiated in five consecutive years, suggests revolution rather than evolution. The question that presents itself, then, is why a substantial number of Americans chose to involve themselves with this new and largely untested institution.

A close analysis of the individuals who planned the hotels, the structures they designed and built, and the way people reacted to them reveals their underlying motivations and agendas. While these were complex and overlapping and resist easy categorization, they reflected four main imperatives: the economic, the sociocultural, the political, and the geographic.

HOTELS AND A NEW ECONOMY

In seeking the motives for the development of the first hotels, it makes sense to begin with the economic imperatives involved. Hotels were, after all, business ventures. They were extremely expensive to build, and investors would not have risked their money unless they expected profits in return. This was especially true in the late-eighteenth-century United States, where still-developing capital markets made credit dear and involvement in failed businesses could compromise people's reputations and damage their creditworthiness. Early American entrepreneurs were a calculating bunch, and the fact that so many of them were willing to invest in hotel projects indicates that they thought them financially viable. They appear to have reached this conclusion by working out both the short- and long-term prospects and the ways that hotels could benefit them both as individuals and as a group.

The men who created the first generation of hotels had in common a single characteristic which more than any other united them and defined their worldview: their role within the American economy. Virtually without exception, they owed their livelihood to oceangoing trade. Samuel Blodget, Jr., had made his initial fortune in the East India trade, and his insurance companies did most of their business writing policies on ship cargoes. The association behind the City Hotel was composed of merchants operating out of the nation's largest seaport, together with the lawyers who tended to their contracts and other legal affairs; the incorporators of the Newport hotel project played a similar role in

Rhode Island. Charles Bulfinch's career had been made possible by the mercantile fortune amassed by his grandfather. And the projectors of Boston's Exchange Coffee House and Hotel had made their money from trading links that stretched thousands upon thousands of miles from Europe to the Americas to East Asia. It would be no exaggeration to say that these men were living incarnations of international capital.

Viewed from the perspective of the twenty-first century, this might not seem at all unusual. After all, commerce is the mainstay of the world economy, and millions of people earn their living facilitating trade. But in the 1790s few people were involved in complex commercial pursuits. Indeed, more than 90 percent of all Americans did the same work: farming. As different as their lives could be in numerous other respects, the working world of yeoman farmers and their families, and of planters and their enslaved workers, involved a repeated cycle of sowing, tending, and harvesting crops, raising livestock, and producing everyday necessities in the home. The hotel builders, by contrast, came from a small minority for whom wealth derived from the workings of commodities markets that depended upon the exchange of goods, supply and demand, time and distance. Merchant livelihoods came, both literally and figuratively, from beyond the horizon.

Merchants in general, and the hotel builders in particular, thus had a vested interest in the speed and reliability of transportation, a fact that made them advocates of internal improvements. Blodget, for example, came from a family that was deeply involved in transportation and trade: his father had established two stagecoach lines and a canal in Massachusetts and New Hampshire, his brother had been a proprietor of the Charles River Bridge, and he had made his fortune in transatlantic commerce. Similarly, Latrobe worked on canals, bridges, and waterways in Philadelphia, Delaware, Washington, and Baltimore. He was also an early enthusiast of the steamboat, and in 1798 made a special trip to New York to inquire into the use of steam pumps and to see an early steamboat that was moored there. Latrobe became so important in the cause that Albert Gallatin, the first secretary of the interior, chose him to prepare a working paper on canals in support of Gallatin's pivotal 1808 report on the need for internal improvements. Their individual efforts were part of a much larger push in the 1790s to improve the nation's transportation and communications infrastructure. In that decade, the number of post offices in America increased from 75 to 903, and the total mileage of roads used for mail delivery went from 1,875 to 20,817.[35]

Against this backdrop, the nation's first hotels can be seen as part of a generalized effort to improve transportation in the early United States. The hotel builders clearly understood that transportation and accommodation were inherently linked. Commerce was dependent upon the movement of goods, but these goods did not move themselves; they required people to load, sail, cart, supervise, and sell them. Any movement of goods, in other words, required movement of people. The hotel form corresponded perfectly to this requirement. Early hotels contained numerous bedchambers, signaling their readiness to receive large numbers of guests and marking them as cosmopolitan institutions. Taverns, by contrast, primarily served a local drinking clientele and tended to travelers only as a secondary matter: as one historian of colonial public houses has put it, "tavernkeepers invested in chairs rather than beds." The sheer size and distinctive architecture of hotels made them easy to spot from a distance, allowing travelers to proceed directly to the place where they knew they could find shelter rather than wandering the streets looking for tavern signs. Meanwhile, the abundant public rooms of the hotel offered meeting places for a merchant class that had for many years been accustomed to doing business in public houses. (Lloyd's of London, for example, originated on the premises of the seventeenth-century coffeehouse keeper Edward Lloyd.)[36]

The grand architecture of early hotels was also intended to serve a second market-related purpose by increasing the value of surrounding property. Speculative building was increasingly popular in the 1790s, and large urban landholders understood that constructing commercially and socially important institutions would increase the attractiveness of nearby land to renters and purchasers. To be sure, Samuel Blodget, Jr., the man behind the Union Public Hotel, was one of the largest land speculators in Washington, and as we have seen, his aggressive acquisition of adjoining tracts of land—including the area now known as Dupont Circle—cost him his job. The same dynamic was at work in New York City, where the City Hotel's managing board included several active traders of Manhattan real estate.[37]

But to see hotels merely as a functional solution to economic imperatives would be to lose sight of their important symbolic role. Hotels' elaborate architecture and ornamentation also served to ennoble the pursuit of commerce in a nation that was still agrarian. Hotels provided not just a setting for merchants to do business, but a grand setting. Rather than just building more public houses to accommodate mercantile activities, the creators of the first hotels used visual spectacle to suggest a future for the nation that was very different from its present. Notably, it was precisely these years that saw the most intense debates over what kind of economy would provide the best underpinning for a virtuous republic. Jeffersonian Republicans worried that too much commercial involvement would detract from the proper agricultural pursuits of the American people, tempting them into a love of luxury and corrupting their sensibilities. Hamiltonian Federalists argued that without a thriving commercial sector, the nation would become economically stagnant and its population, isolated from the civilizing influence of trade, would regress into coarseness and barbarism.[38]

Hotels were in a very real sense an intervention in this debate—one made with money and masonry. The translocal orientation of the Union Public Hotel was perfectly in line with Samuel Blodget's enthusiasm for commercial expansion and his support for Hamilton's economic policies. When the aspiring hotel builders of Newport promised to use all profits from the hotel to build common schools, they expressed their preference for a community that would devote its resources to the pursuit of trade, which in turn would fund public education, resulting in a harmonious social order supporting the twin virtues of entrepreneurial activity and informed civic participation. The Exchange Coffee House was named after the fundamental transaction that undergirded all commerce—"exchange"—and the first Fourth of July celebration held there featured a play entitled *Huzza for Commerce*. The hotel's rooftop telescope also indicated a commercial outlook, since it could be trained on the harbor to determine which merchant vessels had reached the city, or on the horizon to search for imminent arrivals. Hotels were thoroughly symbolic at all levels. In the same way that church architecture emphasized the divine with vertical lines that guided people's gaze skyward and sunlit stained glass that dazzled the eye, hotels focused public attention on the benefits of trade and pointed toward a commercial future for the nation. As the hotel builders surely realized, grand architecture as a mode of discourse also had the advantage of exclusivity: it made statements that were possible only for a small group of people. Unlike other methods of communication, such as speech making, pamphleteering, and rioting, large-scale construction was available only to Americans with access to the capital and financial instruments required to dramatically modify the built environment.[39]

Hotels thus served three complementary purposes in the economic context of their times. Functionally, they facilitated trade by providing shelter and refreshment to an elite traveling public. Financially, they were intended to increase the value of surrounding property. Visually, their imposing architecture symbolized commerce and valorized its pursuit in a republic that was still overwhelmingly agrarian. As a public accommodation for commercial travelers, as a spur to the price of land, and as a monument to mercantile might, the hotel made perfect economic sense as the successor to the tavern in an age of expanding market capitalism.

HOTELS, CULTURE, AND SOCIABILITY

As important as economic motivations were in the creation of the hotel, other vital influences were also at work. For as surely as the exigencies of commerce determined the hotel's structure and function as a travel accommodation, conflicts over culture and sociability defined the shape of its public spaces and the way they were used. If the impressive exteriors of the first generation of hotels symbolized their connection with the movement of people across oceans and continents, their interiors reflected social relations and cultural aspirations in the communities where they were built.

Hotels were part of a long-term trend in England and America in which people grew increasingly preoccupied with beautifying their material surroundings. As the rise of market economies and social mobility began to erode the importance of aristocratic titles and other kinds of hereditary status, people turned to style, décor, behavior, and other visual cues to demonstrate their social standing. Over the course of the seventeenth and eighteenth centuries, a rising class of middling and well-to-do families spent ever larger sums of money on such consumer goods as silverware, clothing, and furniture, and built new homes that were neater and more spacious than those in which they had grown up. This devotion to aesthetics also led communities to build larger and more elegant churches and town halls, and in some cases to design entire cities according to contemporary canons of good taste. This quest for refinement also prompted changes in public houses. In England, sixteenth-century licensing laws codified a hierarchy of alehouses, taverns, and inns, each with its own duties, tax liabilities, and social status. In the second half of the seventeenth century the coffeehouse evolved as an institution committed to the stimulation afforded by caffeine rather than the intoxicating effects of alcohol. And in the eighteenth century, large inns with attached assembly rooms appeared in numerous provincial towns. North America evidenced a transatlantic echo of these processes, with colonial elites fashioning local facsimiles of the royal court in London: this had been the cultural context for Philadelphia's City Tavern and other elegant public houses of the late eighteenth century.[40]

Hotel interiors were perfectly suited to an age in which Americans used refinement in material goods and manners to establish their social status and evaluate that of others. Because displays of elegance depended in large part upon self-presentation in public, they required spaces in which people could go to see and be seen. Courtly surroundings were, after all, the only appropriate venue for the fashionably dressed bodies, cultivated comportment, and witty repartee that served as the social currency of the American bon ton. Latrobe's 1797 sketch of his proposed hotel's grand assembly room (fig. 1.9) perfectly illustrates the intended clientele and use of the space. The ballroom is the ideal setting for spectatorship and self-display: it is brightly illuminated and fitted with long mirrors that enhance and multiply its long lines of sight. (Indeed, the drawing bears a striking resemblance to the world's most famous site of aristocratic pageantry: the Hall of Mirrors at Versailles.) Latrobe would provide the ideal setting for glamorous men and women like the ones in the sketch to dress up in their best attire and seek the approval of their peers. The Exchange Coffee House likewise contained elaborate spaces designed for spectatorship, including a "ball-room" where, one poet observed, "circling mirrors filled with life appear," allowing people to flirt by catching each other's reflected looks; the poet described just such a scene:

> See bashful Beauty like a phantom glide
> Her fair form glancing forth from every side
> And as fond Love a whispering worship pays
> With sidelong glances mark his ardent gaze.

While no reliable images remain to document the appearance of the public rooms at the City Hotel, the cotillions, dancing assemblies, and other genteel events that took place there indicate a similar commitment to refinement.[41]

The regendering of public houses was also a fundamental part of the creation of the American hotel. Taverns were decidedly masculine institutions in which men celebrated and reinforced fellowship and mutual respect through drinking. Women were no strangers to the insides of taverns, but their role was generally limited to waiting on patrons or serving as objects of male sexual attention. As a result, taverns could be unwelcome places for female patrons, particularly if they considered themselves women of quality. A Pennsylvania hospital matron suggested as much in the 1750s when she wrote disgustedly of

1.9   Latrobe's conceptual sketch for the Richmond hotel ballroom reflected his European training and was reminiscent of the Hall of Mirrors at Versailles. The space would have been the perfect setting for the local plantation aristocracy's pursuit of personal refinement and social status. (Library of Congress)

the leers of tavern customers who assumed her to be the kept woman of her male traveling companion. A quarter-century later, Katherine Farnham Hay, who had just been left at a New York tavern, noted in a letter to her sister that the man who had escorted her there had been "very uneasy" about leaving her unaccompanied. "I was in great distress," she wrote, "but what could I do in a publick House, no person to take care of me?" The first hotels, by contrast, welcomed respectable women and sometimes provided them with their own parlors. As women went to hotels to attend the numerous entertainments held there, they transformed traditional expectations of who was welcome in public houses, and in some cases completely reversed the anxieties connected with their presence. When an observer suggested in 1809 that the Exchange Coffee House should "put up Venetian blinds, or lattice work, between the pillars of the colonnade, to secure the ladies from impertinent observation," he made clear that there was no longer any question that women belonged in these new public houses; it was the presence of spectators of an inappropriate social status that was the real problem.[42]

While it is tempting to interpret the inclusion of women as a sign of commitment to gender equality, it was also part of a different sort of exclusion. The egalitarian ideals of the American Revolution had made public houses into conflict-ridden spaces. For most of the eighteenth century, taverns had drawn customers from many different backgrounds. Masters were accustomed to drinking with apprentices, and magistrates with laborers. As long as people recognized and accepted (at least outwardly) their respective social standings, the customary rounds of treating and toasting could proceed without problems. As hierarchy came under attack in the last third of the century, however, roiling issues of status and honor made this much more difficult. Rituals that had traditionally served to smooth the rough edges of interactions between self-identified superiors and their conscious but grudging inferiors threatened to collapse into open antagonism. Men of importance found that their patronizing jokes and affectionate condescension were no longer taken in stride by the common people, who, feeling belittled or disrespected, were increasingly likely to respond with a hurled insult or even a thrown punch.[43]

The spaces of the hotel defused the social tensions endemic to American public houses through a dual strategy of exclusion and compartmentalization. The elegant décor of hotel interiors signaled that they were intended only for those who were appropriately attired, groomed, and mannered; the unwashed and unlettered were implicitly informed that they did not belong. Within the hotel, social discord was dealt with through spatial separation. Different groups of people, whether divided by class or by clique, could simply occupy different spaces within the same public house. The availability of multiple parlors, meeting halls, ballrooms, coffee rooms, and bars allowed for compartmentalized public sociability: whatever the cause of friction among patrons, from social rivalry to political infighting, it was now possible to move to another part of the hotel whenever some people decided that others had crossed the line between mingling and intrusion. A similar principle was at work in the sleeping areas of the hotel: its private bedchambers shielded guests against strangers or other objectionable people who might otherwise have shared their rooms or beds. Hotel interiors thus reflected the cultural logic of an age in which social status was expressed through physical separation and personal appearance.

Patterns of inclusion and exclusion at hotels were more than just marks of social acceptance or snobbery. They also involved a deliberate maneuver in which people tried to redistribute political power by manipulating the physical spaces of public life.

THE POLITICAL SPACE OF THE HOTEL

Public houses were exceptionally important political institutions in eighteenth-century America. By the time of the first hotel projects in the 1790s, taverns had served as focal points of political activity for well over a century. In colonial New England, for example, they emerged as centers of popular opposition to the power of ministers and magistrates who tried to control the drinking that went on in them. Taverngoers congregated regularly to display their defiance of the authority that emanated from the pulpit and the governor's mansion, and their determined resistance foreshadowed the Revolution. In the decade that preceded the Declaration of Independence, city taverns became vital gathering places where patriots organized resistance to the crown. "If the American Revolution was 'cradled' in any place," one prominent historian has noted, "it was in the urban public house." Politicking in public houses survived into the 1780s, a fact attested by frequent public announcements of tavern meetings called to discuss news from abroad, select candidates for municipal office, and hear campaign speeches. Public houses and politics were thus indissolubly linked in the popular mind of the early republic.[44]

When hotel builders planned and built public houses on an unprecedented scale in the nation's largest cities, they surely did so with the expectation that these would be pivotal sites in the new nation's political life. Polite society in eighteenth-century British America was constituted in private settings as much as it was in public. Many people agreed that it was the very privacy of salons and clubs that made possible the highest level of thought and discussion, since only in familiar company could one aggressively challenge a person's ideas without the risk of giving offense. But when it came to standing for office and other forms of political participation, public appearances were a sine qua non. Politics in the early republic remained highly personalistic, depending heavily upon comportment, persuasion, and deference, and requiring that any aspiring public figure expose himself to the scrutiny of the citizenry. This became an important political issue in the 1780s and 1790s, when Republicans and their radical allies found political leverage in the idea that the closed meetings and private entertainments of the Federalists threatened the nation with a reversion to the secrecy and corruption of the courts of Europe. The accusations of aristocracy hurled at societies and clubs like the Cincinnati and the Sans Souci made clear that any political grouping that appeared to be deliberating behind closed doors ran the risk of alienating large numbers of voters.[45]

Understanding this, the creators of early hotels sought to refashion political spaces in a way that maintained their public character yet afforded them clear tactical advantages. In addition to their shared economic orientation, hotel builders also had political sympathies in common: virtually all were Federalists. In New York the party of Alexander Hamilton had entered the 1790s with a political lock on the city. Before long, however, the Federalists were garnering a reputation for elitism and self-interest. The involvement of leading party men in rehabilitating Tories, in maintaining neutrality toward republican France, and especially in precipitating the financial crises of 1791 and 1792 led to the formation of a popular opposition. Democratically minded fraternal societies pursued a politics of explicit class antagonism, warning that the city was threatened by an "overgrown monied importance" and "the baneful growth of aristocratic weeds among us." They also took to the streets in conscious emulation of the French Jacobins, holding regular parades of hundreds of radical Republicans. The Federalist elite was appalled at such out-of-doors populism. They charged their opponents with appealing to the mob, complaining that "demagogues always fix their meetings at the hour of twelve in order to take in all the Mechanics & Laborers—over whom they alone have influence and who in public meetings have a great advantage as they are not afraid of a black eye or broken head."[46]

The construction of the City Hotel was an effort by New York's Federalists to move campaigns off the street and into an elegant space in which politics would be pursued in the rational, refined manner implied by the architecture. If the dirt and noise of the streets were conducive to a rowdy, chaotic mode of politicking, it was hoped that plush furniture and expensive drapery would serve to exclude nonelite political figures or, at the very least, force them to behave themselves. This had not been the first time that the city's merchant elite had deployed grand architecture to establish order. Only two years before, a group of five leading merchants, including two of the hotel's backers, had formed a committee in the aftermath of the securities scandal and panic of 1792, which had badly damaged public trust in the city's stock exchange. This committee constructed the impressive Tontine Coffee House on Wall Street and moved brokers off the street and into the reestablished New York Stock Exchange inside the building. Just as this structure was intended to restore respectability and order to the city's much maligned financial markets, the City Hotel represented an effort to entrench the preeminence of the wealthy and powerful in key political spaces in Manhattan.[47]

The Exchange Coffee House in Boston also existed in a highly charged political atmosphere in which partisans exchanged allegations of snobbery or demagoguery. In response to popular criticism of the hotel, the *Port Folio,* a Federalist journal which used a belletristic literary style to express its social eminence and refinement, published an ode entitled "Lines on visiting the Exchange Coffeehouse in Boston." After three stanzas glorifying the hotel ("Hail to this pile! by struggling genius rais'd"), the poet turned angrily upon the building's critics ("the herd, who every dear design / To each poor self with pigmy soul confine") and subjected them to a thrashing in verse:

> Let then that herd, who, striving to abuse,
> Conspired in vain to thwart thy generous views,
> With envious glance behold thy deeds of fame,
> And with malignant lip asperse thy name,
> Still shall that name mid breathing prose be found,
> And those high deeds by patriot pride be crowned,
> When all those worthless insects of a day,
> Unknown, unhonoured, shall have passed away.

The sneering tone of the poem and its dismissal of its opponents as a "herd" of "worthless insects" echoed much of the political rhetoric of its Federalist audience, who considered themselves a natural aristocracy that embodied the impartiality needed to lead a population of commoners ruled by passion and self-interest.[48]

The "herd," however, had its own criticisms of hotels and the people who built and socialized in them. The symbolic statements of hotel architecture were heard and understood, and did not go unanswered—though the response came in a language different from that of bricks and mortar. The grand opening of the City Hotel, for example, drew scorn from New York's radicals, who decried it as the haunt of would-be aristocrats who favored "the ancient Colony system of servility and adulation." The Union Public Hotel meanwhile became a symbol of the folly of speculation. One visitor to Washington, told of the lottery bankruptcy that had left the structure unfinished six years after its cornerstone was laid, referred to the ethics of the building's creator by suggesting that perhaps "hotel" was an acronym for "*hic omnes turpitudine excedit longe*"—here all baseness is taken still farther; indeed, the collapse of the speculative scheme with which the Union Public was financed generated such widespread hostility toward Blodget that he was still busy defending himself in print a decade later. And when the Exchange Coffee House burned down in 1818, some people gloated openly over the conflagration. The hotel, concluded one observer, "was conceived in sin and brought forth in iniquity, but it is now purified by fire." A newspaper columnist went into greater detail by reminding his readers that the Exchange Coffee House was "erected during the most perfidious periods of speculation"; that it "arose on the ruins of many industrious citizens" and bore "evidences of the fallacious promises, which were too successfully practised on the credulous tradesmen." The palpable class tension highlights the fact that short of outright vandalism or arson (a popular expedient previously and thereafter), the common people could find victory over such architectural statements only in the buildings' decrepitude or destruction.[49]

HOTELS AND THE GEOGRAPHY OF THE STATE

A key question remains, however: why did the hotel appear at the time it did? The aforementioned economic and social imperatives were not unique to the 1790s. How, then, to account for that decade's sudden enthusiasm for hotel building, especially considering that inns and taverns apparently had been sufficient for the needs of European colonists for the better part of two hundred years? The creation of the hotel was occasioned by the establishment of the United States federal government under the Constitution of 1787, particularly the election of the first president, the founding of a national capital, the redrawing of the nation's political geography, and the activity of federal officials. The hotel was part of the project of American nationhood.

The linkage between the hotel and the American state began with the election of George Washington to the newly established office of president in 1788. Washington's elevation to head of state meant that the United States could for the first time be embodied in a single human being. While the notion of personified nationhood might seem fanciful today, at that time most lands in the Western world were still led by monarchs whose physical presence was ideologically identical with their nations. Even in the world's sole republic, only opposition in Congress prevented Washington from being inaugurated as "His Highness." The president was extraordinarily charismatic, and his physical presence invariably caused a public sensation. His inauguration packed the streets of New York City, where people gathered flowers for him and the letters *GW* were emblazoned on doors, pinned onto clothing, and engraved upon personal effects. The visits Washington made on his presidential tours were momentous events in the community life of cities and towns, occasioning elaborate preparations for the reception and honoring of "the Man who unites all hearts" or "Columbia's favourite Son," as banners welcoming the president often called him. As they had before the inauguration, many communities staged highly choreographed processions (fig. 1.10). In New York, Boston, Salem, Newburyport, and numerous other towns and settlements, local authorities posted broadsides informing the community of the proper procedures and sequence of groups in the planned parade. Daytime festivities were followed by grand public dinners complete with long rounds of toasts. In Newport, Rhode Island, these included "Prosperity to the Constitution of America," "The Memory of the deceased Patriots and Heroes of our Country," and, after Washington took his leave, "THE MAN WE LOVE." Evening entertainments were also common: in Charleston, South Carolina, Washington recalled, "the ladies were all superbly dressed and most of them wore ribbons with different inscriptions expressive of their esteem and respect for the President such as: 'long live the President,' etc."[50]

George Washington's presidential travels accentuated the importance of public accommodations to the political life of the new republic while simultaneously demonstrating the inadequacy of the nation's inns and taverns. It was apparent from the outset that there was a problem: so many people traveled to New York to witness the inauguration that taverns and boardinghouses were quickly overwhelmed, forcing many visitors to put up in adjacent settlements or sleep outdoors in hastily improvised campgrounds. Washington's subsequent presidential tours made plain that the problem was national in scope. His determination to be accommodated and entertained in public houses revealed their shortcomings both as travel accommodations and as centers of local sociability. Not only was Washington often dissatisfied with his accommodations, he also realized that he was sometimes being put up at private residences temporarily redesignated as public houses especially for him. Similar arrangements were frequently made for public dinners and receptions: in preference to the local tavern, some towns occupied people's homes or built temporary structures for the reception of the president.[51]

Washington's visits fostered widespread community embarrassment about local accommodations. The president carried tremendous cultural authority. He had begun his travels from the presidential residence in New York City, the national metropolis in politics, finance, and worldly sophistication; and his visiting presence in any other community effectively put it into a national context of culture and competition. The elaborate efforts that townspeople made to accommodate the president reflected their awareness that he had come from a place with the highest standards of material elegance and personal refinement. Washington's various hosts were at pains to honor him properly, whatever

1.10   George Washington was greeted by cheering crowds and elaborately choreographed receptions wherever he went on his official travels. (Library of Congress)

the size of their population or the state of their fortunes: two accounts of the president's visit to Newport tell of a community collection of silverware and dishes in order to secure enough for a full service. Later, there were often feelings of embarrassment at not having been able to offer more cultivated surroundings: the reception committee in Newport openly expressed regret in their welcoming addresses to the president, and one Exeter resident published an open letter taking his fellow townspeople to task for the meager character of their efforts. At one point the governor of South Carolina even wrote directly to Washington to "apologise . . . for asking you to call at a place so indifferently furnished." Individual communities harbored the feeling, in other words, that the president was judging them by their hospitality and comparing them with other towns that he had visited along his route. In the cities and towns of the United States, just as in the villages of Russia or the provincial capitals of the Habsburg Empire, a visit from the head of state was cause for community self-consciousness as much as for celebration.[52]

The chronology and geography of the nation's public houses provide further evidence of linkage with Washington's presidential travels and the structure of the American state. Even before the hotel age began in earnest, important predecessor forms appeared. Shortly after the transfer of the national government from New York to Philadelphia in late 1790, a Pennsylvania merchant and an innkeeper arranged to purchase a defunct school building, which they successfully converted into the Quaker City's preeminent place of accommodation. It had for years been commonly known, however, that by 1800 the entire federal government would be permanently moved to a new national capital on the banks of the Potomac—and it was there that the nation's first hotel project was commenced on the orders of an officer of the new federal government. (This was not the only example of architecture following President Washington; a similar pattern emerged in the design and construction of a presidential residence every time the national government moved to a new city.) The influence of capital-city status on the character of American public houses extended well beyond the federal government: the nation's second, third, fourth, and fifth hotels were built or planned for New York City, Newport, Boston, and Richmond, all of which were state capitals at that time.[53]

The impetus for hotel building closely followed the political geography of the United States government in part because the need for substantial travel accommodations was in a sense built into American governance. The principle of deliberative democracy on the basis of geographic representation required by its very nature that individuals from across a larger territory gather at a single location in order to discuss and resolve matters of public importance. The choice of terminology for these meetings suggested as much: "congress," a Latinate term meaning literally "moving together." The Constitution of 1787, meanwhile, provided for dual sovereignty, with federal and state legislatures meeting in their respective capitals. The planning and construction of hotels in capital cities was thus an architectural articulation of the political logic of federalism.

The linkage between architecture and the new republic was not lost on contemporary observers. "In respect to their buildings," the English traveler and diarist Henry

Wansey wrote in 1794, "I date a new era from their acceptance of the federal Constitution. They then began to feel themselves united as a nation, and all their public works and undertakings seem to have commenced in a more important style." The hotel manifested this linkage in a way that transcended style, however, because it paralleled the integration of local communities into national networks of commerce, culture, and politics. It had been George Washington who first used travel in the service of American nationalism, establishing symbolic connections between small local polities on his presidential tours. It was the hotel, however, that articulated these connections into a new architecture of accommodation that linked local publics to one another through the itineraries of a traveling and trading citizenry.[54]

CONCLUSION: THE HOTEL AS SOCIAL TECHNOLOGY

To say that the hotel had to be invented is to suggest that it was a particular kind of product: an invention, or, more to the point, a technology. The term *technology* usually denotes the application of science to a practical purpose: using steam to propel a ship, for example, or illuminating a room with electrical current. The hotel was a social technology. Its driving force came not from vapor pressure or electrons but rather from a new way of organizing people. This yielded practical results: it provided travelers with a hugely improved standard of hospitality and established the necessary infrastructure for a new age of commerce and human mobility. The hotel also had other uses which, as with all technologies, reflected the values of its creators. Hotels symbolized the desire for a nation that was urban and commercial; supplied new spaces for social display and stabilized status hierarchies; and were designed to reallocate political power by restructuring political space. The intended purpose of the hotel was, in short, to establish a new paradigm for public houses, public space, and public life in America.

How successful was the hotel? It was most effective in its primary function as a public accommodation. The first generation of hotels almost immediately changed the standards of American hospitality. These new standards were not adopted immediately and by all hosts, but signs of change were not long in coming. The tavern remained for some time the most common type of public house, and many travelers preferred the private quarters of the boardinghouse. But soon after the appearance of the first hotels, tavernkeepers began to adopt new practices. For example, publicans began to use the availability of private rooms as a way to distinguish their houses from lesser places of accommodation. A Philadelphia innkeeper explained to his English guest in 1798 that in his establishment, "every lodger had a room to himself," and some years later another promised his patrons "that so much desired gratification, *a single bed room.*" The new form also registered linguistically, as numerous taverns and converted mansions were renamed—the Eagle Tavern might be designated the Eagle Hotel even in the absence of other changes to the establishment—and the use of the word increased dramatically in city directories and newspapers.[55]

Hotels also achieved some of the other objectives for which they had been invented.

They certainly facilitated the continued growth and intensification of commerce in the United States, both as physical infrastructure and symbolic presence. They were also undeniably successful in their role as elegant social space. Elite society embraced the nation's new public houses, adopting them as ideal venues for the refined entertainments that distinguished them from those whom they considered hoi polloi. The exclusionary character of hotel sociability was recognized as such by Americans of less exalted status, who in response scorned their presumed superiors and their new playgrounds.

The political project behind the first hotels, by contrast, was noticeably less successful. Imposing discipline on politics out-of-doors and suppressing radicalism appear to have been beyond the capacity of architecture to accomplish. The hotel certainly did not succeed as a purely partisan exercise. In Boston, newspaper reports indicated that the Exchange Coffee House was used simultaneously by opposing political groupings: on the Fourth of July 1809, for example, the "*Society of Cincinnati* dined together in one of the Halls of the Exchange Coffee House, and the *Young Republicans* of Boston in another." An analogous outcome obtained in New York City. When the local Federalists who had built the City Hotel subsequently erected the Washington Hall Hotel to serve as their political headquarters, they were answered by their Republican rivals, who built the renowned Tammany Hall as their own base of operations. By then, of course, Thomas Jefferson's defeat of the Federalists in the presidential election of 1800 had made it clear that if popular opposition had somehow been stifled in public space, it remained alive and well at the polling place.[56]

The hotel also had uses that its creators had not anticipated. Over the course of the coming century, their innovative social technology would serve a variety of unforeseen purposes. Hotels would anchor new cities along an advancing western frontier, extending settlement across the continent; they would transform the American home by providing new models for urban living; they would give rise to new behaviors essential to the struggle against racial segregation. Before these outcomes could manifest themselves, however, the hotel would have to move beyond the experimental phase of its first generation. And by the 1820s, America was on the verge of a full-scale hotel-building craze.

Two *Palaces of the Public*

The American Hotel Comes of Age, 1815–1840

THE FIRST GENERATION of hotels was in many ways a remarkable achievement. The creation of a new building type demonstrated that Americans had begun to think in innovative and even visionary ways about what kind of accommodations their commercial and republican nation required. The work of hotel building had united the efforts of intrepid entrepreneurs, talented architects, and skilled artisans, who financed, designed, and constructed a number of highly impressive edifices. Hotels had become hugely popular public places, drawing crowds into their lobbies, parlors, and rooms, creating a ready clientele for the shops, offices, and libraries within, and establishing themselves as vital centers of civic life. It seemed very much as if Americans had produced a worthy successor to the tavern.

In other respects, however, the nation's first hotels were failures. As business ventures, they were a collective fiasco. Only a few of the hotels planned in the 1790s and early 1800s were actually built, and almost all went bankrupt: not more than one first-generation hotel survived ten years under its original management. Moreover, the agenda that hotels had been created to symbolize and advance—fostering an urban and commercial future for the young United States—was not moving forward. American cities lagged behind rural areas in population growth during the 1810s. The War of 1812 disrupted commerce, driving numerous merchants out of business. And large numbers of Americans, especially artisans and mechanics, had become suspicious of, even hostile toward, hotels and their clientele. A well-informed contemporary observer might easily have come to the conclusion that the hotel didn't have much of a future.[1]

Appearances proved to be deceiving. Americans were soon to embark upon a hotel-building craze. After tentative beginnings in the aftermath of the war, hotel construction intensified in the 1820s and continued for more than a decade. The idea of the hotel, which had originated in Atlantic port cities, soon manifested itself along eastern rivers before traversing the Appalachian Mountains and spreading throughout the Ohio and Mississippi river valleys and along the shores of the Great Lakes. By about 1840 hotels could be found in most settlements of more than a few thousand people, and the number of hotels in the United States reached into the hundreds.

The success of the hotel also involved changes in political culture. The first generation of hotels in the United States had embodied ideas about social hierarchy and civic exclusivity that were increasingly unacceptable in the age of Jacksonian Democracy. Hotels therefore had to be repositioned within American culture. As they multiplied in the quarter-century after 1815, hotels came to symbolize very different political ideals from the ones that initially inspired them.

EXPANSION, TRANSPORTATION, AND ACCOMMODATION

The stage was set for the second generation of American hotels by the new geographic, political, and economic circumstances that resulted from the War of 1812. Having confirmed its independence from Britain by the peace treaty of December 1814, the nation turned its attention inward. The Louisiana Purchase of 1803 had added hundreds of thousands of square miles of the trans-Mississippi West to the United States, making it almost incomprehensibly large to the Americans of the day. Native Americans had limited white encroachment on their lands, but the withdrawal of British forces and the subsequent collapse of intertribal leadership decisively altered the balance of power. A further frontier awaited the plans of its new rulers, and the rapid admission of five new western states—Indiana (1816), Mississippi (1817), Illinois (1818), Alabama (1819), and Missouri (1821)—made it clear that those plans called for expansion throughout the national territory.[2]

This new political geography fostered corresponding economic opportunities. Land was still the world's most important source of wealth, and the promise of affordable farmsteads with extraordinarily fertile soil drew hundreds of thousands of settlers into the trans-Appalachian West. Manufacturing also played an important role in the developing national economy. War-related disruptions of oceangoing trade had led Americans to develop domestic production in order to supply themselves with many items no longer obtainable from overseas. The combination of cheap and productive agricultural land, early industrialization, and domestic trade, along with the resumption of transatlantic commerce, propelled a faltering national economy into a period of increasing prosperity.[3]

Economic growth could not be achieved without improved transportation. Farmers who hoped to move past subsistence agriculture and pursue profits could do so only by selling their wheat, cotton, tobacco, corn, and other crops in distant markets; the same rule applied to producers of lumber, pelts, meat, and hides. Manufacturers could find customers in their own towns and cities, but real prosperity depended on demand from people in frontier areas farther from the largest settlements.

The American economy had for centuries depended on waterborne transport. Producers and merchants in the East moved goods down the region's many rivers and along the Atlantic coast. Inland commerce floated along the St. Lawrence, Mississippi, and Ohio river systems. Yet these waterways also imposed limitations on trade. They flowed where they flowed and nowhere else, so transporting goods any distance from existing watercourses meant a labor-intensive breaking down of cargo followed by the slow pace and high cost of overland transport in wagons or on the backs of animals. Cold winter weather froze rivers, leaving them nonnavigable for months every year. And even when the weather was mild, rafts and barges could only float with the current, so returning upstream meant slow, lengthy journeys on horseback or on foot.

Conditions of geography and economy thus held out a dual promise: great wealth to whoever could establish new ways to transport commodities, and municipal prosperity to whichever cities could position themselves as the best markets for buying and selling those commodities. Americans devoted a great deal of imagination, labor, state aid, and private capital to these tasks. The process detailed by the historian George Rogers Taylor in his seminal work *The Transportation Revolution* began around 1815 and continued for the following half-century. The earliest efforts centered on the nation's still rudimentary roads. The construction of turnpikes—roads built by state-sanctioned corporations using private capital and charging their users tolls—was a highly popular venture, and by 1830 thousands of miles had been built. The second phase of transportation improvement involved the establishment of a national network of water transportation, using canals to link existing rivers and other waterways. Such projects drastically reduced transportation costs and created expanded regional markets. But it was the harnessing of steam power to water and land transportation that most dramatically reshaped the United States. Beginning in the 1810s, steamboats transformed riverine transport thanks to their great speed, large cargo capacity, and ability to travel upstream as well as down. The locomotive further revolutionized transportation by making it independent of water and weather: railroad tracks could be laid in any direction without regard to the course of rivers, and trains could run around the clock and at any time of year. By 1844 the American railroad system was the most extensive in the world.[4]

Hotels proliferated rapidly in the early nineteenth century because they were an integral part of this transportation revolution, the urbanization that underlay it, and the geographic and economic expansion it facilitated. Transportation and accommodation were inherently linked. Moving goods meant moving people who needed somewhere to stay when they traveled away from home: wagons, boats, and trains had to be driven, and cargoes supervised; and as new forms of transportation increasingly carried passengers as well as freight, the demand for accommodation increased further. Taylor's account of the transportation revolution was an economic history that focused on the movement of goods and said nothing about inns or hotels; tellingly, though, they found their way into the book's illustrations.[5]

Yet hotels were not simply a side effect of the transportation revolution—the first hotels had, after all, preceded it by more than two decades. Rather, both transportation and accommodation were products of the same collective effort to reorganize the national landscape in the interest of commercial growth. They were sponsored by the same people, employed parallel methods of financing, and were justified with similar rhetoric. Whether undertaken in old, established cities or frontier boomtowns, hotels were part of municipal strategies aimed at establishing secure positions in an emergent urban hierarchy. And because they were presented as public projects that would benefit entire communities, hotels began to lose some of their elitist connotations and were recast as "palaces of the public."

HESITATION

The second age of the hotel began rather haltingly. For almost a decade following the War of 1812, hotel construction remained at a virtual standstill. Only a small number of projects were undertaken, all on a more modest scale than the hotels of a quarter-century earlier. These hotels were also geographically disjointed, bearing little relation to one another or to patterns of regional urbanization. The Union Hotel, completed in Richmond in 1816, was the first in the South. The project's location made sense given the existing tradition of planning hotels for state capitals, but it was otherwise anomalous. The hotel stood in a city of barely ten thousand inhabitants at a time when the region's most successful ports were anywhere from two to almost six times more populous. A thousand miles to the west, in the still tiny settlement of St. Louis, two local entrepreneurs oversaw the construction of the Missouri Hotel (1819), a two-story stone building that was the first of its kind in the Ohio-Mississippi river system. In the same year, Hartford, Connecticut, got its first hotel, a purpose-built structure at the center of town that included a reading room, multiple parlors, and separate dining rooms. And in 1823 an 80-by-150-foot columned structure dubbed the Ottawa House was sited in the middle of a Michigan forest at the behest of speculators, who were later forced to dismantle it when their hoped-for city failed to attract either investors or settlers.[6]

The slow pace of new construction did not mean that Americans had no use for hotels. On the contrary, the citizens of many cities and towns sought to re-create hotel-like spaces and functions without building anew. In Washington, for instance, house conversions resulted in numerous small hotels and boardinghouses that were eagerly patronized by elected officials and other government employees. In Baltimore a refurbished eighteenth-century tavern was reopened for business in 1818 as the Indian Queen Hotel. A similar method was used the following year in New York City, where an aspiring host leased two older marble-fronted buildings and renovated them into a hotel. In Philadelphia a group of investors took possession of the thirty-year-old Washington Tavern, which they rechristened the New Theatre Hotel in 1822.[7]

Prospective hotel builders had good reason to hesitate during the first postwar decade. The failure of the first generation of hotels was widely recognized, as was the fate of their projectors: Samuel Blodget's efforts to build the Union Public Hotel had landed him in debtors' prison, and the backers of the Exchange Coffee House had been forced to sell out at less than fifty cents on the dollar. As a later hotel builder remarked in 1830, "The unfortunate experience of those who had previously engaged in similar enterprises was sufficient to deter any individual from undertaking a work of so much labor, cost, and capital." The continued success of older hotels also discouraged further building. The City Hotel served New Yorkers into the 1830s, its ongoing presence promising tough going for any competing establishment, and the Exchange Coffee House remained the center of Boston's social and commercial life for a decade. Macroeconomic factors may also have played a role: economic historians generally view the fifteen years after the trade embargo of 1808 as relatively slack times for the United States economy.[8]

Americans' appreciation for the function of hotels, seen together with their disinclination to build many of them, suggests a significant point of transition. The hotel had progressed beyond the experimental phase, but its status remained probationary. In this respect, the state of accommodation mirrored that of transportation: only historical hindsight allows us to see that a revolution had begun and was about to gain momentum. At the time, though, whatever enthusiasm some people displayed for each new hotel, turnpike, canal, or steamboat, most were still waiting for a sure sign that such internal improvements could be counted on as viable investments.

ADOPTION AND PROLIFERATION

Such a sign was not long in coming, one that transformed people's understanding of the risks and rewards of internal improvements in general and hotels in particular. If the previous conventional wisdom held that hotels were desirable but financially hazardous undertakings, the newer assumption was that the far greater danger was not having a hotel at all. Beginning in the mid-1820s, hotel construction came to be seen as essential to municipal prosperity. As one observer later remarked, "The leading men of the larger towns seem to have realized that the hotel, as a rule, was the index of the place of its location. A good hotel meant a prosperous town, and a public-spirited town would have a good hotel."[9]

The event that catalyzed this realization was the completion of the Erie Canal in 1825. This greatest of all American internal improvements had generated high expectations ever since 1815, when the future New York governor De Witt Clinton first pitched the idea to a group of merchants gathered at the City Hotel. The canal's completion was elaborately celebrated. Governor Clinton headed an official delegation on a ten-day boat trip from the canal's western terminus at Buffalo; upon reaching New York City, he ceremonially poured two casks of Lake Erie water into the harbor and led a procession through Manhattan streets past cheering crowds estimated at more than one hundred thousand people. The excitement proved entirely justified. The Erie Canal transformed the economic and human geography of an enormous section of North America. The linkage of the Great Lakes and Ohio River systems with the Atlantic Ocean drastically reduced the expense of moving goods to and from the West, slashing shipping costs to less than a tenth of their precanal levels. This in turn opened a vast region to profitable cultivation and large-scale settlement as part of a greatly expanded commercial hinterland of New York City.[10]

The Erie Canal also touched off a period of intense competition among the major cities of the East. Merchant elites in every city along the Atlantic seaboard understood that New York's canal threatened their prosperity, and they responded by looking for ways to harness trans-Appalachian hinterlands of their own. Their basic strategy was to preserve their municipal fortunes through massive investment in ambitious transportation projects. Alongside road, canal, and railway projects, urban leaders began building a new generation of hotels. In a striking recapitulation of the suddenness and geographic distribution of the hotel projects of 1793–1797, a grand hotel was opened in one of the nation's leading economic or political capitals each year from 1826 to 1829.[11]

Baltimore's business elite was the first to take action. As the Erie Canal approached completion, the city's leading entrepreneurs were already at work planning two major internal improvements. The Baltimore and Ohio Railroad, begun in 1827, is far better known because it was the nation's first railway; but the city's first big infrastructural project was the City Hotel. The hotel was initiated in the spring of 1825 by two prominent citizens: David Barnum, the former keeper of Boston's Exchange Coffee House, and George Brown, the eldest son of Baltimore's leading banker and the first treasurer of the B&O. That fall Brown bought up several city lots and turned them over to Barnum on a ninety-nine-year lease. Brown financed the hotel by persuading a large group of local merchants to purchase stock in a trust whose largest shareholder was Alexander Brown and Sons. The City Hotel, like the railroad, was understood as a speculative venture that depended on community backing; a local newspaper suggested as much when it called the hotel "a noble experiment." The Baltimoreans who invested in the City Hotel and the B&O were not motivated simply by a desire for profits. They were persuaded to put their money into risky ventures because their city's very prosperity was at stake. Faced with the threat of municipal obsolescence, they understood the necessity of matching their urban rivals in

2.1   Baltimore's City Hotel of 1826 represented the first move in a hotel boom that followed the opening of the Erie Canal and was driven by economic competition among eastern cities. (John Work Garrett Library, The Johns Hopkins University)

infrastructure and prestige. Urban mercantilism was now in full swing, and metropolitan competition became the engine of the new hotel age.[12]

The City Hotel (fig. 2.1) opened for business in the fall of 1826. It covered an entire block, standing six stories tall and containing more than two hundred guest rooms in addition to a full complement of drawing rooms, ballrooms, dining rooms, and stores, and a lunchroom, barber shop, and bar. The interior décor was suitably elegant, with rooms and lounges alike covered with expensive carpets and drapery, all the more easily seen because the entire establishment was brightly illuminated by gaslight. The hotel belonged to a new generation of its type, but it also showed important continuities with the past: in addition to being kept by David Barnum, it was designed by William F. Small, a student of Benjamin Latrobe, the architect of the 1797 Richmond hotel plan. Locals and travelers alike were impressed with the City Hotel and lavished praise upon the hostelry and its keeper. In a clear sign of the competitive character of hotel building, Baltimore's *Gazette and Daily Advertiser* proudly reprinted a letter from a New Yorker who deemed the City Hotel superior to any such establishment in Gotham and expressed the hope that his home city would soon build a hotel to equal it. As it turned out, though, the first response to this implicit challenge was answered not by the national metropolis but by the national capital.[13]

The planning of the National Hotel in Washington, D.C., was under way even before the City Hotel opened its doors. The National (fig. 2.2) resembled its Baltimore counterpart

2.2   The National Hotel in Washington (1827) was part of the capital's effort to become an important commercial center as well as a political one. (Collection of the New-York Historical Society)

in ways that suggested an emerging consensus on hotel architecture. It rose four stories high, fronted an entire city block, and contained 130 single and double bedchambers, an unspecified number of family lodging rooms, 12 parlors, and numerous public rooms. It was completed in less than a year and opened with a lavish and well-attended Washington's Birthday ball in 1827. The hotel represented a collective effort by leading merchants and property owners—most notably the city's prominent Calvert family, which provided essential support—to improve the economic viability and elevate the prestige of their city. Washington's importance was founded on politics rather than on trade, but the Federal City did have a functioning, if small, urban economy, and its business community hoped it could attain a prosperity long predicted but never achieved. The language of metropolitan competition pervaded discussion of the new hotel. One local newspaper boasted that there was "no city in the Union, we believe, so well supplied with Hotels of the first class, both in extent and style of keeping, as the City of Washington." The paper's editors also delighted in quoting the *Baltimore Gazette,* which they conspicuously declared an "unprejudiced source," after it published an article favorably comparing the National to the City Hotel. Such bravado would hardly have been necessary had Washingtonians been content to rest upon the laurels of political prestige, since in that province their city had no rival in the land. Rather, this represented a challenge issued by Washington to much larger Baltimore and based on the grandness of its public accommodations. The hotel race was clearly on.[14]

The next entrant was Philadelphia, a city that, despite its size and economic importance, had continued to receive travelers in converted schools and mansions. The Pennsylvania metropolis had for decades been battling Baltimore for economic control of the Susquehanna Valley. Each city set about improving roads, modifying river channels, and constructing canals and eventually railroads to advance its position as the primary clearinghouse for the area's agricultural produce. Baltimore's City Hotel was only the latest effort to augment its existing geographic advantages, and Philadelphians apparently realized that they, too, needed to improve their city's public accommodations. The United States Hotel (fig. 2.3), a five-story structure that fronted broadly on Chestnut Street, opened for business in 1828. Little information survives regarding its capacity, but the sixty-five windows on its main façade suggest a complement of between one hundred and two hundred guest rooms. Like its competitors elsewhere, the United States Hotel was managed by its city's most experienced host. William Renshaw, for twenty years the keeper of Philadelphia's best mansion-conversion hotel, made the new establishment into the city's preeminent hostelry, a position it maintained for more than two decades. The hotel also attracted the attention of the Pennsylvania Central Railroad, which laid track alongside and established a stop that directly integrated the hotel into a regional freight and travel network. The United States Hotel's timing, historical context, and railroad

2.3   Philadelphia's United States Hotel of 1828 occupied a prominent place opposite another economically important institution, the city's leading bank. (The Library Company of Philadelphia)

2.4 The Tremont House in Boston (1829) has often been called the nation's first hotel, but it is better understood as just one example of a nationwide enthusiasm for hotel building that began four years earlier. (Collection of the author)

link bespoke yet another effort to use transportation and accommodation infrastructure to maintain municipal fortunes and harness a hinterland.[15]

Urban competition also gave rise to the Tremont House, often mischaracterized as America's first hotel.[16] In 1825 a group of wealthy Bostonians secured a charter from the Massachusetts legislature establishing a company authorized to build a hotel worth up to half a million dollars. The Tremont House counted among its subscribers scores of individuals and businesses representing Boston's wealthiest and most eminent mercantile and manufacturing clans, including the Cabots, Quincys, and Lowells. A great many of these Tremont backers were also deeply invested in other internal improvement projects around Boston, reinforcing long-established connections between transportation and accommodation. Notwithstanding an early start and the support of prominent citizens, the project ran behind schedule, and it was only the well-publicized openings of the City Hotel and National Hotel in 1826 and 1827 that pressured the hotel company's leadership into finally beginning construction in 1828. As it stood when completed the following year, the Tremont House (fig. 2.4) was a fine example of Greek Revival architecture, with its granite façade, Doric portico, and domed rotunda. Inside, the hotel contained 170 rooms, including the bedchambers and various parlors, dining rooms, and drawing rooms. The

$300,000 structure was promoted aggressively—in 1830 its leading sponsor published an attractive illustrated booklet that was among the first works ever devoted to a single American building. The Tremont garnered effusive praise from the public, and its architect, Isaiah Rogers, quickly became the nation's most sought-after designer of hotels.[17]

The City, the National, the United States, and the Tremont showed that commercial hinterlands were also human mobility hinterlands. The economic growth of the 1820s and 1830s owed primarily to increased domestic and overseas trade, with cities functioning as markets where commodities were collected and distributed. The primary measures of a city's fortunes were the extent and productivity of its hinterland, which was why people invested so heavily in new modes of transportation that allowed goods to move to market more cheaply and quickly and across greater distances. In harnessing an expanding hinterland, though, a city also became a gathering place for its occupants, who converged in order to buy and sell the things produced there. It was therefore essential for a city to build the necessary infrastructure for this human hinterland. Understood in terms of urban theory, hotels functioned as central places in an economy of human motion. Urban boosters understood this same basic idea in more utilitarian terms, which is why city newspapers celebrated the quality of their local hotels, and why editors and journalists began to emphasize the importance of providing travelers with comfortable accommodations.[18]

New modes of transportation compelled cities to compete with one another through hotel building because every municipality came under increased pressure to make sure it became a stopping place for both goods and travelers. The transportation revolution meant that far more people were moving from place to place than ever before, creating a heightened demand for accommodation. Also important were changes in the ways travelers were distributed across the landscape. Canals, steamboats, and railroads led to an increase in the scale of travel as measured in both distance and volume. Because goods and people could move farther in a day, they bypassed older stopping points along the way and collected in greater numbers at fewer destinations. In 1810, for example, the 675-mile trip from New Orleans to St. Louis would have taken about a month of upriver towing or overland riding and required more than two dozen overnight stays in places like Natchez, Vicksburg, Greenville, Helena, Memphis, Cairo, and Cape Girardeau. By 1830 the distance could be covered by steamboat in several days, the vessel's staterooms obviating any tavern stays at all. Under these conditions, hotel building offered cities and towns a key competitive advantage by making them more attractive places to put up for the night.[19]

This was by no means the first time urbanites had grasped the connection between transportation and accommodation; it had been in play at least since the hotels of the 1790s. What was new was that hotels were now economically viable. The hotel projects of 1826–1829 fostered a frenzy of hotel construction because they represented an important vote of confidence in the hotel. If the most respected and powerful businessmen in the nation's largest cities had been willing to invest their time, effort, and capital, there could be little doubt that hotels were sound businesses; and as the years passed and these hotels remained open and stayed profitable, confidence in the hotel form solidi-fied further. So whenever entrepreneurs, builders, investors, or architects saw crowds of people at big-city hotels or read newspaper reports about meetings or balls held therein, they were reminded once again that the practicality and feasibility of hotels had become a demonstrated fact.

These geographic and economic imperatives were not restricted to the nation's largest urban areas. The hotel craze came to include municipalities in almost every state in the union, with small-town boosters and big-city capitalists alike rushing to build hos-telries that would demonstrate the present importance or future aspirations of their home communities. A systematic analysis of hotel construction in the forty most populous cities and towns in the United States through 1840 reveals the timing and distribution of hotel construction. These municipalities ranged in population from New York City, at more than three hundred thousand inhabitants, to Portsmouth, New Hampshire, with just un-der eight thousand. The results are summarized on a map of the locations and dates of completion for hotels in these communities (fig. 2.5). In 1815 only five of the forty were home to a substantial purpose-built hotel, and ten years later the number had increased only to thirteen. But between 1825 and 1840, the total climbed to thirty-three, with a dozen communities building their first hotels in the decade between 1830 and 1840 alone. A similarly useful indicator of just how enthusiastically American cities adopted the hotel form is the fact that by 1840, 87 percent of settlements of ten thousand inhabitants or more had completed a hotel.[20]

Hotel construction was most intense in the nation's northeastern urban core. Along with the most ambitious projects in the largest cities, the hotel idea spread outward to second- and third-tier cities and ambitious towns. The Rhode Island capital of Provi-dence made available a lot on the city's central square for the Franklin House, which was completed in 1823. The following year marked the opening of New Haven's Tontine Hotel and the four-story Washington Square Hotel in Worcester, Massachusetts. Hotels also appeared in growing industrial towns located along the rivers that punctuated the Atlantic coastline. In Lowell, Massachusetts, for example, a local transportation company financed the construction of the Merrimack House (fig. 2.6), which opened at the busy intersection of Merrimack and Dutton streets in 1832.[21]

The region's newer river and canal cities were not far behind once the Erie Canal had made the Hudson and Mohawk valleys into the nation's fastest-growing commercial corridor. Albany, which had for many years made do with taverns and converted hostel-ries, constructed its first hotel only in 1833. Stanwix Hall (fig. 2.7) was a five-story brick structure that was later enlarged and ornamented with an impressive gilded dome. Troy, New York, whose position along the canal had vaulted it into the ranks of the twenty largest American cities, got its first purpose-built hotel, the four-story Mansion House, in 1828. The somewhat smaller canal city of Utica also saw aggressive hotel-building efforts in these years. Farther west, Rochester built its first hotel, the Rochester House, by the side of the canal in 1826.[22]

2.5 This map displays the forty most populous cities in the United States in 1840 and the year in which each built its first hotel.

Communities in the South also displayed considerable interest in hotels. Throughout the 1830s state legislatures in Maryland, Virginia, North Carolina, South Carolina, Louisiana, Tennessee, and Kentucky issued acts of incorporation for hotel companies seeking to finance construction through public stock offerings. Such legislative acts only measured intentions and aspiration, however, and many did not lead to completed structures. As a result, the region was not nearly as well supplied with hotels as the Northeast. Such hotels as were built, though, were sometimes comparable to those in the North. The geographic pattern was reminiscent of northern precedents, with the largest projects going

2.6   This early image of the Merrimack House in Lowell, Massachusetts, shows its location opposite the train station, emphasizing its linkage with new modes of transportation. (Lowell Historical Society)

up in coastal cities and along major waterways. New Orleans followed Baltimore's hotel-building lead within a few years, with the Crescent City's block-sized City Hotel opening for business in 1831; it was joined seven years later by the architecturally outstanding and much-remarked-upon St. Charles Hotel (fig. 2.8). Norfolk got its first hotel in 1837, Charleston in 1838. The existence in Richmond of the 1816 City Hotel reduced public pressure and structural need for a newer establishment, but a successor was begun in the late 1830s and completed in 1841.[23]

Meanwhile, the people who migrated, resettled, and did business on the far side of the Appalachian Mountains carried enthusiasm for the hotel into the growing cities of the Ohio and Mississippi river valleys. Cincinnati's merchant class had built a modest hotel in 1824, but when it proved insufficient for the city's needs, a newer building was constructed. The Pearl Street House, which opened its doors in 1830, was impressive enough to be compared favorably with the large hotels of the East. Farther downriver, the people of Louisville joined the competition with the sixty-room Louisville Hotel (1832); it was joined in 1835 by the Galt House (fig. 2.9), located a few blocks farther down Main Street. Pittsburgh had by then seen the completion of its Exchange Hotel (1832), which served as the city's premier hostelry until the construction of the much larger Monongahela House in 1840. Because they had built a substantial hotel in 1819, the city fathers of St. Louis did not consider updating its travel accommodations until ten years later, and even then, the conversion of older buildings into hotels delayed further construction. It was not until 1836 that civic leaders finally organized a corporation to finance the Planters Hotel, but their plans were overtaken by the financial disaster of the following year, and the hotel could not be completed until 1841.[24]

The Erie Canal had also facilitated trade and communication around the Great Lakes, and the new cities that emerged on their southern shores soon outgrew their local taverns. Chicago, the smallest of these with only a few thousand inhabitants, became home to the region's first hotel in 1835, when a group of investors devoted one hundred thousand dollars to the building of the Lake House, "the pride of the city and the admiration of strangers." Buffalo mobilized shortly thereafter, augmenting its commanding position at the meeting point of lake and canal with the immense American Hotel (fig. 2.10). Detroiters, whom a local newspaper congratulated for "becoming alive to the importance of an addition to the comforts and convenience of travelers," in 1836 built the National Hotel, which drew praise for "its lofty front, pretentious style and dazzling new paint" and was called "quite the swell house of the city." In Cleveland local editors raised their voices to "respectfully inquire of our capitalists and owners of real estate how much longer the traveling public are to suffer for want of the necessary accommodations for their comfort while sojourning with us." Their entreaties were soon answered by the completion of the American House (1837), a stately three-story brick building occupying an entire city block. That all these projects were commenced and completed in a span of only three years underscores the unanimity of sentiment regarding the importance of hotels to the region.[25]

Hotels were eagerly adopted by the nation's smallest cities and in a considerable

2.7   Stanwix Hall was Albany's first substantial hotel. (National Museum of American History)

2.8   The St. Charles Hotel in New Orleans was one of the grandest hostelries in the country from its opening in 1838 until it was destroyed in a fire in 1851 (The Historic New Orleans Collection)

number of towns with populations below the twenty-five hundred that the census bureau had set as the official threshold of urbanism. In Charlottesville, Virginia, in 1826, a local postmaster built a three-story brick hotel that fronted almost one hundred feet along Court Square and contained a post office and shops on the first floor; as an homage to the recently deceased president, he named it the Jefferson Hotel (fig. 2.11). In Bangor, Maine, a fast-growing settlement that in 1830 had fewer than three thousand inhabitants, civic leaders built a hotel to showcase the wealth the town had amassed in the lumber business. Greatly impressed by Boston's Tremont House, they commissioned its architect to construct a hotel of equal merit in their own community. The result was the Bangor House (1834), a stately stone-fronted structure that still stands today. In the New Hampshire town of Exeter, local merchants erected the Swamscot Hotel (1837), a four-story brick structure sited at the town's commercial center. The construction of substantial hotels in such small settlements suggests just how thoroughly the idea of the hotel had spread through American life.[26]

A large city's first hotel was seldom its only one. Intraurban competition often led to the construction of a number of similar hotels, though this period also saw the beginnings of differentiation into hotel types. Determining the number and character of the

2.9   The Galt House in Louisville, Kentucky, was one of several hotels built in the 1830s in the fast-growing cities of the Ohio and Mississippi river valleys. (The Filson Historical Society)

various hotels within a city can be a complicated task, since the keepers of inns and taverns frequently tried to elevate their status by renaming their premises hotels. It is nonetheless possible to distinguish among establishments by using city directories, urban maps, and illustrations. All available sources point toward rapid multiplication of hotels within cities (fig. 2.12). City directories typically listed all of a municipality's public houses without differentiating among them, but as a service to well-heeled visitors they also frequently included guides to the most prominent hotels. Thus Boston's city directory for 1840 listed forty-six establishments specifically identified as hotels rather than inns, taverns, exchanges, or coffeehouses. M'Elroy's Philadelphia city directory for 1842 likewise listed twenty-three "principal hotels," suggesting that it was only counting establishments of some significance. Urban maps offer further evidence. The 1844 Twichel map of St. Louis featured an illustration of the Planters Hotel and showed the location of eleven hotels. The Boynton map of Boston, also from 1844, listed four hotels among twenty-one named landmarks. Hotel ephemera show the same trend. Various archival collections, most notably those at the National Museum of American History and the New-York Historical Society, contain a plethora of advertising cards, stationery, hotel bills, and other materials that vividly illustrate the many shapes, sizes, aesthetics, and locations of hotels within individual cities.[27]

By 1840 Americans had fully embraced the hotel and made it an everyday part of urban life in the United States. But while the multiplication of hotels on the nation's cityscape demonstrated a new approach to the built environment, there is still more to be said about what kinds of meanings Americans attached to these newly popular institutions. The decades in question brought dramatic transformations in public life and sociability interwoven with changes in the economy, and the hotel's place in American life was also determined by the less quantifiable but equally important influence of politics and culture.

HOTELS AND JACKSONIAN DEMOCRACY

Early in the summer of 1827, as the nationwide surge of hotel building gained momentum, the Washington-based *National Intelligencer* published a brief item entitled "Our Public Hotels." The author applauded recent improvements in the city's public accommodations and situated them within a larger national context: "The splendor of modern Hotels has obtained for them the appellation of 'palaces of the public,' and really the elegance of some of them here, and elsewhere, almost justifies the phrase." In using the words "palaces of the public," the article's author combined two kinds of imagery that were usually set in opposition to each other. *Palaces* recalled the luxury and splendor of European aristocracy but also evoked the exclusionary, antidemocratic character of the Old World social

2.10   The American Hotel in Buffalo was emblematic of the tremendous resources devoted to hotel building in the new cities of the Great Lakes region in the 1830s. (Buffalo and Erie County Historical Society)

order. By contrast, invoking "the public" indicated respect for a citizenry whose symbolic ownership of hotels paralleled the way it controlled its government. The phrase "palaces of the public" suggested that while opulence and grandeur had traditionally been products of monarchical corruption and inequality of status, hotels demonstrated that in the United States, these had now become the property of the common people.[28]

This effort to portray hotels as democratic institutions indicated a concern that they might be incompatible with the changing political culture of the United States. The concern was well founded, in part because of the hotel's unmistakably elitist origins. The first hotels had, after all, been created by groups of wealthy, urban, entrepreneurial Federalists who sought to advance their narrow economic interests and solidify their political dominance. These hotels were intended to exclude much of the population, which recognized the gesture: workingmen expressed their resentment of hotels as soon as they appeared, and as recently as 1818, when Boston's Exchange Coffee House burned down, artisans and mechanics had gloated openly over its demise. The increasing scale and opulence of hotels could hardly be expected to ease three decades of popular suspicion.[29]

Even more important, the political environment of the 1820s and 1830s was increasingly inhospitable to the original purposes of hotels. The Federalist Party had collapsed, and the Jacksonian Democrats were the nation's ascendant political grouping. Jacksonians appealed to the electorate by denouncing would-be aristocrats, railing against special privilege, and exalting the superior virtue of the common man. Andrew Jackson and his supporters advocated equality of political and economic opportunity among white men,

2.11   Hotel construction was not the exclusive province of larger cities. Many towns of just a few thousand people joined in, as well, building hostelries like the Jefferson Hotel, center, in Charlottesville, Virginia. (Albemarle Charlottesville Historical Society)

2.12　By the 1840s Cleveland's main street was lined with hotels and other commercial institutions essential to the city's role as a regional entrepôt. (Collection of the author)

who, given a fair chance to make a living, ought to be able to support themselves and their dependent women, children, servants, and slaves. The problem, as they saw it, was that a monied and politically connected elite was using exclusive institutions like banks and other specially chartered corporations to enrich its members at the expense of the common citizenry. This rhetoric might easily be directed against hotels, since they were unmistakably the creations of rich, well-connected financiers, sometimes with special privileges granted by state legislatures in the form of acts of incorporation. Political ideology in the age of Jackson thus required ways to mediate the contradiction between the opulence of hotels and the aggressive egalitarianism of public life.[30]

But how well did the idea of "palaces of the public" correspond to reality? Probably the most direct evidence of the actual social character of hotels in the quarter-century to 1840 comes from the prices they charged for rooms, food, and drink. If hotels really were democratic institutions, they should have been affordable to a significant proportion of the population. Hotel rates between the mid-1820s and the late 1830s ranged from approximately $1.50 to $2.50 per day. In 1827 rooms at Washington's National Hotel went for about $2 ($1 each to share a double room, $6.50 for a suite for three adults). The Tremont House charged $2 when it opened in 1829, and Holt's Hotel in Manhattan cost from $1.50 to $2 in 1835. These were similar to prices of $3.00 at New York's Bishop's Hotel, $2.50 at the Astor House, and $1.50 at an unnamed Detroit hotel. These rates, it should be noted, included both room and board, since the "American plan" of shared meals at set hours was the established practice at virtually all hotels.[31]

Comparing these prices with prevailing wage and income rates in the 1820s and 1830s suggests that a hotel stay was beyond the reach of most Americans but would have been

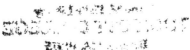

affordable for a small yet significant minority of the population. People who worked with their hands were highly improbable hotel guests. Unskilled male laborers earned about 70 to 90 cents a day and endured irregular employment that often held their incomes down to less than $250 per year; an overnight hotel stay would have required two or more days' wages, a virtual impossibility for individuals and families who lived in or at the edge of poverty and could rarely keep any savings. Artisans like shoemakers, masons, and carpenters did significantly better, their skilled work earning them from $1.30 to $1.90 per day, but this still came in most cases to less than the cost of a night at a hotel, and any savings they might have put away would probably have more urgent uses.[32] The growing middle class comprised a more promising potential clientele. While reliable statistics on their incomes are harder to come by, the best estimates for nonmanual workers like clerks, shopkeepers, and small-scale merchants are in the neighborhood of $750 to perhaps $3,000 annually. With $2.50 to $10.00 a workday to spend, such people could view a hotel stay costing less than a day's wages as at least a possibility, particularly given their ability to save money.[33] Needless to say, the well-to-do and wealthy, including merchants, elite professionals, and large landholders, who took in several thousand dollars or more per year, would have had no difficulty affording even a lengthy hotel visit.[34] Given the occupational and income distribution of the Jacksonian period, then, perhaps 20 percent of white Americans might be expected to be at least occasional hotel guests.[35]

Staying overnight was not the only way to patronize a hotel, however. Bars, dining halls, and assembly rooms offered ways to enjoy a hotel's amenities without having to pay the full cost of a stay. Hotelkeepers, always eager to generate additional marginal income, actively encouraged the local public to spend money on their premises (fig. 2.13). Drinks were priced at a level that would have allowed a small group of friends to raise a glass together for less than a quarter each: English porter could be had at fifty cents a bottle, sherry at one dollar, and even at the luxurious Astor House, the wine list included one-dollar bottles of claret. Meals offered a slightly more expensive but still manageable way to rub elbows with hotel guests, with dinners priced at about fifty cents per person. Hotels also occasionally hosted small exhibitions and minor spectacles with relatively low ticket prices: at Cleveland's American House, one might see "Davenport's Electro Magnetic Engine" or "the celebrated Albino Lady and the Irish Giant" for twenty-five cents; at the nearby Cleveland Hotel, attractions included "Four Egyptian Mummies" and Mr. and Mrs. Booth, "but 40 inches [and] 30 inches high," for only twelve and a half cents. There were also ways of enjoying hotel amenities like well-upholstered furniture, elegant paintings and drapery, and gaslight at no cost whatsoever. Most establishments included a lobby and various lounges and parlors. While these areas were monitored by hotel staff, a reasonably attired and well-behaved white person would probably not be asked to leave for some time, if at all.[36]

This suggests that a significant proportion of whites could have found their way into even the most luxurious hotels. But did they? The preponderance of evidence indicates that hotels were indeed reasonably accessible institutions for white people. Visitors from

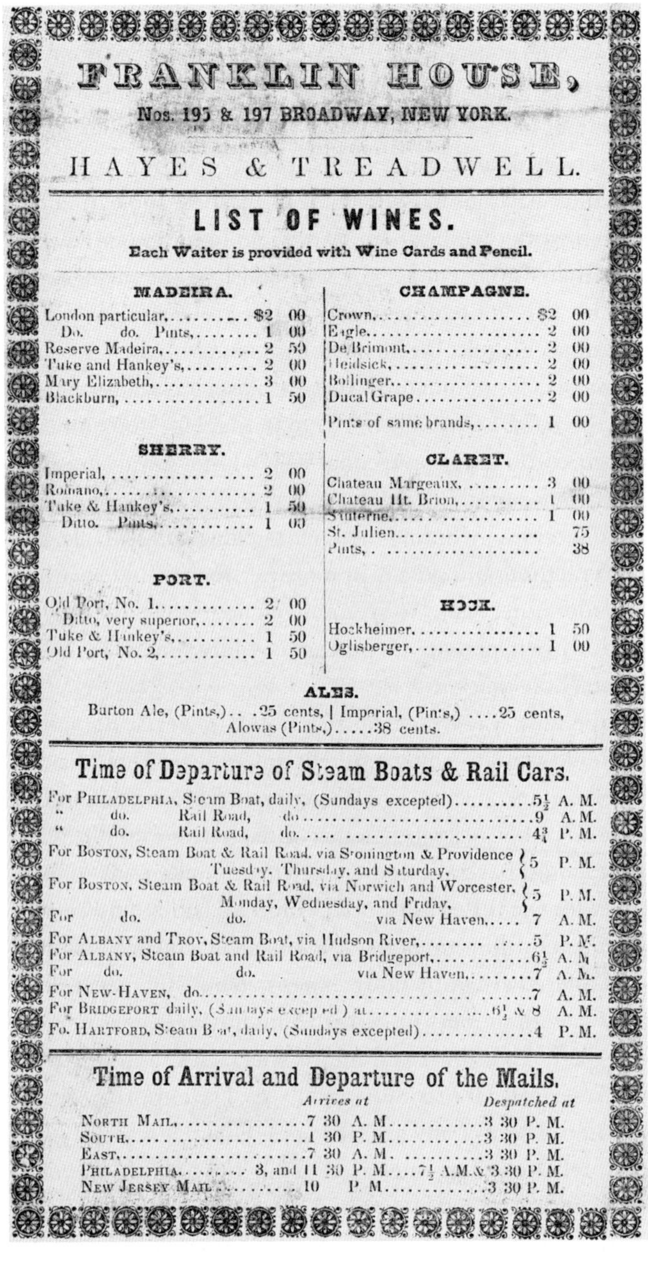

FRANKLIN HOUSE,

Nos. 195 & 197 BROADWAY, NEW YORK.

HAYES & TREADWELL.

LIST OF WINES.

Each Waiter is provided with Wine Cards and Pencil.

MADEIRA.

London particular ... $2 00
Do. do. Pints ... 1 00
Reserve Madeira ... 2 50
Tuke and Hankey's ... 2 00
Mary Elizabeth ... 3 00
Blackburn ... 1 50

SHERRY.

Imperial ... 2 00
Romano ... 2 00
Tuke & Hankey's ... 1 50
Ditto. Pints ... 1 00

PORT.

Old Port, No. 1 ... 2 00
Ditto, very superior ... 2 00
Tuke & Hankey's ... 1 50
Old Port, No. 2 ... 1 50

CHAMPAGNE.

Crown ... $2 00
Eagle ... 2 00
De Brimont ... 2 00
Heidsick ... 2 00
Bollinger ... 2 00
Ducal Grape ... 2 00
Pints of same brands ... 1 00

CLARET.

Chateau Margeaux ... 3 00
Chateau Ht. Brion ... 1 00
Sauterne ... 1 00
St. Julien ... 75
Pints ... 38

HOCK.

Hockheimer ... 1 50
Oglisberger ... 1 00

ALES.

Burton Ale, (Pints,) ... 25 cents, | Imperial, (Pints,) ... 25 cents,
Alowas (Pints,) ... 38 cents.

Time of Departure of Steam Boats & Rail Cars.

For PHILADELPHIA, Steam Boat, daily, (Sundays excepted) ... 5½ A. M.
" do. Rail Road, do ... 9 A. M.
" do. Rail Road, do. ... 4¾ P. M.
For BOSTON, Steam Boat & Rail Road, via Stonington & Providence, Tuesday, Thursday, and Saturday, ... 5 P. M.
For BOSTON, Steam Boat & Rail Road, via Norwich and Worcester, Monday, Wednesday, and Friday, ... 5 P. M.
For do. do. via New Haven ... 7 A. M.
For ALBANY and TROY, Steam Boat, via Hudson River ... 5 P. M.
For ALBANY, Steam Boat and Rail Road, via Bridgeport ... 6½ A. M.
For do. do. via New Haven ... 7 A. M.
For NEW-HAVEN, do. ... 7 A. M.
For BRIDGEPORT daily, (Sundays excepted) at ... 6½ & 8 A. M.
For HARTFORD, Steam Boat, daily, (Sundays excepted) ... 4 P. M.

Time of Arrival and Departure of the Mails.

	Arrives at	Despatched at
NORTH MAIL	7 30 A. M	3 30 P. M.
SOUTH	1 30 P. M	3 30 P. M.
EAST	7 30 A. M	3 30 P. M.
PHILADELPHIA	3, and 11 30 P. M	7½ A.M.& 3 30 P. M.
NEW JERSEY MAIL	10 P. M	3 30 P. M.

2.13 The prices on this 1841 wine and drinks list from a New York City hotel indicate that a substantial proportion of Americans could at least have afforded to share a bottle in a hotel bar. (Collection of the New-York Historical Society)

abroad often commented on the social heterogeneity of American hotels, and while their reactions differed—some were impressed and others discomfited by class mixing—all seemed to agree that hotels exemplified the nation's democratic creed. One British traveler observed in 1833 that Americans of very different conditions and occupations were at ease with one another conversationally, a fact he attributed partly to "the constant amalgamation of the different classes in hotels, boarding houses, and particularly in travelling, in which there are no aristocratic modes." Another remarked that "at the hotels . . . you have frequent opportunities of seeing all classes: from the best and highest (viz., richest), to the needy speculator, and the successful adventurer." Other visitors learned about their American hosts' attitudes toward hotel sociability by accident rather than observation: when they asked to be served meals in their rooms in order to avoid the social mixing and jostling of the common dining table, their requests were often denied, and it was made clear to them that the very idea was improperly undemocratic (though sometimes the service was available for an additional fee). Such historical evidence is not unproblematic. European travel writers were on the lookout for proof of American distinctiveness, and were therefore inclined toward broad generalizations about the democratic spirit of the citizenry.[37]

Yet the same impressions of promiscuous sociability formed a recurrent theme in the writings of domestic commentators as well. A writer for the *New York Mirror,* for example, remarked in 1836 on "the thousands who are constantly passing between the City-hotel and the American [Hotel]" and noted the varied character of the crowd: "The beau, the belle, the merchant and the scholar, the poet, the editor, the Wall-Street broker, ladies to meet their lovers, and tradesmen running to the bank to meet their notes."[38]

Even stronger claims can be made regarding the working-class presence in hotels. There is abundant documentation of mechanics and artisans using hotels for their trade and political meetings. The New York City labor newspaper *The Workingman's Advocate* published dozens of reports on gatherings of workers at various city hotels in the early 1830s. The most frequently used was the North American Hotel, a sizable establishment located on the Bowery. The hotel hosted a wide range of activities: meetings of the General Executive Committee of the Mechanics and Working Men, nominating caucuses for the Working Men's Party, celebrations of the successes of workingmen in other cities, and even protests by splinter groups within the labor movement. (Indeed, during an episode of internecine conflict in 1830, one faction became known as the North American Hotel Committee.) In Boston in 1832, the New England Association of Farmers, Mechanics, and Other Working Men met at the Marlborough Hotel for a convention that drew nearly one hundred delegates from more than two dozen cities and towns across New England. Labor newspapers carried similar notices of workingmen's meetings in many other industrializing cities, including Philadelphia, Albany, Troy, and Newark; and the records of the United States Congress contain repeated references to workers meeting at hotels to formulate requests for their representatives in Washington.[39]

Indeed, with regard to the public image of hotels at a time of emergent class stratification, what is perhaps most noticeable is the lack of criticism directed at them. At a time when political partisanship often bordered on contrariness, one might expect that hotels would come under rhetorical fire, if not from Jacksonian Democrats, then at least from the workingmen who were developing direct critiques of capitalism. Yet there is little or no evidence that resentment of hotels survived into the 1820s and 1830s. Labor newspapers that constantly attacked banks, chartered corporations, and other bastions of special privilege did not include hotels among their targets, instead dealing with them in a matter-of-fact way. For instance, the *Workingman's Advocate* reprinted without comment lists of new arrivals to New York City that were organized according to which hotel the traveler was patronizing. Moreover, when members of the North American Hotel Committee were attacked by their enemies in print, no effort was made to call attention to their meeting place, even when it might have been a convenient way to paint them as aristocrats. And when a Jacksonian radical from Ohio was publicly mocked for staying at a luxury hotel some years later, he retorted that "it is one of the first ideas of a democrat to live upon the best which the country offers [even if he is] a poor one."[40]

There were good reasons why hotels gained widespread acceptance in the Jacksonian period. They had become accessible enough to avoid the impression of exclusion that had dogged them previously, and internal improvements were gaining popularity in American political culture. But there may also have been other, more subtle factors at work—changes in hotels that preceded the opening of their doors or even the laying of the first brick or stone. Methods of financing hotels were changing significantly in this period, and projects that were once the exclusive province of wealthy merchants, bankers, and lawyers increasingly involved broader participation. By the end of the second generation of American hoteldom, the building of a hotel meant something different in both theory and practice than it had before.

FINANCING PUBLIC PALACES

Hotels were just one of the various types of infrastructural projects that constituted the transportation revolution, and from the standpoint of an aspiring hotel builder, the first and most pressing task was to secure the necessary capital. Prospective investors had any number of opportunities before them: they could put their money into a local turnpike or a long-distance canal company; they could also opt for a non–transportation-related concern like a bank. Not all investments were considered equal. Banks were highly regarded because they typically posted high rates of return; by contrast, transportation company stock was less sought after because such concerns sometimes failed to generate any interest or dividends at all. In order to attract investors, transportation companies often had to appeal to local pride or emphasize expected community benefits to compensate for the unreliability of direct profits. As infrastructural improvements, hotels faced considerable uncertainty in early American capital markets.[41]

The builders of the second generation of hotels financed their projects in ways that insulated them from political criticism. To begin with, few hotel companies were state-chartered corporations. A systematic examination of the session laws of five selected state legislatures from 1825 to 1840 reveals a tiny number of hotel company incorporations: none in New York, one in Pennsylvania, four in Ohio, four in Virginia, five in Louisiana. In one sense, this is not unexpected, since most companies in the early United States were single proprietorships or partnerships. It *is* surprising, however, in light of the close connection between accommodation and transportation. Over the same period, these state legislatures issued scores of corporate charters for bridges, turnpikes, canals, and railways; and considering how frequently hotel builders also sponsored transportation projects, it is doubtful that they lacked the wherewithal to obtain a state charter. This organizational divergence between hotels and other kinds of internal improvements may suggest that legislatures were reluctant to grant incorporation to profit-making ventures whose benefits were limited to a single part of the state; it could indicate that the state powers that came with incorporation were not necessary for enterprises that, unlike railroads or canals, did not require the power of eminent domain to secure rights-of-way; or it might simply reflect the organizational preferences of hotel entrepreneurs. From the standpoint of political economy in the age of Jackson, however, it raises the possibility that hotels escaped the condemnation of Jacksonian Democrats because very few enjoyed state-sponsored privileges. Incorporated banks or steamboat lines might fairly be criticized as private monopolies that barred the common people from fair economic competition, and railway corporations could be accused of seizing land, but there was little about unchartered hotel partnerships that could be attributed to special favors from corrupt legislators.[42]

Furthermore, hotel projects enjoyed little in the way of public subsidies. Historians have long recognized that state governments were heavily involved in promoting economic development in the early nineteenth century, and the state session laws just cited contain abundant evidence of legislative allocations for, and state investment in, a broad range of concerns, particularly transportation companies. Yet there is scant evidence of direct public support of hotels, and with rare exceptions, states and municipalities avoided investing in hotel construction. An 1828 controversy over the financing of the Tremont House suggests that this was the case even in Boston, a redoubt of Federalists and Whigs who believed in economically active governance. A week before construction was to begin, the hotel's lead investor, William Havard Eliot, petitioned the city for an allocation of five hundred dollars per year for ten years, a sum that would offset the property taxes on the project. When the measure came up before the Common Council, one member protested against using public funds to aid a project that would benefit only the rich, citing the "danger of the precedent" that would be set by such a subsidy. If the city agreed to aid the wealthy men behind the hotel company, he asked, "Who shall defend the treasury from the assaults of the middling, the poorer, and the numerous classes of society, all of whom abound in projects that promise to increase both the capital and population of the city?" Local newspapers reported on the council proceedings, setting off weeks of arguments in which claims of the hotel's benefit to the community were answered by remonstrances against the favoritism inherent in publicly funding some private projects and not others. Ultimately, the disagreement was decided by the city solicitor, who concluded that Boston could not spend taxpayer dollars on the hotel without specific authorization from the Massachusetts legislature.[43]

The Tremont House investors' failure to secure a public subsidy suggests an emergent consensus on state support of hotels. The Tremont's backers clearly did not need public funding. Their petition was filed shortly before the scheduled groundbreaking, which they surely expected to go ahead whatever the Common Council decided. More-over, powerful financiers who could marshal three hundred thousand dollars for the Tre-mont House were hardly incapable of paying five hundred dollars a year in taxes on their own account. It seems rather as if they were looking for an official imprimatur, a symbolic validation of the public-spiritedness of their undertaking. The opponents of the hotel subsidy were similarly measured in their claims. Their initial objection did assert that the Tremont House was being built for the wealthy, but much of the subsequent argu-ment involved the moderate Jacksonian claim that the project did not deserve taxpayer support because it was an essentially private venture. The denial of state aid here, viewed in conjunction with the generalized lack of public funding for hotels elsewhere, indicates that even as Americans embraced hotels as important and beneficial institutions, they expected them to function without government assistance. Once it had been agreed that hotels would be privately funded, they were effectively removed from the field of battle of Jacksonian politics, a landscape dotted with the remains of abandoned banks and canceled public improvements.

There may also have been another reason why hotels never became targets for Jack-sonian Democrats: because changes in financing had made hotel shares available to a significant segment of a growing population of investors. Though archival evidence is limited to the small number of hotel projects for which acts of incorporation or company records are available, these sources suggest that hotel builders made a deliberate effort to make hotels less exclusionary by altering how they worked as businesses.

Hotel company charters document a generalized trend toward lower share prices. This is significant because it reduced the amount of money a person needed to have to invest in a hotel company and enjoy any corresponding financial returns. In Louisiana, for example, the first two hotel charters, granted in 1831 and 1835, set the price of a single share at $250 and $500, respectively; the three hotels incorporated in 1836 and 1837, however, all issued shares for $100 each. The General Assembly of Virginia issued a hotel charter in 1838 that fixed the share price at $500, but when the incorporation was modified a year later, this was cut to $100; the state's other hotel corporations also set their share prices at $100. And in the famously development-oriented state of Ohio, three hotel corporations sold shares for $50 and one for only $25.[44]

Furthermore, even these share prices overstate the sums required to invest in a hotel company. In the early decades of the nineteenth century, subscribers to stock offer-ings only had to pay 10–20 percent of a share's face value up front. The company would hold the buyer's stock certificate and call for incremental payments as the need arose. In other words, an aspiring hotel investor could go in for as little as $2.50 or $5. Shares in the Baltimore City Hotel (fig. 2.14) paid 5 percent annual interest, and according to the company's business ledgers, stockholders paid just 3 percent per year on a minimum of $100 to maintain their investments. In a period in which banks were highly unstable and savings could be easily lost, the opportunity to become a hotel investor could be a very profitable one. (Indeed, Whigs constructed their appeals to workingmen around the idea

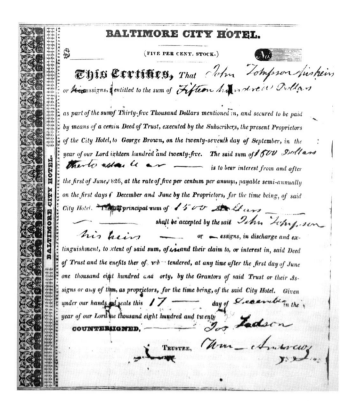

that Jacksonian Democrats' anticorporate politics would end up denying them the benefits of participation in company profits.) The extant evidence suggests, then, that hotel corporations tried to increase their pool of available capital by broadening their investor base to include people with less cash on hand.[45]

This trend can also be seen by comparing the financing of three of Boston's most important hotels. The city's first, the Exchange Coffee House of 1809, had only three exceptionally wealthy investors; the hotel bore a reputation for elitism, and its owners were accused of having cheated the workingmen who built the structure. When it was destroyed by fire and the city's leading entrepreneurs set about erecting a replacement, they took a very different approach. Rather than keeping ownership in elite hands, the financiers behind the Tremont House broadened participation to 144 shareholders, including at least eight artisans. The groundbreaking ceremony also involved a conscious effort to shape people's perceptions of the hotel project. On the Fourth of July 1828, a procession of the hotel's financial backers and members of the Massachusetts Charitable Mechanics Association, an organization of leading artisans, marched to the site of the future Tremont House. There, the hotel's lead investor gave a speech in which he declared that it was Boston's workingmen who had the most "direct interest" in the hotel, since it "promote[d] the advancement of the community in refinement and the growth and improvement of the city." Workers, Eliot emphasized, would be "among the first to receive a share of the advantages which will accrue from it."[46]

This effort to give working Bostonians prominent roles in the event may have been no more than an attempt to preserve the kind of hierarchical mutuality that had been expressed in countless public processions during the colonial and early national periods. But the workingmen evidently took a different message from the event, one manifested fifteen years later in the construction of the Revere House (fig. 2.15).[47] Far from being the creation of a mercantile elite, the hotel belonged to the Massachusetts Charitable Mechanics Association. The association had wanted to construct a Mechanic's Hall as a permanent headquarters, but was unable to raise the necessary funds. Instead, members decided to find investors for "a first-rate hotel," reasoning that the financial returns on such an establishment would enable them to maintain a club and reading room on the premises. The hotel occupied a prominent place on Bowdoin Square, comprised more than two hundred rooms, and featured marble floors, elaborate chandeliers, Brussels carpets, and velvet upholstery. Association members took pride in the Revere House, not least because it had been an excellent financial investment. As one of the association's official histories noted, the hotel was "the very best investment for our funds that could possibly have been found. . . . [It] will continue to pay us a higher rate of interest than we could look for elsewhere." The ownership by mechanics of one of the finest hostelries of the 1840s suggests the extent to which the meaning of the hotel form had changed during the age of Jackson.

Hotels, originally intended as elite projects that would exclude most people, gained acceptance in Jacksonian America less because they truly were "palaces of the public" than because they were useful and accessible enough to avoid generating resentment among the period's white male electorate. Most Americans might not be able to afford a room at a hotel, but hotel lobbies, lounges, dining rooms, and bars were open to a substantial percentage of the population. Meanwhile, the financial underpinnings of hotels were changing in ways that promoted transparency and broadened investor participation, making them unlikely targets for accusations of corruption or conspiracy. Hotels thus formed an egalitarian capitalist answer to monarchical institutions: they might look like aristocratic palaces, yet any white man could walk into one and expect to be served.

CONCLUSION: POPULAR PALACES

The great success of second-generation American hotels owed largely to the fact that they continued to advance the economic aims of the first generation while moving away from its social exclusivity. The primary achievement of the hotel builders of 1815–1840 consisted in transforming what had once been a risky venture into a reliable, and thus reproducible, institutional type. As a result, the hotel form could be easily adopted in a wide variety of locales. Numerous communities were thus able to incorporate themselves into larger networks of commerce and participate in the era's virtuous cycle of infrastructural improvement and economic expansion. Meanwhile, the new methods by which hotels were designed, financed, and managed not only made it possible for them to avoid

2.15   The construction of the Revere House suggests that by 1840 many workingmen and artisans had enthusiastically adopted an institutional type they had once criticized and that had initially been intended to exclude them. (Bostonian Society/Old State House)

the antipathy directed at other developmental corporations but also contributed to their ongoing viability by drawing investors as well as customers. As competing cities reordered geographic space in their own urban image, the hotel demonstrated how perfectly suited it was to a new age of human mobility and political democracy.

The hotel-building frenzy of the 1820s and 1830s was brought to a close only because of the worst economic crisis in the nation's history. The Panic of 1837 began with the failure of a limited number of local banks that had been supported by the speculative value of landholdings. When these banks began to call in their debts, they precipitated a cascading effect in which the collapse of smaller banks spurred larger banks to redeem their own paper, sparking bankruptcies higher up in the nation's financial hierarchy. In the depression that followed, tens of thousands of businesses closed their doors and hundreds of thousands of people lost their jobs. Unlike previous periods of recession, the post-Panic hard times lasted for years, with some regions of the country not fully recovering for a decade. These bleak economic conditions greatly curtailed the availability of capital on which hotel construction depended. Land valuations had plummeted in the Panic, and bank failures left very little reliable currency in circulation. As important sources of hotel financing evaporated, construction slowed. Much the same thing happened elsewhere in the transportation industry: canal and railroad projects were moribund for years after the Panic. The full resumption of hotel building would have to await the economic recovery of the mid-1840s.[48]

By then, however, the hotel had thoroughly proven its utility, and had been so enthusiastically adopted by Americans that its institutional momentum carried through into a decades-long wave of hotel construction. As hard times gave way to a new period of prosperity, the number of hotels in the United States climbed into the thousands, and the basic hotel form diversified into various subtypes. As a result, the nation's hotels were elaborated into a network of accommodations that changed the basic character of travel and opened every part of the continent up to further colonization.

Three   *The Hotel System*

Assembling a Transcontinental Accommodation Network, 1840–1876

DOMINGO FAUSTINO SARMIENTO was lost. The Argentine teacher and journalist, who fifteen years earlier had been exiled from his homeland by a brutal dictator, visited the United States in 1847 to study its innovative public schools; his hope was to use them as a model for public education in South America. When the dictator was overthrown several years later, Sarmiento returned to Argentina and became its most influential educator. Elected president in 1868, he arranged for the construction of more than a hundred libraries and initiated the greatest expansion in school enrollments in the nation's history.

On this particular summer day, however, his object was rather more prosaic. Having nearly run out of money, he needed to rendezvous with Don Santiago Mariano Arcos, a young Spaniard who had offered to provide him with the funds he needed to continue his travels. Upon arriving in Harrisburg, Pennsylvania, Sarmiento recalled, "I inquired the whereabouts of the Hotel United States. I was shocked to learn that there was no hotel by that name in Harrisburg! As there is a Hotel United States in every American city, I had made an appointment with my future traveling companion to meet him in a place I had supposed to exist in Harrisburg." Sarmiento soon hit upon a method for finding his friend: he went from hotel to hotel checking guest registers, eventually finding a message directing him to a nearby city. "With much trouble," Sarmiento explained, "I was able to find out Arcos' whereabouts, as he had left written in the register of the hotel near the station these laconic words addressed to me: 'I'll be waiting for you in Chambersburg.'"[1]

Sarmiento's account provides a suitable point of departure for understanding the establishment of a transcontinental American hotel system. At one level, his statement that there was a Hotel United States in every city and his claim to have been "shocked" not to find one in Harrisburg were simply products of his playful literary wit. At the same time, though, the way Sarmiento and Arcos used hotels to locate each other highlights how hotels had begun to systematize travel and accommodation. By the 1840s Americans had begun to assemble a rationalized and predictable hotel network; the first and second generations of hotels had set the stage for such a network, but it became a reality only in conjunction with subsequent developments in geography, transportation, architecture, and information.

Hotels must be understood as part of a system because they were fundamentally translocal institutions. The basic purpose of a hotel was to provide accommodation to people arriving at a place from somewhere else; without that implicit elsewhere, the hotel would make little sense. Hotels did have many local uses, as any number of politicians, debutantes, drinkers, and prostitutes could have attested. But a hotel was more than just an agglomeration of bar, bedchambers, and ballrooms. Each individual hotel was dependent upon systems that stretched far beyond the horizon. Because every hotel was a node in an extended network of travel, hotels cannot be correctly conceptualized separate from this larger system; to do so would be like writing railroad history by looking only at locomotives and ignoring tracks, depots, and the idea of distance. There is also a practical reason for a system-oriented approach. By midcentury, hotels had become so numerous that it is not feasible to focus on individual establishments. They must therefore be analyzed collectively, in terms of broader types and trends.

The creation of the American hotel system comprised a number of interlinked processes, including territorial expansion, economic growth, technological advancement, the emergence of specialized hotel types, and the compilation of new sources of travel information. These developments transformed the geography of the United States by making travel faster, cheaper, safer, more reliable, and more accessible than ever before. Over the course of the years between 1840 and 1876, the emergent hotel system not only provided the basics of shelter and sustenance, it also allowed Americans to feel at home throughout most of the length and breadth of their continental republic.

The third generation of hotels developed within a changing national geography.[2] As the economy recovered from the Panic of 1837, entrepreneurs, city councils, and state legislatures rediscovered their zeal for internal improvements. The steam locomotive played the most important role in the ongoing transportation revolution. Railroading was scarcely a decade old in the United States when it was disrupted by the Panic, and as of 1840 there were only about 3,300 miles of track nationwide. America's railways comprised little more than a half-dozen local lines designed to connect eastern cities with interior hinterlands, and the longest of these covered a mere 127 miles. With the economy improving, railroad companies could resume their westward push with plans to cross the Appalachian Mountains and drive on toward the Mississippi River. There were limits to Americans' conceptual horizons, however: when in 1846 one promoter proposed a railway from Lake Michigan to the Pacific Ocean, the House of Representatives balked, declaring it "a project too gigantic, and, at least from the present, entirely impracticable."[3]

But the geographic politics of the age had already begun to overtake the conventional wisdom of the day. The United States was undergoing its most dramatic territorial expansion since the Louisiana Purchase of 1803. The Polk administration arranged for the annexation of Texas in 1845 and secured the Oregon Territory through an 1846 treaty with Great Britain. It then deliberately provoked a war with Mexico and in 1848 stripped it of one-third of its territory, adding what would become New Mexico, Colorado, Arizona, Utah, Nevada, and California to the national domain. In just four years, the United States had expanded by more than 1.2 million square miles, an increase of 51 percent.[4]

This new West might have been settled at the moderate pace of previous frontiers but for the convergence of mineral wealth and railroads. The discovery of gold deposits at John Augustus Sutter's sawmill in California in 1848 drew the most migrants to the region, but other parts of the West also had their attractions: there were gold and silver rushes in Colorado, and the entire intermountain region was rich in subsoil resources. Eastern railroad interests, already enthusiastic about profits to be made carrying agricultural produce from the Midwest and the Great Plains, set about building trunk lines to the Pacific, reorienting the national transportation system to run from east to west instead of along predominantly north-south river systems. This facilitated the extraction and movement of natural resources to manufacturing and market centers in the Midwest and East, as well as the flow of people and finished goods westward. These factors combined to reignite the hotel-building enthusiasm of the 1820s and 1830s on a far more extensive and extravagant scale.[5]

The resurgence of hotel construction under these new circumstances intensified— or, to use a more exact term, amplified—many of the trends that had been established by the second generation of hotels. This meant that travelers were able to cross increasingly long distances, leading to a corresponding growth in the scale and spacing of travel accommodations.

The longer process of amplification can be seen cartographically and schematically. In the colonial, revolutionary, and early national periods, destinations located on rivers or seacoasts were easy to reach, but inland travel using horses and stagecoaches was uncomfortable, expensive, and above all slow. This made regular stopping places an absolute necessity, a role admirably served by roadside inns and taverns. A mid-eighteenth-century map of the road between Trenton and Perth Amboy, New Jersey, depicted individual taverns closely spaced on the forty-two-mile route. The geography of commercial hospitality was largely unchanged when Christopher Colles published *A Survey of the Roads of the United States of America* (1789). Colles's maps, which used simple icons to represent churches, townhouses, mills, and taverns, demonstrated a similar distribution of public houses, with a tavern indicated every few miles along the entire route (fig. 3.1). Mathew Carey's *Traveller's Directory* (1802), with its strip maps of the roads between Philadelphia and Washington, likewise shows that wayfarers on these routes were never far from an inn. In sum, eighteenth-century American travel operated on small scales of distance and depended upon ready access to shelter.[6]

When canals, steamboats, and the first railroads were built in the early nineteenth century, American travelers could traverse greater distances with fewer intermediate stops, and they expected to reach many destinations in a single day. For example, the 150-mile Hudson River voyage from New York City to Albany could take several days on a sailing sloop around the turn of the century, but by the 1830s steam navigation had reduced the travel time to less than ten hours. Early railroads were faster still, moving at a clip of up to three times that of steamboats. These new modes created a new geography of inland travel, one that concentrated passenger populations at the endpoints of journeys—that is, in larger cities and towns. Travelers between Albany and Buffalo, for instance, were redistributed from numerous points along the land route to one of three places: aboard a canal boat or in accommodations at either end of its run. The new hotels of the era, with their huge capacity for guests, operated perfectly in this new travel regime.[7]

This meant hard times for inns and taverns. Older public houses did not become immediately extinct, but most were rendered obsolete. The Erie Canal in particular all but destroyed land-based trade and travel across New York. Many of the thousands of complaints and lawsuits against the Canal Board were filed by innkeepers, whose former clientele now spent their nights on canal boats and bought their drinks at the numerous grog shops that sprang up along the banks of the canal. The effect on taverns in the region was so dramatic that even a quarter-century later it was cited by the chief justice of the New York State Supreme Court. "The construction of the Erie Canal," Justice Greene C. Bronson recalled, "destroyed the business of hundreds of tavern-keepers and common carriers between Albany and Buffalo, and greatly depreciated the value of their property, and yet they got no compensation." The rise of the hotel was not without its human and monetary costs.[8]

The ongoing development of transportation, especially greatly lengthened railway runs, furthered the process of amplification. By the late 1850s it was not just conceivable but

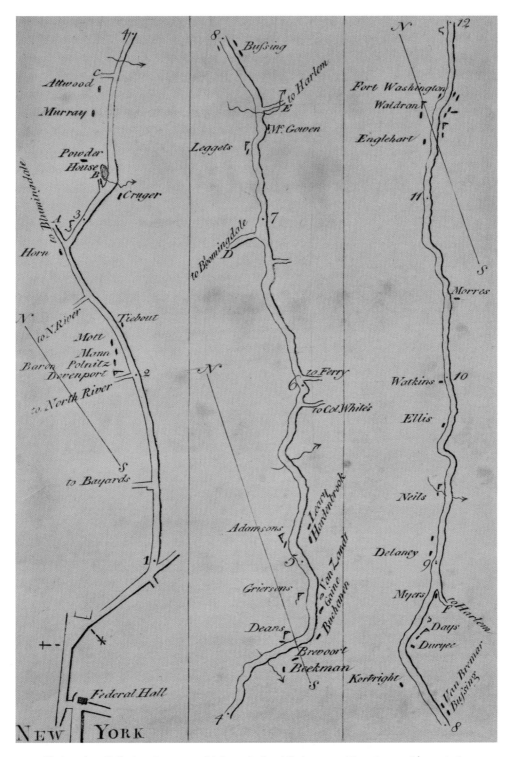

3.1   Christopher Colles's 1789 maps, which marked public houses with an inverted L symbol, displayed the close proximity of inns and taverns along roads in the colonial and early national periods. (The Library Company of Philadelphia)

common for Americans to travel hundreds of miles in a day, sometimes thousands within a week. For example, a person could take the Baltimore and Ohio Railroad directly from Washington to Cincinnati, a distance of more than 500 miles, in twenty-eight hours. More ambitious wayfarers could board a Pennsylvania Railroad express train in Philadelphia and cross the 356-mile distance to Pittsburgh in fourteen hours; they could then transfer to another rail line and reach Chicago, another 467 miles to the west, in nineteen hours more. A further day's travel could take them across Illinois and Iowa to Omaha, Nebraska, on the far bank of the Missouri River, more than 1,250 miles from their point of departure. This process came to a symbolic climax in 1869 with the completion of the transcontinental railroad, which allowed people to traverse the 3,000-mile distance between the Atlantic and the Pacific—a voyage that a generation earlier would have required two and a half months—in an astounding eight days.[9]

The nation's accommodation network developed accordingly. Americans had long found hotels extremely useful, and thanks to the financial success of second-generation hotels, there remained little doubt that they were reliably profitable ventures. In addition, the more recently settled parts of the United States had far fewer taverns to be displaced or to draw custom away from new hotels. Under such circumstances it was hardly surprising that the number of hotels per capita soared after 1850, and that growth was fastest in the West.[10]

While most well-informed people recognized railways as a network from early on, only a few were able to see hotels as part of a network as well. The first of these was Tunis G. Campbell, a New Jersey–born antislavery activist and hotel employee who later worked with the Union Army in South Carolina and during Reconstruction became one of Georgia's first black state legislators. In 1848 Campbell published the nation's first book on hotel management, a two hundred–page volume entitled *Hotel Keepers, Head Waiters, and Housekeepers' Guide.* The *Guide* elaborated Campbell's view of "what is required in every hotel, namely—system. Every thing must be systematized, or nothing can be kept right, but all must be left to chance." While the book dealt mainly with the internal workings of hotels, Campbell also focused on larger networks of transportation and accommodation. He insisted that every hotelkeeper must understand these in great detail: "The proprietor should also travel through the country, and make the acquaintance of all the principal hotel-keepers, steamboat captains, rail-road agents and conductors, and in fact all public men upon the great routes in the country. . . . Having made himself acquainted with all the principal places, wherever he has been, he is of course able to give any information that may be required about the best routes, distances, houses of accommodation, &c., all of which information is invaluable to travellers." The same conception of networks and mobility was evident in Campbell's directives on managing a hotel's dining room, which, he advised, "should be ready an hour before any rail-road cars or steamboats start . . . and for an hour after the arrival of the same." For Campbell, the operation of a hotel always had to be coordinated with the transportation network that delivered so many of its customers.[11]

While Campbell offered by far the most detailed and elaborate conceptualization of how hotels operated as a system, he was joined by others in this line of thinking. Philip Kelland, a Scottish academician who visited the United States in 1858, called "the hotel system" his "first lesson in the enterprize of the States." He concluded that this hotel system was "well adapted to those who lead an unsettled life, and consequently displays the wisdom of the people in accommodating themselves to the part they have so largely to play in the world's history—the part, I mean, of pioneers—of an advanced guard to reduce to their dominion the boundless expanse of forest and prairie land which forms the background of their immediate position." Isabella Bird, the celebrated English travel writer, made a similar point much more amusingly when she drew a parallel between the American systems of transportation, accommodation, and pork production: "As there is a railway system and a hotel system, so there is also a pig system." Both observers recognized hotels as symptomatic of a more general American campaign to occupy and control space, whether in the grandiloquent form of "reduc[ing] to their dominion" the "boundless expanse" of their country or in the simple guise of moving people and pigs from place to place.[12]

At a time when most commentary about hotels emphasized the luxuriousness of their décor or their impressiveness as stand-alone architectural or entrepreneurial achievements, Campbell, Kelland, and Bird had begun to imagine them as part of a continent-spanning urban system. By the 1870s this understanding of hotels was to gain broad acceptance and application. But the first major developments in the creation of a national hotel system involved not so much a theoretical approach as a series of architectural and institutional adaptations.

THE EMERGENCE OF HOTEL TYPES

As Americans deployed the basic hotel form in many different landscapes and adapted it to a range of uses, they created location- and function-specific hotel types. These can be divided into at least seven variants: luxury hotels, commercial hotels, middle-class hotels, marginal hotels, resort hotels, railroad hotels, and settlement hotels. (Residential hotels constitute a different sort of category and will be dealt with in Chapter 9.) While any typology necessarily involves fine distinctions and broad elisions, at least four of these hotel types were classified as such by nineteenth-century Americans. Each variant played a role in processes of specialization and expansion that were essential to the creation of a national hotel system.[13]

Hotels of the first generation and early examples of the second generation belonged to the luxury (also called palace or first-class) variety. They were large, ornate, expensive, and intended for a well-to-do clientele. Luxury hotels like the Exchange Coffee House and the St. Charles were so visually impressive and elicited so much commentary that nearly two centuries later they still capture the imagination and have come to stand for all hoteldom. The American hotel certainly did originate in this most opulent manifestation, but by midcentury, the luxury hotel was no longer representative of the species. For every extravagant caravansary whose opening was front-page news, there were many marginal operations more likely to turn up in police reports; and for every privileged family that stayed in a lavish suite and patronized the downstairs shops, there were a dozen traveling salesmen who could afford no more than a clean bed and a small sample room in which to display their goods. Despite the atypicality of luxury hotels, virtually all the historical and antiquarian literature has focused on them; but a proper understanding of the American hotel must draw upon many different hotel types.[14]

Commercial hotels emerged around 1820 to provide accommodation to business travelers: the salesmen, account clerks, wholesale agents, shopkeepers, and buyers whose ranks were growing as the economy expanded. (Salesmen alone were said to number sixty thousand by 1860 and more than two hundred thousand by 1883.) Commercial hotelkeepers solicited businessmen's patronage quite aggressively, often distributing business cards that were addressed exclusively to the trade: one for a hotel in Bucyrus, Ohio, depicted a salesman, sample case in hand, leading a crowd of his fellows with the words, "All in favor of going to the Monnett House, say I." Hands raised, all respond, "I." Indeed, commercial hotels were so strongly geared to this clientele that they sometimes greeted the rest of the traveling public only as an afterthought. An advertisement for one St. Louis establishment specified that it was "Managed by Mr. J. M. Long, an old time traveling man who knows what the boys want"; it was only in the last line that it halfheartedly added, "The Patronage of the Public is Solicited."[15]

What the boys wanted was basic hotel amenities at affordable prices and sample rooms where they could do their work. With luxury hotels in the 1820s and 1830s charging about two dollars a day or eight to ten dollars per week, a commercial hotel offering hospitality at half the price was a welcome find. Equally important were sample rooms, special spaces reserved for traveling salesmen to display their wares to customers (fig. 3.2). Commercial hotels constantly publicized these facilities in their advertising, promising "suitable sample rooms" or boasting the "Best Sample Rooms in the City." The largest commercial hotels in major cities contained dozens or even hundreds of these rooms.[16]

The architecture and siting of commercial hotels were designed to control costs. While still purpose-built structures, commercial hotels were typically smaller and less ornate than their luxury counterparts. They had dozens of guest rooms rather than hundreds, and their exteriors were only lightly ornamented, if at all. Whereas luxury hotels frequently occupied entire city blocks, commanding two or more street corners and presenting an impressive façade, commercial hotels could occupy as little as a single lot, and did not often stand out from the building line. The Pearl Street House and Ohio Hotel in New York City (fig. 3.3), for example, did feature a columned and pedimented entrance and an arched roof sign, but was otherwise quite plain; it was two lots wide, and its four-story rise was unexceptional for its neighborhood. Commercial hotels were commonly sited on less expensive real estate along side streets, often near wholesaling centers where their clientele did business.[17]

Commercial hotels originated in New York City and spread nationwide. The concentration of merchant travelers in the Pearl Street neighborhood made it the nation's leading commercial hotel district. While boardinghouses had predominated into the 1820s, half a dozen hotels catering to the trade were built by 1834. The Pearl Street House and Ohio Hotel was typical. Its double name not only linked it with the burgeoning trade of Pearl Street but also served to acknowledge and attract the patronage of buyers from the increasingly prosperous Ohio River valley. Similar naming schemes were used for establishments like the Commerce Hotel (1819), the Canal House (1825), and the Merchant's Hotel (1825). This process was repeated in other urban areas, and within a few decades, the business directory of almost every substantial city listed at least one establishment called the Commercial House or the Commercial Hotel.[18]

Others in need of affordable hotel accommodations formed the main clientele of middle-class hotels (fig. 3.4). These were establishments constructed to provide cheaper alternatives to luxury hotels, but which were intended for men, women, and children rather than commercial travelers. Unlike the other hotel types described so far, this categorization was not in use in nineteenth-century America. It is nonetheless useful for encapsulating a large and functionally coherent class of hotels that combined affordability with respectability.

Because they had to be kept affordable, middle-class hotels were less grand and

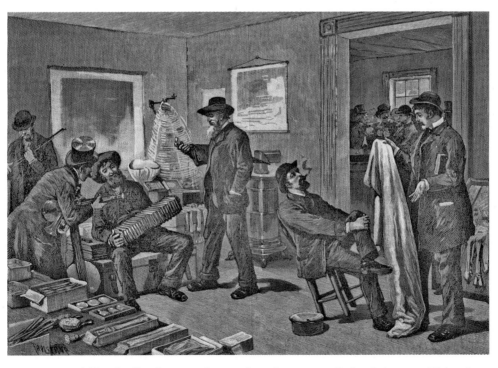

3.2   Commercial hotels offered patrons the use of sample rooms to display their wares. (University of New Mexico Center for Southwest Research)

3.3   The Pearl Street House and Ohio Hotel was a typical commercial hotel located in a district frequented by jobbers and others involved in wholesaling and retailing. (Museum of the City of New York)

offered fewer services than palace hotels. Their façades were relatively plain, more likely of brick than stone; and while most were situated on reasonably busy downtown streets, a few were found along a city's principal boulevard. Inside, the proprietors of middle-class hotels controlled costs through a range of money-saving measures: they offered fewer and plainer public spaces, eschewed opulent draperies and carpeting, bought less and cheaper furniture, provided smaller and less well-appointed bedchambers to maximize income per square foot, maintained fewer baths and water closets, and hired fewer employees per guest. The keepers of middle-class hotels were not shy about their business model, and their promotional materials emphasized thrift. An advertisement for the Occidental House, a Manhattan establishment offering rooms for seventy-five cents to one dollar, averred: "It is the aim of the proprietors to furnish superior accommodations at reasonable rates," adding that its "tables will be supplied with the best the market affords at reasonable prices." Popular practice also reflected sensitivity to price: middle-class hotels were not as well known or easy to locate as palace hotels, and travelers who would be in town for several days might check into a luxury establishment for the first night before transferring to more affordable accommodations.[19]

Middle-class hotels were about more than thriftiness, however: their proprietors also emphasized the respectability that was the cultural hallmark of the middle class. These hotels defined respectability in terms of domesticity, especially their suitability for women and children. San Francisco's American Exchange, for example, distributed cards announcing in large print that it was a "Good Family Hotel" and noting its separate

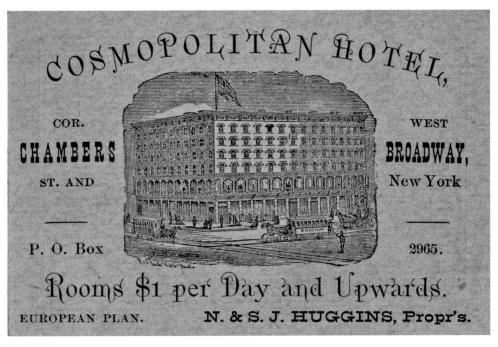

3.4 Middling establishments like the Cosmopolitan Hotel in New York offered modest but respectable accommodations at moderate prices. This hotel is still in business today, serving the same segment of the market. (National Museum of American History)

"Ladies' Entrance." Some midpriced hotels tried to split the difference between their clienteles. The keeper of the Broadway Hotel, an 1860s hostelry that advertised primarily to families but also welcomed commercial travelers, explained: "The house is arranged with rooms in suites for family conveniences; also single rooms for transient men of business. And [the proprietor] feels confident, with this double arrangement, that he can make it pleasant for all."[20]

Middle-class hotels, like commercial hotels, greatly outnumbered luxury establishments. In business directories and hotel guides, the highest-priced hotels—those that charged $2 to $3 in the 1830s, a figure which drifted upward to $3.50 or $4 by the mid-1870s—were consistently outnumbered by a much larger stratum of midpriced hotels that cost about half as much. The urban geographer and historian Paul Groth's figures for San Francisco in subsequent decades have "mid-priced" hotels outnumbering first-class hotels by three to one, with both types together exceeded by other hotels by a factor of more than four to one. This suggests that while middle-class and commercial hotels substantially outnumbered luxury hotels, the great numerical majority of hotels in American cities belonged to a still lower stratum.[21]

The bottom of the socioeconomic hierarchy of American hoteldom was occupied by establishments which for lack of a better term can be called marginal. It might seem odd

3.5 Marginal hotels, like this one on the Bowery in New York City, were often operated in converted tenements and served a working-class and poor clientele. (Milstein Division of United States History, Local History, and Genealogy, The New York Public Library, Astor, Lenox and Tilden Foundations)

to categorize as marginal a hotel type that was far more numerous than any other, but the term accurately reflects their cultural profile. Marginal hotels were architecturally unremarkable and socially inconspicuous, and were ignored by journalists and public officials except as alleged sources of social problems. Such hotels thus have a great deal to say about what the hotel concept meant to people and what kinds of cultural work it did.

Some marginal hotels were considered outside the bounds of respectability simply because they operated in a seedy part of town or served a low-income clientele. Every substantial American city had a cheap-hotel district patronized by peddlers, seamen, drovers, hoboes, and other people whose work took them away from home and paid poorly. The hotels they patronized (fig. 3.5) offered the same basic services as other hostelries, but at the most rudimentary level: their rooms were small and spare, they had no substantial public spaces other than a cramped lobby with a small front desk and a few chairs, and they provided few or none of the amenities that were standard at tonier hostelries. Marginal hotels were often establishments that had once been of a higher class but which, due perhaps to an economic downturn or a shift in the location of the city's business district, had been abandoned by their former respectable patrons.[22]

Other marginal hotels scarcely qualified for the name. Sometimes this was linked to liquor licensing: in New York, the Raines Law of 1896 prohibited Sunday liquor sales except at hotels; in response, many barkeeps set up ten cots in a back room and maintained a pantry in order to satisfy the statute's definition of a hotel. In new settlements and remote areas, the term *hotel* was very loosely applied—for example, to single-story adobe structures in early Anglo California and even to canvas tents in the interior West. And throughout the country, brothel owners applied for hotel licenses in hopes of allaying suspicions as to the men and women who were constantly entering and exiting their premises.[23]

Some marginal hotels were not really hotels at all. By far the most common were low-priced boardinghouses occupied by day laborers, vagrants, and the semihomeless. Such establishments, which did not serve travelers and lacked liquor licenses, were essentially flophouses whose operators kept up their name in a way they could not keep up their premises. These were characterized by minimal compartmentalization and the use of bunk beds (fig. 3.6), shelves with mattresses, or even wooden pallets as sleeping places. Even when there were separate spaces, they often had very thin partitions or consisted of cubicles whose walls did not reach the ceiling. As Jacob Riis commented in his classic 1890 exposé *How the Other Half Lives,* "There is a wider gap between the 'hotel'—they are all hotels—that charges a quarter and the one that furnishes a bed for a dime than between the bridal suite and the everyday hall bedroom of the ordinary hostelry." On the whole, marginal hotels were united by little more than their use of the mental associations summoned up by the word *hotel* to make a claim to heightened status or social legitimacy.[24]

While luxury, commercial, middle-class, and marginal hotels were urban building forms, there were other hotel types that were usually located away from large cities. By far the most prominent of these was the resort hotel. As the word *resort* suggests, these were intended as places to get away, which in most cases meant away from the city and the urban world of work. Yet despite their rural, seaside, or wilderness surroundings, resort hotels were unmistakably part of the urban system. They drew their clientele primarily from among the nation's city dwellers, since other than large slaveholders, they were the only ones whose occupations involved sufficient income and leisure time for pleasure travel. Resort hotels were thus built near enough to cities so that urbanites could get there within a day's travel.

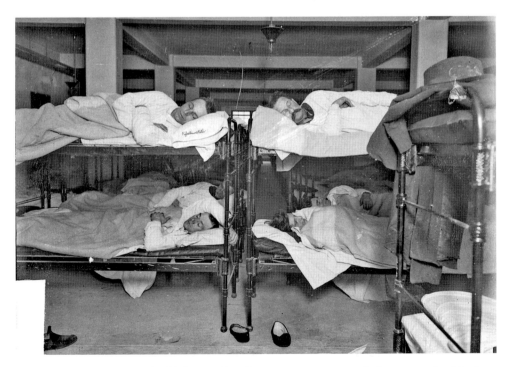

3.6   Chicago's Dawes Hotel, which served low-income customers, crowded numerous bunk beds into shared rooms. (Chicago History Museum)

Resort hotels emerged not long after the urban hotels of the 1790s, though for different reasons. If America's first hotels were successors to city taverns, its early resort hotels were the latest additions to a long-standing tradition of visits to mineral springs and other sites thought to improve health. Spa towns had drawn visitors in Europe for centuries, and at least as far back as the 1760s, European Americans had made organized trips to places like Newton Springs, not far from Boston, Yellow Springs and Bristol Springs, near Philadelphia, and various other springs in pursuit of their supposedly curative properties. Health seekers had built a few small structures at such destinations, but it was not until the early nineteenth century that well-traveled urban entrepreneurs, some of whom had visited leading English spas, began to construct substantial edifices. The first of these was the Sans Souci Hotel in Ballston Spa, New York, a hundred-room establishment that opened in 1806. The idea caught on, and soon others were making similar plans. The first hotels at Stafford Springs, Connecticut, Saratoga Springs, New York, and the Virginia Springs went up in the 1810s. In subsequent decades, Americans found medical or quasi-medical reasons to build many more hotels, including the benefits of sea air, high elevations, and desert climates.[25]

A subsequent and even greater stimulus for resort hotel building involved scenic landscapes and the cultural meanings that Americans attached to them. As early as 1802 Thomas Jefferson proposed erecting a hotel at Virginia's Natural Bridge so that people could come see the geological feature he called "the most sublime of Nature's works." It was only twenty years later, though, that the touristic impulse gained strength. Well-to-do Americans, familiar with the European Grand Tour, strove to demonstrate their own cultural credentials and establish a national identity through travel, and by the 1820s the "fashionable tour" through the Northeast had become hugely popular in elite circles. This was further encouraged by writers and artists who sought relief from urban commerce and early industrialization by turning to natural wonders and pastoral landscapes: literary Romanticism, with its notions of the sublime, the beautiful, and the picturesque, as well as the delicate images of the Hudson River School of painters, provided words, pictures, and concepts that made tourism into something sacred. Americans having thus been set into motion, the profit motive spurred developers to erect large hostelries in their nation's most dramatic landscapes. The peaks of the Catskill Mountains became a popular setting for resort hotels, beginning in 1824 with the Catskill Mountain House (fig. 3.7). In the 1830s Niagara Falls was so densely surrounded by hotels that visitors complained of the difficulty of seeing the cascade without taking rooms. By then, New England was dotted with dozens of resort hotels, especially along the seashore and in New Hampshire's White Mountains.[26]

The social life of resort hotels soon overtook health and scenery as the main reason for their popularity.[27] Resort hotels were unique in drawing enough seasonal patrons to generate a standing community. While a transient guest at a city hotel stayed for an average of three days, resort hotel patrons checked in for weeks and sometimes months at a time: prosperous families could reserve rooms for an entire summer, with the husband return-

3.7   The Catskill Mountain House's mountaintop site commanded extraordinary views of the surrounding countryside. (Library of Congress)

ing to work during the week and the wife and children staying continuously. In order to occupy their guests' abundant available time, resort hotels sponsored concerts, lectures, nature walks, plays, recitals, masquerade balls, and countless other entertainments. These events involved much mingling among young men and women, and resorts became widely recognized as marriage markets where parents could put their eligible daughters and sons

3.8   The Greenbrier Hotel at White Sulphur Springs, Virginia (now West Virginia), displayed the strongly horizontal lines and bucolic settings that characterized resort hotels. (University of Virginia)

on display. All these activities combined to make resorts into places of studied public performance and self-fashioning, with all the attendant potential for emotional drama, petty intrigue, and outright deception. It was no wonder that resort hotels were such popular settings for American writers like William Dean Howells, Edith Wharton, and Kate Chopin, who observed, satirized, or mocked the pretensions of the American bourgeoisie who gathered there. In *The Rise of Silas Lapham* (1885), for example, Howells described how the Lapham women "had gone about to mountain and sea-side resorts, the mother and the two girls, where they witnessed the spectacle which such resorts present throughout New England, of multitudes of girls, lovely, accomplished, exquisitely dressed, humbly glad of the presence of any sort of young man; but the Laphams had no skill or courage to make themselves noticed, far less courted by the solitary invalid, or clergyman, or artist. They lurked helplessly about in the hotel parlours, looking on and not knowing how to put themselves forward."[28]

The architecture of resort hotels showed considerable uniformity in terms of materials, layout, and size. They were almost always built of wood, a material that was both inexpensive and well suited for light, uninsulated structures that operated during warm weather. They were relatively horizontal in their massing, reflecting both the low cost of rural land and an effort to avoid disrupting the bucolic character of the surrounding countryside. Many resort hotels thus presented long, low façades that offered guests views of the local landscape, as with the Catskill Mountain House's clifftop panorama or the leafy environs of White Sulphur Springs, Virginia (fig. 3.8). Resort hotels were typically large, and became more so over time. The nation's first resort hotel, at Ballston, was already more than one hundred rooms, and by the second half of the nineteenth century, there were many, including New York's Lake Mohonk Mountain House, Michigan's Grand Hotel on Mackinac Island, and West Virginia's Greenbrier, that were several times larger. The substantial size of the resort hotel was intended to impress well-to-do patrons and attract enough guests to create a large and desirable society "scene."[29]

Resort hotels bore a complex and changing relationship to their surroundings. Though positioned as antiurban, they offered their guests a wide range of amenities and technologies; in their first several decades, their exteriors tended to feature formal neoclassical styles, and their interiors were no less well appointed than those in luxury hotels (fig. 3.9). By the 1870s, however, architects had begun to apply more rustic visual vocabularies, such as the Stick style used on J. Pickering Putnam's Manhattan Beach Hotel (1876) or the West End Hotel (1878) at Bar Harbor, Maine. Still later, around the turn of the century, bucolic styling was increasingly used inside, with many resort hotel lobbies and lounges featuring unfinished timbers, rough-hewn furniture, and field-stone fireplaces (fig. 3.10). Whatever their aesthetic character, almost all resort hotels deliberately blurred the boundary between their comfortable interiors and the natural landscape outside. Wide verandas allowed guests to be out in nature yet sheltered from the elements, and gardens, lawns, footpaths, and other carefully designed grounds provided a gradual transition from manicured flora to untamed wilderness. This openness was, of course, illusory. Resort

3.9   The United States Hotel in Saratoga Springs, New York, catered to urbanites seeking to escape the commotion of the city, but it offered the same state-of-the-art amenities as any first-class urban hotel. (Collection of the author)

3.10   Resort hotel interiors, like this one at the Old Faithful Inn at Yellowstone, often used rustic décor to emphasize their function as a respite from the competitive world of urban work—this despite the fact that they were part of an extended city system. (Collection of the author)

guests had paid for proximity to nature and the company of fashionable strangers but were insulated from contact with social undesirables by barriers of price and distance.[30]

Resort hotels emerged out of the same conditions that had given rise to other hotel types—commercial capitalism, rapid urbanization, and improved transportation—but played a very different role in the hotel system. Resort hotels were not crossroads in networks of travel; they were more in the nature of terminal points, places that people arrived at rather than moved through. They formed a refuge from the heterogeneity and hubbub of city life, and in this sense they stood in opposition to the democratizing trends that characterized other American hotels. Indeed, to the extent that resort hotels served as an escape from urban hoi polloi, they were the lineal descendants of the exclusive British resorts that had inspired them. They represented a new economy of travel: one based not on moving goods, workers, or information but rather on transporting people to safe, pleasurable surroundings where they could occupy and consume the land in new ways.

The structural requirements of long-distance rail transport gave rise to railroad hotels, establishments that were built to facilitate the operation of railways and would not have existed but for their presence. As the short rail lines of the 1820s and 1830s gave way to the lengthy routes of the 1840s and after, runs of hundreds of miles became increasingly common. Railroad companies were thus faced with new operating requirements: locomotives needed fuel and maintenance, and passengers had to have food and shelter. Because American railroading began in the densely populated East, such facilities could at first be placed in existing settlements. But as rail lines extended over the Appalachian Mountains, across the prairies, and into a new and sparsely populated West, they called forth a series of way stations along the tracks.

Locomotives were exceptionally complicated machines that demanded elaborate support systems: steam engines had to be refueled at regularly spaced coaling and watering stations; locomotives and train cars also needed constant maintenance to avoid on-track breakdowns that would idle the entire rail line until the train could be moved onto a side track. In order to facilitate this essential work, and to ensure that a broken-down train was never too far from help, railroads typically planned a breaking point and workshop for every hundred miles of track. Such facilities were continuously staffed by rotating shifts of mechanics and engineers who needed food and shelter, and hotels were built to satisfy this need.

Passengers had requirements of their own. Until railroads introduced dining cars in the 1860s, trains made meal stops at which travelers would leave their carriages, proceed into a dining room, eat, and then return to their seats. Passengers also needed to sleep, and with the longest voyages lasting days, trains stopped every night at a place where riders could find available beds. This practice persisted until sleeping cars became common in the 1870s. These considerations provided railroad companies with an additional incentive to build hotels.

Railroad hotels soon began to multiply. The Baltimore and Ohio Railroad and the North Carolina Railroad offer excellent examples. While the B&O was a largely private company and the N.C.R.R. a government enterprise, both recognized the need for railroad hotels. Initially, they sited their facilities at division points in existing settlements like Cumberland, Maryland, and Wheeling and Martinsburg, Virginia. But in the 1850s the B&O began to lay the groundwork for its own system of hotels, one that lasted for more than half a century. The first of these was a brick hotel at Grafton, Virginia, a fifty-room establishment built hard by the tracks in 1852. The N.C.R.R. established a machine shop near the Haw River in 1855, and later that year the company granted a private concession to open a hotel there for work crews, railroad officials, and passengers. Notably, efforts were made in the early 1860s to make the Company Shop site, as it was called, into a permanent town. The N.C.R.R. attempted to sell town lots and turn the place into "a large manufacturing or industrial center," but there was little interest, and when the railroad began to run sleeping cars, it was forced to assign a salaried manager to operate the hotel just to accommodate shop employees. Similar examples of hotel building by railroad companies included the Pennsylvania Railroad's Logan House at Altoona and the Erie Railroad's Susquehanna House in central Pennsylvania.[31]

Architecturally, railroad hotels ranged greatly in size and form. The Berkeley Hotel, for example, was built around 1850 when the B&O reached Martinsburg. The four-story brick structure, which remains standing today, contained a ticket office and dining room on its first two floors and several small guest rooms above. About twenty years later, the Union Pacific Railroad built the Laramie Hotel in Laramie City, Wyoming (fig. 3.11), a much larger structure whose horizontal design was in keeping with the greater availability of land in the West. The Union Pacific's promotional materials noted that "one thousand persons can be comfortably accommodated at table," and ambitiously but implausibly claimed that "its dining room will compare very favorably with those of the best buildings for like purposes in any State of the Union."[32]

But the foremost example of the railroad hotel remains the Hotel Florence (fig. 3.12), an 1881 structure that still stands in the town of Pullman, just south of Chicago. The hotel was part of a planned town that George Pullman, the inventor and manufacturing magnate of the railroad sleeping carriage, established as a model community for the industrial workers who built his cars. The four-story Florence, named for its creator's favorite daughter, was an integral part of Pullman's plan to manage and showcase the town. The hotel included a large suite for Pullman's exclusive use, smaller suites for visiting company executives, and fifty rooms for travelers, including the tourists who Pullman expected would come to see his model town. The Florence contributed to practically all the functions of its parent company: not only transportation and maintenance but the production of railway carriages and the promotion of tourism as well. Viewed in conjunction with the extant parts of the factory next door and the surrounding railway roadbed, the Hotel Florence is a durable monument to the symbiotic relationship between the American railroad and hotel systems.[33]

3.11   The Laramie Hotel was built alongside the tracks of the Union Pacific Railroad in Laramie City, Wyoming. (Beinecke Rare Book and Manuscript Library, Yale University)

3.12   The Hotel Florence, built in 1881 as part of the model railcar-manufacturing town of Pullman, Illinois, is the quintessential surviving example of a railroad hotel. (Historic Pullman Foundation)

The seventh and final hotel type was the settlement hotel, a structure constructed to serve a newly established town or, in some cases, an older community experiencing sudden growth. These hotels were designed to be affordable, quick and easy to build, and ultimately disposable if a town's ongoing development required a larger hostelry. While they might take any number of shapes and styles, the great majority shared certain common characteristics. Most settlement hotels were wood-frame structures with pitched roofs, almost universally painted white; but their most distinctive and consistent features were long balconies that extended along each story, sometimes wrapping around three or more sides of the building.

Settlement hotels were purpose-built adaptations of a building type that became common in the early nineteenth century in the new hill towns and provincial market centers of the Northeast. The settlement hotel was subsequently carried along the same routes of migration that had brought other hotel forms westward. Numerous photographs and drawings depict settlement hotels in New England (fig. 3.13), and they figured regularly in the early histories of small towns on the prairie and the plains. Judging by the available visual evidence, however, they were most popular in the far West. Settlement hotels were a constant feature in early prints of towns in California; one collection of 1850s letter sheets pictured dozens of them. The Gold Rush was one of the first events in American history to be widely photographed, and settlement hotels—easily identified thanks to their bright white paint and because they were among the few structures not built shotgun style, with their eaves facing the street—appeared not only in early images of California (fig. 3.14) but also in daguerreotypes of remigrations into Nevada and Colorado.[34]

Settlement hotels functioned particularly well in the far West for many of the same reasons they had in the East. They could be built quickly and inexpensively, since they required little specialized skill, and because the primary construction material was abundant in both ecosystems. The settlement hotel's porches offered sheltered outdoor space for social interaction, and its balconies served as platforms for announcements and speech making; they also offered an elevated perspective on the surrounding landscape. In places where settlement was more permanent and local communities were generating greater wealth, people built larger, more durable structures. But in the first decade or so of white migration, the settlement hotel was the modal form of commercial hospitality.

Some of these seven hotel variants also existed in temperance and ethnic subtypes. Temperance hotels emerged around 1830 in connection with the rise of the antiliquor movement. Hotels made extensive use of their special privilege of selling strong drink, and people who saw alcohol as the leading cause of social pathology in America grew

3.13   A settlement hotel in New England. (New Hampshire Historical Society)

3.14   The National Hotel was a settlement hotel in Forbestown, a Gold Rush town in 1850s California. (University of California Libraries)

alarmed that in a highly mobile nation people were being offered liquor at every stop on their travels. Temperance advocates therefore proposed to break the link between travel and alcohol by establishing "dry" travel accommodations. They discussed the idea in movement publications and soon took action. Within a decade or two, most city directories listed establishments either bearing names like "Temperance House" or "Temperance Hotel" or parenthetically denoted as such. Hotel advertising documents numerous examples of new or converted proprietors announcing that their premises would be "run on strict temperance principles" or handing out trade cards (fig. 3.15) or other notices to the same effect. Sometimes hotelkeepers were compelled to operate on a temperance basis, as in the dozen states where legislatures enacted statutes modeled on the famous Maine Law of 1851 outlawing the sale of intoxicating liquors. Temperance hotels accounted for only a small proportion of establishments, in part because it was difficult for a hotel to stay profitable without liquor receipts. (In a revealing incident from the 1840s, the leading antiliquor reformer Edward C. Delavan sold his Albany temperance hotel to a new keeper only to see it revert to selling alcohol.) Nonetheless, temperance hotels maintained a constant presence throughout the century and into the next.[35]

Hotels also existed in ethnically specific forms to serve people in their own language or culture. Antebellum Milwaukee, for example, was home to Irish, English, and numerous German establishments. The nation's largest linguistic minority was particularly intent upon familiar cooking and Gemütlichkeit. An 1857 article in the *New Yorker Staats-Zeitung* emphasized the importance of proper German hospitality: "German hotels in New York that really deserve the name of 'hotels' are of recent origin. They are not known much by Germans in the South and West, so they stay in American hotels. The reason is that they probably believe German hotels are not so respectable, not so 'noble' as American hotels. . . . But this is no longer the case, since German hotels are not only erected on a 'fine footing,' but also have restaurants." The article then listed six of the largest German establishments in the city and concluded, "Our readers in the country will see from this list of German hotels that when they come to New York, they will not lack the opportunity to stay in good German houses where they will enjoy not only German kitchens and German food, but also German facilities, and can be cared for in real German fashion." Other ethnic minorities in the United States also established hotels of their own, and city directories and advertisements document hostelries operated by and for immigrants from Ireland, France, and Italy, among other countries.[36]

People who were excluded from hotels also built establishments of their own. The

3.15   Temperance hotels like this one in New York State's evangelical "burned-over district" offered accommodations to people who wanted to avoid supporting establishments that tempted travelers with strong drink. (Collection of the New-York Historical Society)

most prevalent example involved black people, who were routinely barred from hotels throughout most of the nineteenth century and much of the twentieth. Black travelers were thus forced to arrange in advance to stay with family, friends, or people of goodwill. In response, black businesspeople opened hotels to serve travelers of color (fig. 3.16). These hotels were sufficiently numerous that by the early twentieth century, there was a regularly updated national guide to hotels for black people.[37] A far less widespread but still significant pattern of exclusion led American Jews to establish their own hotels. When many resort hotels declared themselves "restricted" beginning in the 1870s, Jewish entrepreneurs set about creating alternate vacation destinations, most famously in the Catskill Mountains of New York, where many hotels continued to serve a predominantly Jewish clientele into the second half of the twentieth century.[38]

Hotel types formed an essential part of a national system because they facilitated personal mobility for a growing proportion of Americans. As hotels diversified beyond the luxury variety, the availability of more affordable establishments allowed people of different income levels access to identifiable and reliable travel accommodations. Meanwhile, the evolution of hostelries with specialized functions and facilities allowed the basic hotel form to serve in many different landscapes and locations by occupying profitable niche markets. Operating in tandem with the nation's expanding transportation network, hotels made it convenient for Americans to travel to places that had been previously inaccessible, and to occupy, enjoy, or exploit them. The evolution of distinct hotel types was a decentralized process that proceeded without conscious national planning or coordination. Before long, however, Americans came to recognize hotels as a coherent system and began to redefine and reorganize them as such.

A NATIONAL SYSTEM

The first signs of a truly national understanding of public accommodations emerged shortly after 1870. The preceding decade had been a slack period for hotel projects because the Panic of 1857 and the Civil War had largely halted the aggressive hotel building of the 1840s and 1850s. In one sense, the sustained hotel construction of the 1870s and after represented the resumption of a longer trend. Yet it was more than that, because when Americans took up the project that they had left aside years earlier, they did so with a new conception of transportation and accommodation. They could now see hotels as part of an integrated national system that could offer wayfarers predictable, dependable hospitality.

This new pattern of thought and action was crucially influenced by the Civil War, which set millions of Americans into motion. Men from throughout the nation were transported hundreds or thousands of miles to battlefronts in places like Virginia, Georgia, Louisiana, and Tennessee. Farmers, husbandmen, cartmen, and slaves, whose work would rarely have taken them far from home, grew accustomed to marching, sailing, or riding from state to state and region to region. These experiences broadened their horizons, making faraway states into places they had personally visited rather than just names heard

3.16 Persistent racial discrimination in white-owned hotels prompted black Americans to establish hostelries of their own, like the Union Hotel in Chattanooga, Tennessee. (Library of Congress)

in conversation or read in newspapers. Moreover, veterans' organizations recast this once-in-a-lifetime experience of travel into a regular part of former soldiers' lives by sponsoring yearly encampments, ritualized events in which men journeyed great distances to spend time together at the battlefields where they had fought.[39]

The war's influence also operated through small but powerful elites whose military work taught them new ways of organizing human mobility. The deployment and redeployment of huge armies in a continental theater of war produced new kinds of logistical and geographic knowledge. For example, when its forces were surrounded by Confederates at Chattanooga, Tennessee, in the fall of 1863, the Union Army transported more than twenty thousand soldiers from eastern Virginia in railway cars. Confederate forces were caught off guard and defeated because none thought that troops could be deployed so quickly: a reinforcement that should have taken a month's hard marching had been accomplished in eleven days. Officers on both sides of the conflict were quick to learn the new logistics of large-scale, long-distance, steam-driven transportation, and lessons learned on the battlefield were sometimes turned to civilian use after the war.[40]

The Union Army's officer corps played a significant role in restructuring postwar business practices, particularly in railroading, and the elaboration of national markets was inflected by what they had done in uniform. More generally, the Civil War prompted Americans to think in different terms about travel. The basic idea of transportation networks was not new: the government-sponsored internal improvements of the antebellum period had, after all, been thought of in terms of statewide transport. But these projects had been fueled by urban mercantilism and the assistance of state governments; efforts at federal coordination of a truly national transportation policy had been destroyed by the localistic politics of Jacksonian Democracy and had never recovered. In a conceptual analog to the oft-cited post–Civil War transition from the plural "these United States" to the singular "this United States," Americans came to see the nation rather than the state as the relevant geographic unit of trade, travel, and accommodation.[41]

The appearance of nationwide hotel directories was the clearest manifestation of the conscious and deliberate nationalization of the American hotel system. Hotel guides for individual cities had been published in earlier decades, but there was little in the way of national coverage. In the 1870s, however, entrepreneurial publishers suddenly produced numerous titles, including *Boyd's Hotel Directory and Tourists' Guide* (1872), *Statia's Hotel List Guide* (1874), and *Gazlay's United States Hotel Guide* (1875).[42]

These compact but comprehensive guides (fig. 3.17) typically measured about four by six inches, small enough to carry in a pocket or purse, and at twenty-five cents each, they were very affordable. Hotel directories offered a fairly standard set of information about each location. *Boyd's* was typical in providing the name and population of each city or town, the railroad or railroads that served it, distances to nearby communities, and the names, room rates, and meal plans of the principal hotels. Not surprisingly, large cities got elaborate treatments and numerous hotel entries: Boston, for instance, merited thirty-two lines of text and a dozen listings for hotels costing from $3 to $4.50 per day. More unexpected, though, were numerous smaller communities that supported what were, judging by their prices, reasonably good hotels. Newburgh, New York, a town of 17,000 residents, was home to hotels charging from $2.50 to $3.00 per day for room and board; Great Barrington, Massachusetts, population 4,320, had three hotels charging from $2.00 to $2.50 with meals; and Wells River, Vermont, with only 750 inhabitants, boasted four hotels, all priced at $2.50 per day inclusive. Other than twenty pages of hotel advertisements at back and front and a few city maps, these hotel directories went on methodically in the same way, in small print at two columns per page for two hundred to three hundred pages.[43]

National hotel directories, used together with railway guides, rendered the entire national territory knowable, navigable, and predictable. With nothing more than two booklets costing only a quarter each, people could plan journeys of any length or complexity throughout the United States. They could formulate an itinerary with a full understanding of every route and every distance. They could work out a schedule knowing how long each leg of their trip would take, every departure and arrival time, and the hour of each transfer. They could calculate an accurate and detailed budget that accounted for every

GAZLAY'S

UNITED STATES

HOTEL GUIDE

FOR 1875

CONTAINING THE NAME AND ADDRESS OF THE VARIOUS HOTELS
IN ALL THE PRINCIPAL CITIES, TOWNS AND SUMMER RESORTS
THROUGHOUT THE UNITED STATES AND CANADA, ON THE
VARIOUS LINES OF TRAVEL BY RAIL AND WATER,
CONDUCTED ON THE EUROPEAN OR AMERICAN
PLAN; RATES PER DAY, POPULATION OF
CITIES, TOWNS, VILLAGES, ETC., ETC.

☞ *The whole making a much-needed, cheap and convenient* POCKET REFERENCE BOOK *for the use of* TRA-
VELERS, HOTEL MEN, *and the public generally.*

REVISED MONTHLY.

PUBLISHED BY
THE FRANKLIN PUBLISHING COMPANY,
67 LIBERTY STREET,
NEW YORK.

Entered according to Act of Congress in the year of our Lord one thousand eight
hundred and seventy-five, by THE FRANKLIN PUBLISHING COMPANY, in the
office of the Librarian of Congress at Washington, D. C.

3.17 The first national hotel
guides were published in
the 1870s. (General Research
Division, The New York
Public Library, Astor, Lenox
and Tilden Foundations)

railway ticket and hotel bill. They could send messages ahead by mail or telegraph to
reserve hotel rooms and railcar seats. And at every intermediate destination, they would
know exactly where to find a hotel that suited their needs. Traveling under these conditions was a far cry from several decades earlier, when departures were uncertain and daily
progress unpredictable, and when wayfarers often arrived in town at dusk and were faced
with having to seek out a hanging tavern sign in fading light.[44]

Hotel directories demonstrated that the hotel system was not a conceptual abstraction but a matter of everyday practice. The sudden profusion of national guides meant that
entrepreneurs in a number of cities—Boyd and Gazlay in New York, Bradford in Chicago,
and Statia in Portland, Maine—had wagered that there was money to be made by compiling
such information and offering it to travelers. The guides' low prices suggested furthermore
that their creators were aiming at a fairly broad market. Most important, the popularity of
the guides meant that these entrepreneurs had judged the situation correctly and found
steady customers: in subsequent decades, numerous publishers would print a variety of

regional and national hotel directories on a regular basis, with guides like *The United States Official Hotel Directory* and the *Hotel Red Book* issued annually into the 1960s.[45]

The growth of the hotel system was also recorded in government sources. The Census Bureau enumerated publicans beginning in 1850, first under the rubric "innkeepers" and after 1860 as "hotelkeepers." The census counts indicate two related trends: an ongoing increase in the number of keepers and a decline in the ratio of publicans to population. The number of professional hosts rose from 22,476 in 1850 to 25,818 in 1860 and 26,394 in 1870, followed by an unprecedented jump to 32,453 in 1880. But the number of keepers relative to population fell steadily: one host for every 1,031 Americans in 1850, one for each 1,217 in 1860, one per 1,450 in 1870, and one for every 1,545 in 1880. These figures suggest absolute numerical growth as well as a gradual increase in the average size of each establishment; this probably encompassed both a rise in the guest capacity of individual hotels and the obsolescence of small inns and taverns.[46]

These inferences are supported by census data on hotel clerks and hotel workers. In the 1870 and 1880 returns, the census supplemented its enumeration of hotelkeepers with counts of both "hotel clerks" and "hotel employees." These categories comprised workers who were needed only when an establishment was large enough to require full-time workers for guest registration and other duties around a hotel. Hotel workers multiplied even faster than their employers in these years. The ranks of hotel clerks grew from 5,243 to 10,916, an increase of 108 percent and a rate of growth almost five times as fast as for proprietors. Over the same decade, hotel employees increased from 23,438 to 77,413, a rise of 230 percent and a rate of increase fully ten times as great as for their employers. The Census Bureau abandoned these categories in 1890, but this decadelong sample demonstrates the trend toward more hotels, and larger ones, in the third generation of American hoteldom.[47]

While Americans were building hotels nationwide, they were not doing so with equal enthusiasm in all parts of the country. When the census data for 1850 to 1880 are broken down by state, they reveal considerable regional variation. The Northeast enjoyed by far the densest distribution of public accommodations, with states like Massachusetts and New York having the most establishments per square mile and Pennsylvania and Connecticut following close behind. Because this region was also very heavily populated, however, the ratio of hotels per person was only slightly higher than the national average. The Midwest's hotel network was somewhat more sparse, mostly because the area had been settled more recently and less densely, though in some states, most notably Minnesota and Iowa, there were more hotels per capita than in much of the Northeast.

The South and West were the most noticeable outliers. By any available measure, the South was less equipped to provide for travelers than any other part of the country. A few states in the region, like Virginia and Arkansas, had one inn or hotel for every 3,000 to 4,000 inhabitants by the 1870s, but more typical were North Carolina and Florida, with one per 7,000 to 9,000 in those years; there were also exceptionally commercially inhospitable states like Alabama, at one per 8,600 to 9,900, and South Carolina, at one per 10,000 to 14,000 from 1870 to 1880. In dramatic contrast, almost every part of the West was generously supplied with inns and hotels by the 1870s, boasting exceptional ratios like those in Oregon (one per 580 to 810 residents), California (one per 500 to 550), and Nevada (one per 310 to 350).

These regional variations corresponded closely with transportation and urbanization. The East and Midwest had the most elaborately developed transportation grids in the nation, and their density of public accommodations was exceeded only in the West, a region that been tied into the national railroad network relatively recently but was still the most urbanized part of the United States. The relative paucity of hotels in the South could be explained by its strongly rural character and underdeveloped railways, though there may also have been cultural determinants. Southerners took pride in private hospitality, and apparently valued fixity of residence: in an 1860 essay glorifying the region, the proslavery apologist D. R. Hundley gave specific thanks that "the bane of hotel life and the curse of boardinghouses have not as yet extended their pernicious influences to our Southern states." While the emergence of hotel types and the informational rationalization of the nation's accommodations did extend the reach of travel, not all places were equally well served by the American hotel system.[48]

A MOBILE CENTENNIAL

The development of the nation's systems of transportation and accommodation reached a culmination of sorts in 1876 with the Centennial Exhibition at Philadelphia. The world's fair celebrating the hundredth anniversary of the Declaration of Independence was a pivotal cultural event in the nation's history, one that revealed much about how far the United States had come and where it was headed.

The idea of commemorating the centennial with an international exposition had first been raised in 1864, but it was not until 1870 that local promoters secured the endorsement of the Philadelphia city council and persuaded Pennsylvania legislators to lobby for the project in Washington. The following year, Congress established a United States Centennial Commission and appropriated $1.5 million for the event once enough private money had been raised to stage it. The commission decided to fund the exhibition by raising $10 million through the sale of stock. While many individuals did purchase shares in the fair, the great majority of stock was held by corporations: notably, three railroad companies alone controlled more than 66 percent of the voting shares.[49]

The Philadelphians were ambitious. The United States had never participated seriously in the international exposition craze that had begun with the Great Exhibition in London in 1851 and continued as European capitals hosted five more world's fairs over the following two decades. New York had made a modest effort with its Crystal Palace of 1853, but the event had been almost totally derivative of the London fair of two years earlier, and its size and attendance were but a small fraction of European expositions. Cognizant of this fact, the Centennial Commission sent a fact-finding mission to Vienna's Weltausstellung of 1873. The great success of the Vienna exhibition, which boasted attendance figures that surpassed all previous fairs save Paris's Exposition Universelle of 1867, made it clear that the Philadelphia affair would have to be planned and executed on a tremendous scale if the United States hoped to compete in international circles.[50]

Consequently, the Philadelphia exhibition plan was grand indeed. The event would occupy Fairmount Park, which at 2,470 acres was the largest in the United States. The fairgrounds were to include five main exposition buildings, seventeen structures erected by state delegations, nine edifices for exhibits from foreign countries, and dozens of smaller buildings. The principal structures were colossal: the Main Exhibition Hall measured 1,880 feet long by 464 wide and covered 20 acres, and the second largest building was fully two-thirds as capacious. All told, the fair's official buildings covered 75 acres of ground, an area half again as extensive as the next largest previous fair.[51]

Exhibition organizers and local entrepreneurs understood that hosting an event on this scale would involve a huge influx of visitors to Philadelphia, and they took action to ensure adequate accommodations. By opening day, downtown Philadelphia boasted fifty-one hotels of more than fifty rooms each, with eight hotels immediately adjacent to Fairmount Park (fig. 3.18). The Grand Exposition Hotel, which opened shortly before the fair, billed itself as the "Largest Hotel in the world; 1325 Rooms" and highlighted its location "Within FIVE MINUTES Walk of THE CENTENNIAL BUILDINGS." The operators of the

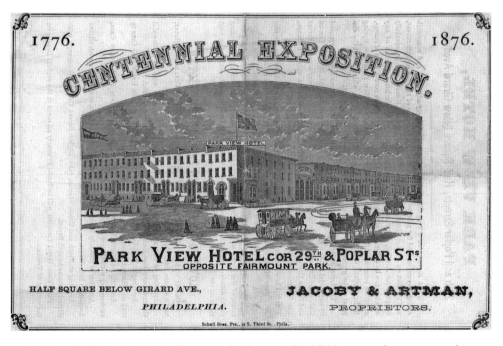

3.18 A handbill for a hotel built adjacent to the Centennial Exhibition grounds to accommodate some of the nearly ten million visitors to the fair. (Collection of the New-York Historical Society)

Trans-Continental Hotel emphasized its siting "Opposite Main Entrance to Centennial International Exposition Grounds," and later claimed to have "accommodated over 72,000 guests in about five months." Even large hostelries like these were overshadowed by the Globe Hotel, built to accommodate 3,500 guests, and the aptly named Atlas Hotel, with room for 5,000. Like many of the buildings erected for the exhibition, these two hotels were temporary structures that were torn down after the gates closed, but they nonetheless set a precedent for world's fair hotels in decades to come. Hotelkeepers beyond Philadelphia also used the centennial celebration in their advertising. New York City's Grand Union Hotel, for example, advised travelers to the exhibition of the convenience of a route through Manhattan; taking a slightly different approach, a hotel in Wernersville, Pennsylvania, emphasized its proximity to the fair, a generous interpretation given the town's location almost seventy-five miles west of Philadelphia.[52]

It was almost immediately clear that the Centennial Exhibition would be a runaway success. On the first day alone, almost 187,000 people came to the fairgrounds, and on the busiest day, more than 250,000 visited. Over the course of 160 days, nearly ten million people passed through the gates, making Philadelphia's the most widely attended of any of the fairs in the world up to that time. Given a United States population of fewer than fifty million, attendance represented a number equal to more than one-fifth of all citizens. By way of comparison, its admissions were more than fifteen times higher than for the New York fair held a quarter-century earlier. But its significance for travel in the United States was more fundamental, for it had become the most widely and eagerly attended event in American history; only the involuntary military mobilization of the Civil War had put anywhere near as many people into motion. Indeed, some saw the fair as a national gathering for the purpose of sectional reconciliation: before opening day, one prominent Pennsylvania minister had distributed a letter predicting that "people from all parts of our recently divided country will meet around the old family hearthstone of Independence Hall and pledge anew heart and hand in a social and political brotherhood never to be broken." Whatever the cultural meanings of the fair, mobility on this scale demonstrated not only the extraordinary complexity and capacity of the nation's networks of transportation and accommodation, but also the extent to which Americans had become willing to travel (fig. 3.19).[53]

The Centennial Exhibition also exemplified another important shift in travel patterns by drawing large numbers of families. Prints and photographs of visitors at the fair often depicted women and children (fig. 3.20), an unusual sight at a time when most urban scenes showed heavily male crowds. These visual representations were corroborated by the fair's record keepers, who reported 504 incidences of children being separated from their parents and brought to local officials. (Happily, all were quickly reunited with their families.) This was a departure from earlier patterns of travel in the United States. While the appearance of hotels eighty years earlier had made it possible for respectable women to take to the road, most descriptions of travelers and hotel guests around midcentury suggested a predominantly male clientele, and made only infrequent mention of children.

3.19 An 1876 cartoon from *Harper's Weekly* illustrates the rush at hotel desks as eager guests arrived in Philadélphia for the centennial celebration. (University of New Mexico Center for Southwest Research)

The presence of so many families at the Philadelphia exposition signaled a new set of expectations. Traveling was no longer thought of as risky or even particularly rigorous, and many Americans moved about *en famille,* confident that the most vulnerable members of their party could be accommodated in comfort and safety.[54]

CONCLUSION: PROSPECT AND RETROSPECT

The Centennial Exhibition was full of portents for the United States in its second century. Contemporary observers predicted, and historians have confirmed, how particular attractions foreshadowed things to come. The Corliss engine, a 45-foot-tall, 112,000-pound "athlete of steel and iron" that powered the Hall of Machinery and formed the centerpiece of the fair, foretold America's coming industrial dominance. The French sculptor Frédéric Bartholdi's immense torch-bearing arm, which would later form the apex of the Statue of Liberty, prophesied the coming waves of immigrants. And Alexander Graham Bell's transmitter telephone heralded the nation's leading role in an international community bound together by instantaneous voice communication.

But there were other emergent trends in evidence at the 1876 fair. Among these was Americans' increasing propensity to travel and corresponding demand for commercial hospitality. The Centennial Exhibition had been the biggest travel event in the history of the

3.20 An evening crowd at the Centennial Exhibition; note the women and children in the foreground. (University of New Mexico Center for Southwest Research)

United States, but it was only the first of a decades-long series of world's fairs that was to include Chicago's World's Columbian Exposition of 1893, Buffalo's Pan American Exposition of 1901, St. Louis's Louisiana Purchase International Exposition of 1904, San Francisco's Panama Pacific International Exposition of 1915, and several others lasting into the 1960s. These fairs drew tens of millions of people to their host cities, and every event was accompanied by intensive hotel construction. In the decades after the Philadelphia fair, not only would Americans travel more, but more of them would travel, setting the stage for an age of broad-based tourism that would augment the influence of travel on life in the United States.

This had become possible because by the time of the centennial, the American network of transportation and accommodation was the most extensive, elaborate, and refined in the world. The citizenry's enthusiasm for mobility manifested itself in tens of thousands of miles of railroads and waterways, thousands of hotels of many different types, and the timetables and hotel directories needed to coordinate their use. Had Sarmiento and Arcos returned to the United States thirty years after their 1847 visit, their cleverly improvised means of finding one another would have been unnecessary; the change in their pockets would have bought them guidebooks they could use to determine with great ease and precision their relative locations, their transportation options, and the addresses of hotels where they could meet. Americans had never been sedentary, and had not become entirely rootless; what they had done was to reorganize their national space in a way that allowed them to leave their homes and set out for faraway places feeling assured that when they reached their destinations, they could find safe, reliable, comfortable, and affordable accommodations.

Four *Imperial Hotels and Hotel Empires*

Tourism, Expansion, Standardization, and the
Beginning of the End of a Hotel Age, 1876–1908

THE TREMENDOUS SURGE of travel to Philadelphia for the Centennial Exhibition heralded the dawn of mass tourism in the United States. In the final quarter of the century, the democratization of pleasure travel led to new uses of hotels on the nation's frontiers and fostered innovative modes of hotel building and management in the cities.

The rapid growth of tourism created a new relationship between hotels and cities. For more than eighty years, hotel construction had followed capitalist urbanization. Commerce, agriculture, manufacturing, and mining had dictated where and when people would settle, and hotels helped anchor communities and tied them into networks of transportation and communication. Beginning around 1880, however, hotels became an indispensable part of tourism-driven migration to the West, with pleasure travel helping to determine where some prosperous Americans made homes and built cities. Hotels thus formed a leading edge of urbanization on the frontier. This did not mean the end of trade-driven hotel construction: as westward expansion turned into imperial ambition, hotels again became outposts of commercial capital and political power, this time in colonies overseas.

Back in America's urban-industrial core, the increasing popularity of travel restructured the market for commercial hospitality. While wealthy Americans still traveled far more than their less well-to-do compatriots, mass tourism meant that the rich made up a declining proportion of hotel guests. Hoteliers, attentive as always to the changing character of their clientele and the needs and wants of their guests, began to reorganize their establishments to suit a broader customer base. E. M. Statler, the leading proponent of this new approach, turned away from the ostentation of grand hotels, instead using standardization to generate efficient economies of scale and lower the price of hotel accommodations. In so doing, he became the most influential hotel manager in America and helped establish a new business model for hotels in the twentieth century.

Meanwhile, the American pursuit of mobility culminated in yet another transportation technology: the automobile. At first, automobiles were intended only for the rich; in this, they echoed the first hotels. But then Henry Ford, another apostle of rationalization and standardization, made automobiles affordable enough for a mass consumer market. The coming of the motor age transformed the nation's travel patterns and brought the century-long developmental arc of American hotels to an end.

IMPERIAL HOTELS

Americans had engaged in pleasure travel since the eighteenth century and had established numerous resort areas in the antebellum decades, but even during the peak years of the "fashionable tour," long-distance travel remained an unfamiliar experience for most people. Only a small proportion of Americans possessed the money and time necessary to move around much beyond what was economically necessary. Moreover, while the United States offered wayfarers an unmatched travel infrastructure, it had not developed a full-fledged culture of tourism. The idea of travel for the sake of pleasure was often viewed with suspicion, and not just by people who celebrated the virtues of hard, continuous work and self-denial; even those most directly involved with travel seemed to share this sentiment. Travel writers often felt the need to distinguish pleasure travel from outright idleness or purposeless leisure, travelers' guides of the late 1860s still emphasized business rather than enjoyment, and railways had only just begun to run observation cars. Railroads did offer special excursion fares, but in a sign of their priorities, company managers worried that these would drain revenues by prompting their main clientele of commercial travelers to schedule necessary trips for excursion days.[1]

Beginning in the 1870s, however, Americans started to embrace tourism. Economic change was the first cause and necessary condition for the rise of tourist culture. The growth of clerical and managerial occupations and the efforts of organized labor meant that many white-collar families and a few craft workers could expect time off from their jobs, sometimes with pay. Vacationing received sanction from labor-relations experts who asserted that leisure, far from being time lost to employers, actually increased the productivity of workers. As one observer commented, vacations had become recognized "not as a luxury, but as a necessity for those who aim to do a large amount of high-grade work." Sensing a new business opportunity, entrepreneurs began to organize travel agencies. The nation's first, which opened in 1874, was the U.S. branch of Thomas Cook and Son, whose founders had grown wealthy arranging tours for British and European travelers. It was followed in 1879 by Boston's Raymond and Whitcomb, and a few years later by E. M. Jenkins, the Cooks' former American partner. The public responded enthusiastically, and by the early 1890s, competition among travel agencies had become so intense that some took to disparaging each other in newspaper advertisements as a way to gain new clients.[2]

While tourists continued to flock to older resorts in the Northeast, South, and Midwest, the most significant new development was the establishment of an archipelago of resort and recreation areas in the far West. Tourism to the West was driven by many of the same factors as in other regions. By far the most important cause was the effort of railroad corporations to make their new transcontinental lines more profitable by encouraging tourism and pursuing land development. Nationalistic writers and journalists promoted the extraordinary landscapes of the West as worthy rivals to Europe's architectural monuments and cultural cachet, and the region's mountain and desert climates were much ballyhooed as treatments for respiratory distress and nervous exhaustion. Finally, the increasing ease and affordability of travel had made the resorts of the East into crowded places, and many wealthy travelers sought to avoid their presumed inferiors by vacationing in places where few could afford to go. The extension of recreational travel into the West made resort hotels into instruments of a large-scale effort by Anglo-Americans to settle vast territories that had for centuries been home to Native and Hispanic people. This was an unmistakably imperial project: not only did it involve geographic expansion and control, it also entailed the expropriation or commodification of these populations.[3]

In some cases, resort hotels in the West recapitulated processes that had long been operative in the East. In eastern resorts like Saratoga, White Sulphur Springs, and Newport, hotels were essentially seasonal projections of urbanism into rural or wilderness areas. They served as recreational outposts for prosperous city dwellers and did not significantly alter the region's urban geography.

Resorts around San Francisco followed the same dynamic. Faced with the hectic pace and discomfiting social mixing of downtown, the Bay City's wealthy elite sought out havens where they could enjoy mountain views and sea air in exclusive company. For many years they went to the Cliff House, a hotel overlooking the rocks near the Golden Gate, but this was hardly far enough from the city to ensure a clientele limited to high society. The new plans of the Southern Pacific Railroad created the opportunity for a resort hotel at a proper remove from San Francisco. In the mid-1870s, the Southern Pacific decided to construct a rail line southward through California's Central Valley, and one of its subsidiaries subsequently purchased several thousand acres of land on the Monterey Peninsula about one hundred miles south of San Francisco. The company planned a grand hotel–centered resort that could compete with any in the nation, and by 1880 it had completed the large and luxurious Hotel Del Monte (fig. 4.1). The hotel's grand opening was attended by a large group representing "the flower of San Francisco's aristocracy," a fact that promoters used to advertise the resort throughout the United States and Europe. The Del Monte quickly became "the fashionable and favorite watering place of California" and a choice destination for wealthy tourists from farther afield. Geographically, though, it remained a satellite of San Francisco rather than a self-sustaining settlement.[4]

A similar example is offered by the Fred Harvey hotels of New Mexico and Arizona. Harvey was an English immigrant who had worked in restaurants in New York and St. Louis and managed a number of railway eateries. In 1876 he signed a contract with the Atchison, Topeka and Santa Fe Railroad to operate restaurants and hotels along its line. Over the following half-century, the Fred Harvey Company opened numerous hostelries; these included the Montezuma Hotel (1882) (fig. 4.2) and the Castañeda Hotel (1899), both in Las Vegas, New Mexico; Albuquerque's Alvarado Hotel (1902); and El Tovar Hotel (1905), perched at the edge of the Grand Canyon in Arizona. Harvey provided reliable, standardized hospitality, perfectly personified by the "Harvey Girls," hostesses and servers whose appearance was regulated by the company in every detail, from their starched

4.1   The Hotel Del Monte was the first great resort hotel in the West, and the first of many essentially imperial hotels to be given a Spanish name. (Collection of the author)

4.2   The Montezuma Hotel in Las Vegas, New Mexico, was one of many Fred Harvey hotels offering reliable service to travelers in the Southwest. (The Old Print Shop, New York City)

black-and-white uniforms to a workplace prohibition against jewelry and makeup. The company also aggressively marketed travel through the Southwest by emphasizing the region's Native and Hispanic cultures: Harvey hotels, for example, were built in identifiably Spanish or Pueblo styles. The Harvey-A.T.S.F. partnership channeled an unprecedented number of people through the region, accelerating white settlement and fostering a culture which, despite its increasing hybridity, was nevertheless presented as "authentically" Indian or Spanish. Notwithstanding the increased Anglo presence, the region's principal cities and towns continued to be centered on the places where their Native and Hispanic inhabitants had settled centuries before.[5]

In other areas, however, tourist resorts established a very different relationship between hotels and urbanization. Some resort hotels precipitated rapid settlement in frontier areas. In his influential book *The Urban Frontier*, Richard Wade proclaimed that the "towns were the spearheads of the frontier." In a roughly parallel process that played out on a farther frontier than Wade's, hotels became an essential part of tourism-driven settlement.[6]

In 1870 William Jackson Palmer, a surveyor and executive with the Union Pacific Railroad, sought investors for a new railway line that would serve southern Colorado, New Mexico, and eventually Mexico. His proposed railroad would require towns and

4.3 The Antlers Hotel was only the most famous of several hotels that helped Colorado Springs develop from a tourist haven into one of the largest cities in Colorado. (University of New Mexico Center for Southwest Research)

cities to control and gather resources, and he platted entirely new settlements along its route. The first of these was Colorado Springs. "When I found the magnificent Pike's Peak towering immediately above me," wrote Palmer when he first saw the site, "I could not sleep any more with all the splendid panorama of mountains gradually unrolling itself. . . . I am sure there will be a famous resort here." In contrast with the mineral resource–driven development of Denver, the growth of Colorado Springs was avowedly touristic from the very beginning. Palmer and his partners marketed the settlement to wealthy Americans and Europeans by comparing it to existing resorts while emphasizing its unique location in the western wilderness. Promotional literature called it "Our New Saratoga" and "Newport in the Rockies," and one cooperative guidebook author explained how visitors "exhausted the vocabulary of laudatory phraseology in attempting to describe the grandeur, beauty, and sublimity of the mountain and valley scenery." The Colorado Springs Hotel, which one local newspaper praised as "the most elegant hostelry between Chicago and San Francisco," opened in 1872 and was followed by many others, most famously the Antlers Hotel (1883) (fig. 4.3) and the Broadmoor (1892). Colorado Springs enjoyed booming growth almost immediately, and its subsequent worldwide fame as an exclusive resort attracted hundreds of thousands of visitors annually and an increasing number of permanent residents. By century's end, it had grown into the state's third-largest city. This

4.4   Pasadena's Hotel Raymond, named for the leading travel agency serving the region in
the 1880s, spearheaded residential settlement of southern California. (Collection of the author)

hotel-dependent strategy of growth through tourism was imitated on a smaller scale by
towns elsewhere in the region, as with the Colorado Hotel in Glenwood Springs and the
Inter-Laken Hotel near Aspen.[7]

      An analogous process played out in southern California. The region remained
relatively underdeveloped into the 1870s because San Francisco dominated the state's
economy, drawing the lion's share of capital and migrants and thus limiting opportunities
in other areas. In the following decade, however, the development of tourism, anchored
by a new generation of resort hotels, created a new impetus for settlement. The pivotal
event was the breaking of the Southern Pacific's regional monopoly by the Atchison, Topeka and Santa Fe in 1883. As the price of railroad passage to the region plunged, tourist
promoters sprang into action. Seeking to replicate the success of the Del Monte and the
hotels of Colorado Springs, the Raymond and Whitcomb travel agency and the A.T.S.F.
immediately joined in constructing an enormous new resort hotel to accommodate the
expected influx of tourists. The Hotel Raymond (fig. 4.4), an immense structure that
dwarfed the rest of the still tiny town of Pasadena, opened in 1886; it was followed by others, including the still standing Hotel Green. These hotels, which brought in their staffs
en masse from New York and Chicago, played host to a veritable flood of guests and made
Pasadena another of the region's thriving tourist destinations. Many visitors decided to
move to the area, often staying in the hotels for months or years as their homes were built
nearby, or becoming permanent hotel residents. Farther south, this process was repeated
in San Diego when the railroad arrived in 1885. Alert promoters staked out a stretch of

4.5   The Hotel Del Coronado, like its Pasadena counterpart, helped establish a foothold for Anglo settlement by drawing large numbers of tourists to the region. (Library of Congress)

land on a peninsula in the bay and built the Hotel Del Coronado (fig. 4.5), the largest hotel in the West, which became an instant success, drawing huge numbers of guests to the area. Southern California was soon to become a major area of urban settlement and to develop a diversified economy based on oceangoing commerce, manufacturing, and military industries. But in its early days, the hotel-driven growth of tourism and the concomitant surge of speculation in residential real estate were indispensable parts of the large-scale settlement of the region.[8]

But the most elaborate example of hotel-driven settlement took place on a very different kind of frontier: the sparsely populated coastal areas of southern Florida. This was the work of Henry M. Flagler, a partner in John D. Rockefeller's Standard Oil Company. Flagler's interest in hotels began in 1878 with his first trip to Florida, which he undertook because his wife, Mary, suffered from a respiratory ailment and physicians had advised him to take her to a warmer climate during the winter. The Flaglers stayed at a hotel in Jacksonville because there were no good hotels farther south. Mary did benefit from the Florida climate but refused to stay there when her husband returned to New York City that spring. She died two years later.[9]

Flagler became fixated upon Florida. He learned that the state had recently begun making substantial land grants to encourage settlement and economic development. Returning to Florida in 1883 and again in 1885, Flagler noted the presence of other wealthy New Yorkers avoiding the winter cold and decided that he would build a hotel in St. Augustine. The luxurious Hotel Ponce de León opened in 1888, followed within a year by the somewhat more affordable Córdova Hotel and Alcázar Hotel (fig. 4.6). In order to service his properties, Flagler built a southern extension to the railway network of the East. He then set about developing the tiny settlement of Palm Beach into another resort community built around the Royal Poinciana Hotel (1894) and the Breakers Hotel (1895). Flagler continued the same pattern of hotel building and railway extension all the way to Miami, where in 1896 ground was broken for yet another grand hotel, the Royal Palm.[10]

By the turn of the century Flagler had established a string of tourist enclaves extending more than three hundred miles along Florida's eastern coast. While these began as exclusive and seasonal communities, they soon developed into more diverse permanent settlements. High room rates, the enforcement of Jim Crow, and a predominantly out-of-state clientele notwithstanding, the tony demographics of Flagler's towns were substantially illusory. Hotels required large amounts of cheap labor and thus attracted many poor people, both black and white, to the area. Meanwhile, well-to-do travelers who had initially come as refugees from northern winters grew fond of the balmy conditions of the Florida seashore and decided to make homes there. As more guests stayed throughout the year, a corresponding population of workers did as well. Flagler's hotels thus set the stage for rapid growth in a state that at the turn of the twentieth century had only slightly more than half a million inhabitants. What had begun as a leisure-based seasonal community gradually became a mature zone of settlement, the geographic vanguard of what would later be known as the Sun Belt, the newest urbanizing region of the twentieth-century United States.[11]

Tourism-driven, hotel-dependent settlement of the nation's frontier areas led almost inevitably to the dispossession of longtime inhabitants. In order to draw travelers to their resorts, promoters presented western tourism as an extension of Manifest Destiny, claiming that white Americans were fated to visit and settle in the West and naturally belonged there. The construction of resort hotels was an architectural manifestation of such appeals, one that allowed guests to experience "wilderness" while enjoying the familiar comforts

4.6   This panoramic view of Henry Flagler's three hotels in St. Augustine, Florida, displays both their picturesque architecture and the creation of a concentrated touristic zone that formed the heart of new settlements in south Florida. (Library of Congress)

and conveniences of "civilization." But at a time when the U.S. Army's wars against numerous Indian tribes were turning large parts of the West into combat zones, western tourism necessitated more than just advertising and architecture; it required that Native Americans be removed from any area where a resort was being built. In the early 1870s, for example, Utes who had long used the mineral baths around Colorado Springs were forced to abandon them. In Yellowstone National Park, the superintendent's concern that resident Indians would discourage the construction of hotels and other facilities led to the removal of all the park's Native peoples by 1879. In these and other instances, the arrival of tourists meant exile for inhabitants.[12]

In other times and places, tourism promoters preferred to turn local residents' cultures into salable commodities. Because western resorts and the railways that promoted them competed with one another for customers, they tried to provide distinctive attractions or otherwise make themselves unique. Many resorts offered visitors "exotic" surroundings and experiences. Their hotels were built in appropriately vernacular architectural idioms: Spanish Mission style in California, Spanish Pueblo style in New Mexico, log or rustic Stick construction in the national parks. Tour directors also arranged for guests to have personal contact with human representatives of colorful local cultures, whether "disappearing" Indians or "romantic" Spanish Americans. This necessarily involved cultivating or controlling surrounding populations. The Fred Harvey Company's Hopi House (1904), a company-built, Hopi-inhabited community established for the amusement of guests at El Tovar, became a signature attraction at the Grand Canyon. The Harvey Company established an entire Indian Department, while the Atchison, Topeka and Santa Fe advertising division promoted Pueblo and Navajo ceremonies as spectacles and marketed their crafts as commodities. Other hotel concerns paid Indians to play-act for guests. Officials and promoters at Yosemite established Indian Field Days, a festival at which local Native people were paid to dress up like Plains Indians in buckskins and feathers. The lodges at Glacier National Park similarly employed Indians to serve and entertain guests while wearing ceremonial garb; at the same time, however, they were excluded from the Glacier backcountry. While these and many other instances of cultural exploitation were certainly less brutal than outright expulsion, they were coercive nonetheless because they shifted control over ritual practices and craft production away from local populations and toward outsiders.[13]

Resort hotels constituted an indispensable part of a new age of domestic tourism that brought enormous numbers of white Americans to remote areas they might otherwise never have visited, in some cases hastening permanent Anglo settlement of entire regions. This was not the last time that hotels would facilitate expansionism: they soon became advance outposts for overseas empires.

As the United States government and the nation's commercial interests moved to establish political and economic dominion in Latin America, the Caribbean, and the Pacific, hotels served as headquarters for diplomats, business magnates, and expatriate workers. Some of the same people were responsible for hotel-dependent expansion

4.7 The Hotel Colonial in Nassau was a perfect example of American hotel interests expanding overseas, in this case into the Caribbean. (National Museum of American History)

both domestically and internationally. One early-twentieth-century letter sheet listed the managers of the Flagler hotels of eastern Florida as the backers of a new venture that extended the southward thrust into the Caribbean: it announced the completion of a new hotel on the Bahamian island of Nassau, the frankly named Hotel Colonial (fig. 4.7). Subsequent American ventures were also accompanied by new hotels. The Panama Canal project gave rise to the 1906 Tivoli Hotel (fig. 4.8), which, explained a contemporary travel guide, was "built for the threefold purpose of furnishing quarters to employees who had arrived on the isthmus and had no quarters assigned to them, for the use of persons whose business with the canal administration forced them to come to the isthmus, and the recreation of employees." A parallel situation emerged on the Anglo-Hispanic frontier around 1910. Mining corporations' international projects drew geologists, engineers, accountants, and other professionals into the U.S.-Mexico borderlands, and their employers sponsored the construction of American-style hotels to accommodate them. Analogous projects, such as the Manila Hotel in the Philippine capital, were undertaken in the nation's new Pacific protectorates.[14]

The United States was not the only nation to use hotels in colonial projects overseas; indeed, it was not even the first. European countries adopted the American hotel form on their own soil and subsequently reexported it. Early hotels in Europe featured exceptionally beautiful façades, but by virtually every other standard they were less impressive than their counterparts across the Atlantic. The 1838 Queen's Hotel at Cheltenham (fig. 4.9), which one visitor called "the first of all the hotels of English spas" and a local newspaper deemed "the grandest hotel in Europe," was quite modest compared with its American contemporaries. The four-story, thirteen-bay structure contained little more than one

4.8   In another example of how hotels spearheaded U.S. expansion, the Tivoli Hotel was built by American interests in order to house high-status workers and government officials involved with the construction of the new Panama Canal. (Library of Congress)

hundred bedchambers, the principal dining room seated only forty to fifty people, and its coffee room measured only twenty-six feet by fifty; moreover, contemporary descriptions made no mention of internal plumbing. In 1830s Paris the leading hotel had only twenty-five suites of two to five rooms each, none with private bathrooms.[15]

Foreign observers acknowledged the United States as the world's trendsetter for commercial hospitality. Around midcentury, Alexander Mackay wrote of hotels in England, "It is seldom that, in their appearance, they stand out from the mass of private houses," and some years later, one of his countrymen referred to the American hotel as "a 'peculiar institution' of this country." Upon seeing the 482-bedroom Mount Vernon Hotel in Cape May, New Jersey, in 1854, a British magazine correspondent described it as "so stupendous that an Englishman has some difficulty in believing that such a structure can be a hotel. It exceeds in size anything we can even dream of as a Hotel in England." And in 1861 George Augustus Sala opined that "the American hotel is to an English hotel what an elephant is to a periwinkle" and added that he considered hotels in the United States to be at least a century ahead of those in England.[16]

Europeans gradually moved toward constructing hotels on a comparable scale, sometimes with explicit reference to American establishments. French builders were responsible for the largest of these, the Grand Hôtel du Louvre (1855) and the Grand Hôtel de l'Opéra (1862), Parisian hostelries boasting as many as seven hundred bedrooms each. English hoteliers also erected several large hotels beginning around 1860, typically on a slightly smaller scale of two hundred to three hundred rooms. Dutch hotels attained a similar size around 1860, with German and Austrian hostelries following only in the

1870s. In terms of size, amenities, and organization, European hotels often took their cues from across the Atlantic. For example, when English newspapers like the *Illustrated London News* and the *Building News* reported on two newly built London hotels of the late 1850s, they specifically noted one establishment's American bar and mentioned its "hair-cutting saloon" as "another American luxury," and described the other as being on "the admirable scale [of hotels] of the American cities." In 1885 a German author observed that "in England in some hotels the American system of bedroom and own bathroom has been imitated."[17]

This Atlantic crossing marked the beginning of the globalization of the American hotel. Hotels were firmly ensconced in English and continental cities (fig. 4.10) by the late nineteenth century, just as European colonialism entered its most energetic phase. As Europe's imperial powers established or expanded colonies around the globe, they found the hotel to be as useful in overseas expansion as Americans would some years later. The cruelest aspects of colonialism—the expropriation, brutalization, and sometimes mass killing of local populations—were kept well out of sight of the citizenry back home. Imperial hotels were part of the public face of empire. British colonial hostelries like Raffles Hotel (fig. 4.11) in Singapore and Shepheard's Hotel in Cairo and French operations like the Hôtel Continental in Saigon were grandiose structures that served twin purposes. At a functional level, they provided comfortable, familiar accommodations to the civil

4.9   The 1838 Queen's Hotel in Cheltenham, England, was considered the finest hotel in Europe. While it was aesthetically impressive, by every other measure it was modest compared to establishments being built in the United States at that time. (National Monuments Record, English Heritage)

4.10 The Victoria Hotel, located on Berlin's Unter den Linden thoroughfare, was emblematic of the internationalization of the American hotel form. (Library of Congress)

servants and commercial agents who ran the business of empire; it was a measure of their success in this that many Englishmen, for example, could refer familiarly to Raffles as if it were a local inn rather than a colonial outpost thousands of miles away. Symbolically, imperial hotels implied a transfer of wealth from metropole to colony: they made it look as if colonizers were bringing "civilization" to the locals when in fact they were taking resources away from them.

By the early twentieth century, colonialism had made the American hotel the global standard for commercial hospitality. But this was an odd sort of hospitality. The first hotels were constructed by residents of long-settled communities in order to welcome outsiders and thereby stimulate commerce. As the nation expanded into the West, however, Americans built hotels to welcome *themselves* into areas where they did not already live. This new generation of western resort hotels might be interpreted as no more than an effort to attract travelers who were accustomed to the hotels of the East. Yet it was not so benign as that. Hotels became unmistakably imperial when outsiders built them to accommodate guests who required the subordination or ejection of local residents. The hard lesson that was first learned by Native Americans in the western United States soon became apparent to people in Latin America, Asia, and the Middle East: when newcomers built their own hotels, they would be dedicated to self-imposition rather than hospitality; when it was the guest who controlled the character of the welcome, the entire calculus of the custom had changed.

A NEW APPROACH

Meanwhile, back in the urban centers that gave it birth, the hotel form continued to evolve. The unregulated economic growth of the Gilded Age generated enormous fortunes for the upper echelons of American society, and leading hoteliers responded by creating the most elegant establishments the world had ever seen. Toward the end of the century, however, there emerged a countervailing trend in hotelkeeping, one that pointed toward a very different future for commercial hospitality in the United States.

Underlying these contrasting approaches was the unmistakable fact that hotels were still multiplying in number and increasing in size. All available evidence indicates ongoing expansion in this period. The federal census recorded persistent increases in the number of hotelkeepers nationwide: from 26,394 in 1870 to 32,453 in 1880, 44,076 in 1890, 54,931 in 1900, and 64,504 in 1910. City directories documented corresponding increases in hotels from 1880 to 1910: 136 to 357 in Chicago, about 550 to more than 1,000 in San Francisco. Much of this increase resulted from the continued proliferation of small establishments, but individual hotels were also growing larger. The introduction of steel-frame construction (fig. 4.12) in the 1880s and its growing affordability in the decades that followed meant

4.11   Raffles Hotel in Singapore was beloved of generations of British imperial officials, merchants, and literary figures. (Raffles Hotel)

4.12 The adoption of steel-frame construction, like that used in the building of Chicago's La Salle Hotel in 1908, allowed hotels to rise to unprecedented heights and enormous capacities: in this case, twenty-two stories and one thousand rooms. (Chicago History Museum)

ever-taller hotels, and by shortly after the turn of the century, even many small cities boasted huge ten- or fifteen-story hostelries with hundreds of rooms.[18]

This continuing construction boom included hotels of all kinds, but its most visible manifestations were the luxury establishments. In a crowded and competitive industry, leading hotel builders sought ways to make their houses stand out from the rest, and the most obvious solution was to erect structures that were distinctively ostentatious. Economic inequality was reaching unprecedented levels, and in the absence of a federal income tax, the richest Americans were flush with cash and made for an appealing prospective clientele. In the national metropolis of New York City, such imperatives gave rise to two hotels whose names became synonymous with opulence. The massive and ornate Waldorf-Astoria Hotel (fig. 4.13) was built in two parts by scions of one of the nation's wealthiest families: William Waldorf Astor financed the construction of the Waldorf Hotel, which opened in 1893; four years later, his cousin John Jacob Astor IV presided over the opening

4.13   The Waldorf-Astoria Hotel, built at the height of socioeconomic inequality in the United States, catered to the wealthiest Americans, offering them elegant architecture and extravagant service at a correspondingly elevated price. (Library of Congress)

of his own adjacent and equally eponymous palace hotel, the Astoria. The two halves of the thousand-room caravansary were linked by a three hundred–foot–long marble-faced corridor that became such a favored venue for self-display among the wealthy, beautiful, stylish, and famous that it garnered the nickname Peacock Alley. Five years later, three leading Manhattan investors joined forces with a nationally prominent hotel architect and the manager of two Flagler hotels in Florida to finance, build, and operate the Plaza Hotel (fig. 4.14). The seventeen-story edifice, which was stylistically inspired by the châteaux of France, was completed in just over two years at a cost of $12.5 million and opened in October 1907. Correspondingly lavish hotels were built in these years in major cities across the nation. Prominent examples included Denver's Brown Palace (1892), Philadelphia's Bellevue-Stratford Hotel (1904), San Francisco's Fairmont Hotel (1907) (fig. 4.15), and Chicago's Blackstone Hotel (1908) (fig. 4.16). Indeed, the leading hostelries of this era were so extraordinary that some remain their cities' most prestigious hotels a century later.[19]

While establishments like these certainly were attention-grabbing, they were hardly indicative of the future course of the industry. The true innovators of the period were hoteliers whose business models aimed for a far broader customer base. Transportation costs had been declining for several decades, making travel available to an increasing proportion of Americans; and there had been a corresponding fall in the price of hospitality, especially as architectural diversification gave rise to more affordable hotel types. What was new about the turn-of-the-century hotel industry was its organized attentiveness to middle-class travelers and its corporate response to the changing market for commercial hospitality.

While allowing a single individual or company to stand in for an entire industry runs the risk of oversimplification, the career of E. M. Statler exemplifies some of the most important changes in hotel management. Statler got his start in 1876, when at the age of thirteen he was hired as a bellboy at the McClure House in Wheeling, West Virginia. After rising through the ranks of attendants and desk clerks, Statler turned entrepreneur, borrowing money to refurbish and operate a billiard room and railway ticket office in the hotel. Over the following twenty years, he expanded his operations to include a private bowling club, barbershop, and lunchroom in Wheeling and a five hundred–seat restaurant in Buffalo. But it was the national appetite for world's fairs that set the stage for Statler's rise to fame. In 1900 he persuaded the planners of the Pan American Exposition that Buffalo needed additional hotel space and arranged for the construction of a temporary two thousand–room hotel, which, while it stood, was the world's largest. Despite the fair's financial failure due to inclement weather and the assassination of President William McKinley, Statler reported a small profit on the venture. Two years later St. Louis businessmen offered Statler a concession for the 1904 Louisiana Purchase Exposition, and he directed the construction of an even larger temporary hotel. This time, the enthusiastic public response to the fair translated into large profits for the hotel. These projects established Statler's reputation in financial circles, allowing him to find investors for a permanent hotel built to his specifications and managed according to his methods.[20]

Statler's approach to business management was based on pursuit of a mass clientele

4.14   The Plaza Hotel, located on Fifth Avenue in Manhattan, is the most famous establishment
in a generation of hostelries that marked the zenith of luxury hotel architecture in the United States.
(Photography Collection, Miriam and Ira D. Wallach Division of Art, Prints and Photographs,
The New York Public Library, Astor, Lenox and Tilden Foundations)

and cost cutting through economies of scale. Statler's Buffalo restaurant was designed to bring in a huge volume of diners, who could be fed inexpensively thanks to the efficiencies of bulk purchasing, large-scale food preparation, and fast service. When the restaurant initially failed to draw enough customers, he cut costs further by firing some employees and advertising even cheaper meals; these measures kept its doors open long enough to develop a regular, and eventually an enthusiastic, clientele. Statler's world's fair hotels similarly encouraged thrift and standardization. Both were designed to last for only a single year of heavy, continuous occupancy and then to be demolished and sold for scrap. He therefore built on the cheap, using fireproofed wood that was plastered over to give the appearance of permanence and choosing cut-rate plumbing and fixtures. Organizationally, Statler constantly sought out the smallest service efficiencies, since with upward of two thousand fairgoers per night, saving a few cents on each translated into meaningful sums. For instance, in order to avoid delays in checking people in and out, he devised a system of rotating clerks and bellhops that could process scores of guests per hour.[21]

Statler's first permanent hotel, the Buffalo Statler of 1908, provided the perfect opportunity to develop his methods on an ongoing basis. Statler sited the hotel off the city's main street, choosing a less desirable block and applying the resultant savings on real estate costs to the building budget. His conception of the project went against conventional understandings of what a city's principal hotel should be: when his lead architect expressed doubt that Buffalo could sustain a luxury establishment, Statler replied, "Who said anything about a luxury hotel? This is to be a commercial hotel for traveling salesmen and for families. But it's going to offer service and comfort and privacy beyond anything ever before offered." Statler devoted his full attention to the design and furnishing of the hotel, using new arrangements of rooms, service corridors, and plumbing to lower costs. The savings allowed him to equip all guest rooms with certain standard features, including private baths, telephones, clocks, full-length mirrors, reading lamps, and stationery. As Statler envisioned it, a hotel that set new standards of comfort at a reasonable price would garner unprecedented customer loyalty. Indeed, he had already come up with an easily remembered slogan: "A bed and a bath for a dollar and a half." The building itself was quite plain, lacking the ornate exterior detail common to its luxurious contemporaries; but this demonstrated a certain architectural honesty, as it was a straightforward reflection of Statler's operational philosophy.[22]

The Buffalo Statler was a tremendous success, both as a business and as an exemplar of a new approach to hotel architecture and management. The hotel won such broad and enthusiastic public patronage that it required a 150-room addition in its first year. It was also lauded in the trade press, with the *Hotel Monthly* calling it "the most remarkable hotel, from a serviceable point of view, that has ever been constructed" and, despite its plainness, "one of the best known hotels of the world." Statler followed up by building similar-looking hotels (fig. 4.17) in other cities, including Cleveland (1912), Detroit (1915), St. Louis (1917), New York (1919), Buffalo again (1923), and Boston (1927). These hotels became proving grounds for further refinement of his management techniques, but even after some of the newer hostelries had been built, the *Hotel Monthly* noted that it was still the Buffalo Statler that served as "the mecca of architects and hotelmen seeking new ideas."[23]

Statler hotel architecture was based on standardization. Guest chambers were designed so that every individual room had a door to the hall and thus could serve as a single bedroom; alternatively, these could be grouped together into suites. This allowed Statler hotels to reconfigure and renovate their guest areas to accommodate special requests and, more important, to respond to gradual shifts in the needs and wants of travelers. The same principle could be applied to all aspects of a hotel. As Statler's lead architect explained in a series of *Architectural Forum* articles in 1917, the basic idea was to reduce the various hotel spaces to a manageable number with standard features. Each floor of a Statler hotel should house only one function: bedchambers were grouped with bedchambers, sample rooms with sample rooms. Similarly, passenger and service elevators were arranged together and thus required only a single bank of machinery; bathrooms were built back to back so that they shared a single plumbing shaft, saving space and making repairs easier. Instead of constructing highly individualized hotels, the architect explained, it made more sense to redeploy a single successful model. These methods were closely observed by other architects, with Statler hotels regularly featured in professional journals.[24]

Purchasing and labor practices at Statler hotels were also standardized. When choosing carpets for his hotels, for example, Statler reduced the number of different patterns, sacrificing visual variety in the interest of ease of replacement and bulk discounts in pur-

4.15   The Fairmont Hotel, which began construction atop San Francisco's Nob Hill just before the earthquake and fire of 1906, survived the catastrophe and has for more than a century been one of the city's premier hotels. (Library of Congress)

4.16   Chicago's Blackstone Hotel, which was named for the stockyard and railroad magnate on whose property it was built, helped anchor a growing Michigan Avenue hotel district. The hotel was home to the original "smoke-filled room" and has been designated a historic landmark. (Collection of the author)

chasing. Statler's approach to labor relations demonstrated his enthusiasm for uniformity in personal service, in pursuit of which he employed methods that were alternately callous and paternal. Statler issued detailed written instructions which employees were told to memorize and were required to carry on their persons; he made frequent secret or surprise inspections and resorted to mass firings or threats thereof. Yet he also instituted paid vacations, free health care, and profit sharing. Indeed, as we shall see, Statler's management techniques had a great deal in common with those of Henry Ford, a man whose zeal for standardization and mass production made him the most important businessman of the twentieth century.[25]

Statler succeeded not only in building and managing several profitable hotels according to his notions of standardization and affordability but also in establishing a very different set of criteria for excellence in commercial hospitality. As a writer for the *Hotel World* observed in 1917, "If I were compelled to describe the new Hotel Statler of St. Louis in five words I would write: *It is a Statler Hotel.* Any man who has seen the Statler Hotel of Buffalo, Cleveland, and Detroit, and particularly in the latter two cities, will recognize a Statler Hotel as far as he can see one, and entering it he knows instantly that he is in one of the Statler public palaces. . . . Statler has created a *type.*" This approach did have its discontents: some patrons and critics complained that his hotels were too uniform and repetitive. But Statler was unmoved. As long as his hotels were "the best," he responded, "there is nothing wrong with standardization." Statler defined the success of his ventures in very different terms than his predecessors did. "If I wanted to," he once remarked, "I could run a so-called luxury hotel or a resort hotel . . . but I don't operate in that field. To hell with it; I'm not interested in it . . . mine will be at a price ordinary people can afford." Statler thus broke with the socially exclusive hotel-as-monument approach that had predominated among leading hotel builders since the 1790s.[26]

In so doing, Statler became enormously influential throughout the hotel industry. His name entered the professional lexicon of hoteliers, who made regular use of the term "Statlerization." As early as 1917 even the manager of the Waldorf-Astoria—a hotel that had once represented the ne plus ultra of luxury and extravagance—was enthusiastically repeating Statler's mantra of standardization and efficiency; and by then, hotel designers had made cost-effectiveness one of their highest priorities. By the time of his death in 1928, Statler was universally regarded as the most respected hotelkeeper in America, and as late as 1950 hotel executives surveyed by one industry journal still named the long-deceased boniface as "The Hotel Man of the Half Century."[27]

With regard to the other defining feature of his operations—organizing hotels into a chain—Statler was more of a bellwether than an innovator. As early as the 1850s there were three family partnerships that managed a number of hotels in northeastern cities, and in that same decade, the New England–born hotelier Paran Stevens oversaw the operation

4.17   The repetitive architecture of E. M. Statler's hotels led some critics to complain that "Statlerization" meant stultifying sameness. (Collection of Lisa Pfueller Davidson)

of six hotels in New Hampshire, Boston, Mobile, New York, and Philadelphia. Beginning in the 1880s, several incorporated hotel companies ran multiple establishments and often featured the names of all their properties on their stationery, and in the same years, the Fred Harvey Company became famous managing various hotels in the Southwest. What was distinctive about Statler was his demonstration of how a hotel chain could extend economies of scale beyond a single property and create a brand identity that would attract customers both regionally and nationally. The number of hotel chains in America remained small until the late 1910s, when it began to grow into the hundreds; by midcentury, chains accounted for about 20 percent of nationwide hotel revenues, the figure increasing to 50 percent thirty years later. It is thus possible to see in Statler's career the clearest expression of a new paradigm for the service industries of the twentieth century's developing consumer culture.[28]

THE AUTOMOBILE AND THE END OF AN ERA

The same zeal for mobility that had led Americans to adopt so many new technologies of travel in the first half of the nineteenth century drove them at century's end to yet another innovation: the automobile. Building on the work of German engineers who constructed the first modern automobiles in the 1880s, American inventors began designing their own cars in the early 1890s. Newspaper-sponsored races and motoring events at resort areas generated a great deal of public attention and participation by fledgling manufacturers, but automobiles remained unreliable and extremely expensive. Past the turn of the century, almost everyone assumed that cars would remain amusements for the very wealthy rather than feasible means of transportation for the masses.[29]

Within a decade, however, that assumption was rendered invalid by the new manufacturing techniques of Henry Ford. In the early 1890s, after ten years of working in Detroit-area machine shops and engine plants, Ford set about developing a workable automobile. Shortly after forming the Ford Motor Company in 1903, he decided that the way to succeed in the automobile business was to undertake large-scale production of a light, standardized, and above all affordable car model for a mass consumer market. Ford's business philosophy and management methods were very similar to Statler's, and in fact the two became friends and kept informed about each other's companies. Both men pursued a mass market and used standardization and large-scale production to reduce costs. Both paid high wages and offered profit-sharing incentives to employees in exchange for managerial control of the work process. And both made their big move in the same year: the Buffalo Statler and the Model T both debuted in 1908. The Model T was the most advanced car of its day and by most measures the most successful model in automotive history: over the following twenty years, Ford would produce and sell more than fifteen million units. As the fast-growing automobile market began to make America into a nation of drivers, it decisively altered the business of commercial hospitality.[30]

Automobility transformed transportation in the United States by adding roads to rails. Car manufacturers and drivers worked in concert with bicyclists and postal officials to catalyze road construction by successfully lobbying Congress to pass the Federal Highway Act in 1916. The law allocated $50 million to constructing the first national road system and facilitated federal-state cooperation in planning and engineering. Five years later, continued growth in automobile ownership encouraged further federal action in the form of plans for a national highway network to link American cities together. The resultant routes largely paralleled the existing railway networks, and while most people continued to favor trains for long-distance travel, the nation was seeing the emergence of a popular road-and-car culture. The rise of automobiles meant that a fast-growing number of Americans could go from place to place in small, self-selected groups and along itineraries of their own choosing. The passenger car soon began to compete with the railroad carriage as the basic unit of travel, and by the late 1940s roads ran to more places than train tracks and trucks rivaled railroads as carriers of freight.[31]

Systems of commercial hospitality changed in response. A growing proportion of the traveling public took to autocamping: automobilists slept in tents pitched near their cars or reserved space at rudimentary campgrounds designated for drivers. Estimates of the number of autocampers varied greatly, from nine million to fifteen million around 1920, growing to ten million to twenty million five years later; but whatever the counting method used, there was general agreement that more and more people were opting out of hotel stays. Other developers created the motor hotel, or motel, a new travel accommodation that, instead of being located in cities and other travel destinations, was sited on inexpensive land along the roads in between. The leading historians of the motel estimate that there were roughly three thousand of them in the United States in 1928, a number that had more than tripled by 1935 and quadrupled by 1939. This means that the number of motels probably surpassed that of hotels in the late 1930s or early 1940s, though hotels doubtless contained more total rooms until at least a decade later. In one sense, this twentieth-century order of public accommodation harkened back to the eighteenth-century geography of roadside inns and taverns, with numerous establishments lining the roads between settlements. Indeed, an early-twentieth-century surge of nostalgia for the quaintness of "ye olde inne" inspired well-to-do and predominantly Anglo-Saxon motorists to follow two-century-old routes in the Northeast and rediscover the charms of their ancestors' public houses (fig. 4.18).[32]

The American hotel reached the end of a long developmental trajectory just after the turn of the twentieth century. The hotel had come of age in the era of steam and steel and was fundamentally linked with and designed around distinctly nineteenth-century modes of travel characterized by collective, long-distance, point-to-point water and rail transportation. The automobile did not put an end to the hotel age. Hoteliers saw the writing on the wall, and adapted accordingly: in an effort to secure the patronage of drivers, existing hotels added parking facilities, and new establishments incorporated them into their building plans. Just as inns and taverns did not vanish in the nineteenth century, hotels by no means disappeared in the twentieth. Hotel construction continued unabated until the Great Depression—by which time the Census Bureau counted more than seven-

4.18   This early-twentieth-century poster humorously juxtaposed the modern automobile and colonial visitors at a rustic inn, suggesting how automobility was changing the character of American commercial hospitality. (Art and Architecture Collection, Miriam and Ira D. Wallach Division of Art, Prints and Photographs, The New York Public Library, Astor, Lenox and Tilden Foundations)

teen thousand substantial hotels in the United States—and accelerated rapidly amid the unprecedented prosperity of the postwar decades.[33]

But long before hotels adopted the logic and forms of twentieth-century industrial capitalism, they had played a significant role in the elaboration and expansion of nineteenth-century commercial capitalism. For as surely as American cities served as centers of control and nodes of exchange in the national economy, hotels functioned as headquarters and outposts for an urbanizing commercial system. Hotels helped facilitate a transportation revolution that was substantially responsible for the rapid growth of trade. They served as footholds and anchors in the expansion of the United States urban system. And they formed part of a rationalized, regularized, nationwide system of public accommodations that made travel into a safe and predictable undertaking. In all these ways, and in others still to be described, hotels were invaluable in helping metropolitan merchant capitalists and capital reach out over the tremendous distances of the North American continent. In so doing, the hotel had successfully served the purposes of its eighteenth-century originators: to establish the United States as an urban and commercial nation.

Part Two   Hospitality

IN PART ONE, WE SAW that hotels could be viewed collectively as elements within larger networks of transportation and accommodation. But a history of hotels must also reveal how they functioned individually as purveyors of hospitality. The hotel was not the first institution to provide shelter, sustenance, and services to travelers and others willing to pay; it was only the most recent in a long line of hostelries. But hotel hospitality was distinct from any that had come before. Accommodating travelers and strangers always raised thorny questions: Who would provide hospitality? On what basis would they do so? And most problematically, to whom would hospitality be offered, and from whom would it be withheld? The hotel was the place where these issues would find a definitive resolution.

Hospitality is the name given to an array of rituals for dealing with strangers. While hospitality comes in any number of guises—there are at least as many forms as there have been cultures—they all share a similar underlying structure. As the cultural anthropologist Julian Pitt-Rivers has defined it, hospitality is a "rite of incorporation" by which one status is temporarily exchanged for another. Through a ritual of hospitality, "it is the status of the stranger which is lost and that of the community member which is gained." As an outsider, the stranger has an uncertain status. He or she may be a danger to the community or a benefit to it, but either way is ignorant of its rules and cannot be trusted to behave appropriately. The stranger must therefore be assigned some sort of knowable role. This means not that the stranger becomes a member of the community but rather that he or she enters an intermediate status between outsider and insider. He or she takes on the role of guest.[1]

A guest requires a host, and the first step in a ritual of hospitality is to identify a community member who will take on that role. This can be accomplished in any number of ways: the ancient Greeks washed the feet of their guests and anointed them with oil, native Alaskans traditionally staged an exchange of blows to the face between host and stranger, and today most people simply share a drink or a meal. However this connection is established, the host thereafter serves as the link between the community and the person who was previously a stranger to it. Hosts are answerable for the welfare of their guests and responsible for their behavior.[2]

Rituals of hospitality are inherently precarious because they are performed along borders that separate communities and cultures—places where misunderstandings can easily give way to discord or even violence. Even in a society with well-established codes of conduct, conflicts can emerge over small disagreements. Not a few travelers have quarreled with their hosts over the price of rooms, unexpected surcharges for meals or other items, or the speed or quality of certain services. In intercultural encounters, the parties involved lack a set of shared understandings and expectations of proper behavior, making it easy for people to give or take offense.

Indeed, the very language used to describe the elements of hospitality demonstrates these underlying tensions. The modern English term *hospitality* and the words *host* and *guest* (and, of course, *hotel*) are derived from closely related or identical linguistic roots. Traced back through intermediate tongues like Middle English, Middle High German, Old French, Old Norse, and Old English, they find their origin in the Latin forms *hospes* and *hostis*. Intriguingly, these terms indicated not only "host" and "guest," but also "stranger," "foreigner," and "enemy." The basic lexicon of hospitality thus expresses the combination of trust and suspicion involved in the relation of host and guest. Hosts are confronted with people who are unknown or foreign, and may be hostile, yet they are expected to welcome them into their homes and communities. Guests, meanwhile, are in an unfamiliar place or foreign land but are compelled to trust their hosts enough to eat and sleep on their premises. These etymologies mark hospitality as a ritual fraught with difficulties.[3]

However problematic the work of accommodating strangers, it at least helped that the difficulties of hospitality were historically limited by the relatively small number of people involved. As long as mobility was narrowly subscribed and travel was undertaken only rarely, traditional modes of hospitality were adequate to the task. As time passed, however, it became apparent that transience was becoming a common condition in the Atlantic world.

In the early nineteenth century, writers in Europe and America became preoccupied with strangers. Whether in the singular form of the unknown individual or the plural form of the anonymous crowd, the stranger became one of the representative figures of the age. In an 1822 short story entitled "My Cousin's Corner Window," the German author, composer, and dramatist E. T. A. Hoffmann described a homebound invalid sitting alone in his Berlin apartment and observing the masses of people moving about the streets. At first, the cousin perceives only an undifferentiated throng, but he soon takes up a pair of opera glasses that allow him to pick out individuals. Though he can see them clearly, they remain unknown to him, and so he scans their appearances for clues to their identity and guesses at their intentions. The works of the French poet Charles Baudelaire, especially *The Flowers of Evil* (1857) and *Tableaux parisiens* (1861), contain numerous depictions of Paris crowds, and *The Spleen of Paris,* his 1864 collection of prose poetry, opens with a short dialogue called "The Stranger":

> Whom do you love most, enigmatic man, tell me, your father, your mother, your sister, or your brother?
>
> I have neither father, nor mother, nor sister, nor brother.
>
> Your friends?
>
> You are using a term whose meaning has to this day remained unknown to me.

Extended treatments of the stranger and the crowd also appeared in the works of Victor Hugo, Honoré de Balzac, Søren Kierkegaard, and Fyodor Dostoevsky, among others, and became an archetypal setting in Western literature for the rest of the nineteenth century and into the twentieth.[4]

A fascination with the interplay between the person and the multitude emerged simultaneously in the United States. In 1818 a visitor to Pittsburgh wondered at the anonymity that prevailed among the city's residents. "A next door neighbor is, with them, frequently unknown," he remarked, "and months and years pass, without their exchanging with each other the ordinary compliments of friendship and goodwill." The novelist and abolitionist Lydia Maria Child expressed a similar sentiment a quarter-century later in a plaintive passage from her hugely popular *Letters from New-York.* "For eight weary months," she wrote, "I have met in the crowded streets but two faces I had ever seen before. . . . At times, I almost fancy I can feel myself turning to stone by inches." Edgar Allan Poe's short story "The Man of the Crowd" (1840) described its narrator lounging about a hotel coffee room where "dense and continuous tides of population were rushing past the door." Suddenly, the face of a single stranger "at once arrested and absorbed my whole attention," spawning "a craving desire to keep the man in view—to know more of him." Poe's narrator follows the stranger across the busy downtown, into a crowded bazaar, and through poverty-stricken tenements. After a pursuit that lasts all night, throughout the day, and into the following evening, the narrator realizes that the stranger, despite his attraction to crowds, is terribly alone: he has not met any acquaintance, exchanged a word with anyone, nor so much as acknowledged a single person. Herman Melville elaborated the theme of the stranger into an entire novel in *The Confidence-Man: His Masquerade* (1857), in which the title character takes advantage of the anonymity of urban crowds, using various disguises and the opportunity of casual contact and conversation to swindle the unsuspecting.[5]

Behind this wave of literary impressions lay changes in both everyday life and political ideology. These changes are usually discussed in terms of urbanization, the rise of capitalism, and the advent of industrialization. It is essential to recognize, however, that these familiar processes were themselves predicated on a more generalized shift in human geography in which people were increasingly decoupled from place. This new geography emerged most clearly in the late-eighteenth-century age of revolutions and continued to expand throughout the nineteenth century and after. Human mobility increased most markedly in the Anglo-American context, where it manifested itself in a number of concrete ways. The first was the massive increase in oceangoing trade in the late seventeenth and eighteenth centuries, a commercial revolution marked not only by its soaring absolute volume but more importantly by its rich material variety and increasing penetration into areas well beyond Atlantic port cities. This was soon followed by the invention and deployment of various transportation technologies that greatly amplified the range and ease of travel within nations. The English pioneered the construction of roads, canals, and railways in the eighteenth century, and the people of the United States followed suit in the nineteenth, building internal improvements on such an ambitious scale that North America soon boasted the most extensive and elaborate transportation network that the world had ever seen.[6]

Meanwhile, emergent liberal political ideologies came to include new claims about human mobility, in particular the assertion that individuals possessed a natural right to move from place to place. This idea was a substantial preoccupation of Enlightenment thinkers in eighteenth-century Europe. An early version of this principle was issued in William Blackstone's *Commentaries on the Laws of England* (1765–1769), for more than a century the most authoritative statement of English law. Blackstone interpreted traditional English liberties as protecting "the personal liberty of individuals," which "consists in the power of loco-motion, of changing situation, or removing one's person to whatsoever place one's own inclination may direct." Similar statements of such rights were promulgated in revolutionary France. In 1789 the Estates General asserted that "every sojourner in this life must be left undisturbed in his legitimate possessions . . . and therefore that each must be free to move about or to come, within and outside the Kingdom, without permissions, passports, or other formalities that tend to hamper the liberty of its citizens." This opposition to involuntary sedentariness was not surprising, given that Enlightenment philosophy had emerged in antagonism with the feudal ancien régime, with its commitment to restricted mobility. The declaration of a right to travel, however, also ultimately raised the question of the legal status of strangers. The National Assembly's first constitution, issued in 1791, listed as the first "natural and civil right" the freedom "to move about, to remain, [and] to leave."[7]

This intellectual commitment to freedom of movement set the stage for the Kantian theory of hospitality noted in my Introduction. When Kant asserted that world peace required "conditions of universal *hospitality*," he was thinking within a new paradigm of human mobility. His intervention was particularly innovative because he saw that it would not be enough for governments simply to stand aside and allow people to travel; nations would also have to deal with the problems generated by mobile citizenries. If states could no longer restrain people from moving around, they would have to take positive action to ensure that wayfarers moving across borders did not become the cause of international hostilities.

The material and ideological changes of the late eighteenth and early nineteenth centuries were gradually matched by changes in governance that removed barriers to mobility. The process played out most quickly in the United States and was epitomized by such legal changes as the state-by-state abrogation of entail (a body of restrictions on the sale and transfer of landed property that had long served to tie families to their landholdings) and the gradual collapse of locally enforced restrictions on movement. American attitudes toward personal mobility were highly innovative for their time, and foreign travelers often made note of the United States as a place where people could come and go in ways that they could not in Europe. As early as 1798 the Polish traveler Julian Ursyn Niemcewicz could note: "There are no eagles, nor customs, nor sentries, nor do they stop nor ask who one is, whence one came, and for what purpose. They do not inspect nor put their seal on trunks. A traveler goes a thousand miles in America and nowhere will he be held up nor inspected nor tormented. In Europe one can not travel a score of miles without being exposed to all this unpleasantness."[8]

As the nineteenth century progressed, many European governments gradually moved in the same direction as the United States by abolishing or easing restrictions on movement, most notably the requirement that travelers carry internal and international passports. These changes set the stage for further decoupling of people and place in the Atlantic world. The various abolitions of slavery—first by nations in Spanish America, then in Europe, and finally in the United States and Brazil—meant the end of labor regimes that were defined in part through lack of freedom to leave one's assigned place of work; the end of serfdom in Europe had similar implications for human mobility. The mass migration of millions, and later tens of millions, of Europeans to the Americas further attenuated the people-place linkage, as did the expropriation of the Native peoples who were forcibly displaced in the process. These transformations made constantly moving populations into an accepted fact of life, and in so doing foreshadowed the even more intensive globalization of the twentieth-century world.[9]

These changes made many parts of the Atlantic world, especially its cities, into a world of strangers. There, people increasingly found themselves in contact with unknown individuals who could arrive from over the horizon one day and disappear beyond it the next. It had become increasingly common, and increasingly acceptable, for people to move from place to place, and so to encounter, and become, strangers. This new everyday social reality put pressure on existing forms of travel accommodation and soon gave rise to new forms and styles of commercial hospitality.[10]

Five *The House of Strangers*

The Transformation of Hospitality and the Everyday Life of the Hotel

HOTELS WERE sophisticated hospitality machines. While they served the same basic purposes as inns and taverns—providing shelter, food, and refreshment to travelers and others away from home—they did so in a fundamentally different way. This new order of hospitality recast the host-guest relationship, restructured the architecture of accommodation, and reorganized the work of welcoming strangers.

Understanding the transformation of hospitality means going inside hotels, and accordingly, in this chapter I will focus on everyday hotel life. Hotels were characterized by a permanent state of coming and going, of constant contact between people unknown to one another. There were other spaces in which Americans regularly encountered strangers: trains, steamboats, and trolleys were crowded with people on the move; shops and theaters profited from a regular turnover of patrons; and busy city streets guaranteed much rubbing of elbows among the urban masses. But hotels occupied a special place in the nineteenth-century world of strangers because they put transient individuals into contact for days rather than just minutes or hours, and because such contact often took place in domestic and even intimate spaces like parlors and bedrooms. Hotels thus required that people constantly establish, maintain, and renegotiate myriad contacts and relationships.

The challenge of providing hospitality to a world of strangers yielded both new methods and unexpected outcomes. The ongoing work of managing transient populations fostered a process of innovation and refinement that resulted in an elaborate array of services and an increasingly complex architecture. In the process, hotelkeepers also achieved something more: instead of responding to the problems of transience and anonymity by emphasizing privacy and keeping people separated, they created a sense of community among guests, residents, and locals, imbuing hotels with a resolutely public culture. Hotel hospitality did have its discontents. The replacement of the personal hospitality of inns and taverns with the institutional accommodation of the hotel disrupted social and economic hierarchies, creating friction between patrons and employees. But by the third quarter of the nineteenth century, American hotels had won the admiration of domestic travelers and foreign visitors alike and established a new international standard for hospitality.

HOSPITALITY TRANSFORMED

Hotels represented a new paradigm for hospitality. Hotel hospitality differed from older modes of accommodation in a number of specific ways, but in general terms, hotels replaced a household model of hospitality with an institutional model. In place of a household hospitality that was offered by a proprietor-patriarch, incorporated members of his family, and involved personalized attendance, the new hospitality was characterized by hotels that were operated by professional managers, employed large numbers of wage workers, and provided rationalized, efficient service (fig. 5.1).

Hotel hospitality entailed the restructuring of architectural space. The first step in the move away from household hospitality came when hotel builders discarded the private house as the architectural model for guest accommodation. This was not a case of total abandonment. The people who designed the first hotels did not start from either a blank slate or an abstract ideal. Rather, they took the traditional house form and broke it apart, disaggregating its spaces and functions and reconfiguring them into a new building type.

A house or dwelling is a collection of spaces that serves the residential needs or wants of the people who occupy it. A simple house might contain only one or two rooms. For example, the hall-and-parlor houses of colonial America (fig. 5.2) consisted of two rooms. A person would enter directly into the hall, which contained the hearth and was used for cooking, eating, and sociability. The parlor, separated from the hall by a doorway, was more often devoted to family, rest, and intimacy. More elaborate houses might assign

5.1   This cutaway view of the Astor Hotel reveals the great complexity of its operations and spatial arrangement. (Museum of the City of New York)

one or more rooms to each of these functions and add additional spaces designated for particular purposes. This 1772 Georgian-style home in Delaware (fig. 5.3) contained a first-floor parlor, a formal dining room, a drawing room, and a kitchen, among other spaces. Different functions were sometimes located on different floors, but all were grouped together for the use of one family.[1]

Colonial American inns and taverns were architecturally indistinguishable from dwelling houses because the vast majority were simply homes with liquor licenses and makeshift bars. Hospitality was thus provided in domestic spaces: guests shared bedrooms, ate food prepared at the family hearth, and drank and socialized in converted living rooms (fig. 5.4). In this respect, inns and taverns were typical of a colonial American architecture that comprised a limited number of building types. Because the household was the basic unit of economic production and social reproduction, the built environment was mostly

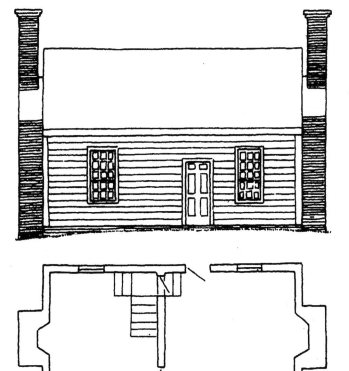

5.2 A simple hall-and-parlor house separated the home into two parts, each of which was a multipurpose space. (Henry Glassie, *Vernacular Architecture*, Indiana University Press)

composed of simple structures that served as both dwellings and workplaces. These were joined by a few specialized edifices, including churches, market houses, warehouses, and town halls, but it was only in the early national period that Americans began to build additional purpose-specific architectural types.[2]

When Americans set about creating a new kind of public house, they transformed the space of hospitality. The most dramatic reconfiguration of the household involved the sleeping areas, which were greatly multiplied in number and placed side by side in the form of dozens or scores of hotel bedchambers. These guest rooms remained individuated private spaces that were separated from the more public functions of hotels by being placed on upper floors or in separate wings. The other functions of the household underwent a very different transformation: they were reduced in number but greatly amplified in size and capacity so that they could be used in common by the hotel's numerous guests. There would be only a single hotel kitchen, but it would be very large; private dining rooms gave way to huge common dining halls. Similarly, the family-size halls and parlors of the private house expanded into sitting rooms and lounges big enough to accommodate large groups; reading rooms became libraries, hallways became galleries. These more public areas remained together, usually arranged on the lower floors of a hotel.

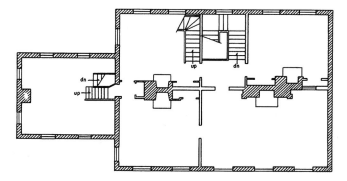

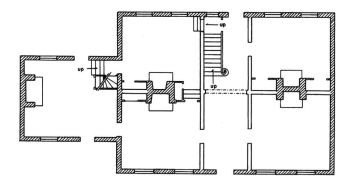

5.3 More elaborate urban dwellings like this 1772 house in Delaware contained more purpose-specific spaces arranged on multiple levels for a single family. (Drawn by Gabrielle Lanier after John A. H. Sweeney, *Grandeur on the Appoquinimink,* Johns Hopkins University Press)

This reconfiguration of space was evident in the hotel projects of the 1790s and is documented by architectural plans of hotels built in the 1800s and 1820s. Descriptions and images of Washington's Union Public Hotel and New York's City Hotel indicate upper stories filled with numerous small bedchambers and main and second floors equipped with large dining rooms, spacious ballrooms, and other shared spaces. A set of measured drawings of the Boston Exchange Coffee House and Hotel (fig. 5.5) displays in detail how its architect resized and redistributed household functions. The "Basement Story" includes two cellars and a kitchen, each measuring close to one thousand square feet, and a "Servant's Hall" only slightly smaller. The "Principle [*sic*] Story" includes a "Parlour" and a "Family Parlour" of several hundred square feet each and a "Drawing Room" and "Reading Room" both in the range of one thousand square feet. The upper stories are occupied by numerous small guest rooms of about one hundred square feet each. A similar arrangement of space can be seen in a plan of the main floor of Boston's Tremont House (fig. 5.6), which clustered the bedchambers in a projecting wing that was separated from the large public areas grouped to the front of the structure; additional guest rooms were located on upper floors.

Hotels were also shaped by commercial and government buildings. Business architecture increasingly featured floor plans based on a grid system, with interchangeable cells

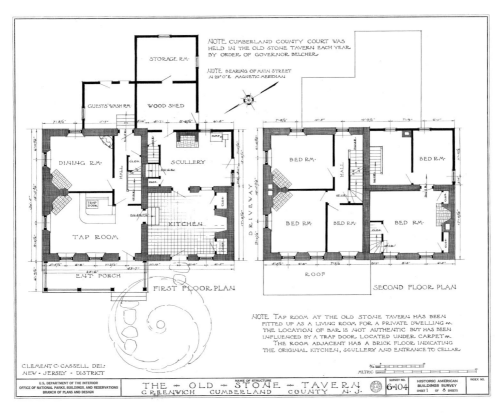

5.4   The floor plans of early American taverns indicate an essentially homelike division of space and labor. (Historic American Buildings Survey)

or units repeated in long arrays, as in the Philadelphia Arcade (fig. 5.7) from around 1825. This trend had emerged some years earlier in public building design, which was moving away from largely residential forms like governors' mansions and toward multicelled plans. A government office building (fig. 5.8) from 1814, for example, comprised a series of identical administrative spaces, each with its own door to the hallway, a plan that resembled the arrangement of early hotel bedchambers. The influence of public buildings on hotel architecture was also evidenced externally: the domes, cupolas, porticoes, and colonnades that graced so many hotels were Enlightenment-inspired gestures that expressed rationality and deliberation and had become standard features of civic structures.[3]

Hotel architects continued to modify floor plans throughout the nineteenth century. They experimented with various design elements, repeating or expanding those that worked best and discarding others. A prime example is the double-loaded corridor, in which rows of rooms open onto both sides of a central circulating hallway instead of rooms opening one onto another. The only regular double-loaded corridor in the 1809 Exchange Coffee House served a dozen rooms along a hall at the back right of the fourth gallery; the hotel's other rooms were arranged in irregular plans that varied from floor to floor. Twenty

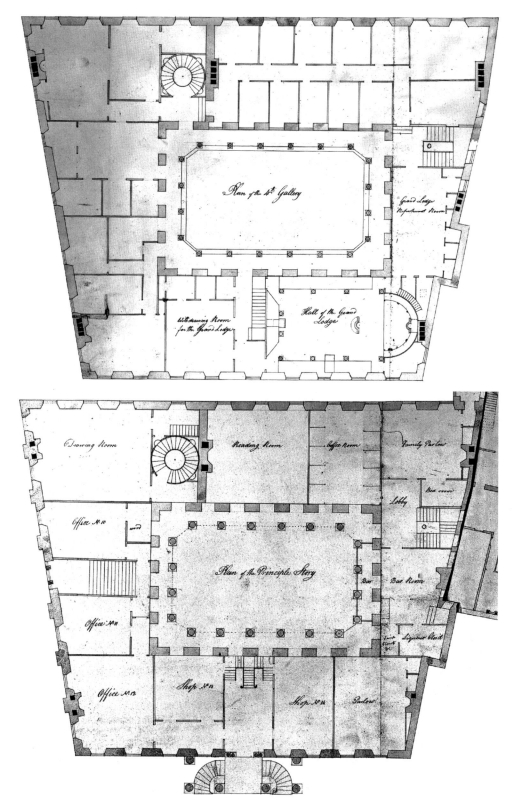

5.5   Asher Benjamin's Exchange Coffee House and Hotel (1809) displays the basic spatial innovation of hotels: the disaggregation of the private household. Individual bedchambers were placed on the upper stories, shared public spaces on the ground and second floors. (Bostonian Society/Old State House)

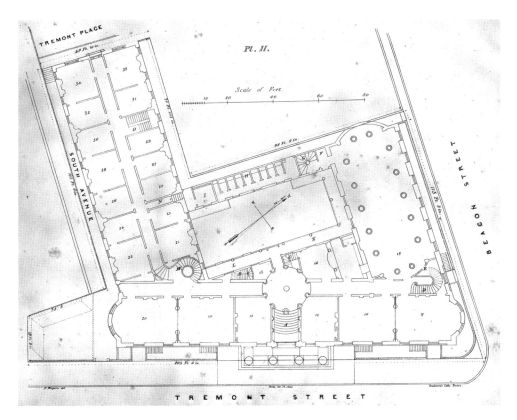

5.6   Isaiah Rogers's 1829 Tremont House grouped small guest rooms together in their own wing at left, separated from the reception area, parlors, and ballrooms of the hotel's main section. (Bostonian Society/Old State House)

years later, the main floor of the Tremont House included an entire double-loaded corridor wing at left, and its upper stories probably housed more such corridors. This marked a transition from experimentation based on a domestic vernacular to a maturing modern institutional building type. By the late nineteenth and early twentieth centuries, hotel plans were dominated by double-loaded corridors, as with the United States Hotel, a resort establishment in Saratoga (fig. 5.9), or any of Statler's mature hotel plans (fig. 5.10).

Another example of experimentation in hotels involved privately held halls and offices. The Exchange Coffee House floor plans show many rooms marked "Office" and "Shop" on the basement and principal floors, and halls held by the "Grand Lodge" and "St. John's Lodge" on the upper floors. These rentable or owned spaces were probably in-tended to generate additional income for the owners of an early, experimental hotel at a time when they were unsure of the reliability of receipts from the guest rooms. Later establishments maintained some of these uses, with ground-level shops and offices for rent becoming a regular part of hotel architecture, but privately owned areas largely vanished from upper stories in later hotels, which typically reserved these floors exclusively for guest

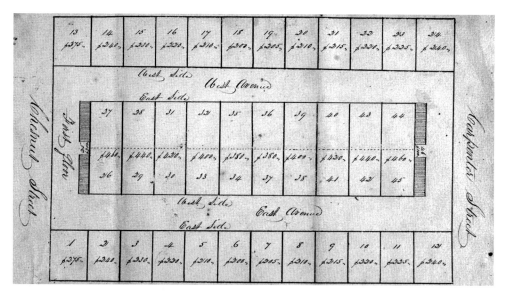

5.7   The Philadelphia Arcade (c. 1825) displayed the gridlike arrangement of rooms that was increasingly common in early-nineteenth-century commercial architecture. (The Historical Society of Pennsylvania)

rooms. So while many of the main features of hotels were well established by the early nineteenth century, others were still being worked out over the following decades.

Hotels were part of a larger transformation in American architecture. As the architectural historian Dell Upton has shown, the early decades of the republic were a time of constant innovation in which architects refined older building types, created new ones, and worked out many of the spatial arrangements that became basic design elements of the nation's built environment. As a result, other institutional buildings that followed the emergence of the hotel displayed similar architectural tendencies, especially repeating cells and the use of corridors. The ground floor of the 1814 Philadelphia mental asylum (fig. 5.11), for example, departed from the previous practice of placing patients in shared wards and instead assigned individuals to their own small, identical rooms. These rooms opened onto long corridors forming men's and women's wings that projected from a center section containing shared areas like sitting rooms, parlors, and an office (a configuration that in many respects anticipated the T-, C-, and E-shaped hotel plans of a century later). These kinds of individuated spaces were also used in prisons and almshouses, and repeating cells soon found their way into the designs of schools and factories.[4]

In hotels, the new interior architecture corresponded to major changes in the organization of work. Household hospitality had depended on a familial system of labor: the head of household owned the premises, obtained the liquor license, greeted guests, and made business decisions; spouses or children helped cook, serve, and clean, sometimes with the help of one or two domestic servants. The larger scale of hotels made such arrangements impractical. Even a modest establishment of twenty or thirty rooms required more labor than most families could supply, and a hundred-room hotel called for an entire house staff. The use of large-scale wage labor for hospitality quickly grew from the ad hoc hiring of helpmeets into an elaborate system of employment with specialized tasks, tiered authority, and time discipline. In many respects this mirrored the contemporaneous rise of the factory system of manufacturing, which moved production out of the household, subdivided it, and contracted it out according to the demands of a new economic rationality. Indeed, the advent of the hotel might also be interpreted as the industrialization of hospitality—but here, the process was conceptually and functionally separate from commodity production and instead devoted to the provision of services.

Just as industrialization restructured the master-servant relationship, the transformation of hospitality rendered host-guest relations increasingly impersonal. As the change in the scale of public accommodations attenuated the household model, the patriarchal role of the host was also weakened. While it was possible for the hotelkeeper in a small establishment to greet every guest personally, this was not the case in a larger hotel. As a result, it was mostly the hotel staff who dealt directly with guests. Other changes followed. The presumption that a guest would recognize the host's authority eroded considerably, and as we shall see, the host's employee-proxies faced considerable hostility when they tried to exercise authority in his stead.[5]

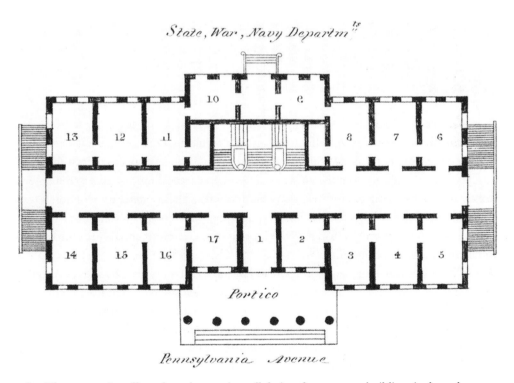

5.8   These executive offices show the growing cellularity of government buildings in the early national period. (Oberlin College Library Special Collections)

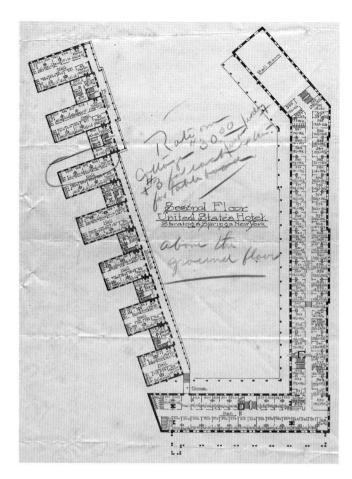

5.9 Like many other hotels in the mid- to late nineteenth century, the United States Hotel arrayed guest rooms along lengthy double-loaded corridors. (National Museum of American History)

This new mode of hospitality was perfectly suited to a nation that was becoming steadily more mobile. While one might interpret the hotel as a response to the advent of the transportation revolution and the consequent growth of travel, it is essential to remember that hotels preceded major advances in transportation. The first generation of hotels was built well in advance of demand, and the building type failed economically. But when the technology of transportation caught up with that of accommodation, both could thrive and facilitate still more mobility.

The result was manifested in crowded byways and a flood of wayfarers into the nation's cities. Available evidence of the volume of travel suggests that it was large and constantly increasing. The effect was most pronounced in the nation's northeastern urban core. An 1835 "strangers list" for New York City, which purported to have counted all visitors over 270 days, recorded 59,700 people, or more than 1,500 arrivals per week. Ten years later, the *American Railroad Journal* stated that the number of passengers traveling between Hartford, Connecticut, and Springfield, Massachusetts, exceeded 3,000 per month—and in small cities like these, with populations of 10,000 to 12,000, a weekly influx of 350 people per city would have been very noticeable indeed. Another 1845 estimate put the number of railway and steamboat passengers between Boston and New York City at from 19,000 to 22,000 per month, or about 2,400 people per city per week. The comparable figure for travel between New York City and Philadelphia was some 30,000 people per month, or 3,500 per city per week. And the number of steamboat passengers up and down the Hudson River was an astounding 100,000 per month.[6]

The remarkable mobility of the American people was also reflected in hotel patronage. In 1852, for example, the *Daily True Democrat* reported that in Cleveland, then a city of only about 17,000 inhabitants, a hotelkeeper had "entertained 457 strangers at the American House" over the course of four days. A decade later, by which time the city had nearly tripled in population, the same hotel was said to have welcomed "between eight and nine hundred" registered guests in a single week, and "over fifteen hundred visitors during the State Fair week." Even much smaller hotels played host to a constant stream of guests. Cleveland's midsized Angier House, for example, welcomed 96 guests over two days in August 1861. In larger cities, the numbers were substantially higher. James Drew, an Englishman who visited New York City in 1845, put the number of customers at hundreds per day: "Probably 200 would be the average number to be attended to in Howard's Hotel, while at the Astor House, and many other Hotels, the average number may be from 300 to 400." (These estimates seem too high for travelers alone, and probably also included dinner guests and other locals.) A decade later, immense establishments like the St. Nicholas Hotel regularly greeted nearly 1,000 new overnight guests each week.[7]

Accommodating so many guests made hotelkeeping an exceptionally difficult business; it was no accident that in nineteenth-century parlance, the expression "he can keep a hotel" meant that the person was extremely capable. A hotelkeeper's challenges began with the sheer size of the premises. While an inn or a tavern could be run on the same basis as a private household, operating a hotel of fifty or one hundred rooms or more involved a completely different order of logistics. Simply keeping track of all these rooms and their

5.10 The upper floors of Statler hotels were dominated by long double-loaded corridors, a room layout that had become standard in large hotels by the early twentieth century. (General Research Division, The New York Public Library, Astor, Lenox and Tilden Foundations)

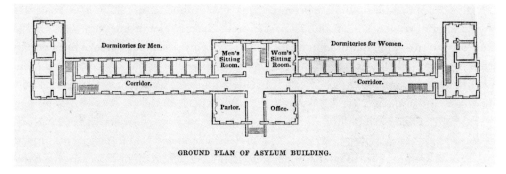

5.11   Many other institutional buildings, such as the Philadelphia Asylum for the Relief of Persons Deprived of Their Use of Reason (1814), adopted some of the same architectural configurations as hotels. (The Library Company of Philadelphia)

contents was a formidable task that involved countless items like keys, number-plates, rugs, mattresses, curtains, chairs, tables, inkwells, and bowls and pitchers. There were also elaborate purchasing responsibilities: daily procurement of food, drink, and ice; weekly deliveries of fuel for cooking, heating, and lighting; and occasional orders for linens, towels, dishes, silverware, and stationery. Most complicated of all, there was the matter of labor, which confronted every proprietor with the intricacies of hiring, training, coordination, payment, and firing. Hotelkeepers had to manage every one of these areas successfully just to keep their doors open.

Added to this were exigencies that arose from the microeconomics of hotelkeeping. Hotels, like many other businesses in what would later be called the service sector, had very high startup costs but relatively stable fixed costs. Because hotels ran to tens or hundreds of thousands of dollars in building costs alone, they were almost always owned by groups of investors. The usual practice was for these owners to hire a professional hotelkeeper to manage the establishment. The hotelkeeper typically paid a fixed annual sum on a multiyear rental contract and was responsible for all expenses and receipts. Such contracts were potentially very lucrative, but also quite risky. If a hotelkeeper's revenues greatly exceeded his expenses, the owners of the hotel had no claim on any profits beyond the rent, and he could pocket considerable sums of money. On the other hand, if he failed to turn a profit, he stood to lose all monies spent on furniture, supplies, and wages, and even then he remained responsible for the rent.[8]

Compounding the logistical and microeconomic challenges of the hotel business was the fact of increasing competition. As long as most cities had only one first-rate hotel, keepers could hold prices at two dollars per day despite public complaints about gouging. Notably, hotels cost the same throughout the East, suggesting strong demand; otherwise, hotelkeepers in less wealthy cities would have charged less than in New York or Boston. As midcentury approached, however, the rapid proliferation of hotels in individual cities triggered fears that an oversupply of rooms would drive keepers out of business. In

Philadelphia in 1857, for example, a leading newspaper published "The Hotel Folly," a lengthy argument between developers and hotelkeepers over a proposal to build a huge new hotel in the city. Many city directories did indeed record high rates of turnover: in New York, two or three different people were often listed as the keepers of a given hotel over the course of several years, with the name of a hotel sometimes changing as new proprietors reopened it on new terms at the same address; and in Louisville, Kentucky, half the hotels listed in both the 1848 and 1851 city directories had changed ownership in those three years. The ledgers of R. G. Dun and Company, the premier credit reporting agency of the period, show numerous entries in which hotelkeepers were deemed unworthy of further credit, often with subsequent notations indicating a bankruptcy or decision to sell out and leave the business. By the 1880s competition was so fierce that New York's opulent St. Nicholas Hotel, which charged up to five dollars for some rooms, also had accommodations available for as little as one dollar; apparently, even the keepers of the most luxurious establishments were hungry enough for revenue that they would not concede even the low end of the market to their competitors.[9]

Hotelkeepers thus operated under conditions that made them extremely dependent upon public favor, and they spared no effort in establishing and preserving what they called "the consideration of the public." Every hotel manager knew that if people stopped coming through the door, revenues would plunge and he would be out of business in a matter of weeks. In response, hoteliers constantly strove to attract customers with more comfortable rooms, better-trained staff, a wider variety of services, innovative technologies, and in-house spectacles and entertainments. The result of this combination of competition and innovation was a rapidly advancing standard of hospitality. The first generation of hotels had established the basic features of the building type, but the level of service was often lacking. It was primarily in the 1830s and 1840s that hotelkeepers worked out recognizably modern standards of hotel hospitality, and many of the methods and protocols familiar today had been introduced by the late 1850s. In order to see how this worked, it helps to know what it was like to stay at a hotel in a large city sometime around the third quarter of the nineteenth century.

SECURING ACCOMMODATIONS

Visitors arriving in town would first have to decide where to stay. They might already have chosen a particular hotel because a friend, family member, or business contact had suggested one, or on the basis of a recommendation from a train conductor or the previous night's hotelkeeper. Even if they arrived knowing nothing about local hotels, they would soon have plenty of information—the city's hotelkeepers had paid good money to see to it. Managers of the top hotels in large cities could take it for granted that people would know the names and locations of their establishments, but few others could, and so they advertised aggressively. Newspapers and magazines were filled with notices that combined unabashed puffery ("the best house in America") with promises of comfort ("the best accommodations available") and assurances of safety ("the house is absolutely fireproof"). Hotel trade cards (fig. 5.12) were placed on train seats or thrust into travelers' hands as they climbed down from passenger cars. And a phalanx of hotel runners—men and boys paid to direct people to a particular establishment—accosted visitors on the platform, in the station house, and on the street and tried to haul them and their luggage to their employer's hotel. "Porters and boys of every size soon made an irruption into the cars, recommending different hotels in Cincinnati," wrote one wayfarer in 1855. "I selected one who wore a label showing that he belonged to the far-famed Burnet House hotel; and I was assured . . . that I might trust him with my forty-two brass checks with which to claim my baggage."[10]

Visitors could also find a suitable hostelry without assistance. Hotels' distinctive architecture and siting had been intended to make them easy to locate, and in many cities the leading house could be seen from the deck of an approaching steamer or through a train window. Hotels typically clustered on main thoroughfares: Broadway and Fifth Avenue were the primary hotel streets in New York City; in Cleveland they were St. Clair and Superior, and in San Francisco, Montgomery and Market. A person could tell a great deal about a hotel at first glance. A prominent location, an elaborately ornamented façade, or liveried porters served as an invitation to the well-to-do. A more affordable establishment might stand on cheaper real estate along a side street, its function indicated only by large lettering painted on a simple brick front. Hotelkeepers knew that customers were attracted by visual cues, and they used fresh paint, polished surfaces, and prominent signboards to ensure that they would not be overlooked.[11]

Any uncertainty about the hotel's character would have been dispelled as visitors went inside. The aesthetic choices on display in hotel interiors were in effect appeals to class and culture. A large lobby with smartly dressed people lounging on abundant and well-upholstered furniture would indicate a hotel for prosperous and respectable patrons (fig. 5.13). A modest, low-ceilinged entry hall might mean only that this was a midpriced house, but other visual cues, like an all-male clientele (fig. 5.14), would suggest a commercial hotel favored by traveling salesmen or local workingmen. A shabbily dressed crowd of men would indicate a flophouse, though a person would not likely have entered such an establishment accidentally.

Having decided that this was the right kind of hotel for their purposes, the visitors would establish themselves as guests. While in some early hotels the bar doubled as the front desk, by the 1830s most substantial establishments placed the registration area directly inside the entrance and staffed it with a new kind of employee: the hotel clerk. As prospective guests approached the front desk, the clerk quickly sized them up and decided whether they were acceptable patrons. If they were suspicious looking, intoxicated, inappropriately attired, or African American, the clerk might pretend not to see them, keep them waiting indefinitely, or inform them that there were no rooms available. If, by contrast, they were people of particular importance, he might summon the hotelkeeper for a personal welcome. Most arrivals were judged unremarkable but inoffensive. Once the clerk had agreed to accommodate them, he would turn the guest register around and ask them to sign in.

Virtually every hotel had a guest register. Whether it was a palatial caravansary in the national metropolis or a small establishment in a provincial town, it kept track of its guests in the same way. Hotel registers were large and impressive leatherbound volumes measuring about twenty inches high by thirty wide as they lay open (fig. 5.15). Each page was divided into rows and columns with boxes for guests' names, room numbers, places of origin, and lengths of stay; some registers also left space for comments. While guests signed their names in the register and filled in any other required information, the hotel clerk selected rooms for them. Most guests hoped for a reasonably sized room, one with a street view for maximum light, and preferably on a lower floor, since this would obviate repeated stair climbing. Some people were in the habit of requesting particular rooms or demanding them outright, but this was widely considered unwise, since the clerk had all but absolute discretion over the process, and if provoked, he could always find a reason to put guests in an undesirable location. Once the clerk had decided, he would turn the register back around, fill in the room number, select the corresponding key from behind the desk, and slide it over the counter. This small ritual of signature and exchange formally established the relationship of host and guest.[12]

Guests would probably need help getting to their rooms. Even small hotels had fairly complex floor plans, and larger hostelries invariably featured labyrinthine corridors that made it easy to get lost. There was also the question of luggage. Most hotel bedchambers were located on upper stories, and carrying bags or trunks up flights of stairs could challenge the strength of even fit and vigorous travelers. (Elevators were a relatively late addition to hotel architecture. A few establishments used steam-driven mechanisms to carry baggage beginning in the 1830s, but the first passenger elevator entered service only in 1859, when New York's Fifth Avenue Hotel began using its "vertical railway." Even though elevators appealed to hotelkeepers because they made upper-story rooms as attractive as lower-story ones, their considerable expense and operating requirements limited them to a small minority of hotels until the 1880s.)[13] Hotel managers responded by creating another new category of hotel employee. While such workers must have been on the scene from the first generation of hotels, they were mentioned mainly in the 1820s, when travelers made note of the Tremont House's "rotunda men"; the terms *bellhop* and *bellboy* came into use only in the 1850s, when the desk bell became the standard way of summoning them.[14]

These workers led the way in establishing the practice of tipping in hotels. Early-nineteenth-century political ideology frowned upon gratuities as unrepublican remnants of an aristocratic past, but in practice tips were routinely asked for and almost as routinely given. This irritated some guests, who felt they were being unfairly dunned for cash. The British tourist Emily Faithfull noted, "The traveller who expects to be comfortable in an American hotel without a free distribution of dollars will soon be disenchanted. . . . In most hotels four bell-boys reign in each corridor; on their sovereign will depends the

ONLY FIRE-PROOF HOUSE IN THE UNITED STATES.

THE PALACE HOTEL } **PALMER HOUSE,** { POTTER PALMER,
OF THE WORLD. } CHICAGO. { Owner and Proprietor.

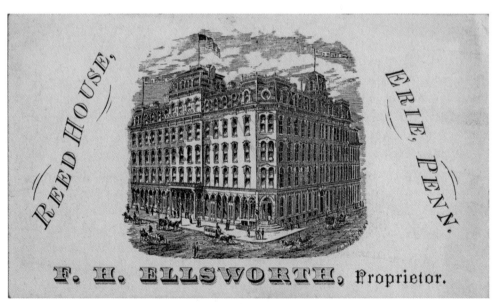

REED HOUSE, ERIE, PENN.

F. H. ELLSWORTH, Proprietor.

5.12 Hotels printed trade cards and distributed them at ticket offices, railroad stations, steamboat landings, and similar locations in an effort to drum up business. (National Museum of American History)

AMERICAN EXCHANGE,

SANSOME STREET,

Opposite American Theatre,   SAN FRANCISCO.

THE EXCHANGE IS A

Good Family Hotel,

— CONTAINING —

185 HARD FINISHED ROOMS

Extending from Halleck to Sacramento Street, and is

FIRE - PROOF.

Ladies' Entrance Corner of Sansome and Halleck Streets.

PRICES MODERATE.

JOHN W. SARGENT, Proprietor.

PLANTERS HOUSE

ST. LOUIS, MO.

KELSEY & STICKNEY, Proprietors.

The R P Studley Comp? St Louis.

kind of service you receive." Some hotelkeepers forbade their employees to solicit tips, but workers' low wages and constant resistance ensured that tipping gradually became an expected, if not fully accepted, part of a hotel stay. So after bellhops had guided their charges to their rooms and placed their belongings inside, the guests would probably have searched for a small coin and handed it over.[15]

The ritual of establishing the host-guest relationship had to be repeated many times per day at a hotel, and as a result it became increasingly rationalized. A few hotelkeepers continued to greet customers personally, but at larger houses this gave way to an impersonal, institutional procedure that often left guests feeling as if they were being processed rather than welcomed. The reformer and landscape architect Frederick Law Olmsted expressed precisely this sentiment in an 1853 description of his experience at the National Hotel in Washington. "Clerk No. 4," he wrote, "suddenly catches the Register by the corner, swings it round with a jerk, and throws a hieroglyphic scrawl at it, which strikes near my name. Henceforth I figure as Boarder No. 201. . . . Clerk No. 4 whistles and throws Key No. 201 upon the table. Turnkey No. 3 takes it and me, and my travelling bag up several flights of stairs, along corridors and galleries, and finally consigns me to this little square

5.13   A well-furnished lobby, like this one in Denver's Brown Palace, was designed to attract the well-to-do to a hotel intended for them. (Denver Public Library)

5.14 This hotel lobby, also in Colorado, was marked both by décor and gender as something less than respectable. (Denver Public Library)

cell." The prison metaphor was a durable one: three decades later, another guest depicted hotel life as "an alternation of the penitentiary systems carried out at Philadelphia and at Auburn." But hotelkeepers and their staffs could spare little time for delicate feelings, especially while there were so many other visitors lining up at the front desk and calling for rooms of their own.[16]

UPSTAIRS IN THE HOTEL

Hotel bedchambers varied as much as hotels themselves. Large luxury establishments contained well-appointed parlor-and-bedroom suites and spacious multiroom apartments, the most opulent of which were lavish indeed (fig. 5.16). On an 1879 visit to the United States, the English journalist George Augustus Sala marveled at his quarters in Chicago's Grand Pacific Hotel: "Height at least 15 feet; two immense plate-glass windows; beautifully frescoed ceiling; couch, easy chairs, rocking chairs, foot stools in profusion, covered with crimson velvet; large writing table for gentleman, pretty *escritoire* for lady; *two* towering cheval glasses; handsomely carved wardrobe and dressing tables; commanding pier-glass

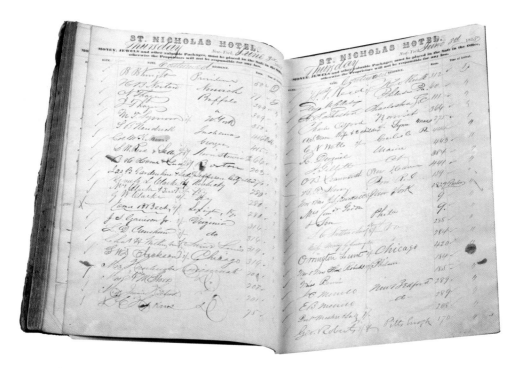

5.15   This 1858 register from New York's St. Nicholas Hotel displays the same basic format as guest books from other hotels across the nation. (Collection of the New-York Historical Society)

over mantelpiece; adjoining bath-room beautifully fitted; rich carpet; and finally the bed, in a deep alcove, impenetrably screened from the visitor's gaze by elegant lace curtains." But this was one of the most sumptuous hostelries in the country; it was highly atypical of hotels generally, even those built during the unabashed excess of the Gilded Age. Guests who compared their rooms to prison cells were probably more representative of hotel patrons generally, many of whom found their rooms unexpectedly small.[17]

A more representative sample of hotel rooms reveals considerable variation within a context of relatively modest accommodations (fig. 5.17). Available floor plans suggest an average size of about 150 square feet, with commercial and middling hotels having rooms of 80 to 145 square feet and only a few large houses having many guest quarters larger than 450 square feet. Early luxury hotels still had small rooms: in the Exchange Coffee House, for instance, bedchambers measured about 110 square feet. As the century progressed, hotel builders constructed larger rooms, like the 325-square-foot chambers at the Tremont House. But establishments like these were far outnumbered by hotels with smaller rooms. At the Cosmopolitan Hotel, an 1851 commercial house on West Broadway in Manhattan, most rooms were about 125 square feet, and in many marginal hotels there were long corridors of rooms as small as 65 square feet. Indeed, even after the turn of the century, some of the finest hotels that contained large suites also incorporated small single rooms at the back of the house, as indicated by architectural plans of New York's renowned Ansonia Hotel of 1902.[18]

The furnishings and amenities available in hotel rooms varied so widely with the quality of the house that it is difficult to make meaningful generalizations. At minimum, all but the most marginal hotel rooms provided some sort of bed, usually (but by no means always) with linens or blankets. A more respectable house would include a proper mattress, bedclothes, a chair or two, and a mirror; more upscale establishments might add a table and chairs suitable for eating, an upholstered couch, a carpet, window drapes, and the like. The kind of elaborate chambers that Sala described were offered in only a tiny percentage of American hotels.[19]

Lighting and heating fixtures also showed great variability. For the first half-century of hoteldom, bedchambers were lit by sunlight during the day and candles or oil lamps at night; the latter method presented a constant fire hazard, however, and hotelkeepers tried to minimize their use. Gaslight—pressed coal gas directed through tubes into hand-lit wall or ceiling fixtures—offered a much safer and brighter form of illumination. Hotels were among the earliest adopters of the new technology when it entered service in the 1810s, but high installation costs limited its use to public areas until the 1840s; nonelite

5.16   The most elaborate suites at luxury hotels, like this late-nineteenth-century example at the Waldorf-Astoria, could be sumptuous indeed. (Library of Congress)

BED ROOM.

5.17 Most accounts and images of hotel rooms focused on first-class houses with large, luxurious rooms, but small, simple bedchambers were far more representative of hoteldom generally. (University of New Mexico Center for Southwest Research)

establishments switched to gaslight years later, as it became more affordable. Electric lighting, which became available in the 1880s, was likewise adopted only gradually, with luxury houses wired first but most other hotel rooms going without lightbulbs until the twentieth century. Room heating followed a similar path. Most early hotel rooms were unheated, leaving guests to keep warm using blankets. Radiant steam heat made some headway beginning in the 1840s, but was restricted to the common areas of hotels. For most hotel guests of the nineteenth century, warmth was supplied by small wood- or coal-burning parlor stoves or fireplaces.[20]

Water and waste systems also differed greatly from hotel to hotel and over time. Because indoor plumbing was both uncommon and very expensive, nineteenth-century hotel rooms seldom had private sinks or toilets. The Tremont House, for example, lacked running water in its rooms and relied on privies located in the basement or outside the main building at the back of the hotel's lot; only a few water closets were available at the

Astor House and the other leading hotels of the 1830s. Such establishments typically included shared bathing rooms. This meant that guests must have made extensive use of bowls and pitchers for in-room ablutions and chamber pots for nighttime relief. Even when indoor facilities became the standard for well-appointed hotels in the 1840s, guests were still expected to share bathrooms located on every floor. In more modest hostelries, of course, guests were still making trips outside the building, as they would for decades thereafter. The grandest big-city hotels began to offer in-room bathrooms beginning in the 1850s, but guests were expected to pay a premium for what was still regarded as a special privilege. A number of primarily residential hotels advertised baths in every room in the 1870s and 1880s, but it was only after 1900 that a hotel made a private bathroom available to every guest.[21]

The limitations of these fixtures and facilities meant that guests required constant resupply from outside their rooms. In most hotels, patrons had to walk the halls in search of water, soap, towels, candles, oil, and coal. Guests at first-class houses could simply summon chambermaids and other housekeeping staff by calling out, ringing a hand bell, or, in houses with the most advanced technology, pressing the button of an annunciator, a device which connected rooms to the service desk and sounded chimes or dropped numbered disks to let managers know what to send to which room.

However much nineteenth-century hotel rooms varied, there is one generalization that applies to almost all: hosts did not expect people to spend many waking hours in them, and guests tended not to. Architects made most rooms rather small, and the fact that few had separate parlors meant that respectable Americans would not have considered them appropriate places to receive visitors. The state of domestic technology meant furthermore that bedchambers were dark at night, cold in winter, and stuffy in summer, subtracting further from their appeal as social spaces. It is indicative how little attention guest rooms received in print and visual culture. At a time when writers and journalists were composing numerous lengthy articles on hotels, bedchambers received only minor treatment compared with the public areas featured in such pieces. Travel writers made slightly more mention of the quality and contents of hotel rooms, but they, too, devoted most of their prose to other parts of the hotel. Likewise, while newspapers and magazines published innumerable images of hotels, these almost always involved building exteriors or views of dining rooms, lobbies, and lounges; guest rooms were seldom pictured. Even more revealing is the fact that hotelkeepers were typically quite restrained in their efforts to furnish guest rooms; when they improved their establishments, the lion's share of their funds and effort went to the public spaces.[22]

THE PUBLIC SPACE OF THE HOTEL

A hotel's public spaces were the heart and soul of the establishment: the places where people spent their time, the part observers said the most about, the areas of the liveliest sociability and innovation. Unlike the guest rooms, which were regarded as private, public spaces were always open to contact among the hotel's three principal clienteles: transient guests, residents, and locals. The social organization of these spaces was essential to the everyday operation of a hotel because it allowed people to carefully manage their interactions with strangers—an important consideration in a culture whose rules of interpersonal contact remained uncertain.[23]

Lobbies were the most public spaces in hotels. Whether through the willingness of hotelkeepers or the insistence of the local public, as early as the 1830s it was accepted practice that white people could enter hotel lobbies and spend time there without having to explain themselves. Architects and proprietors devoted considerable effort to making lobbies spacious and inviting. Palace hotels always featured elaborate décor, with expensive carpets, stylish wallpaper, elegant drapery, fine paintings, large mirrors, and richly upholstered furniture distributed liberally throughout the room. Other, less expensive hotels had more modest lobbies, but even small establishments typically contained a medium-sized room with a few chairs and tables scattered about.[24]

American hotel lobbies were famously given over to local public use, whether for meeting friends, transacting business, discussing the news of the day, getting warm, or simply loitering (fig. 5.18). Images of hotel lobbies usually depicted them as thronged with passers-through, as did the writings of journalists, traveloguists, and novelists. Anthony Trollope observed in the late 1850s that the nation's hotel lobbies were always "full of men who are idling about, sitting round on stationary seats, talking in a listless manner, and getting through their time as though the place were a public lounging-room. And so it is. The chances are that not half the crowd are guests at the hotel." A visiting British Navy captain provided more evocative details: "The great entrance is liberally supplied with an abundance of chairs, benches, &c., and decorated with capacious spittoons, and a stove which glows red-hot in the winter. . . . The human species of every kind may be seen variously occupied—groups talking, others roasting over the stove, many cracking peanuts, many more smoking. . . . One feature is common to them all—busy-ness; whether they are talking, or reading, or cracking nuts, a peculiar energy shows the mind is working."[25]

Hotel lobbies became community stages, convenient venues for public self-fashioning and performance. Local notables often spent time in hotels with no apparent purpose other than to put in an appearance. In 1870, for example, a Nebraska merchant who constantly visited his local hotel waxed humorous in the guest register, sometimes signing in as "an Irish Jew from Cork" or a traveler from "Pekin, Celestial Empire." Hotel-going could also have a more desperate flavor. In *Sister Carrie,* Theodore Dreiser depicted the downwardly mobile Hurstwood attempting to recapture the experience of being well-off: "He knew hotels well enough to know that any decent looking individual was welcome to a chair in the lobby. This was the Broadway Central which was then one of the most important hotels in the city. Taking a chair here was a painful thing to him. To think he should come to this! He had heard loungers about hotels called chair-warmers. He had called them that himself in his day. But here he was . . . shielding himself from the cold and the weariness of the streets in a hotel lobby."[26]

5.18   Hotel lobbies, like this one in 1890s Chicago, were often used as temporary refuges, whether from the elements or from the noise and dirt of city streets. (Collection of the author)

Lobbies were gendered spaces. Most large hotels maintained a ladies' entrance separate from the main entrance, though their actual use was more complicated than these designations suggest. The ladies' entrance was for women and parties that included women: husbands and wives, fathers and daughters, or ladies with escorts. The main entrance was for unaccompanied men. While the main entrance opened directly into the lobby, ladies' entrances often led to separate sitting rooms where women could wait for their male companions to secure rooms on their behalf. This kind of gendering was a characteristic of many other arrangements of hotel space. Unmarked public areas were not closed to women by either house rules or custom, but the commonsense assumption was that any respectable woman who entered must be protected from unmonitored interaction with strangers. That said, hotel space was often gendered by women themselves: men who intruded into female-designated space could be asked to leave, while women who ignored these rules were usually permitted to do so.[27]

There were some rooms into which no respectable woman would normally venture. Chief among these were hotel bars. These were resolutely masculine spaces, defined not just by the absence of women but also by unrestricted entry for non–hotel guests, the constant consumption of alcohol and smoking of tobacco, and a general disregard for proper manners. Hotel bars were almost always located on the ground floor, usually directly off the lobby for easy access; in some cases, bars also had a separate street entrance. While hotel barrooms varied tremendously in their size and décor, the basic elements were fairly consistent across different hotel types: racks of liquor bottles and glassware arrayed behind a long bar with a footrail and stools, the whole built into a room filled with tables and chairs. The interior design of bars was determined not just by the scale of the hotels but also by the importance of liquor receipts to hotelkeeping. Selling drinks was by far the most profitable operation in a hotel, and it often supplied the marginal income that kept accounts in the black. Hotelkeepers thus strove to hire talented barkeeps who could make their bars welcoming places and keep them filled with paying customers. The finest hotel bars (fig. 5.19) were richly furnished and presided over by bartenders who prided themselves on their knowledge of imported wines and fancy cocktails: "Lovers of such beverages," explained one diarist, "can procure 'toddy,' 'nightcaps,' 'mint julep,' 'gin sling,' &c."[28]

Of all the hotel's spaces, the dining rooms attracted the most attention. Observers from abroad seized upon them as the places where Americans revealed their true national character. The defining feature of the hotel dining room was the custom of the table d'hôte, or host's table. Everyone ate together at hours set by the hotelkeeper; the kitchen staff announced the beginning of each meal by ringing a bell or sounding a gong. The rules of the table d'hôte were also enforced by the structure of billing: hotel rates included both room and board, with no discounts made for meals taken elsewhere. This practice, which was also known as the American plan, was exceptionally durable: while some hosts adopted the European plan of separate room charges and à la carte meals during the nineteenth century, most hotels in the United States remained on the American plan into the 1910s, and it was not abandoned entirely until the mid-twentieth century.[29]

The table d'hôte made hotel dining into a hugely sociable affair. Hotels served meals to overnight guests, of course, but they also seated local residents, many of whom used hotels essentially as restaurants, sometimes for every meal. Americans embraced the busy sociability of hotel dining (fig. 5.20). As the popular poet and essayist N. P. Willis remarked in 1844: "There are some republican advantages in our present system of hotels which the country is not yet ready to forgo. Tell a country lady in these times that when she comes to New York she must eat and pass an evening in a room by herself, and she would rather stay home. The going to the Astor and dining with two hundred well-dressed people, and sitting in full dress in a splendid drawing room with plenty of company—is the charm of going to the city!" For most people, the point of hotel meals was to enjoy eating in public rather than to display refinement. Hotel dining was hardly conducive to good table manners; one commentator echoed many others when he noted, "The meal is devoured with a rapidity which a pack of fox-hounds, after a week's fast, might in vain attempt to rival." This lack of decorum may have been due to hotel guests on the American plan wanting to make sure they got enough to eat, while local diners who paid by the meal had to compete to ensure that their own stomachs were filled.[30]

Hotel dining varied with the size and class of the establishment. Smaller hotels often preserved remnants of the household mode of hospitality, with the host sitting at the head of the table, carving the meat, and guiding conversation. Such personal hospitality became impracticable as the number of guests grew into the dozens, but some hotelkeepers liked to maintain this honorific position. "The keepers of American hotels," noted one traveler during the Civil War, "take pride in entertaining their guests. They sit at the head of the

5.19   The bar at Philadelphia's Continental Hotel, 1861. (Hagley Museum and Library)

5.20   Hotel dining rooms, like this one at the Fifth Avenue Hotel in New York, were proportioned to accommodate huge volumes of travelers and other guests. (Collection of the author)

table, and invite the President, the Governor of the State, or distinguished foreigners, to take wine with them. They have the manners, not of a head-waiter, but of a gentleman of fortune dispensing the hospitalities of his mansion."[31]

Most guests were served on an institutional basis. Tunis Campbell, in his 1848 *Hotel Keepers, Head Waiters, and Housekeepers' Guide,* stated that the best kind of hospitality involved personal attention from the host, but he acknowledged that the scale of many hotels made this impossible. Campbell's program for managing hotel dining rooms was exceptionally detailed, comprising more than one hundred pages of text and ten full-page diagrams of place settings and waiter choreography. "The work of a dining-room ought to be divided so that each man would have his regular work," Campbell explained, subdividing the necessary tasks so that they could be assigned to groups of waiters. Individual areas of responsibility included "cups and saucers," "bread and napkins," "cheese, cake, and milk," "hot covered dishes," "lamps for alcohol," "the dish for meat," "tea and coffee, hot urns, &c.," and "dessert of all kinds." His methods were exceedingly systematized, with uniformed waiters walking in step and learning to uncover all the dishes on a table simultaneously. Indeed, Campbell's training regimen was explicitly modeled on the military: he proposed that dining-room staff should perform service drills five days a week and wrote of "lieutenants," "squads," "right flank and left," and "march and countermarch."[32]

There are good reasons to believe that Campbell's *Guide* accurately represented everyday hotel procedures. Campbell had held the position of headwaiter at major establishments like Howard's Hotel in New York and the Adams House in Boston, where he developed and applied his methods. More important, numerous travel writers described equally elaborate hotel service. One English traveler of the 1850s observed: "After all the company are seated, say twenty or thirty of these waiters are ranged, one half on each side of the table, behind the guests, in military line. At a given signal, each one reaches over his arm and takes hold of the handle of a dish . . . at another signal, they all at the same moment lift the cover, all as if flying off at one whoop, and with as great exactness as soldiers expected to 'shoulder arms.' This is the case in the $2 and $2.50 houses in the large cities."[33]

Hotel food drew nearly as much public attention as the manner in which it was served. Opinions on the quality of hotel cuisine varied widely, but there can be no doubt as to the abundance and variety of hotel fare. In urban centers that were markets for huge crop- and livestock-producing hinterlands, hotels made impressive outlays of comestibles. One 1850s visitor at Boston's Revere House was so impressed that he "transcribe[d] the bill of fare as a specimen of the variety in the commissariat department of American hotels":

> Broiled.—Beef steaks—pork steaks—mutton chops—calf's liver—sausages—ham—squabs. Fried.—Pig's feet—veal and mutton kidneys—sausages—tripe—salt pork—hashed meat. Fish.—Cod-fish with pork—fish balls—hashed fish—fresh salmon—broiled mackerel—broiled smoked salmon—Digby herring—halibut—perch with pork. Eggs.—Boiled—skinned—fried—scrambled—dropped. Omelets.—Plain, with parsley, onions, and ham—kidneys—cheese. Potatoes.—Stewed—fried—baked. Bread.—Hot rolls—Graham rolls—Graham bread—brown bread—dry and dipped toast—hominy—fried Indian pudding—cracked wheat—corn cake—griddle cake. And for beverage, tea, coffee, cocoa, chocolate, and iced milk.

Even offerings like these were sometimes overshadowed by more esoteric delicacies. The most avidly publicized culinary events at American hotels involved the delivery of huge sea turtles whose sad fate was to be made into soup and served in their own shells at one or another special banquet. It was not just big-city hotels that offered elaborate meals. Even in much smaller settlements, hotelkeepers depended upon local farmers, ranchers, and hunters to supply their tables with a broad range of foodstuffs. Hotel meals were generally offered as set menus, and bills of fare (fig. 5.21) rarely included prices. Rather than selecting dishes to be served to them individually, guests would call for a particular platter or bowl already on the table or sideboard. Hotel dining thus transposed the shared meal, a traditional element of hospitality, into a large-scale event that could be enjoyed in common by dozens or hundreds of people.[34]

Most hotels also contained lounges, parlors, or sitting rooms. It was common for

5.21   An 1857 hotel menu suggests the kinds of food available at a typical meal around midcentury. Note that table d'hôte service meant that no prices were indicated on the menu. (Collection of the New-York Historical Society)

hotel guests to retire to such rooms after meals, but they were also in use throughout the day as people received formal visits, brought their children to play together, or simply chatted. Lounges were less open to nonguests than the hotel's other public spaces. In order to insulate guests and residents from outsiders, lounges were usually placed at the back of the main floor or on the second floor, away from the flow of people through the hotel (the exception being waiting rooms for those checking in or meeting guests). Hotels with multiple lounges usually designated them by gender (fig. 5.22); as with entrances, the division was between unaccompanied men and women with male companions. The semiprivate and gendered space of hotel lounges was somewhat permeable, however. One observer noted: "Any one travelling in America would be far better off with a lady. . . . He will have the entrée of the ladies' saloons, from which single men are rigidly excluded, and should he arrive late at night at a crowded hotel he will readily get a room, and not be, with scant civility, told to take his chance." A female diarist agreed, advising men that if they wished to mingle with the women in the ladies' lounge, they could "enjoy the privilege of entrée equally well, by acting as escort, real or nominal, to any female acquaintance they may possess." Women, by contrast, seem to have enjoyed meaningful control over their interactions in hotels. As a New York journalist concluded in 1853, "No lady [at a hotel]

5.22   This print of the ladies' parlor at the Fifth Avenue Hotel illustrates that people in hotels preferred to socialize in large, shared public spaces rather than spending time in their rooms. (University of New Mexico Center for Southwest Research)

need see or be seen by a half a dozen persons out of her own set in the course of a winter unless she chooses to be."[35]

Some hotel spaces were organized around business rather than sociability. Many hotels featured a reading room (fig. 5.23) or library that held domestic and foreign newspapers, magazines, price lists, shipping reports, and the like; a smaller number housed business exchanges (fig. 5.24). Such rooms had their origins in the long-standing use of public houses by merchants and were present in the earliest hotels: New York's City Hotel, for example, hosted a reading room and a lending library that was the largest in the United States. These rooms provided another place of mixing between guests and locals, and operated on much the same basis as dining rooms: guests were permitted at their leisure, but locals were required to pay a regular membership fee for the privilege. Many did—travelogues described hotel reading rooms as constantly packed with men doing business and discussing politics.[36]

Its thoroughly public character made American hotel hospitality distinctive. Some visitors, notably those from Europe, found this disagreeable. One such traveler bemoaned the impossibility of being left alone at meals or in a sitting room at large hotels. There,

5.23   Nineteenth-century gender norms made reading rooms some of the most male-dominated of a hotel's public spaces. (Picture Collection, The Branch Libraries, The New York Public Library, Astor, Lenox and Tilden Foundations)

he explained, to decline to participate in conversation was "a species of neglect, if not offense.... You may sin and be wicked in many ways, and in the tolerant circle of American Society receive a full and generous pardon. But this one sin can never be pardoned." A French visitor who groused that "many of the hotels make no provision for privacy" and that resort hotels "offer hardly more privacy than bee-hives" found ready agreement from his English and German counterparts, who disapprovingly noted the lack of private parlors. (Similar remarks were made about American railway passenger cars, which had rows of seats in a single, open space rather than individual compartments in the European style.) Not all visitors found the promiscuous sociability of American hotels disagreeable, however. Domingo F. Sarmiento, the Argentine educator and statesman, struck a more charitable and wittier note in 1847 when he joked that the people who thronged hotels were so unselfconsciously inquisitive that "if the buttons on your overcoat have deer, horse, or boars' heads in relief, everyone who spies them will come up to you and go over them one by one, turning you about from left to right to better examine the walking museum." Sarmiento's embrace of spontaneous and unmediated interpersonal contact made his understanding of hotel space much more akin to that of most Americans, whose enthusiasm for the social possibilities of the hotel drew them into its environs day after day for decades on end.[37]

HOTEL SERVICES

Because hotel guests spent so much time in public, they needed help preparing themselves for constant social interaction. Hoteliers responded by hiring employees and building facilities to assist patrons with their everyday needs. This was yet another manifestation of hotels' role as homes away from home: just as households readied their members to participate in the outside world, hotels provided support for their guests' public performances. The difference was that hotels required cash payment for the work involved, again applying the rules of the market to domestic tasks.

Personal cleanliness was the focus of most of these services because that virtue was so difficult to achieve while on the road. Even after transportation had been revolutionized by new technologies, traveling continued to be a dirty affair. Steamboats and railroads were fast and efficient, but their engines constantly belched soot, some of which invariably settled on passengers. In addition, stuffy cabin interiors and railcars packed

5.24   The business exchange at Philadelphia's Continental Hotel, 1861. (Hagley Museum and Library)

with wayfarers could become quite ripe, especially in hot and humid weather. Further filth awaited at the end of the beaten path. Most nineteenth-century cities were unpaved, and their most important source of short-distance motive power was horses. Streets were thus caked with mud and manure that invariably found their way onto shoes, dress hems, trouser legs, and luggage.

Consequently, travelers' first priority after securing accommodations would likely have been to clean themselves up. In their rooms, they could change clothes and perform simple ablutions like washing hands and faces or tending to unruly hair. Before venturing out in public, however, they might feel the need for a more thorough cleaning. Laundry service was available in some form in all but the most remote or down-at-heel establishments because it required little in the way of facilities and labor: all that was needed was water, soap, a sink or tub, a line for drying, and a person to do the work. Simple arrangements like these were used in small or modest hotels throughout the nineteenth century and into the twentieth.

Larger establishments devised more elaborate services, most notably specialized, in-house laundry facilities. Such additions were made only gradually. Available plans for first-generation hotels bear no evidence of spaces specifically assigned for the purpose, though the harshness of winter weather outside the South makes it likely that washing was done in hotels' large basement- and ground-level service areas or sent out to laundresses. This began to change with the second generation of hotels. The Tremont House contained a simple basement-level laundry where washerwomen did their work by hand. Less than a decade later, the Astor House installed an innovative facility with a steam engine that powered washing machines and large-capacity clothes dryers. By the early 1850s such technologies had evolved into large, fully rationalized laundries with industrial-size steam-cleaning technology and high-speed drying and ironing machines designed to service hundreds of guests. New York's Metropolitan Hotel contained an in-house mechanized laundry that reportedly handled four thousand items per day and could wash, dry, and iron an article of clothing and return it to its owner within fifteen minutes. Decades before steam laundries became common elsewhere in American life, they were standard issue in hotels.[38]

Hotel employees and hotel-based independent operators provided many other personal services. The most common of these was the barbershop or tonsorial parlor, usually located adjacent to the lobby, where attendants stood ready to do guests' hair, groom their nails, or provide them with a fresh shave. Many hotels maintained in-house tailors, who made a living mending or altering guests' clothing. Shoeshining services were also popular. Guests would leave their footwear in the hall outside their rooms at bedtime, and a worker would take them away on a wheeled cart, clean and shine them, and have them back by morning; there were also shoeshine stands in the lobby. While each of these services cost money, travelers were away from the households that customarily provided them for free; they thus had little choice and might well look upon hotel offerings as a welcome convenience.[39]

Even more essential to the operation of a hotel was another category of service: housekeeping. Hotels hired numerous employees to work in lieu of whoever maintained guests' living spaces at home. Chambermaids made up beds, perhaps even with fresh sheets (the more elegant the hotel, the more frequent the changing of the linen); swept floors, emptied trash, and dusted furniture; rinsed and refilled bowls and pitchers and scrubbed sinks; placed clothes on hangers and hung them in wardrobes or on wall hooks; and replenished wood, coal, candles, or oil for heating and lighting. As with a hotel's other services, housekeeping helped guests fulfill their public roles by making it unnecessary for them to spend time and effort maintaining their own private spaces.

Hotel services also involved the work of mediating guests' interactions with the surrounding city and its residents. Most transient hotel guests were visitors from elsewhere and thus unfamiliar with their new surroundings. A hotel functioned as a staging ground for forays into the urban environment, and its staff as gatekeepers interposing themselves between visitors and locals. For hotel guests who arrived knowing where they needed to go and whom they wished to see, clerks and concierges could provide directions or advice on how to get there, perhaps directing them to the appropriate omnibus or streetcar line or hailing a carriage to carry them privately.[40] The hotel staff could also be useful to tourists by suggesting which local points of interest were most worth seeing. At a Kentucky hostelry, reported an English visitor in 1857, "There are guides appointed who provide lanterns and torches for visitors who wish to examine the Mammoth Cave. . . . Rough clothing is provided at the hotel, the excursion being one of scramble and difficulty." In addition, many large urban hotels maintained permanent contacts with theaters, pleasure grounds, excursion companies, and other entertainment promoters interested in attracting out-of-town customers; indeed, some of the grandest big-city hotels maintained permanent ticket offices or kiosks in their lobbies. A former hotel worker's observation regarding clerks might easily have been applied to any of a number of hotel personnel: "[One] must be a walking encyclopedia, directory, railway and steamship guide, and, in short, a universal fountain of knowledge and information."[41]

Hotels also helped their guests manage contacts with locals, mostly by relaying messages and facilitating visits. Travelogues contain numerous references to visitors calling on hotel guests and either being told where to find them or being allowed to leave a note with a clerk or manager. "Behind the counter," observed one visitor, "we perceive a large case of pigeon-holes, with a number over each, and appropriated for receiving letters or cards left for the guests. Knowing your particular number, you have only to glance at the little depository under it, to know if any one has been calling, or if any letters have arrived for you." Sometimes hotel staff interposed themselves between guests and visitors, usually because they had been asked to do so by the guests. While the urban environment outside hotels could be disorderly and unpredictable, hotel workers helped guests control their own social milieu within.[42]

The last service that hotels provided for their patrons was that of seeing them off. Once guests had concluded whatever business or pleasure had set them into motion

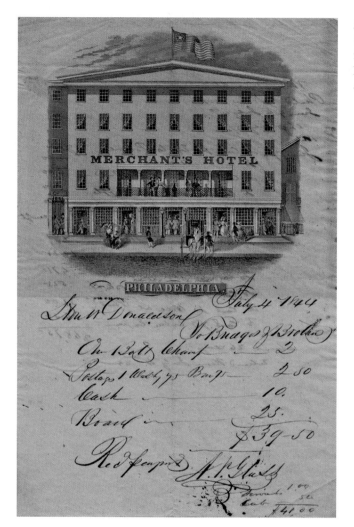

5.25 Hotel bills were typically made out on stationery featuring images of the house. (National Museum of American History)

and their stay had come to an end, they would pack their bags and send a message to the front desk indicating their readiness to depart. After they carried their luggage down to the lobby or paid a bellhop to do so, it would be time to check out. The clerk would total up their days of lodging, the meals and other services they had consumed, and any other expenses recorded in the register. He would then present guests with their bills, probably on preprinted hotel sheets (fig. 5.25), and they would provide payment. This exchange of invoice, money, and receipt would signal the end of the host-guest relationship. The travelers' belongings would then be taken to the dock or station, and they could be on their way.

Hotels promised a great deal. Whether a hotel was luxurious or rudimentary, its keeper predictably insisted that guests could expect a worthy home away from home where they would be accommodated in comfort. In order to serve the needs of their clientele, hotel proprietors had to hire and manage large numbers of workers, which from the employer's standpoint usually meant trying to keep their wages low while getting them to perform arduous labor, smiling all the while for the customers. Yet there were ways in which even the most capably managed establishments failed to satisfy the public. A close look at hotel guests' complaints reveals a great deal about how Americans responded to the transformation of hospitality and the new, market-based relationships that underlay it.

The operation of a hotel depended upon enormous numbers of workers doing a wide variety of tasks. Nineteenth-century hotel employees included, but were not limited to, managers, clerks, bookkeepers, doormen, porters, cooks, bartenders, stewards, waiters, dishwashers, launderers, housekeepers, janitors, plumbers, coal loaders, mechanics, and elevator operators. The number of employees and the division of labor varied with the size and rank of the hotel. The labor historian Daniel Levinson Wilk's painstaking census research shows that the largest New York City hotels of 1850 each had more than three hundred employees on the premises, a figure he suspects of being an overall underestimate because many workers lived elsewhere. Even in smaller establishments, he finds forty to sixty in-house employees. These numbers grew over time as hotels became larger and more complex and their keepers offered more services. In 1877 *Frank Leslie's Popular Monthly* informed its readers that luxury hotels in the 1850s had employed one worker for every six guests, a ratio that reached one per three guests in the 1860s and as many as two per three in the 1870s. These figures, which are consistent with Levinson Wilk's census-based estimates, would mean that by the third quarter of the century, when the largest hostelries accommodated more than one thousand guests, individual hotels could employ upward of six hundred people.[43]

The individual jobs done by hotel workers varied greatly in their duties, income, and conditions. The more desirable of these were front-of-the-house positions that involved direct contact with guests. At the top of the hotel world were supervisory jobs like hotel manager, head clerk, and headwaiter. Positions like these paid middle-class compensation or better and were filled through regional or national labor markets: hotel industry trade journals regularly published announcements of high-level employees taking up new jobs at hotels in different cities. Less prestigious and well paid was semiskilled work done in public. While lower clerks, waiters, doormen, and bellhops needed no formal education and could be trained in a matter of days or weeks, they did need a certain amount of behavioral polish, since they dealt directly with customers and thus helped determine their hotel's public reputation. The bottom of the hotel work hierarchy were people who labored in the back of the house, intentionally kept in the hotel's service areas and away from guests. With the exception of mechanical maintenance workers and line cooks, these employees performed mostly unskilled or domestic tasks and were thus easily replaced. They were the most likely to work twelve- to fourteen-hour shifts and live on site, where they could be called on at any hour. Such workers were also the lowest paid. Chamber-maids, for example, often got "no more than $6 or $8 per month wages" in the 1870s, little more than a fifth of what a regularly employed unskilled man could earn at that time, and even people sympathetic to the needs of hotelkeepers acknowledged that these and most other low-level employees were badly underpaid.[44]

These positions were filled by workers from many different ethnoracial backgrounds and of both sexes. Within this diversity, however, hotel employment was stratified by identity. Levinson Wilk finds that all managerial and most staff jobs were exclusively male; with few exceptions, women were hired only to do housekeeping work like cleaning and laundry. Clerks, because they served as the public face of a hotel and exercised a certain amount of authority, were white and mostly Protestant. Employees in more subservient roles, like waiters, could come from less advantaged groups: travelogues and census data suggest that Irishmen and blacks predominated. The work of cooking, which was skilled and important but still back-of-the-house, was often done by European immigrants (especially French and Swiss), mostly due to the more refined culinary culture of Europe but also because linguistic barriers posed less of a problem in nonpublic jobs. Except for a few head housekeepers, women hotel workers were drawn from the people with the fewest employment options: travel accounts depict them as almost exclusively Irish or black. Hotel employment did offer workers a few significant advantages. The workplace was a large one, allowing for greater sociability and less isolation than was common among private domestics. The particular characteristics of hotel labor may have helped give rise to a remarkable cross-racial coalition that led an 1853 strike by hotel workers in New York, Boston, and Philadelphia, an action that presaged more than a century of sporadic but active unionization in the hotel and restaurant industry.[45]

However hard hotel managers and workers applied themselves, guests still found reasons to complain; they groused about a lack of cold or warm water, the price of a meal, the stuffiness of a room, and the like. Such complaints were usually simple, occasional, and focused on a particular hotel (since people's grumblings necessarily implied their having had better at another hostelry). But some were repeated so often and in such an unchanging form that they took on a folkloric quality that elevated them to the level of a cultural trope or categorical critique.

Easily the most common of these were directed at hotel clerks. Throughout nine-teenth-century American fiction, journalism, travel writing, cartoons, and folklore, they were stock characters, their unhelpfulness and arrogance making them a constant source of grievances. The popular author Henry Hooper referred to the hotel clerk in 1874 as "the supercilious embodiment of Philistinism," and a traveling salesman added that an encounter with a hotel clerk provided a useful corrective "whenever I feel that I need taking down a peg or two, and that I am getting too big for my clothes." In *Roughing It*

(1872), Mark Twain characterized the species by writing about the "nice American hotel clerk who was crusty and disobliging, and didn't know anything about the time tables, or the railroad routes—or—anything—and was proud of it." And an aggrieved contributor to *Harper's Weekly* asserted in 1857: "The chief aim of the hotel clerk is not to seem to earn his money. . . . [He] devotes his life to trying to look as if he was in the office entirely by accident. He hands you your key as if he was in a dream, and rarely condescends to answer any question that you may address to him. He spends his days like his master, reading the paper, picking his teeth, and indulging occasionally in a little light conversation with some particular friend who is staying in the house, and who you may be sure has the best room in it."[46]

Other observers alleged that hotel clerks constantly ridiculed and intimidated guests. One commentator recalled that the hotel clerk was "feared by the general public" and was "the one being in existence before whom the free-born American quailed." His willingness to casually insult patrons underlay the punch line in an 1874 cartoon (fig. 5.26). But the most comprehensive defamation of the hotel clerk came from the pen of William Dean Howells, whose satirical 1872 novel *Their Wedding Journey* included the following passage:

> It was with a sudden sinking of the heart that Basil beheld presiding over
> the register the conventional American hotel clerk. He was young, he had
> a neat mustache and well-brushed hair; jeweled studs sparkled in his shirt-
> front, and rings on his white hands; a gentle disdain of the travelling public
> breathed from his person. . . . He did not lift his haughty head to look at the
> way-farer who meekly wrote his name in the register; he did not answer him
> when he begged for a cool room; he turned to the board on which the keys
> hung, and, plucking one from it, slid it towards Basil on the marble counter,
> touched a bell for a call-boy, whistled a bar of Offenbach, and . . . wrote
> the number of the room against Basil's name. . . . When I reflect that this
> was a type of the hotel clerk throughout the United States, that behind un-
> numbered registers at this moment he is snubbing travellers into the dust,
> and that they are suffering and perpetuating him, I am lost in wonder at
> the national meekness.[47]

Chambermaids were also subject to a certain amount of textual abuse. What people most feared from them sprang from what they could not see them doing. The more conventional of these fears was that chambermaids would steal guests' belongings. For example, Eliza Leslie, the author of a successful series of etiquette manuals, noted in an 1853 edition that many patrons were "afraid to trust the chambermaid alone, lest she should steal something." More revealing than popular anxiety about theft, though, were fears that centered on more primal, personal, bodily concerns—in particular, the possibility of uncleanness and contagion. This species of fear was epitomized by the anonymous

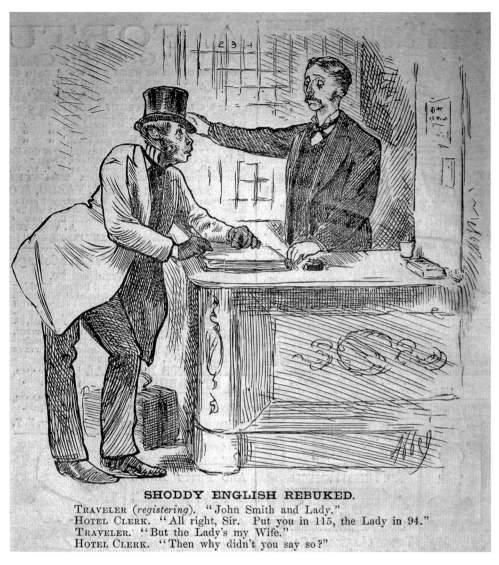

SHODDY ENGLISH REBUKED.

Traveler (*registering*). "John Smith and Lady."
Hotel Clerk. "All right, Sir. Put you in 115, the Lady in 94."
Traveler. "But the Lady's my Wife."
Hotel Clerk. "Then why didn't you say so?"

5.26   A cartoon from *Harper's Weekly* displays the popular view of the hotel clerk as arrogant and insulting. (University of New Mexico Center for Southwest Research)

author of a sensationalistic 1884 pamphlet entitled *Horrors of Hotel Life. By a Reformed Landlord.* The author explains: "Arriving at a hotel, travel-stained and weary, the guest is shown at once to his chamber, where he may either sleep or dress. Whichever he does he is confronted at once with dangers and dirt, not apparent to the eye, indeed, but a thousand times the worse for being concealed under apparent cleanliness. . . . The guest finds certain indispensable things in his room. Things he must use. Things that will come in contact with certain parts of his body." The author then proceeds with a litany of stomach-turning examples of unclean bodies and unpleasant personal habits, confronting readers with extremely graphic accounts of spitting, oozing, probing, and wiping. Chambermaids stood accused of such practices as using towels as cleaning rags, reusing dirty dishes and soiled linens without washing them, and deploying dinner napkins in place of sanitary napkins.[48]

Even the hotel manager himself was not above criticism. The writer from *Harper's Weekly* of 1857 lamented: "Time was when, if a weary traveler arrived at the door of a hostelry, he was not off his saddle before a portly white-aproned figure filled the entry, and welcomed him with a good hearty welcome. It was the jolly, well-fed, bustling, attentive, hospitable landlord." But in the mid-nineteenth-century hotel, things had changed. The writer continued: "Would you ever imagine, on entering the Bunkum House, that the portly, insolent-looking man, smoking his cigar in the public hall with his feet on a chair, and reading the morning paper—would you ever imagine that this immense being, radiant with diamonds and huge chain, was the landlord? He is. Go and ask him for a room, and be instantly withered with a glance of offended dignity. Speak to him at all, if you are a stranger, and you will soon learn better than to address this Jove of Olympian attic rooms on a short acquaintance."[49]

What are we to make of this? It is difficult to believe that clerks or managers could really have been so indifferent or hostile, or chambermaids so slovenly, since hotel owners would surely have removed such employees from the payroll. The key to deciphering the folklore of hotel employees is to focus on how their status and responsibilities changed in the transition from household to institutional hospitality. Generally speaking, guests were unprepared for the replacement of a patriarch and his household dependants with wage laborers who, despite their economically subordinate status, still commanded authority or required quasi-familial trust. Hotel clerks, for example, were especially mocked for living beyond their means, and critics described them with phrases like "resplendent autocrat of sleeping accommodations" and "haughty and unapproachable despot." Charges of misplaced aristocratic aspirations were one way that nineteenth-century Americans, proud of their republican heritage, mocked those who they thought were getting too uppity. The folklore of chambermaids, which emphasized their low status through accusations of thievery and filth, seems at first glance to be a completely contrary line of criticism, but it expressed a similar discomfort: distrust of chambermaids followed the cultural logic of nostalgia for the home because it was precisely the lack of household connection between maids and guests that was bothersome. And criticism of hotel managers was explicit in deploying the jovial tavernkeeper of yore as the opposite number of the indifferent modern host. These and many similar complaints were elements of a sort of cultural holdover, one that afflicted people who were used to the home as a governing social metaphor and were willing to accept the authority of an actual head of household but who resented being ordered around by a hireling, a person with neither property nor standing.[50]

However anxiety-inducing the transition from the old hospitality to the new, the glorification of the tavern smacked of historical amnesia. In their eighteenth-century heyday, taverns had elicited far harsher invective for their dirt, bedbugs, bad food, uneven service, and chronic overcharging than was ever directed at hotels for their impersonality. Nostalgia notwithstanding, by midcentury, Americans were building and staying in hotels in ever-larger numbers, voting with their feet, money, and bricks in favor of this new order of hospitality. Far from turning their backs on hotels, Americans were in the process of embracing them even more tightly, and in so doing pulling the market and the home ever closer together.

CONCLUSION: MODEL HOSPITALITY

Hotels represented a new hospitality paradigm that was ideally suited to the remarkable mobility and transience of the nineteenth-century United States. Over the course of several decades, hotel managers and workers devised elaborate methods for welcoming, accommodating, and serving the masses of travelers and strangers who passed through and inhabited the nation's cities. In so doing, they helped establish a distinctly American urbanism predicated upon the constant movement of people, goods, and information, conditions that would have been difficult to sustain had hospitality remained limited to the traditional household.

Notwithstanding my use of the phrase "sophisticated hospitality machines" in the first sentence of this chapter, the advent of hotels in American life involved far more than an alteration of scale and a triumph of rationalization and efficiency. The development of the hotel was indeed characterized by processes of subdivision, individuation, and exploitation familiar to labor and business historians, and hotelkeepers and guests did fashion a new culture of hospitality that rejected the organic wholeness of the household in favor of depersonalized service. But the story to be told here is not one of modernization, isolation, alienation, and anomie. On the contrary, the everyday culture of the hotel was a resolutely public one in which people emerged from their guest rooms and converged from points across the city to partake of the social dynamism of this singular institution. While Americans did value their privacy, they also celebrated hotels for the way they put people into contact with one another, and they made hotel lobbies, parlors, and ballrooms into important gathering places. An institution where the paths of travelers and citizens crossed so regularly soon became a place where people sought each other out, and hotels became an indispensable part of the urban fabric of every American city.

Contemporary observers understood these changes as progress. Americans tended strongly toward boosterism, holding hotels up as examples of their nation's egalitarian culture and growing prosperity. While the persistence of celebratory coverage makes it difficult to gauge changes in public attitudes toward hotels, people's actual behavior—the enthusiastic patronage that made hotels into profitable ventures and the resultant expansion of hotel construction—demonstrates how they felt far more conclusively than textual evidence. One might also add that in measurable terms, hotels offered an unmistakably improving standard of service at prices that rose very slowly: adjusted for wage inflation, the two-dollar rooms of the early 1830s were only slightly less expensive than the four-dollar rooms of fifty years later, and the newer hotels far outstripped their predecessors in every measurable index of comfort, convenience, and safety, from room size, indoor plumbing, steam heat, and electric lighting to upholstery, elevators, fireproof construction, and communications facilities.[51]

European commentary offers a particularly revealing look at hotels because its tone and content changed over the decades in ways that illustrate the increasing sophistication and influence of the American hotel. Visitors from across the Atlantic had long been impressed by some aspects of hotels in the United States, especially their large size and the corresponding scale of their operations. At the same time, most Europeans continued to criticize the American way of hospitality, which they found insufficiently deferential and excessively impersonal. A Scottish traveler complained in 1855 of "the inconvenience of these great establishments," where "the proprietor could not personally attend to everything and every one; perhaps he did not attend to anything or any body. . . . I found no great wish to oblige in the matter of the bed-rooms, and a saucy independence as to the terms." Another visitor echoed these sentiments five years later. "The English traveller," he groused, "must be content to give up all idea, or, at least, all assertion of individual importance; and, if he would enter into the spirit of American life under such circumstances, resign his fondly cherished exclusiveness and reserve in favour of more social sentiments. The hotel system is the most levelling of all American 'institutions.'" The guest, he explained, "must not look for "the obsequious attentions which greet a new arrival at an English hotel [or] the double doses of flunkeyism administered by shrewd continental Bonifaces to flatter the pride" because "particular attention to individuals is . . . out of the question where guests are booked by the score and dined by the hundred." In sum, the initial European stance was that however impressive American hotel buildings were, the hospitality they offered was inferior to that in Europe.[52]

By the last third of the nineteenth century, however, transatlantic visitors increasingly conceded that American dominance in hotel architecture had been matched by leadership in the provision of hospitality. "In the United States," explained an English visitor in 1875, "the hotel is literally an 'institution.' The system, initiated here some forty years ago, has revolutionised the hotel system throughout the world." A decade later, another British traveler seconded this proposition when he remarked that Americans "certainly have succeeded in placing themselves far away first as hotel keepers." Well before century's end, many European hosts had begun to imitate the methods of their American counterparts, and hoteliers from the United States moved to open their own establishments in the cities of Europe. This combination of emulation and expansion demonstrated the international influence of the American system of commercial hospitality and foreshadowed the U.S.-led globalization of the hotel industry in the twentieth century.[53]

Six

The Law of Hospitality

The Common Law of Innkeepers and the

Public Space of the Hotel

HOTELKEEPERS CREATED an impressive array of services and amenities for their guests, making hotels into some of the most elaborate business enterprises of their day. But hotel hospitality was not simply the outcome of a dialectical relationship between entrepreneurs and customers in which the supply and demand for services and goods resulted in constant revisions and improvements. While proprietors and clients were undoubtedly the main influences on the everyday operation of the hotel, it would be a mistake to assume that hoteliers were free to set the terms of accommodation, or that guests could negotiate any conditions they wished. Hotels were more than just private businesses that functioned according to the rules of the market. They were also public institutions that were subject to extensive regulation. In particular, they were required to adhere to a specific set of laws governing the provision of hospitality.

In this chapter I explore the origins and development of the American common law of innkeepers, a code governing the relations of host and guest in public houses. Hotels and other travel accommodations were sites of contestation in which proprietors and patrons sought to impose their conflicting prerogatives. Over the course of several decades, the hotel—originally the creation of a narrow elite seeking to impose control over city life—was remade into one of the most widely used and easily accessible public spaces in the United States.

Innkeeper law became a disputed terrain because when hotel proprietors and patrons quarreled, they constantly went to court in hopes of using the power of the state to get their way. The regulation of hotels thus became a judicial matter. Judges gradually refashioned centuries-old legal traditions into a definitively American common law of innkeepers, one that upheld a broad public right of access and strict protections for the property of guests. This revision of innkeeper law eventually served as the basis of a century's worth of struggles over the civil rights of black Americans, a subject to be explored in detail in Chapter 10.

These everyday disagreements were about more than just the use of hotels. They begin to suggest how the legal relation of host and guest shaped urban space. This chapter sets up one of the larger arguments made in this book: that hospitality served as a point of articulation between the operation of the market and the character of daily life. As we examine how the laws governing hotels changed, we can see how the hotel became an important patterning agent for other aspects of the American scene.

THE COMMON LAW OF INNKEEPERS

Public houses were the creations of governments. In both Britain and British North America, a public house was defined by its having been granted a license by municipal, county, or state authorities. No other type of establishment shared its privileges: a private citizen might take in travelers or boarders but could not lawfully sell alcohol at retail; a person vending drinks without a license was guilty of a criminal offense, and he would be prosecuted and his premises promptly shut down. Public houses were thus fundamentally legal entities because they were called into existence and permitted to operate only by a positive act of law.[1]

The authorities who created public houses also established their basic purpose. The linkage of their two essential functions—sheltering travelers and selling strong drink—was effected not by common practice but by governments. Colonial and early national statutes made clear that public houses were intended primarily for the use of travelers. In some cases this was implicit, as in a Maryland law of 1674 which stipulated that "noe rates of prices of anie accommodacons be set or ascertained, but such only as are of absolute necessity for sustaining and refreshing travelers." Other statements of this principle were more explicit: the preamble to the New Jersey licensing law of 1739 avowed that "the true and original design of taverns, inns and ordinaries, was for the accommodating of strangers, travelers and other persons" and for business and reasonable entertainment, "not for the encouragement of gaming, tippling, drunkenness and other vices so much of late practiced at such places, etc." The same assumption underlay state laws in the early national period. The New York licensing statute of 1799, for example, made it unlawful to grant an innkeeper's license "unless it appears to be necessary that an inn or tavern ought to be kept at such a place for the actual benefit and accommodation of travellers." The theory behind these and similar laws was that the only reason to permit the sale of alcoholic beverages was to ensure that wayfarers would have access to safe accommodations.[2]

In the eyes of the law, hotels, taverns, and other public houses were thus set pieces: their basic legal status and functional role were fixed from the moment they were licensed. They might provide any number of additional services and could be housed in buildings that ranged from small shacks to multimillion-dollar city blocks; legislatures and magistrates might also impose other rules and requirements upon them. But legally speaking, these were mere accretions that in no way changed their status as public houses—a status that implied additional regulatory conditions.

The oldest and most widely observed of these was a set of rules known in legal circles as the common law of innkeepers. Before we move on to the details of innkeeper law, we need to understand the general concept of the common law.

The common law was (and is) a body of precedent-based legal rules used to decide matters left unresolved by existing legislation. According to the traditional understanding of the common law, a judge who is faced with a legal question for which there is no clear answer will consult law books to determine how similar cases have been decided in the past; the judge will then render a decision in keeping with previous practice. (Statutes—laws passed by legislatures—normally supersede judicial pronouncements, but there are many instances in which no statutes have been adopted, or in which existing statutes provide insufficient guidance on some issues.) Over the years, jurists compiled treatises on particular aspects of the common law, making some into recognized subcategories of precedent. For example, there were common-law regimes for contracts, hunting animals, canals, inheritance, and seduction and bastardy.[3]

There was also a common law of innkeepers, a body of rules applied to inns, taverns, and, later, hotels. The three basic components of innkeeper law were rendered in the phrase "bed, board, and hearth." The first common-law duty of innkeepers was to provide available accommodation ("bed") to any traveler willing to pay a reasonable price. In a few cases, this requirement was codified in postindependence state statutes. The Massachusetts code of 1786, for example, stipulated that any innkeeper "convicted of refusing to make suitable provision when desired, for the receiving of strangers, travellers, and their horses and cattle" would "be deprived of his or her license."[4] More often, though, enforcing the duties of innkeepers was the responsibility of the courts. Common-law practice was that an innkeeper's refusal to provide lodging gave the excluded party the right to sue for damages. For example, if a traveler's goods were stolen or damaged by rain because an innkeeper refused to offer shelter, that innkeeper would have to pay the traveler at least the full value of the loss. Innkeepers were thus required by two separate sets of regulation—the public law of the state and the private law of damages on suit—to provide accommodation. In this way, early American law sought to ensure that the primary purpose of the inn was fulfilled by all keepers.[5]

The second common-law responsibility of the innkeeper was to offer guests food and refreshment ("board"). States heavily regulated publicans to ensure that they plied their trade faithfully and fairly. Vermont required that innkeepers "at all times be furnished with suitable refreshments, provisions, and accommodations for travellers, their cattle and horses," and Delaware required the provision of food for people and hay for their animals from every innkeeper in the state. Moreover, state governments sometimes set maximum prices, presumably to protect travelers from overcharging, as was the case in Massachusetts, Maryland, North Carolina, and other states.[6] Notably, existing laws prohibiting taverns from serving alcohol on the Sabbath were explicitly waived for travelers. A strict New Hampshire law employed language seen in many other statutes when it forbade innkeepers to "suffer any of the inhabitants of the respective towns where they dwell, or others, not being strangers, or lodgers in such houses, to abide or remain in the houses . . . drinking or idly spending their time on the Lord's day"; Maine made similar exceptions for "travellers, strangers, or lodgers in such houses." These laws made clear the intention of the authorities to ensure that travelers were protected from extortion and left unobstructed in their way.[7]

The vulnerability of travelers was particularly at issue in the third obligation of the innkeeper, which was to safeguard the property of guests (that is, to offer them a metaphorical "hearth"). If a traveler's possessions or goods were lost while at an inn, the keeper was presumed responsible and would be obligated to compensate the guest for their full value. The purpose of this requirement was to provide protection to wayfarers, who were away from their communities and in unfamiliar surroundings and thus singularly vulnerable to collusion between innkeepers and local thieves. As the influential American jurist James Kent explained it, "Travellers . . . are obliged to rely almost implicitly on the good faith of innkeepers; and it would be almost impossible for them, in any given case, to make out proof of fraud or negligence in the landlord." Indeed, the imperative of protecting the traveler was so powerful that innkeepers were to be presumed answerable for all thefts on their premises even though this conflicted with Anglo-American law's traditional presumption of innocence. While this was indeed a heavy burden of responsibility, explained the leading treatise writer Joseph Story, the condition of the traveler created "an extraordinary temptation to fraud" and a "danger of plunder" that required a "policy of subjecting particular classes of persons to extraordinary responsibility."[8]

Legal provisions like these made it clear that innkeeping was regarded not simply as a private business pursued by a profit-seeking individual but as a public calling requiring community oversight. The law of innkeepers was part of the tradition of a well-regulated society based upon communal governance and the people's welfare.[9] Statutes regulating innkeeping contained repeated references to public necessity and the common good. Like practically all other states, Massachusetts restricted entry into the trade, imposing limits upon who could do business and granting licenses for only as many inns as were "necessary for the public good." By the same token, Connecticut permitted the issuance of additional tavern permits only when town selectmen "shall judge it to be of public convenience and necessity." The same idea was expressed in treatises on innkeeper law. Chancellor Kent, for example, justified the heavy legal obligations placed upon innkeepers as "founded on the principle of public utility, to which all private considerations ought to yield." These repeated expressions of concern for the public good were not simply idle or ornamental—they represented serious intellectual and jurisprudential commitments. Then as now, lawyers and judges chose their words with extreme care because they knew that when the time came for application and enforcement, their phrasings would be parsed for their precise meaning.[10]

The public, communal character of innkeeping also dictated that the privileges granted to guests by the common law were not "rights" in the modern sense of the term. (This is a crucial point, particularly in light of the pivotal role of common-law precedents in later debates over civil rights.) The protections of innkeeper law did not apply to everyone; they were regularly withheld from entire classes of people. Many state innkeeper codes included provisions like the one in the Pennsylvania statutes which forbade innkeepers to "receive, harbor, entertain, or trust any person under the age of twenty-one years, or any apprentice or servant." Moreover, courts regularly ruled that the mere presence of black patrons was sufficient grounds for ordering an inn closed. These exceptions demonstrate the partial and situational nature of innkeeper law: travelers enjoyed privileges and innkeepers bore obligations, but nobody possessed automatic entitlements.[11]

Innkeeper law was the legal expression of an ethic of hospitality at least two millennia old. Western cultures traditionally placed great value on hospitality, promising temporal or spiritual rewards to those who properly welcomed strangers and bad fortune to those who did not. Ancient Greek texts were so filled with episodes involving hospitality that classicists recognize them as representatives of a literary type-scene. For example, the kidnapping of Helen, which precipitated the Trojan War, was primarily an offense against the hospitality of her husband, Menelaus; similarly, the slaughter at the end of the *Odyssey* has been interpreted as an act of retribution against guests who had abused the hospitality of their absent host.[12] Early Hebrew culture also valorized hospitality. Abraham's reception of three angels in disguise and Lot's refusal to surrender his guests to the crowd in Sodom exemplify this attitude, as do the numerous rules for hosting and protecting strangers that are scattered throughout the Hebrew Bible.[13] Early Christianity made regular reference to the importance of hospitality, both implicitly in the gospel writer Luke's stories of the Nativity and the Good Samaritan and explicitly in various New Testament admonitions to be hospitable. These recurrent scenes of sheltering strangers document a continuous preoccupation with hospitality that passed from one tradition to another over the centuries.[14]

The earliest evidence that this deeply rooted ethic of hospitality had gained the force of law in civil society comes from sixth-century Rome. In 530 CE, the emperor Justinian ordered a compilation of laws, the *Digest,* which included two separate titles requiring that innkeepers not refuse travelers and that they be responsible for safeguarding guests' possessions. Because the Romans controlled a vast extent of territory, these rules were disseminated throughout Europe and Asia Minor. They appeared in medieval writings and persisted into the early modern era, when they became part of the legal systems of monarchical states, as outlined in such influential treatises as Nicolas Delamare's *Traité de la Police* (1722) and William Blackstone's *Commentaries on the Laws of England* (1765–1769). English law was the direct progenitor of American innkeeper law: the common law of England had been observed in British North America since the beginnings of colonization in the early seventeenth century, and with the coming of independence, courts in the United States adopted many aspects of English common law.[15]

This was not a wholesale embrace, however. Each society that had enforced the law of hospitality had done so in a way appropriate to its particular circumstances and political culture, and nineteenth-century Americans did the same. They reinterpreted the common law of innkeepers at a time when the legal system of the United States was in flux and the nation's jurists were elaborating new doctrines in vital areas like contract, employment, and commercial law. It was in the legal arguments, verdicts, and treatises of lawyers, jurisprudes, and judges that a new variant of innkeeper law emerged.[16]

INNKEEPER LAW IN AMERICA: BED

The innkeeper's duty to accommodate all paying travelers was the most important part of the law of hospitality. It was also the one that underwent the most significant changes. Over the course of several decades around the middle of the nineteenth century, American courts extended its range of application beyond travelers and to the general public. At the same time, it was transformed in a more subtle but equally consequential way: its situational privileges were recast as individual rights. These changes constituted a distinctly American common law of innkeepers.

The Americanization of innkeeper law is most easily seen in contrast with English law. The basic doctrine of the English common law of innkeepers had been set forth in 1612 in *Calye's Case,* which specified that "inns are instituted for passengers and wayfaring men" and that therefore "a neighbour, who is no traveller . . . shall not have an action" against any innkeeper.[17] Cognizant of the importance of traveler status, plaintiffs' lawyers in England took particular care to make clear that their clients were indeed wayfarers. Usually this was accomplished by the prominent use of such phrases as "who was travelling" or "then being a traveller," though in one case from 1844, a barrister employed various forms of the word six times, including the amusingly tautological yet purposeful clause, "the plaintiff then being a traveller, and then being and travelling in a certain carriage, then drawn by a certain horse, then driven and used by the plaintiff in that behalf."[18]

English lawyers were right to emphasize travel, since judges assumed that all prospective guests must be wayfarers. Justice Coleridge of the Oxford Circuit, for instance, affirmed in 1835 that inns were established "for the reception of travellers" and concluded that "if the traveller conducts himself properly, the innkeeper is bound to admit him."[19] Judges also made a further distinction: that the privilege accorded to travelers was contingent upon their desire to secure accommodations. In other words, a person who simply wished to spend time in an inn without actually taking rooms had no right to do so. The judge stated in the 1844 ruling that innkeepers must admit only those who "apply peaceably to be admitted as guests" and charged the jury that the legal issue turned upon the question of whether the plaintiffs "wanted to be admitted as guests or not."[20]

An Englishman's status as a traveler became even more pivotal in the latter part of the nineteenth century, when the definition of the term *traveler* came under greater scrutiny. In an 1877 case before the Sussex county court, one W. Cramer sued James Rymer, the keeper of the Royal Sea House Hotel, for having refused him and his St. Bernard mastiff access to a refreshment bar attached to the hotel. The hotelkeeper was convicted, whereupon he appealed to the Queen's Bench on the grounds that Cramer "was a local resident and not a traveller, and therefore there was no obligation" to serve him. All five justices agreed, quashing the conviction in concurrence with Justice Kelly's notably annoyed admonition: "I need hardly cite authorities to shew that it is essential to such a prosecution that the prosecutor should be a traveller. . . . Here the prosecutor was not a traveller in any sense whatever."[21]

English courts in the late nineteenth century further limited the right of accommodation at an inn by defining the term *traveler* in stricter terms. In the most notable of these cases, a Mrs. Lamond checked into the Hotel Metropole at Brighton and remained there as a guest for ten months. When asked by the hotel manager when she planned to depart, she replied that she would stay as long as she liked, apparently offending him enough that he asked her to leave within two days. When she made no move to check out, he had her belongings packed up and removed and refused to readmit her. In the resultant lawsuit, the county judges ruled that an innkeeper's obligation existed "only so long as the person is a traveller," adding that otherwise, a guest "might be entitled to call on the innkeeper to entertain him for life." When Mrs. Lamond appealed the case, Justice Chitty of the Queen's Bench dismissed her claim and ridiculed her lawyer, characterizing his arguments as an assertion that "if a person once enters an inn as a traveller he can remain there in that character as long as he likes."[22]

English judges thus limited the common-law duty of innkeepers both by restricting it to travelers only and by imposing an effective time limit on the privileges of people who were already guests. This left English travelers with less and less legal recourse as the century progressed.[23]

The American common law meanwhile proceeded in precisely the opposite direction, extending the legal protections accorded to travelers to a broad range of people in and around taverns and hotels. *Markham v. Brown* was the most elaborate and explicit judicial statement of the Americanized common law of innkeepers, and the case cited as the key precedent in virtually all subsequent rulings. It began with a dispute in a New Hampshire tavern in 1835. Brown, the operator of a new line of stagecoaches, wanted to solicit customers in the parlor of Markham's tavern. The tavernkeeper, however, had already granted other stagecoach drivers the exclusive privilege of looking for passengers in his establishment. Brown's attempts to drum up business resulted in "frequent altercations" with the other drivers, leading Markham to forbid him to return to the premises. Brown did so anyway, and a scuffle broke out between him and another stagecoachman, whereupon Markham again ordered Brown out of the tavern.

Markham then sued Brown for trespassing. Brown, for his part, claimed that he had a right to enter the tavern to seek the trade of the guests, even without Markham's consent. When a local jury found for Brown, Markham moved for a new trial. In the appeal to the New Hampshire Supreme Court, the tavernkeeper's attorney cited the "ancient strictness" of English common law in support of his position, contending that "none but travellers have a right in a common inn; every right in an inn must be claimed by a traveller . . . or by some person who acts at the request, and under the direction of such a traveller, for a reasonable purpose." Justice Parker, ruling for the court, disagreed. Since an innkeeper was bound to admit travelers, he reasoned, "he may likewise be held, under proper limitations, to admit those who have business with them as such." Moreover, he continued, an innkeeper who allowed some people to enter who had business with his guests could "not lawfully exclude others, pursuing the same business, and who enter for a similar object." The court thus turned aside the plaintiff's attempt to bring the American common law of innkeepers into alignment with narrower English norms, electing instead to use the existing "right of the traveller," as Justice Parker put it, to imply an extended right of entry which applied to a broader portion of the public.[24]

A few judges wanted to rein in such extensions of the law of hospitality but were unable or unwilling to modify the emergent logic and assumptions of American innkeeper law. In *Commonwealth v. Mitchel* (1850), for example, Judge Parsons of the Pennsylvania Supreme Court ruled on a case much like the New Hampshire precedent just discussed. M. P. Mitchel, the proprietor of the United States Hotel in Philadelphia, had for personal reasons informed one Mr. Potter that he was never to enter the hotel again. When Potter returned a few days later, Mitchel sent for a policeman and laid his hand on Potter's shoulder to direct him off the premises. Potter departed, but pressed criminal charges against Mitchel for assault.

Judge Parsons clearly hoped to make the case into a legal landmark. He explained that because taverns and hotels "affect[ed] a large class of citizens engaged in an important business in the community, and in fact the public at large," the court would "give a written enunciation of the law" so that "all should understand their rights." But rather than focusing on the privileges of travelers, Parsons emphasized what he called "the rights of the proprietor of a hotel, as to the control of his own house, and of those who enter it." In his view, the real danger at hand was that limiting the innkeeper's rights "would expose all well regulated public houses to the constant intrusions of the idle, dissolute and abandoned in the community," allowing the "pickpocket, the burglar, gambler, and horse-thief [to] come and take his seat by the side of the most virtuous man in the community in the gentleman's common parlour at the hotel." "Nor would the line of distinction be drawn here," concluded Parsons in a flourish of social anxiety, since "the filthy and unclean would claim the same right." Notwithstanding the judge's obvious desire to insulate respectable society against the socially and economically marginalized, his ruling did little to check the ongoing broadening of the right of entry. Parsons did rule that a hotelkeeper could eject a person who was disorderly or offensive to guests. He also stated that the proprietor would not be *criminally* liable for doing so. Yet he confirmed that a *civil* liability still existed. Moreover, he conceded a broad duty to admit guests. The fact that Potter was a resident of the city rather than a traveler was never mentioned, and Parsons allowed that, according to his understanding, an innkeeper's duty to provide accommodation extended to "all *strangers* and *travellers*" seeking entertainment.[25]

Subsequent rulings further broadened the right of entry. In *State v. Whitby* (1854), the Delaware Supreme Court convicted a publican of assault and battery for removing a vendor from his hotel. "All persons have the right to go to an inn," explained the court, "as guests, or for the purpose of selling any thing." The court added that as long as the person behaved properly while selling goods, he had the right to remain on the premises.[26] A later verdict from Maine's highest court further limited innkeepers' discretion in deciding whom to exclude from their premises. *Atwater v. Sawyer* (1884) involved an innkeeper who had refused to serve drinks to two members of the Maine militia on the grounds that other militiamen had "behaved in a disorderly and insulting manner" in his establishment earlier in the day and "threatened to turn him and his house into the street." In rejecting the defendant's claim that he was justifiably apprehensive about how other militiamen would comport themselves, the justices ruled that the plaintiffs had a "right to entertainment" that the innkeeper could not abridge without more compelling evidence that they were "evil disposed toward him."[27]

As noteworthy as the rulings themselves were the defendants' pleadings. In the Delaware case, the defense could have argued that the plaintiff was not a traveler, even though it might have been expected that the judge would cite *Markham v. Brown* and conclude that a vendor did indeed have business with the hotel's guests. But in the case of the Maine militiamen, it is difficult to imagine why an attorney would decline to point out that the militiamen had no business with any of the guests and were not themselves seeking accommodations, and therefore could not claim rights explicitly delineated in earlier cases. The most plausible explanation for these omissions is that by then it had become clear to all involved that the right to enter a hotel or tavern had become generalized to the public at large.

This broadening of access to public houses involved a subtle but hugely important shift in the law of hospitality: the privileges of travelers were refashioned into the rights of individuals. In place of an earlier understanding of innkeeper law in which state and local authorities regulated the behavior of hosts and guests in the name of the common good, American courts gradually created an individual entitlement that could not legitimately be abridged by governments or other individuals. Early-nineteenth-century cases tended to employ words connoting relations of responsibility and privilege: innkeepers were deemed "chargeable," "liable," or "answerable" for the losses of their guests, and patrons received "license" or "permission" to enter inns. Toward the end of the 1830s, and more noticeably after the 1840s, judges were inclined to use a more individualistic language of possession and right. The ruling in *Markham v. Brown* typified this trend, with the justices declaring a "right of the traveller" where once there had only been an assigned privilege. The same tendency was evident in *State v. Whitby,* in which the "right to go to an inn" was proclaimed without reference to reciprocal duties or special conditions. These new linguistic usages precisely tracked the legal content of the rulings, leaving little doubt that they accurately reflected new ways of thinking about the law of hospitality.[28]

Why did American judges reinterpret the common law of innkeepers? The most important factor was probably the influence of everyday practice. Hotels pioneered a new kind of commercial hospitality that served both wayfarers and the local public. Hotel-keepers made ends meet by leasing floor space for newsstands, barbershops, ticket offices, cigar stands, banks, telegraph offices, retail stores, and other concerns (figs. 6.1, 6.2), in addition to their offerings of ballrooms, assembly halls, private meeting chambers, com-mercial display rooms, and lounges. All these facilities were patronized as much by the local community as by travelers, and as a result, hotels constantly played host to a bustling and often free-spending public whose patronage was essential to keeping hotel lobbies, barrooms, and restaurants full. The broadened right of access to public houses was in large part an unintended consequence of hotelkeepers' success in popularizing the hotel as a public resort. To the extent that they had made their hotels into public places, hotel-keepers effectively surrendered their authority to decide who could come in. The judicial declaration of a general right to enter can thus be interpreted as a classic common-law process: judges were simply acknowledging a customary practice and transforming it into a legally supported right.[29]

This redefinition of innkeeper law was also part of a larger transition in American legal culture that influenced many different areas of jurisprudence. In the early nineteenth century, law was an expression of community self-rule, an active and collective effort by citizens to preserve public order and promote the general welfare. Legal rules were thus based on mutuality, public authority, and the common good. Any claim of a right was constrained by a person's duties or obligations to others, and the interests of the commu-nity outweighed the prerogatives of individuals. As the century progressed, however, this common-law vision of a well-regulated society came under pressure from the gathering influence of classical liberalism. This newer conception of the rule of law was predicated upon property, individual rights, and limited government. As a result, liberalizing judges sought to replace the common law's customary protections and traditional rules with a streamlined legal regime that privileged unfettered private action, economic development,

6.1 A photograph of Cincinnati's Burnet House shows the various ticket offices that did business within the hotel. (Collection of the author)

and formal equality. In the case of innkeeper law, this combination of customary protections and liberal jurisprudence led to a broadened conception of who could claim the special privileges of the traveler and a refashioning of those privileges into individual rights.[30]

This trend in American jurisprudence was in turn related to a larger political context. The reinterpretation of innkeeper law began at a time when a new generation of judges appointed by Jacksonian Democrats were exerting considerable influence on appellate courts. The same political ideology that led Americans to democratize the hotel may also have persuaded judges that the best way to subvert it as an aristocratic project was to open it to a wider public. No such agenda was explicitly declared from the bench, since that would have exposed judges' use of legal language to cloak political decision making in the raiment of putatively neutral judicial principles. Yet the affinities with Jacksonian politics are difficult to miss. The revised version of innkeeper law followed a particular kind of economic logic: defining equality and rights in terms of freedom to participate in the market. This construction of citizenship was second nature to Jacksonians, and a similar ideal of equality defined in terms of economic participation was behind their opposition to corporate privilege, especially in the form of banks. While a definitive conclusion would require direct evidence of ideological rhetoric or political influence in the leading cases on the subject, there is at least circumstantial evidence that the transformation of innkeeper law reflected new political claims on the space of the hotel.[31]

INNKEEPER LAW IN AMERICA: BOARD

The innkeeper's responsibility for providing guests with food and drink had different legal origins than did the other aspects of the law of hospitality. It lacked the classical pedigree of the duties of bed and hearth, not having been included in Justinian's *Digest*. There can be no doubt, however, that it was firmly established within American innkeeper law. Not only did virtually all state statute books in the early United States mandate that food and drink be available at public houses, they also specified the prices at which they could be sold. These laws were based less on judicial rulings than on the long-standing practice of government regulation of the economy. From the beginnings of European settlement, state authorities had routinely set such common standards as the size of bread loaves and barrels, the price of flour and wood, the proper method of producing goods and services, and the allowable times and places for buying and selling them.[32]

The basic requirement that publicans provide their guests with sustenance and refreshment was not seriously questioned in the nineteenth century. There is scant evidence in appellate legal records that this part of innkeeper law was litigated, except as part

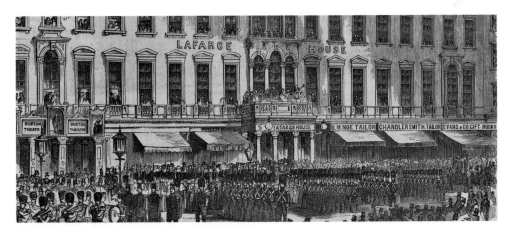

6.2 A newspaper illustration of the La Farge House in New York City displays a ticket office, bookseller, tailors, and other small businesses that served the public there. (General Research Division, The New York Public Library, Astor, Lenox and Tilden Foundations)

of lawsuits over the right of access to an establishment. The main reason for this was the importance of food and especially alcohol sales to proprietors. Tavernkeepers had been avid bartenders but indifferent cooks: they devoted great effort to profitable liquor sales but provided little more or better food than was necessary to fill their guests' stomachs—hence the frequent complaints about tavern fare. Hotelkeepers operated under very different conditions. They had to work hard to compete for patronage, especially in cities with multiple hotels; one way they tried to attract customers was to offer them superior food and drink. Moreover, hotel kitchens and bars were essential to business survival well beyond their usefulness in drawing overnight guests. As contemporary observers pointed out, earnings from room charges would take a hotel only to the break-even point; its proprietor would have little hope of turning a profit without the additional marginal income earned at the table and the footrail. So as long as hotelkeepers' bottom lines depended upon food and drink, and as long as travelers and locals lined up to buy, the second duty of innkeepers needed little enforcement and would be maintained voluntarily for economic reasons.[33]

Such resistance as there was to this requirement of innkeeper law involved not so much the presence or absence of food and drink as the price at which they were sold. Hoteliers and tavernkeepers occasionally attempted to circumvent state regulation. In *State v. Wynne* (1821), for example, a North Carolina innkeeper was indicted for keeping a tavern without a license and for charging more for refreshment than was permitted by the county court's official rates of fare. Despite Wynne's plea that his lack of a license absolved him of the latter charge, the court ruled that he could not "shelter himself under his own double wrong of disobeying the law and defrauding the revenue." To underline the point, the judge added, "To what end is the law made, if any man may set up a tavern, without a license, and sell at rates established by himself?" In the 1830 case of *Commonwealth v. Shortridge*, a Massachusetts court affirmed that under the state's tavern licensing statute, county court judges who were empowered to "fix the rates and prices to be paid at all taverns . . . for liquors, lodging, diet, stableage, provender, and pasturage" could "accommodate the rates . . . as often as they might think proper." In subsequent decades, such challenges gradually disappeared from the court reports. As liberal economic theory gained influence late in the century, an increasing number of states repealed or ignored their price-setting statutes. Unlike other parts of the host-guest relationship, then, the prices of food and drink were increasingly outside the ambit of government regulation.[34]

INNKEEPER LAW IN AMERICA: HEARTH

The duty to safeguard the property of guests was by far the most litigated aspect of the common law of innkeepers in the United States. In one authoritative nineteenth-century index, lawsuits seeking compensation for lost property outnumbered all other innkeeper cases by a margin of more than five to one. This large volume of case law resulted from the many legal intricacies and situational variations on the basic rule at hand. Was an innkeeper responsible for thefts committed by other guests as well as his own employees?

Would a guest's carelessness exculpate the innkeeper? If a guest lost property which did not belong to him, could the actual owner recover? Were some kinds of property exempt from common-law requirements? Judges faced a potentially endless array of permutations of these questions and the many others that arose in court proceedings involving innkeeper law.[35]

Hoteliers, tavernkeepers, and their lawyers used such complicating factors as they attempted to evade their responsibilities at common law. They sought to have plaintiffs' claims dismissed on grounds that ranged from the plausible to the shameless. Many proprietors, upon being sued, declared their premises boardinghouses—to which the common law of innkeepers did not apply—because some of their lodgers had lived for some time at their establishments, or because the plaintiff had requested a room for a fixed period rather than from day to day.[36] Others argued that guests' property had been lost in bars or restaurants within a hotel, rather than in the part of the building where the guest accommodations were located.[37] Still others tried to disclaim the host-guest relationship entirely, pleading that the plaintiffs had not been guests at all because they had taken meals elsewhere or had been away from the hotel for a full day during their stay.[38] Reasonable claims were treated with equanimity, but when presiding judges thought lawyers were deliberately obfuscating, they became impatient and occasionally displayed outright disdain. For example, in an 1867 case in San Francisco, district court judges repeatedly rejected a defense attorney's requests for jury charges, ruling that his statements were "not correct as a proposition of law" and accusing him of formulating them in a way "calculated to mislead" the jury.[39]

Statements like these were indicative of most rulings in cases of lost property: judges and juries seldom failed to hold hotelkeepers and taverners responsible for the goods of their guests. Addressing a wide variety of special circumstances, American courts disallowed hotelkeepers' attempts to reclassify their guests as boarders, rebuffed assertions that losses in some parts of hotels were not recoverable, overruled arguments that servants who had lost their masters' property had no standing to sue, ignored pleas that guests' drunkenness attenuated the duties of hosts, and disregarded claims that hotelkeepers were not responsible for luggage carried by porters before check-in or after check-out. Judges refused to recognize these and many other technical, situational, and evidentiary excuses made by proprietors.[40]

This is not to say that there were never any legal grounds upon which courts would limit or dismiss charges against hosts. In some states, judges or legislatures acted to place constraints on the common-law responsibilities of innkeepers. In a few states in the South, courts ruled that guests could recover for the loss of only those goods that were of real necessity on their travels: luggage, clothing, personal effects, business materials, and a reasonable amount of cash. This was, however, a minority opinion, and the more influential state courts in the North and West affirmed that innkeepers were answerable for all moveable goods brought into their premises.[41] A more common means of limiting the liability of hosts came from state legislatures: a number of states passed laws under which some valuables could be exempted from common-law protection unless they were placed in the hotelkeeper's safe. Such statutes did offer proprietors some measure of relief, but they could not escape responsibility for properly deposited goods: when in 1865 burglars stole 396 ounces of gold dust and $1,500 in gold coins from a safe at San Francisco's What Cheer House, the state's courts ordered its keeper to provide compensation. Moreover, judges and juries regularly held hosts responsible for valuables not placed in hotel safes on the grounds that guests had not been actively and adequately informed that they should do so. While these limits on liability did insulate hosts somewhat, they did not substantially attenuate the heaviest burdens of the common law.[42]

Courts also entertained the possibility that certain findings of negligence could not just limit the amount of an innkeeper's liability but cancel it outright. In some jurisdictions, appellate judges ruled that while innkeepers were presumed responsible for all missing property, they could avoid liability by proving that neither they nor their employees had been negligent in guarding guests' possessions. As with the limitations just discussed, though, this was not the opinion of most state courts, which continued to find that only war, natural disasters, civil disorder, or overwhelming force could excuse innkeepers from their legal duties.[43] A more prevalent legal standard exempted hosts from responsibility for lost goods if they could demonstrate sufficient contributory negligence on the part of the guest. This doctrine did offer a certain amount of legal cover to hotelkeepers, but in practice, judges and juries often set a high standard for a finding of contributory negligence. In some cases, courts ruled for the plaintiffs despite strong evidence of negligence. An 1859 ruling from Kentucky found an innkeeper liable for a valise stolen from a barroom, this despite the innkeeper's request that the guest take the valise to his bedchamber and the guest's refusal to do so. Similarly, in a number of cases from different states, courts ruled that guests could collect for property stolen from their rooms even when they had failed to lock their doors. Taken as a whole, negligence doctrine suggested that another possible avenue of relief for innkeepers was limited by the action of courts.[44]

The most common courtroom plea used to avoid responsibility for lost property was the claim that a plaintiff had not been *infra hospitium*—literally, "under the hospitality"—of a host. Courts held, for example, that a man who checked into a hotel with a prostitute who he claimed was his wife was there illegally and could not recover for stolen money; that a person who entered a hotel to enjoy a meal with a guest, but who was not a guest himself, could not recover for a lost coat; and that those who went to hotels to attend parties or other functions were not *infra hospitium*, whether they had been invited by the hotelkeeper or a third party. Exceptions like these demonstrated judges' recognition that not everyone in public houses was entitled to the special protections of innkeeper law.[45]

But the legal grounds for denying *infra hospitium* status were shrinking. It was here that the "hearth" provision of innkeeper law was being transformed—in its range of application. In a process analogous to the emergent right of access to public houses, judges often extended common-law property protections to a wider public. While there are relatively few reported cases from the republic's early decades, the available evidence suggests a gradually broadening trend. In the 1793 case of *Quinton v. Courtney,* the attorney for a plaintiff who had lost his saddlebags at a North Carolina tavern emphasized that his client was a traveler, stated that "inns were instituted for the benefit of travelers," and warned that if the proprietor were not held responsible for the loss, it "would destroy the utility of the institution in a great measure"; the court agreed and issued a £109 verdict. An 1823 ruling in a Maryland appeals court specified that innkeepers were responsible for the property of "travelers and guests received by them," a phrasing which might be read as broadening the protections of the common law beyond wayfarers. A more detailed explanation of the responsibility of innkeepers, however, awaited the 1830 case of *Mason v. Thompson,* which involved a woman whose horse harness had been stolen from a Boston tavern. Though the woman had stayed at a different person's house and left only her horse and chaise at the inn, the influential Supreme Judicial Court of Massachusetts ruled in her favor, declaring it "clearly settled that to constitute a guest, in legal contemplation, it is not essential that he should be a lodger or have any refreshment at the inn." Some subsequent rulings involved an even broader reading of the common-law duties of innkeepers. In *McDonald v. Edgerton* (1849), a New York appeals court ruled that simply purchasing liquor made a person a guest. In *Read v. Amidon* (1868), a Vermont court ruled that a person who had gone to an inn for a legal hearing and eaten dinner there, but who did not stay overnight, should still be able to recover for lost property.[46]

In sum, the pattern of enforcement of the host's responsibility for the goods of guests put hotelkeepers in a difficult position. Most verdicts held proprietors liable for lost property, and even when some cases went their way, they operated under conditions of considerable uncertainty. They faced the possibility that a local jury or district court might find them answerable for property losses on their premises, whether suffered by a traveling overnight guest or a local tippler quaffing drinks at the bar. The nation's hotelkeepers thus had to guard carefully against theft throughout their establishments, since in actual practice, any of the people under their roofs might also be found to be legally under their care and protection.

CONCLUSION: EXPANDING HOSPITALITY

The law of hospitality showed signs of both continuity and change. Its persistence over centuries suggested a highly durable belief that relations between hosts and guests were so important that they required a distinct set of rules to govern them. The adoption of these rules by people in many different societies also indicated the cross-cultural utility of the special duties and obligations of travelers and those who sheltered them. In the American context, the observance of innkeeper law bespoke a widespread consensus that hotels and other public houses must not operate exclusively according to the rules of the market. Hotels certainly were business ventures that functioned within a capitalist marketplace. But judges, legislators, and the citizenry recognized that unregulated private enterprise could not provide travelers and the public with the safe, reliable accommodation they needed. Even as the ideology of the market gained ascendance in the United States, then, people understood that they must enact and enforce certain nonmarket values—the ancient ethic of hospitality in particular—in order to ensure the feasibility of travel and the maintenance of public order.

The transformation of the common law of innkeepers, meanwhile, is best understood as a generalization of the law of hospitality beyond travelers and to a wider public. Travelers were among the classic personifications of modernity: deracinated, away from their homes and communities, among strangers, and therefore particularly vulnerable. It was no mere accident that American courts used the special privileges of travelers as a legal model for broader rights in precisely the same years when the transportation revolution was making long-distance travel a common experience. The nineteenth-century United States was the most mobile society of its time and one of the most quickly urbanizing. As a result, travelers were no longer the only strangers on the national scene; cities were increasingly populated by people unknown to one another. Under such circumstances it might not be surprising if the legal protections offered to wayfarers—talismans, as it were, against the dangers of being unknown and individuated—were extended to every person in a society of strangers, and if the traveler were thereby becoming the universal American.

Seven

Unruly Guests and Anxious Hosts

Sex, Theft, and Violence at the Hotel

SOME PEOPLE WENT TO hotels for the wrong reasons. Hotel-keepers and their employees worked hard to make their establishments welcoming and comfortable, and showed tremendous resourcefulness in creating ever more sophisticated methods for efficiently receiving guests, providing them with shelter and sustenance, and offering them a variety of personal services. Yet the very same qualities that made hotels appealing to their desired clientele also attracted people whose intentions were less than legitimate. As much as their proprietors would have liked to deny it, hotels were home to a great deal of illicit activity. Adulterers, seducers, and prostitutes sought out their paramours in hotel bars and public parlors before heading upstairs to make use of the guest beds. Burglars and confidence men mingled among the throngs of people who came and went, stealing from those who were distracted or careless and preying upon the unwary and unsophisticated. And people contemplating acts of violence calmed their nerves and made ready their plans in the privacy of their rooms.

Hotelkeepers thus faced something of a dilemma. Their businesses depended upon attracting a paying clientele, and they were legally obligated to offer accommodations to anyone who could afford them. The very openness of hotels, however, endangered their smooth operation. The hotel business was an extremely competitive one, and it was thus essential that an establishment maintain its reputation by avoiding undesirable publicity or unflattering rumors. If word spread that a downtown palace hotel was attracting rakes or thieves, it might rapidly lose customers to rival hostelries and be forced to close its doors. Nor was this a problem only for respectable houses: a marginal hotel patronized by sex workers and gamblers could suffer the same fate if its employees were overly inquisitive about guests' activities or too ready to share what they knew with the police. Hotelkeeping thus demanded a careful balance of supervision and discretion.

The tense and unruly environment of the hotel was a microcosm of a broader problem of social control that accompanied the advent of modernity in the Atlantic world. By the early nineteenth century, the penetration of capitalist logic into human relationships was well under way, dissolving traditional bonds between people and places. Transience became an everyday fact of life, with people coming into contact with unknown individuals as never before. This presented a problem because strangers were difficult to discipline. In the premodern world of small towns and villages, people's conduct was moderated not only by the presence of elders, magistrates, and religious figures but also by the knowledge that serious misbehavior would be remembered by one's neighbors and answered with shaming or ostracism. Travelers, however, existed outside the usual forms of community-based social control, and thus presented a constant threat of disobedience and disruption.

In much the same way that modern societies struggled to find ways to manage the behavior of strangers, hotelkeepers who presided over establishments filled with transients had to find solutions for both accommodating and controlling guests who could arrive and depart in a matter of days or even hours. The nineteenth-century hotel was a bustling, vibrant place (fig. 7.1) that required considerable surveillance and discipline, and as a result, every hotelkeeper's welcoming smile beamed beneath vigilant eyes.

ILLICIT SEX: CRIMES AGAINST PROPRIETY

The first word on sex in hotels belongs to the minister who preached that hotels were immoral. Asked why, he replied that any establishment that sold liquor and contained so many beds had to be sinful.

While this story has the ring of the apocryphal, its authenticity is less important than the way it encapsulates why hotels were such popular venues for illicit sex. The

7.1   Precisely because hotels presented themselves as orderly, disciplined places, they served as the perfect settings for the kinds of raucous comedy evoked by this 1899 showbill. (Library of Congress)

availability of private rooms with private beds offered a convenient realm of seclusion perfectly suited for trysting; and because these spaces were temporary, evidence of misbehavior was quickly removed by the cleaning staff. Meanwhile, hotel bars made it easy for guests to use strong drink to dissolve their inhibitions and embolden themselves for the escapades ahead (fig. 7.2). With these inducements added to the hotel's status as a place of transience and anonymity, it is easy to see why the most common type of misconduct in hotels was sexual in nature.

Illicit hotel sex must have been quite common, though it is difficult to be sure how common. Most liaisons of this kind went undetected, and even affairs that were discovered were unlikely to become part of the written record. Still, many of them did, with legitimate newspapers and scandal sheets alike printing numerous accounts of hotel-based affairs every year. Such accounts offer detailed glimpses of the sexual possibilities of hotels.[1]

Possibly the most elaborate instance of illicit hotel sex ever recorded was revealed in a divorce proceeding initiated by O. O. Woodman against his wife, Caroline. The affair apparently began in New Orleans in the winter of 1856. Mr. and Mrs. Woodman were spending the season in the city, probably to escape the cold weather of their home in New York, and perhaps also to spend time nearer to Mrs. Woodman's family, who lived

FUN IN A HOTEL.

7.2 Nineteenth-century newspapers, most notably the *National Police Gazette*, constantly published lurid accounts of illicit sexual liaisons that took place in hotels. (Library of Congress)

in Mississippi. The Woodmans took rooms at the St. Louis Hotel, where a man named Gardner Furniss, a cousin of Mrs. Woodman's, was also staying. As Mrs. Woodman's maidservant later described it, Furniss "visited Mrs. Woodman quite often at her parlor," usually after Mr. Woodman had left the hotel for the day and before he came back for supper; she never saw Mrs. Woodman receive any other visitor but Mr. Furniss, and the visits always took place behind closed doors. She recalled that "notes passed between" Mrs. Woodman and Furniss, and while she could not say what they contained, she testified that one of the hotel chambermaids had shown her a letter, apparently in Mrs. Woodman's hand, which began with the greeting "Dear Pet" and was signed "Carry." A second witness denied ever having seen Furniss in Mrs. Woodman's room but admitted that she had "heard many scandalous reports" about the pair. A third witness, who had seen the two together at a different hotel, reported that "Mrs. Woodman had acted quite immodestly, while staying at the St. Charles Hotel, toward Mr. Furniss." Other witnesses came forward to corroborate these accounts.[2]

The liaison continued the following year in Boston. While Mrs. Woodman was staying with the Hazard family for two weeks that summer, she was called upon every day by Furniss, whom she introduced by the name Victor Destrian. She soon took rooms at the Winthrop House, where Furniss continued to visit her regularly. The Hazards' eighteen-year-old son, who often dined with Mrs. Woodman at the hotel, testified that on one occasion, she had turned him away at her door, asking him to come back in half an hour; when he returned slightly earlier than expected, he "found Mr. Furniss there." The next day, the Hazard boy visited Mrs. Woodman in her parlor and heard what he thought was a groan from the attached bedroom. Finding a pretext to escort her to a public room, he returned alone to her chambers, where he "pulled the curtain aside, and looked under the bed, and saw Mr. Furniss there." Not surprisingly, Mrs. Woodman asked him to say nothing about what he had seen. Others at the Winthrop House added equally damning testimony, with a guest and a chambermaid both saying that they had seen a man in her bed. One man's deposition stated that he had seen Mrs. Woodman at another Boston hotel, the Revere House, where she had "acted outrageously with Furniss" in her room, "sitting on the sofa, Mrs. W. in her nightdress and F. in his shirt." The man also noted that he had "heard several reports against them from the servants and a gentleman from New Orleans who occupied the next room."[3]

The end of the affair came in New York City. Mrs. Woodman left Boston after sending Furniss a secret message regarding her destination. She took rooms at the New-York Hotel on Broadway, and shortly thereafter Furniss arrived and asked to be taken to her room. Meanwhile, Mr. Woodman, who apparently had found out about the affair, turned up at the hotel, checked the register, and demanded to be taken to his wife's room. Finding her partially dressed, and with a man's clothes still draped across the armoire in the bedroom, Mr. Woodman drew a pistol and went in search of the seducer. He was intercepted by the police (who had been summoned by the hotel clerk), disarmed, and sent home. The clerk later found Furniss hiding in a water closet wearing only a shirt; he retrieved the terrified man's clothing and sent him out a side door. Apparently undaunted by his brush with death, Furniss later attempted to contact Mrs. Woodman but found that her husband had confined her to a private asylum.[4]

This account offers a wealth of detail about the role hotels could play in adulterous relationships. To begin with, hotels afforded Mrs. Woodman and Furniss places to carry on their affair clandestinely, even during family trips or in their own hometowns. The pair also used hotels to communicate, sending and receiving notes carried by hotel staff and leaving messages for each other as to the time and place of their next rendezvous. In addition, Furniss's narrow escape from Mr. Woodman suggests that even once they were found out, the hotel's numerous rooms and corridors provided places to hide that would not have been available in a private home or other small building.

But the episode is even more revealing of the limitations of hotel-based infidelity, for as it turned out, the hotels at which Mrs. Woodman and Furniss stayed were not nearly so private as expected. Despite what must have been at least a minimal effort to be discreet, they had been seen in flagrante delicto by numerous people at various hotels; and these witnesses had not been limited to quick glimpses but had seen enough to provide considerable detail about particular acts and states of undress. In addition, mentions of "scandalous reports" and other whisperings demonstrate that when hotel workers and guests saw things that raised their suspicions, they readily shared their discoveries with others. Boarders and other long-term residents were especially attentive in this respect, since they already knew one another and either relished the fun of gossip or wanted to root out misbehavior in what was, after all, their home. In some cases, hotel observation became active snooping, as with chambermaids who read confidential messages and showed them to others. Hotel employees may also have been involved in passing along sensitive information, since even in a city with scores of hotels, Mr. Woodman had known exactly when and where to find his wife and her lover. Of course, the hotel's informal system of supervision had not worked entirely against the interests of the amorous couple; had the hotel clerk not called the police, the infuriated cuckold might well have found Furniss and shot him to death.

While the Woodman-Furniss affair was unusual in its intensity and geographic range, in other ways it was fairly typical. Many other accounts of hotel adultery followed the same basic narrative of one spouse discovering that the other had been meeting with a third party in hotel rooms for immoral purposes. Often the key piece of evidence was having signed into a hotel as a married couple, an action that would be necessary for one reason only. In an 1888 case, for example, Jennie Schneider sued her husband for divorce on the basis of "drunkenness, cruelty and non-support and also . . . having gone to the Hotel Brunswick with one Teresa O'Donnell in June, 1887, where they registered as man and wife and were guilty of adultery." A case from 1899 involved a wife who applied for "a decree of divorce upon the charges of cruelty and infidelity" after finding that her husband, a hotelkeeper, had been involved in "improper conduct" with a sixteen-year-old girl who had worked at the hotel.[5]

Hotels were also prime locations for seduction. In nineteenth-century America, the term *seduction* indicated a sexual liaison just inside the boundaries of consent: one in which the female partner was somehow deceived into having sex. Because most people were unwilling to believe that a respectable woman would voluntarily consent to sex outside of an engagement or marriage, the term was applied very broadly, and what would be considered consensual today might then have been understood in terms of a woman tricked or otherwise misled. The most common scenario involved a younger, unmarried woman or girl who had "surrendered her virtue" on the basis of some sort of subterfuge, whether intoxication or a false promise of marriage.[6]

The folklore of seduction often featured a famous transient figure of the age, the traveling salesman. Stories circulated in which the wily and rakish traveling man breezed into town and attempted to seduce women in his hotel room. One popular 1880s stage play, George Jessop's *Sam'l of Posen; or, The Commercial Drummer,* had a playbill featuring a "Drummer's Balance Sheet" that included the following entries: "Been to church . . . 0; Accompanied girls from church home . . . 17; Girls flirted with . . . 42; Agreed to marry . . .

2." At a time when failure to make good on a promise of marriage was a legally actionable offense that regularly landed men in court, the sexual connotation of agreeing to marry on two separate occasions could not have been lost on anyone.

Nor was this merely folkloric. An 1884 newspaper article detailed one commercial traveler's apparent effort to seduce a local girl at his hotel. The story ran under the headline "WHERE ARE YOUR DAUGHTERS?" and recounted a misadventure involving the daughter of a prominent Iowa family. At about ten o'clock on a summer night, a young woman entered one of Davenport's best hotels with a man who was "not a resident of the city, but comes here three or four times a year as agent of an eastern manufactory." The two proceeded upstairs to his room, and shortly thereafter "a bottle of champagne was ordered." When the hotelkeeper learned of the situation from the clerk who had taken the order, the boy was immediately "ordered back to say that [the man] and the young woman must leave that room and the hotel immediately." The traveling man descended from his room alone, confronted the hotelkeeper in the lobby, and "protested that he was doing no wrong, that the lady with him was respectable, that they had been to an entertainment together, and merely came to his room to enjoy some cool wine." Unmoved, the proprietor replied "that it could not be so—that no respectable girl would accompany a young man to any such place for any such purpose." After much fruitless pleading, the young man agreed to leave, and the hotelkeeper saw to it that the young woman was discreetly escorted out of the hotel by a side entrance and returned home to her family. The article's author carefully recorded the reaction of the hotel proprietor, who declared that "there is too much carelessness of this sort in Davenport," adding that had the community learned the identity of the woman, there would have been "utter ruin, ghastly ruin, before her" in the form of "the certain loss of her good name."[7]

In numerous other cases, however, seducers escaped detection by the hotel staff and successfully achieved their ends. In 1869 a Miss Cairnes took a man named Nicholas McComas to court "for breach of promise of marriage" after they had consummated what she thought was an engagement in a Maryland hotel. An Ohio woman named Jenny Droz explained to police during a trial that Major Fisk, the keeper of the Cliff House hotel, had "used every artifice possible for a period of eight months and finally succeeded in seducing her," as a result of which she "caught a loathsome disease from him, which incapacitated her for any kind of work." And in Lancaster, Pennsylvania, in 1896, Bertha McConnell told friends of her "deception and betrayal" at the hands of a traveling salesman named Harry Thompson, who, she explained, had "deceived and ruined" her in a hotel.[8]

Prostitution was another exceptionally common context for sex at hotels. In the nineteenth-century United States, the exchange of sex for money was ubiquitous. Practically every city had a known vice district where residents and visitors alike could find sex for sale; in some cities, booklets were published under titles like *Butt Ender's Prostitution Exposed* (1839) that purported to be exposés of urban vice but which offered detailed descriptions and street addresses that made them more useful as guides for the sexual tourist. Despite the efforts of purity reformers and working women's advocates to unmask, reduce, or even eliminate houses of prostitution, people in urban America could scarcely avoid seeing, hearing, or at least knowing about the sex trade.[9]

Hotels were magnets for prostitution (fig. 7.3). As surely as big cities were emporia for goods, they also served as marketplaces for sex, and nobody understood this better than prostitutes and their cohorts. In New York City, for example, the urban historian Timothy Gilfoyle has shown that the hotels built along Broadway in the 1830s were complemented by brothels on nearby side streets, and within two decades nearly 80 percent of houses of prostitution on Manhattan's west side were located within two and a half blocks of a large hotel. Particular brothels even became associated with specific hotels: Mary Benson's establishment on Church Street, for instance, was said to be preferred by guests at the Astor House and the American Hotel. Broadway's grand hotels were favored sites of solicitation for sex workers and pimps, with the latter garnering the nickname "Broadway statues" because they seemed never to leave their places. Later in the century, observers made explicit note of the connection between hotels and prostitution. James D. McCabe, Jr., wrote that "fallen women of the higher classes abound at the hotels," and George Ellington called prostitutes hotels' "very best customers." As Ellington saw it, "The rich miner of mines, the oil speculator, . . . the merchant from the Western city, . . . and the capitalist seeking for an investment,—all these have an overplus of money, and all put up at the very best hotels in the city. It is not long before Anonyma finds them out."[10]

7.3   An illustration in an 1879 issue of the *National Police Gazette* depicted two men being solicited by prostitutes, wined and entertained in an elegant hotel room, and robbed in their sleep. (Library of Congress)

Prostitution was not, of course, limited either to large hotels or to big cities. The cultural historian Sharon Wood's work on Davenport, Iowa, provides a detailed account of how hotels, especially small ones, figured in the city's sex trade. In the fall of 1894 two young men and two teenage girls were arrested after signing into the Slate House Hotel as married couples spending the night together. When the girls told the police that they had visited the hotel earlier in the week with two different men, the mayor ordered a full-scale investigation of unregulated prostitution in the city, which at that time had a system of licensed brothels. This resulted in a number of grand jury indictments, including three against hotelkeepers. In subsequent trials, a picture emerged of how hotels in the Bucktown district were being used as houses of assignation.

In these small establishments, as in much larger ones, the everyday business of hotelkeeping served to hide the regular exchange of sex for money. Lodgers at the Slate House testified that they had never seen any evidence of immoral conduct, but a police detective described the establishment as the haunt of "women of bad character" and described other illicit couplings that took place there. The jury convicted the hotelkeepers, and the judge fined them for renting rooms "for immoral purposes." In another trial, a local proprietor described the Metropolitan Hotel as having "a bad reputation," and a seventeen-year-old girl testified, "I have been there several times and I have occupied rooms and beds with various gentlemen who have at such times paid the bartender for our use of the rooms." Another witness who also used the hotel stated that its keeper "knew that we occupied the room for purposes of prostitution and she received $3.50 a week for its use." In yet another case, a witness claimed that the proprietors of a downtown hotel (in this case the term was used broadly, for the structure was little more than an extended private residence with a liquor license) had actively recruited her and other girls into prostitution. "Mrs. Jacobsen came for me and told me there was some nice fellows in the wine room, and for me to come and drink with them that there was some money in them," she testified. "Afterwards I went to bed with one of them. He paid me two dollars, and he paid Mr. D[avid] Jacobsen a dollar for the use of the room." The world of hotel prostitution, it seems, extended from the grandest establishments to the most marginal of operations.[11]

The hotel's distinctive combination of privacy, anonymity, and transience made it a highly sexualized space, its lobbies, bars, and bedchambers charged with both possibility and peril. But sexual misbehavior was by no means the only kind of illicit activity going on in America's hotels. They also lent themselves to other kinds of lawbreaking.

THEFT: CRIMES AGAINST PROPERTY

"Probably no more prevalent or more popular branch of dishonesty exists at this time," wrote Allan Pinkerton, "than the robbery of hotels." Pinkerton was in a position to know. He was, after all, the most famous detective of the century. After getting his start in the 1850s pursuing counterfeiters and spying on railroad workers, he aided the Union Army during the Civil War by heading an espionage operation in Virginia. Pinkerton soon returned to private practice, his National Detective Agency growing quickly and becoming so widely known that its emblem of an all-seeing eye and its motto, "The Eye That Never Sleeps," helped popularize the term "private eye." So it is a fact of some significance that Pinkerton's posthumously published autobiography, *Thirty Years a Detective* (1884), devoted an entire chapter to "Hotel Thieves."[12]

Pinkerton was right: there was a great deal of stealing going on in hotels. The historical record contains a wealth of evidence of hotel theft, with thousands of newspaper articles reporting hotel burglaries and robberies, recounting the arrests of hotel thieves, and describing the tricks of their trade. Theft posed a far greater danger than illicit sex to the orderly operation of hotels. Sexual misbehavior was mostly private and consensual, and all parties directly involved had good reason to hide what they were doing. Theft, by contrast, invariably involved an aggrieved individual who would want to call attention to the crime in an effort to catch the offender and recover the stolen goods. And the duties imposed by the common law of innkeepers meant that whenever a guest was unable to recover property, the host would have to pay for the loss. Every instance of hotel theft thus threatened a hotelkeeper with a direct and immediate financial cost, leaving him in a difficult position indeed.

Hotel thieves, meanwhile, enjoyed practically every advantage. To begin with, the social character of hotels meant that most people were able to wander freely about the premises in a way that would generate suspicion in most other settings; moreover, the hustle and bustle of a hotel's lobby and public rooms could provide thieves with a sort of urban camouflage. "A hotel thief has all the advantages in the world," explained one police detective, "because so many strangers come and go at the big hotels that but little attention is paid to any individual guest." This is not to say that any person could go into any hotel and pass as a patron. In the more elegant and expensive establishments that were the preferred target for hotel thieves, a shoddily dressed person would seem out of place, and so a successful heist required somewhat more preparation. Some hotel thieves developed elaborate outfits and techniques. An 1854 newspaper article described the modus operandi of an "expert robber" whose methods were representative of "a new system of robbing the guests of our hotels":

> The operator generally dresses richly, is arrayed with jewelry, viz.: diamond studs, pins, rings, and watch and chain, of the most costly qualities. The acquaintance of some respectable gentleman stopping at one of the leading hotels is then sought, and if made, the rogue manages to appear very agreeable, and continues to court the friendship of his new acquaintance. The fellow is noticed by the officers of the house as being intimate with some guest, but he may or may not stop at the same house. Under these disguises he has full liberty to loiter about the parlors, drawing-rooms, and elsewhere about the premises.

7.4   A plate from Allan Pinkerton's *Thirty Years a Detective* (1884) illustrates how hotel thieves obtained access to guests' rooms. (University of Chicago Libraries)

Using these and a host of other ruses, thieves made themselves a constant presence at American hotels.[13]

Once inside a hotel, a thief was presented with a number of opportunities. The most promising was burglary. Hotels were the destination of a steady stream of travelers who arrived with their clothing, goods, and personal effects conveniently packed into portable units in the form of baggage. Moreover, in an age before traveler's checks and credit cards, those on a journey had to carry enough cash to get them from city to city, making their billfolds and purses particularly rich prizes. Guests kept their belongings in their rooms, where they were separated from public corridors by no more than the width of a door; they spent few waking hours in their rooms, and there were no effective hiding places for the possessions they left behind while away. Hotel patrons would have been notified that they should deposit their valuables in the hotel safe, and while some would have done so, there were always others who were careless or in a hurry: said one observer of the ubiquitous posted notice, "no one ever as much as reads it, or follows the good advice." Finally, the everyday comings and goings of a hotel meant that a person walking out with a bag, even a very large one, would arouse no suspicion. As a result, one person's luggage could quickly become another's loot.[14]

Hotel burglars devised numerous means of gaining access to guests' rooms. One young man arrested in a hotel in 1858 was found to be carrying a set of skeleton keys. Pinkerton's autobiography included an illustration (fig. 7.4) depicting a hotel thief using a complex device to spring the lock on a hotel room door, and the most dedicated hotel thieves had entire sets of instruments. A suspect collared in New York City in 1884 carried with him "a very neat and very perfect 'kit' of hotel thieves' tools" that was designed to fit "in a man's trousers pocket." The kit included "a pair of 'nippers,' a gouge, a gimlet, a brad-awl, a 'pull-back' for bolts, a sharp, flat jeweler's file, skeleton keys, blank keys, and a tiny bottle of oil."[15]

Having gained entry, an industrious thief could take advantage of the privacy of the room to work unobserved. A relatively unlucky intruder might find only everyday items or petty cash, like the burglar who ransacked several trunks for a few personal articles and twenty-eight dollars in cash, the burglar who purloined a man's empty valise, or the exceptionally unfortunate Eugene Roland, who in 1869 was sentenced to seven and a half years' imprisonment "for having stolen two shawls and a quantity of laces and embroidery" from a hotel bedchamber.[16] Burglars occasionally managed larger hauls, as when one took from the room of two German jewelers "32 diamond rings, single stones . . . 11 diamond rings, with black morocco cases . . . 2 heavy gold sealing rings . . . 4 gold ladies' necklaces . . . [and] 2 diamond breast-pins."[17] In rare cases, enormously valuable goods could be stolen. A traveling salesman staying at a Baltimore hotel lost "solid gold watch-chains, valued at from $8,000 to $10,000," and one extraordinarily successful burglar managed to get away with $60,000 worth of gold dust from a San Francisco hotel frequented by prospectors late in the Gold Rush.[18]

There were also defensive advantages to burglarizing hotel rooms. One of these was the availability of a quick escape. A hotel thief could easily leave the scene of the crime and disappear into the crowd; and because hotels had to be convenient to railroad stations and steamboat landings, he could leave town even before his victims knew that they had been robbed. Indeed, the existence of a nationwide network of hotels meant that thieves who were willing to travel widely could go from city to city repeating the same crimes without being recognized. Other hotel burglars preferred to stay within the hotels they targeted, renting rooms to which they could quickly retreat and thereby getting themselves and their stolen goods out of sight. Remarkably, even when thieves were discovered in guests' rooms, they could sometimes talk their way out of the predicament by claiming that there had been some kind of misunderstanding. A burglar caught in the act by a clerk at a hotel in Cincinnati, for example, managed to escape "by persuading the clerk of the belief that he had gotten into the room by accident, and that he was entirely innocent of any evil intentions."[19]

When it was not possible to burglarize hotel rooms, thieves stole directly from the persons of hotel guests. There were any number of distractions which might leave hotel patrons and passersby vulnerable to a light-fingered sneak thief. Whether because they had to mind their children, juggle bags and coats, or check into their rooms, guests' attention sometimes wandered. Some thieves took this opportunity to simply walk off with luggage. At New York's Astor House during the Civil War, a hotel thief named Benjamin Graig "picked up a carpet-bag belonging to one of the guests" and attempted to walk out with it, but was immediately apprehended. The following year, a traveling Philadelphian had his carpetbag filched from atop a counter at his hotel. A far more common object of theft was people's clothing, especially their coats. A Cleveland judge had his overcoat stolen while he dined at the American House, and later that year one Major Goodspeed lost his coat under the same circumstances. A man arrested in New York City for trying to steal an overcoat from a hotel billiard room was found to be in possession of a number of claim tickets for other coats he had stolen, and the *New York Times* reported in 1854 that "from one hotel alone we learn that over fifty overcoats have been stolen within the past four or five weeks."[20]

It was not always necessary to wait for a person to become distracted before attempting a robbery. Some hotel thieves adopted precisely the opposite strategy, introducing themselves to hotel guests or employees as a prelude to swindling them. Confidence men, knowing that hotel guests included no small number of country visitors unaccustomed to the schemes of the big city, found their marks in hotel lobbies (fig. 7.5). A man from the small town of Webster, Iowa, was "seduced into a monkey show" and lost $130 in "one sitting of an hour, at a game of chance, played with cards," and another $250 "at a game played with dice." A rather different kind of ruse was commonly attempted on hotel cashiers. In 1857, for example, when a visitor at the American House in Cleveland obtained $400 from its proprietor using false documents, the governor of Ohio managed to trace him to Boston and have him arrested there.[21]

GRAFTERS IN HOTELS
ARE NOW
PICKING OUT VICTIMS

They Invariably Look Upon Spring Visitors From Out of Town as Their Legitimate Prey.

HOW MANY OF THEIR LITTLE SCHEMES ARE WORKED

Carelessness in Handling Jewelry and Valuables a Great Help to Them---There Are Clever Women Grafters, Too.

7.5   Headlines like this one warned Americans of the miscreants who lurked in hotels in hopes of robbing or defrauding guests. (Library of Congress)

Hotels also offered opportunities for theft that had nothing to do with the guests—the accoutrements of the establishment itself were also ripe for the picking. A woman named Hester McGowan in 1856 stole a number of spoons from a hotel, for which she was fined and briefly imprisoned. In 1862 and 1865 Manhattan hotels were hit by a series of thefts in which young men checked in for a night and paid their bills the following day, but in the meantime helped themselves to the bedding. And in 1874 a man entered the Cataract House in Cleveland and tried to make off with a quantity of cigars and whiskey. Employees, too, sometimes supplemented their income by taking things from hotels. John W. Emmery, who in 1852 worked at the Irving House in New York, was charged with stealing "a lot of silver tea spoons" from his employer, along with his gold watch. The proprietor of the Windsor Hotel complained to police in 1876 that "servants were systematically robbing them of table-linen, silverware, and other property," and in response a police detective went about checking the city's pawn shops for the missing goods. But the most industrious thievery of this kind was the work of a bookkeeper at the immense St. Nicholas Hotel who managed to embezzle tens of thousands of dollars before being detected.[22]

A final form of hotel theft that deserves attention is the theft of services. Deadbeats, guests who left a hotel without paying their bill, were common. Because the customary arrangements between host and guest dictated that the bill was paid only at the end of a hotel stay, it was not difficult for a patron to steal away, leaving the proprietor in the lurch. In most cases this was simply a matter of departing undetected, usually after having assumed a false identity to make it more difficult for authorities to follow. This was the method of a "Dr. J. F. Lawrence," who claimed to be an "eminent oculist and aurist" before he "skedaddled from the American House" without having paid. He had a kindred spirit in "Henry C. Smith, *alias* Williams, *alias* Johnson," who quit the Prescott House "leaving behind him a large unpaid board bill." Other ruses involved payment with false money or notes: witness a man stopping at Cleveland in 1854 who "paid his bill with a $20 note which had been altered from a one dollar note," or the guest at that city's Birch House who tried to pay his bill with "a draft purporting to be drawn on the First National Bank" but which "proved to be a forgery." In a few cases very elaborate deceptions were contrived. In 1859 a middle-aged man managed to cheat several New York City hotelkeepers by claiming that he was a Savannah merchant who had lost his trunks, which contained his money, drafts, and letters of reference, through which ruse he "obtained free board at several hotels."[23]

Hotelkeepers operated at a difficult intersection of custom, architecture, labor markets, and law. It was virtually impossible to detect any but known criminals among the guests, and practically anyone in a hotel, from barflies to boarders to employees, could be involved in thievery. Yet as much of a financial threat as they might pose to a hotel's orderly operation, there were still more serious crimes that menaced the very lives of the people who worked, lived, and stayed there.

Violence in hotels was less common than illicit sex or theft, but the threat of bodily harm made it the most damaging kind of breach of order that could occur in a public house. Many Americans might wink at the incidence of immorality at a hotel, and others could comfort themselves by leaving valuables in the hotel safe, but violence had an immediate, personal, and above all random quality that was less easily dismissed. The cities of the nineteenth-century United States were exceptionally violent places, and most had no municipal police forces until after the Civil War; as a result, most law enforcement was performed by constables and magistrates who depended upon personal knowledge of their neighbors to control crime. In this environment, hotels were seen as safe havens for travelers in a sea of urban disorder. If a hotelkeeper wanted to stay in business, he had to preserve the public image of his establishment as a secure enclave.[24]

This was often difficult to achieve, however. Hotel space by its very nature brought people together under unfamiliar or tense conditions, leading to conflicts among guests. In 1855, for example, negotiations for the purchase of a sailing ship ended when, as the victim recalled, his attacker "drew a cowhide from his breast and commenced striking me across the face; a struggle then commenced between us, which was terminated by our being thrust apart." Some years later at the New-York Hotel, a traveling author broke up a card trick and in response was attacked and beaten. And in 1869 at the Osburn House in Rochester, New York, two groups of guests involved in a bitterly fought lawsuit "engaged in a rumpus" involving a thrown water pitcher and clock. Guests also sometimes turned in anger upon hotel employees. Not long after the end of the Civil War, a man named Willie Hickey was convicted and fined five dollars "for brutally assaulting John Sweeney, an employee of the American House." Workplace tensions could even lead to violence among the staff. At Cleveland's Angier House, for example, one fifteen-month period saw two newspaper reports of violence among the employees, with a waiter attacking a chambermaid and a cook assaulting the barkeep. In the spring of 1858, after the prominent New York hotelkeeper Hiram Cranston fired his house physician over a disputed diagnosis, Dr. Gallardet "seized a full bottle of champagne standing in front of a gentleman seated near Mr. Cranston, and struck him twice with it on the top of the head, the first blow shattering the bottle, and stunning Mr. C.; the second felling him to the floor."[25]

Hotelkeepers did their best to maintain order on their premises by remaining vigilant and learning the arts of quiet persuasion and diplomacy. Often they were able to avert dangerous confrontations, but in some cases their efforts themselves escalated into violent situations. Walter Osborne, the keeper of a seaside hotel in Gloucester, Massachusetts, was trying to settle a dispute over a five-dollar hotel bill when he "was knocked down and beaten" by his interlocutor, his wife also suffering a blow as she pulled him to safety "behind a barrier of women." Guests were especially resentful when asked to leave the premises. During the Civil War, when a Cleveland hotelkeeper put a recently recruited soldier out of his hostelry, the man returned with comrades from his regiment and made "serious threats" against the proprietor. But the greatest danger came from burglars caught in the act of stealing. A thief who was surprised by the proprietor of a Brooklyn hotel "endeavored to throw Mr. Dieter down the stairs. A scuffle ensued, during which the intruder drew a large knife, and attempted to stab Mr. Dieter." The hotelkeeper managed to dodge the blade, but the trespasser escaped into the night. Similarly, when in 1856 the Ohio hotelkeeper George R. Bronson intercepted a burglar in the American Hotel, the intruder drew a pistol and "fired several shots, none of which hit their mark," before being overpowered and arrested.[26]

Many violent episodes involved a factor intrinsically related to the hotel milieu: the ready availability of alcohol. In 1858 a newspaper editor complained of raucous behavior in hotel bars. "The first object which attracts the attention of our foreign travelers in this country," he noted, "is the hotel bar-room of our great cities"; but the beauty of the hotel bar stood in stark contrast with its patrons, who were "either strangers or loose young men about town." Focusing on recent incidents in Washington, he pointed an accusing finger at the baneful effects of alcohol:

> The greater part of the disgraceful rows which take place at the national capital have their origin in bar-rooms, where, under the excitement of drink, and the rowdy influences of the place, men are led to commit acts that are abhorrent to them in their sober moments. . . . And what a picture it represents of the half-civilized state of society at our national capital when a party of honorable gentlemen, the representatives of sovereign States, meet in a public bar-room, and while taking a "Kentucky drink" together fall to fighting like a parcel of savages or drunken coal-heavers![27]

A disproportionate share of the various reported incidents of violence in hotels did indeed occur in or around the bar or involved drinking in guests' rooms. In 1858, for example, an employee of the Northern Hotel in Manhattan was accosted by a local ruffian and "without provocation" was "shockingly beaten and kicked . . . in the bar-room of the hotel." Six employees of Brooklyn's Brighton Beach Hotel were arrested on a summer night in 1878 after a drunken brawl with three men who dared to cross the hotel's piazza on the way to another destination. And in an 1889 incident in the nation's capital, a United States senator broke up a fight in the Metropolitan Hotel after "[a] young man named J. A. Gardener entered the hotel and, being somewhat under the influence of liquor, he proceeded to assault a young man named Popham."[28]

The role of strong drink was even more apparent in cases where hotel violence involved deadly force. Newspaper reports from the 1850s alone offer a litany of variations on this single theme. In 1852 one Mr. Fuller, a hotel clerk at the Weddell House in Ohio, was entertaining a friend in his room, both of them enjoying "several drinks," when "shots were heard and Mr. Fuller was found wounded and bleeding." In Baltimore in 1855 "a party of five disorderly persons entered the Washington Hotel" for a few drinks; a scuffle broke out

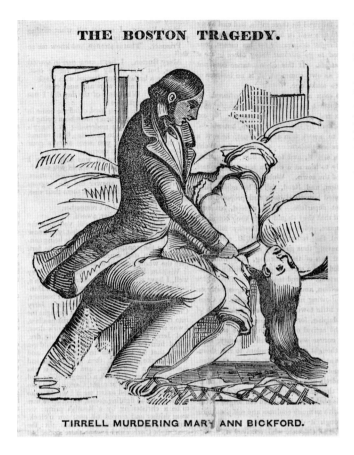

THE BOSTON TRAGEDY.

TIRRELL MURDERING MARY ANN BICKFORD.

7.6   Illicit sexual relationships sometimes went sour and led to murder, as in the 1845 case of a man who cut his lover's throat after carrying on an adulterous affair with her "at several respectable hotels" in Boston. (Beinecke Rare Book and Manuscript Library, Yale University)

as one of the proprietors ushered them out; guns were drawn, and one of the party, "taking deliberate aim with a pistol, fired at Eugene Broaders . . . and in a few minutes [he] was a corpse." In the spring of 1858 a small group of guests at New York's Brandreth House ordered several rounds of whiskey and brandy punch brought to them in their rooms; one picked up a pistol and was joking with the hotel waiter that "I will fire the pistol off if you don't bring up the drinks quick" when the weapon accidentally discharged, striking the waiter in the groin and causing him to bleed to death.[29]

Sex was another key precipitant of violence in hotels. The combination of frequent public mixing, amorous attentions, and nineteenth-century notions of gender, honor, and the legitimate use of force formed a mixture that could be quite volatile (fig. 7.6). For example, one hotel boarder's habit of staring at another's wife in the hotel restaurant in 1878 prompted a "light and harmless" slap "in the face with his kid-gloved hand"; when this failed to deter the masher, the husband "turned furiously and struck a vigorous blow with his clinched fist" before the two were separated. In an earlier, more serious incident, a Mr. Hoffman was observed "deliberately attempting the seduction of Mrs. Baker," who lodged at the St. Charles House in Manhattan. As Hoffman's invitations to "theatres and places of amusement" gave way to "indelicate advances," Mrs. Baker notified her husband, who armed her with a pistol. When Hoffman dared to seek out Mrs. Baker in her hotel room, she fired two shots, sending him running into the street, where he was intercepted and severely beaten by Mr. Baker and three other men who boarded with their families at the hotel.[30]

In a culture willing to condone violence in defense of female virtue, some people took extreme measures in retaliation for its loss. There was one subcategory of hotel violence that became almost a set piece: the murder of seducers by their victims. Such cases were distinct from almost all other kinds of violence at hotels. Far from being committed on the spur of the moment or under the influence of alcohol, they were premeditated and usually perpetrated in a hotel's public rooms in front of witnesses. These were deliberately public acts that were intended to emphasize the abandonment and desperation of the women involved, and perhaps also to put potential seducers on notice that the women they ruined might be left with no choice but to take a similar revenge. The Miss Cairnes mentioned earlier in the section on hotel seduction later "shot and killed Nicholas Mc-Comas" in front of "twenty persons [who] were seated on the porch of the village hotel." Jenny Droz, the hotel worker from Ohio, obtained a pistol and shot her seducer to death in his own hotel. Bertha McConnell, the Pennsylvania woman seduced by the traveling salesman, lured him to the Keystone House, where she shot him in the head and left him for dead. Indeed, incidents like these were so familiar to nineteenth-century Americans that Mark Twain and Charles Dudley Warner used a woman's public murder of her seducer in a hotel lobby as one of the climactic scenes in their enormously successful 1873 novel *The Gilded Age.*[31]

Violence at hotels also included acts that people committed against themselves. Hotel suicides and suicide attempts were reported at least as early as the period when hotels first began to multiply in American cities. In the summer of 1833 a Boston wine merchant who had shown "symptoms of mental alienation" threw himself out of the window of his room at the Tremont House and fell upon the iron points atop the hotel's fence. In 1836 a man described as "insane" was seriously injured after jumping from the fourth floor of the Astor House. Other hotel guests ended their lives in their rooms. Bill Nye, a journalist and humorist popular in the 1880s, observed of one hotel: "The door of our room is full of holes where locks have been wrenched off in order to let the coroner in." This was no exaggeration. Suicides were a common feature of hotel life and were regularly reported in newspapers: the *New York Times,* for example, ran stories on hotel suicides practically every year between 1850 and 1900.[32]

A number of factors contributed to the prevalence of hotel suicide. Deeply depressed people were sometimes attracted to hotels because there they could avoid friends and acquaintances and keep odd hours, yet still find shelter, food, and basic services at arm's length through the impersonal service of the staff. In addition, the hotel setting meant that a person could commit suicide knowing that the corpse would be found by an anonymous hotel worker rather than a family member or friend. But the most specific reason involved a common hotel amenity: gaslight. Coal, when heated, releases an invisible gas that burns with a light between five and ten times brighter than a candle. Hotels were among the earliest adopters of gaslight, and an increasing number of establishments were fitted with pipes and wall and ceiling fixtures. However, manufactured coal gas contains highly toxic carbon monoxide. While its strong odor served as a built-in warning system, a determinedly suicidal person could ignore the smell. This use of gas was later immortalized by Theodore Dreiser in the final scene of *Sister Carrie* (1900). Hurstwood, abandoned, disgraced, and nearly penniless, checks into a skid-row hotel and goes to his dingy room alone. After sealing the space under the door, Hurstwood "turned the gas on again, but applied no match" and "stood there . . . while the uprising fumes filled the room. When the odour reached his nostrils, he quit his attitude and fumbled for the bed. 'What's the use?' he said, weakly, as he stretched himself to rest."[33]

Hotel workers faced with the emotional strain of discovering dead bodies often resorted to gallows humor. Clerks proverbially told bellhops: "Show this gentleman to Room 248, and see that he doesn't blow out the gas." One hotel proprietor reportedly posted a public notice that read: "Guests contemplating suicide while stopping at this hotel, will please notify the clerk, and a room exclusively set apart for the accommodation of self-murderers will be assigned them." Another, addressing a string of suicides at his establishment, quipped,

> We have never written letters to prospective suicides at other hotels inviting them to come with us at reduced rates, and yet, when a man feels it is time for him to shuffle off this mortal coil, it seems perfectly natural for him to drift into our hotel, unostentatious as it may be. It is a comparatively easy class of trade to satisfy. They do not stop to inquire whether the plumbing is modern or antique. They do not ask whether their rooms are decorated in the style of the First Empire or the Seventh Ward. Give them a good six-foot gas burner, about fifteen hundred feet of illuminating gas at $1 a thousand, and a few uninterrupted moments and they are content.[34]

KEEPING ORDER AT THE HOTEL

Faced with the triple threat of illicit sex, theft, and violence, hotelkeepers struggled to keep order at their establishments, using a variety of procedures and personnel to guard against misbehavior and crime. In this, the development of the hotel paralleled the coming of modernity in America: as small towns grew into cities, long-standing modes of community discipline began to fail, necessitating entirely new modes of public regulation. As it turned out, the methods worked out by hotelkeepers depended upon the same cultural innovations as became common elsewhere in the Western world during the nineteenth century.

Hotel guests began to be monitored as soon as they requested rooms. The least-recognized means of surveillance was the guest register. In addition to its essentially clerical purpose, having guests sign the register required that each one self-identify by name and appearance, since the desk clerk and others witnessed the signing. ("As the name is written," observed Anthony Trollope in his 1862 travelogue *North America*, "half a dozen loungers look over your name and listen to what you say.") A person could provide a false name, but even then a handwriting sample was recorded and the attempt to pass under an alias entered into permanent physical evidence. The surveillance function of the hotel register was vividly illustrated in *Running a Thousand Miles for Freedom,* an 1860 slave narrative written by William and Ellen Craft. Having saved sufficient money to pay for passage to the North, the Crafts took advantage of Ellen's light complexion to pose as a white person and a slave. This permitted them to pass undetected and stay at hotels in Charleston and Richmond on their journey, but the hotel register threatened to expose them: as a slave, Ellen had been forbidden to learn how to read and write. In order to avoid raising suspicion, Ellen kept her right hand bandaged, a feigned injury that allowed her to ask the desk clerk to sign for her. A similar disciplinary function was accomplished through the assignment of guest rooms. When a clerk handed a key to a guest, a one-to-one relationship was established between a particular person and a particular space, usually one with a number. The guest was entrusted with control over a private room, but with the understanding that the hotel staff would know its exact location and be able to connect it to the identity and appearance of the person occupying it.[35]

Hotel workers served as the eyes and ears of the institution. Employees kept a constant and close watch over guests; whether they did so out of professional obligation or merely prurient interest is immaterial to the effective level of surveillance. And whenever it seemed that patrons' behavior posed a threat to the good order of the hotel, these employees regularly took action by notifying managers, contacting spouses, calling police, or taking other steps that brought the weight of the authorities or the simple fact of public shame to bear on the situation. In addition to workers whose main tasks were to tend to guests, hotelkeepers who could afford to do so also retained dedicated security staffs. As Allan Pinkerton noted in his memoir: "Every possible precaution has been taken by the proprietors of these establishments to prevent the depredations of . . . midnight marauders. . . . Private officers, watchmen, and detectives have been placed on every floor assigned to sleeping rooms." Yet despite these precautions, he noted, hotel crime had "been abated but not abolished." Pinkerton's hedging indicates that as important as managerial measures surely were in disciplining the lobbies, parlors, hallways, and rooms of American hotels, employees could not effectively patrol every part of even a fairly modest establishment.[36]

Much of the work of maintaining order in hotel space was accomplished by hotel guests themselves. People in hotels were constantly monitoring their own behavior and that of others, effectively policing the premises thereby. This species of public surveillance leaves few documentary traces but has been identified in a number of settings, from the "eyes on the street" described by Jane Jacobs in *The Death and Life of Great American Cities* to the prisons analyzed in Michel Foucault's *Discipline and Punish.* The key feature of this type of discipline is that it does not just emanate from governments and their law-enforcement agencies but is diffused throughout a society and depends upon the attitudes and actions of the entire citizenry. This mode of keeping order has become so continuous and internalized that it has rarely been named by those practicing it, much less written down. One place in which this practice of collective self-policing remains visible, however, is in the promulgation of special standards of etiquette for people in hotels.[37]

Nineteenth-century etiquette books commonly described rules of personal comportment to be observed in hotels, with some guides devoting a chapter or more to the subject. Historical sources like these belong to the category of prescriptive literature—they do not necessarily describe how people actually behaved, but they do reveal how their authors and readers thought people *should* behave. Etiquette books suggest that respectable Americans were keenly aware of the kinds of threats posed by hotels. They also demonstrate that these people did not look to hotelkeepers, their employees, or constables and police officers to make hotels safe and moral places; rather, they emphasized what hotel guests themselves must do to avoid trouble, resist temptation, and ward off disrepute.[38]

As the authors of etiquette books saw it, the basic social problem of the hotel was the difficulty of regulating encounters among strangers. Elizabeth Leslie, a writer for the highly influential magazine *Godey's Lady's Book* and the creator of a series of behavior guides published from the 1830s to the 1860s, devoted more than forty pages of her popular volume *The Behavior Book* to advice on proper comportment in hotels. A chapter entitled "Deportment at a Hotel" opened by "offer[ing] some hints on the propriety of manners that ought to be observed in places where you are always exposed to the inspection and to the remarks of strangers."[39]

The possibility of improper contact between men and respectable women was the primary concern of those giving advice on hotel etiquette. The admonition that was issued earliest and repeated most often was that it was improper for a woman to converse with or otherwise permit the attentions of a stranger. "Ladies at hotels," advised the 1853 edition of *The Behavior Book*, "should be specially careful not to make acquaintance with gentlemen of whom they know nothing." Aware that her female readers might hesitate to stay aloof for fear of appearing rude, its author emphasized that it was "better to thus keep off an objectionable man, (even with the certainty of offending him,) than weakly to subject yourself to the annoyance and discredit (perhaps, still worse) of allowing him to boast of his intimacy with you." The "Hotel Etiquette" section in S. A. Frost's *Laws and By-Laws of American Society* (1869) similarly specified that "no lady will stare around the room" while dining in a hotel, and that if she "accepts any civility from a gentleman . . . she must thank him; but by no means start a conversation with him." For a woman to invite or allow an unfamiliar man to approach her, the guides made clear, was a breach of propriety that could easily damage her reputation. Even a man to whom a woman had been properly introduced could present a problem, since excessive attention to him might lead others to question her virtue. "No lady," asserted Leslie, "can remain long in the drawing-room talking to a gentleman after all the rest have retired for the night, without subjecting herself to remarks which it would greatly annoy her to hear—whether merited or not. Neither is it well for her to be seen continually sitting at the same window with the same gentleman." This passage also highlights the importance of self-control, visual surveillance, and reputation in the enforcement of hotel etiquette: a woman was expected to withdraw from company voluntarily in order to avoid being left unobserved in the company of a man; otherwise, she could be fair game for speculation as to what might have transpired while nobody was watching.[40]

The addition of alcohol to unwelcome overtures only heightened the magnitude of a man's indiscretion toward a woman. A stranger's offer of a shared drink was so improper as to be worthy of open disdain—a strong reaction indeed in the genteel milieu of etiquette advice. "If a stranger whom you do not know, and to whom you have had no introduction, takes the liberty of asking you to drink wine with him," recommended Leslie, "refuse at once, positively and coldly, to prove that you consider it an unwarranted freedom. And so it is." Indeed, even familiar men were to be kept at a distance when alcohol was involved. A woman was advised that if so invited, "if you are acquainted with the gentleman, or have been introduced to him (not else), you may comply with his civility, and when both glasses are filled, look at him, bow your head, and taste the wine." Leslie noted, however, that it was "not customary, in America, for a lady to empty her glass,—or indeed, to take wine with the same gentleman after the first day," a practice which she characterized as "improper, indelicate, and we will say mean."[41]

The advice given to women on how to behave in hotels was pervaded by sexual tension. While usually it lay just below the surface, in some cases it was quite apparent. In one instance, Leslie opined: "We are always sorry to hear a young lady use such a word as 'polking' when she tells of having been engaged in a certain dance too fashionable not long since; but happily, now it is fast going out, and almost banished from the best society. To her honour be it remembered, that Queen Victoria has prohibited the polka being danced in her presence. How can a genteel girl bring herself to say, 'Last night I was polking with Mr. Bell,' or 'Mr. Cope came and asked me to polk with him.' Its coarse and ill-sounding name is worthy of the dance." The imagery here is both elaborate and evocative. The polka had been popularized, among other venues, at numerous hotel parties, and many polkas had been named after particular hotels, with their names and images featured on the sheet music. The word *poke* was a common slang term for sexual intercourse. A pun about men and women "polking/poking" in hotels thus laid bare the sense of sexual danger that characterized them in the middle-class imagination.[42]

Not all contact between men and women in hotels was necessarily improper, but sexual danger lurked even in the most decent and honorable of gestures. Nineteenth-century bourgeois culture held that the inherent vulnerability of the female sex meant that women required the constant aid and protection of men, perhaps never more so than when the former were away from home and thus without the guardianship of a fatherly or husbandly patriarch. Cecil B. Hartley, the author of *The Gentleman's Book of Etiquette and Manual of Politeness* (1860), reminded men of the "many little courtesies which you may offer to a lady when traveling, even if she is an entire stranger to you." Well-mannered men, he explained, should always stand ready to escort women through the unruly city and into the safety of their accommodations. "When arriving at a hotel," instructed Hartley, "escort your companion to the parlor, and leave her there whilst you engage rooms. As soon as her room is ready, escort her to the door, and leave her, as she will probably wish to change her dress or lie down, after the fatigue of traveling." The reader was further advised to ask to escort a woman to meals and otherwise offer his aid. Yet if a man appeared too eager to help a woman, he invited suspicion. "Be careful however," warned Hartley, "not to be too attentive, as you then become officious, and embarrass when you mean to please." Even the "duty of Christian courtesy" championed by the evangelical etiquette writer George Winfred Hervey could easily become problematic. "The pious traveller," he explained in 1852, "should not take a female stranger under his protection, any further than to defend her against insults—to offer her his hand in alighting from a stage-coach, and to perform for her other common offices of kindness." After all, women, too, could be other than what they seemed in an anonymous urban milieu, and a gentleman's "officious attention to females, of whose character he knows nothing, may endanger his reputation." Nobody, it seemed, could be above sexual suspicion.[43]

The promiscuous sociability of the hotel put respectable reputations at risk even in the absence of contact with the opposite sex. In the house of strangers, character often had to be judged at a glance on the basis of appearance or comportment, a circumstance that made it all too easy for improper impressions to be formed. "Any bold action or boisterous deportment in a hotel," warned one etiquette expert, "will expose a lady to the most severe censure of the refined around her, and may render her liable to misconstruction, and impertinence." And because hotels were leading headquarters of the sex trade, such "misconstruction" could be of the most dire sort. Sexual restraint was among the most important elements of middle-class American women's self-image, and prostitutes symbolized everything that a reputable woman must not be.

Remarkably, etiquette-book advice on hotels demonstrated palpable anxiety over the possibility that a lady might be mistaken for a sex worker. Because prostitutes were thought to seek a temporary legitimacy and avoid detection by associating with respectable women, these latter were advised to "have little to say to a woman who is travelling without a companion, and whose face is painted, who wears a profusion of long curls about her neck, who has a meretricious expression of eye, and who is over-dressed. It is safest to avoid her." Notwithstanding the alleged reliability of these signs, though, respectable women were warned to take additional precautions. "A lady alone at a hotel," one authority warned, "should wear the most modest and least conspicuous dress appropriate to the hour of the day. Full dress must not be worn unless she has an escort present." Moreover, because prostitutes solicited trade through loitering and eye contact, respectable women were admonished not to "linger in the halls of a hotel, but pass through them quietly, never stopping alone for a moment," nor to be seen "lolling or lounging in a public parlor," nor to "stand alone at the front windows of a hotel parlor . . . out on the porch, or, indeed, in any conspicuous place." In a world of commercial sexuality and easy self-transformation, respectable women found themselves struggling to distance themselves from their moral nemeses.[44]

Of course, most violations of hotel etiquette were far less serious than being mistaken for a prostitute or a lothario. Even minor infractions could scuff a person's reputation, though, and advice givers were ready to help. The author of *The Handbook of the Man of Fashion* (1845) cautioned against overeagerness at the dinner table, calling it "a vulgar determination to 'get the full worth of [one's] money.'" The anonymous author also counseled readers to avoid gaffes like disturbing other hotel patrons by speaking too loudly, singing in public, or playing the piano. The guide even went into detail about what to do if one suspected hotel employees of having stolen something, the proper method for leaving a greeting card, how to pay a visit to one hotel resident so as to avoid offending another, and why it was a faux pas to return to one's room while it was being cleaned.[45]

But what these catalogues of missteps and ways of avoiding them most clearly demonstrated was that nineteenth-century Americans were trying to learn how to behave in close quarters and among unknown people. Those involved, from etiquette-book writers to their anxious readers, were doing something more generalized than regulating the social space of hotels. They were also acclimating themselves to, and finding social protocols appropriate for, new conditions of urban modernity.

CONCLUSION: DISCIPLINING MODERN SPACES

The various kinds of misbehavior and crime endemic to hotels, and the means devised to impose order upon them, attest to the importance of the term *social* in the social technology that was the hotel. The difficulties that attended the rise of the hotel as the dominant form of public hospitality in America had much to do with the particular architectural form of the hotel, but at base they were questions of human behavior in a transformed national landscape. In other words, the primary difficulty consisted not in the way people interacted with hotels themselves but rather in how the space of the hotel—itself a product of human creativity and responsiveness to change—allowed people to interact with one another. Recognizing this fact makes it easier to understand the nature of discipline in modernity.

Among the key innovations of the hotel was the way it depersonalized the provision of hospitality, replacing the patriarchal figure of the innkeeper and his subordinate family with a salaried hotel manager and a corps of employees. This, combined with a tenfold increase in the size of public houses in the transition from taverns to hotels, meant that proprietors were no longer in a position to personally supervise their establishments. This transformation was concurrent with the gradual decline of royal autocracy in Western societies and its replacement with parliamentary democracy—a farewell to kings, who were succeeded as sovereign by an active, voting citizenry. In both instances, authority and discipline emanating from a single human being became impracticable, whether at the human scale of a hotel or the geographic scale of an entire nation. What gradually emerged in its place was a new regime of surveillance in which people's greatest concern was not that their misbehavior would be discovered and punished by the sovereign and his minions. Rather, it was that their society, with its new political structures and fragile sense of civil order, might collapse unless they were successful in minding the behavior not only of their neighbors but also of their own errant selves.

Part Three   A Nation of Hosts and Guests

WE NOW TURN TO THE influence of the hotel on American society more generally. In Part One we explored the origins of the hotel form, the reasons it evolved from an experimental building type into a ubiquitous presence on the national landscape, and its subsequent development domestically and overseas. Part Two focused on the internal workings of the hotel, from the everyday experience of hotel life to the laws governing hospitality and the difficulty of maintaining order. In Part Three I take up the question of how the hotel's particular operational, architectural, social, and legal characteristics shaped the American scene.

This section also marks the beginning of an interpretive shift from artifact to agency: we now begin to consider how hotels themselves changed the United States in ways that were distinct from how the nation was being reshaped by the same large-scale transformations that occasioned the hotel form itself. To use the term *agency* to describe the influence of hotels is in one sense problematic, since intentionality can hardly be assigned to inanimate objects like buildings. Still, it is possible to argue that the spatial arrangements and social behaviors specific to hotels led to or at least favored particular historical outcomes. The hotel was a symptom of certain epochal shifts, most notably the weakening of ties between people and places; but it was also a deliberate creation intended to advance an economic and political project. Winston Churchill famously remarked: "We shape our buildings; thereafter they shape us." Part Three is an exploration of how this worked in the case of the hotel.

Hotels were engines of modernity because they served as successful models for various aspects of urban life. The hotel functioned as a sort of patterning device, an institution in which people developed expectations and behaviors appropriate to new modes of city living. This process was not without conflict. Even as nineteenth-century Americans eagerly constructed innovative systems of transportation and accommodation, their effect on cherished notions of community and domesticity often generated considerable anxiety. As it turned out, though, it was precisely those characteristics of hotel life that most agitated the hotel's detractors—its institutional trust of strangers, its visual and social opacity, and its potential to transcend the limits of the traditional household—that made it into a useful template for urban living. In the end, despite critics' misgivings and public apprehension, Americans' experience with hotels helped teach them how to adapt to the world of strangers that was the modern city.

Eight *American Forum*

Hotels and Civil Society

"THERE IS ONE COUNTRY in the world which, day in, day out, makes use of an unlimited freedom of political association," observed Alexis de Tocqueville after his 1831 visit to the United States. "And the citizens of this same nation, alone in the world, have thought of using the right of association continually in civil life, and by this means have come to enjoy all the advantages which civilization can offer." The aristocratic young Frenchman, who had come in search of clues as to what the rise of equality might mean for Europe, found much to admire in the United States; but it was the citizenry's distinctive "capacity to pursue great aims in common" that inspired some of the most superlative language in Tocqueville's classic text *Democracy in America*. The people of the nineteenth-century United States were indeed avid associators, banding together in pursuit of all manner of objectives, from claiming title to valuable land on the frontier to electing political representatives to holding dances and sponsoring lectures. In the terminology of political theory, the nation boasted an exceptionally vibrant civil society.[1]

The various forms of action that make up civil society necessarily require gathering places, since associational activity involves people meeting one another, recognizing shared interests, fostering feelings of belonging, discussing goals, and formulating plans of action. All urban societies have created spaces of special importance to civic participation: the ancient Greek agora and the Roman forum were the prototypes in Western civilizations, their functions assumed in subsequent centuries by town commons, marketplaces, piazzas, greens, and courthouse squares. In the nineteenth-century United States, hotels were hugely popular places of assembly, hosting such a broad range of activities that they became vitally important centers of civil society. They were admittedly not unique in this respect, since there were other institutions that served some of the same purposes, including clubhouses, churches, fraternal lodges, union halls, saloons, and the streets themselves.[2]

But hotels were different. They played a distinctive role in organizing civil society because they functioned simultaneously as gathering places and travel accommodations. Hotels brought local people together, put them into contact with strangers and outsiders, and tied them into larger networks of commerce, politics, and association; this allowed citizens to transpose their local activities into organized action on a regional or even national scale. By focusing and projecting the power of direct personal contact—a species of influence that worked more directly than traffic in goods, money, or information—hotels became epicenters of new, translocal modes of affiliation and exchange appropriate to a modern nation that was highly complex yet still operated primarily on the basis of face-to-face interaction.

HOTELS IN THE COMMUNITY

Hotels were important centers of community life. Local people went to hotels for a wide variety of reasons ranging from celebration to mourning. This owed in large part to their central locations in cities and towns: hotels, especially first-class establishments, occupied prominent places within the urban fabric, marking and in many cases defining the districts with the densest crowds and the heaviest pedestrian and vehicular traffic. As a result, residents often passed through or stopped at hotels on the way to appointments or while out strolling. But the local significance of hotels involved more than just the sum total of peoples' individual movements. Organized groups made hotels into leading venues for both private functions and public events because they offered unparalleled facilities for associational life and civic engagement. Hotels helped clubs, societies, and other associations overcome spatial and financial limits on their activities. By renting or informally using hotels, groups could escape the relatively cramped spaces of private homes and instead hold large public meetings; moreover, they could do so even if they had too few members or too little money to build permanent clubhouses or headquarters.

Cleveland's unique combination of regional representativity and archival sources makes it the perfect place to illustrate how hotels functioned as local gathering places. Platted in 1796 and incorporated as a village in 1814, Cleveland remained a small frontier town until the completion of the Ohio and Erie Canal in 1832 made it a key market center for the northern half of the state. Like many other urban areas around the Great Lakes, it gained population rapidly, reaching 43,000 by 1860, 160,000 by 1880, and more than 380,000 by century's end. Decades later, the Ohio Historical Records Survey Project, a team of New Deal–sponsored researchers, compiled *Historic Sites of Cleveland: Hotels and Taverns,* a 750-page index of newspaper articles, official records, and other primary sources that offers unparalleled access to the role of hotels in the life of a growing community.[3]

Many of the uses to which Clevelanders put their hotels revolved around the local economy. Numerous individuals opened shops or offices or otherwise did business in hotels. The American House alone was the workplace of booksellers, physicians, dance instructors, barbers, opticians, an instrument and music retailer, a fabric salesman, a banker, an elocution teacher, a hoop skirt and corset maker, and the operators of a newsstand, a hack service, and a billiard hall. Hotels also hosted meetings of entire trade groups and corporations. In the summer of 1843, for example, "merchants, forwarders, and produce dealers" were called to the American House "to take measures to organize a Board of Trade." A few years later, a group of local businessmen met at the newly constructed Weddell House to establish a telegraph line, and three weeks later the hotel became home to the city's first telegraph office. In January 1850 the stockholders of the recently organized Cleveland, Columbus, and Cincinnati Railroad convened one of many meetings held at the Weddell House and American House. Later in the decade, local insurance underwriters held a three-day meeting at the American House to set rates and tonnage limits for policies on steamboats. Throughout the century, Cleveland hotels continued to be meeting places of choice for innumerable local business groups, including typesetters, saloonkeepers, lumber dealers, traveling salesmen, beekeepers, schoolteachers, homeopaths, wool growers, and beer brewers.[4]

Hotels also attracted political activity (fig. 8.1). They figured in local politics down to the ward level, with parties meeting at hotels to nominate candidates for city council, county convention, and state legislature. Cleveland newspapers regularly printed notices like a March 1839 announcement of "the name of C. M. Gidings, for councilman in the second ward, at the ensuing election, in obedience to the nomination made at the City Hotel, Saturday evening, 23d ult." Hotels also hosted speeches and rallies. In 1852, for example, Mayor Case of Cleveland gave a speech from the balcony of the American House, as did a group of "Democratic orators" who spoke to the local "Irish Catholic population" who gathered in front of the hotel on an autumn evening four years later. Presidential elections were invariably followed by victory parties at local hotels. In 1848 the *Daily True Democrat* reported "a Whig jubilee banquet" to celebrate the election of Zachary Taylor; eight years later, a Whig newspaper reported, "Our Democratic friends had a jolly time last night, celebrating the James Buchanan victory at the American House.

. . . We like to see folks happy, but should like it better in a better cause." Hotels were also important sites of nonelectoral mobilization. Women involved in antiliquor reform sometimes staged demonstrations at hotels because they served alcohol. In 1871 the *Cleveland Leader* reported that "the ladies of the Women's Temperance league of the iron ward assembled at the Presbyterian church . . . then advanced upon the Cataract House," where they demanded that the proprietor close the bar. Activists often rewarded hotelkeepers who stopped selling liquor by renting rooms at their establishments for their meetings. Local hotel-based activities like these formed key building blocks in developing national political systems.[5]

But the most common local uses of hotels were driven less by business or politics than by sociability and associationalism. All manner of groups held events in the public rooms of Cleveland hotels. The American House, for example, played host in the 1840s and 1850s to meetings, fairs, dinners, and balls organized by the Cleveland Fire Department, the Cleveland Foreign Missionary Society, the Cleveland Light Artillery, St. Paul's Episcopal Church, the Cleveland Hibernian Guards, the Society of St. Andrews, the Cleveland Yagers, the Odd Fellows, St. George's Benevolent Society, the managers of the Ohio State

8.1   New York's Tammany Hotel was the headquarters of the most famous political machine in American history. (Milstein Division of United States History, Local History, and Genealogy, The New York Public Library, Astor, Lenox and Tilden Foundations)

Fair, the Cataract Engine Company No. 5, the Cleveland Grays, the Alert Hose Company No. 1, and two groups of spiritualists—this in addition to numerous weddings, cotillions, and assemblies. Even organizations that had their own buildings found them unsuitable for some events and instead used hotels as temporary auxiliary spaces: congregations that worshiped at their church but would not hold a fair there, or fire companies disinclined to have a dance at the firehouse. These two cases also demonstrated a shared belief that hotels were central to community life: the associations thought it important to hold functions in the public eye, and hotelkeepers allowed some groups to use ballrooms free of charge if their efforts were charitable or otherwise served the common good. As with business and politics, hotels would soon make it possible for locally based associations to grow into regional and national networks of convention-holding organizations.[6]

These local uses of hotels in Cleveland were paralleled in cities nationwide (fig. 8.2). Archives, newspaper indexes, and special collections held in state, county, and city historical societies across the United States document analogous uses of hotels for business, political, and associational purposes; the New-York Historical Society's Quinn Collection, for example, includes thousands of items detailing myriad uses of hotels in Gotham. Similarly, when city boosters published celebratory municipal histories in the late nineteenth and early twentieth centuries, they made frequent mention of hotels as prominent centers of civic life, often including sections devoted entirely to public houses and the important events that took place in them. And many historians writing urban community studies have—sometimes directly but more often in the course of addressing other subjects—noted the importance of hotels as local gathering places. There can be little doubt that hotels were among the most important physical and social spaces in American cities throughout the nineteenth century and into the twentieth.[7]

HOTEL HINTERLANDS

Hotels played a distinctive role in American urbanism because they served as points of contact between local communities and the national urban system. Travelers were indispensable in maintaining these links between the local and the national. While there were many places in cities and towns where people gathered, only hotels allowed local populations to interact constantly with travelers, strangers, and other outsiders. In so doing, hotels amplified the power of human mobility to integrate communities into regional and national networks. Every hotel sat at the center of a travel hinterland—an extended geographic area from which it drew people in and put them into direct personal contact.

The idea of hinterlands is used by urban geographers and historians to explain the development of cities and their relationship with the surrounding countryside. Michael Conzen has demonstrated that the geography of banking activity, especially the correspondent linkages among cities of different magnitudes and their financial hinterlands, reveals the economic underpinnings of the urban network and its maturation around the turn of the twentieth century. William Cronon has shown how Chicago became a regional

8.2   Richard Caton Woodville's 1848 painting *War News from Mexico,* which used a hotel entrance as the setting for its depiction of a community receiving news that the nation was at war, became one of the most popular prints of the nineteenth century. (Private collection, on loan to the National Gallery of Art, Washington)

metropolis by serving a vast ecological hinterland: the city established itself as the leading western market for grain, lumber, and meat, and grew wealthy by coordinating the flow of commodities from fields, forests, and ranches to wholesalers and consumers. The broader conclusion of these hinterland studies is that the most successful nineteenth-century cities prospered by controlling the collection and distribution of capital and commodities throughout the surrounding territory. What these studies underplay somewhat is the importance of the people who coordinated these economic processes. Nineteenth-century business was absolutely dependent upon travelers because human labor was required to transport goods and carry information. As surely as a town or city could not prosper without access to commodities and capital, it would wither away without visits from entrepreneurs, teamsters, and salesmen. In a travel-dependent economy, hotels played the same role in facilitating human mobility that banks played with respect to capital and warehouses, lumberyards, and stockyards did with respect to commodities.[8]

Travel hinterlands can be studied in much the same way as capital and commodity hinterlands. Travel itineraries were never measured in the same way as flows of money and goods, which were tabulated in numerous state industrial reports and economic censuses. There exists, however, an untapped source of historical evidence on human mobility: hotel registers. Throughout the nineteenth century and well into the twentieth, hotelkeepers required guests to sign the register when they checked in. Many such registers have been preserved in state and local historical societies. Each one contains a comprehensive and systematic survey of a hotel's guests, including their names, places of residence, and dates of arrival, and can be used to generate a map of the shape, extent, and concentration of a hotel's travel hinterland. Every guest register is thus a detailed historical-geographic portrait of how individual hotels tied their communities into regional, national, and sometimes international networks of travel.

In trying to understand how hotels connected local communities into larger networks of travel, we will consider three hotels in cities of varying size and importance: Plattsmouth, Nebraska; Richmond, Virginia; and New York City. The first of these was a small hotel in a small community shortly after its integration into an important system of transportation: the Platte Valley House in Plattsmouth in 1870 and 1871. Plattsmouth was first settled by European Americans in 1853. As its name suggests, it stood at the place where the Platte River emptied into the Missouri River, making it an important stopping point for people who were traveling west. It gradually became a local market center for farmers, and its first grain elevator was built in 1868. By 1869 it was a stop on the Burlington and Missouri Railroad, and as of 1870 its population had grown to a modest 3,500. The Platte Valley House was a three-story settlement hotel, eight bays wide and six deep, built of wood and painted white, and probably contained no more than two dozen rooms. This was anything but a high-profile palace hotel in a large city, and as such gives a better sense of the operation of any number of small-city hotels in the national interior.[9]

A map (fig. 8.3) of the places of residence of guests who checked into the Platte Valley House on fifty-three evenly distributed days from September 1870 to April 1871 reveals the two main characteristics of its human hinterland. First, the hotel was strongly subregional. More than half of its guests came from its own state and the one adjacent: 35 percent from Nebraska (two-fifths of these from Plattsmouth itself, another two-fifths from Omaha, Lincoln, Nebraska City, and Ashland, and the remaining fifth from about fifteen towns across the state) and 19 percent from Iowa (about half from its Missouri River cities and the other half from smaller towns farther east).

Second, even though Plattsmouth was a small and relatively remote town, its hotel

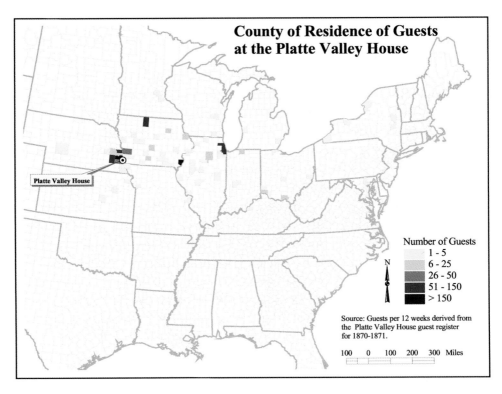

**County of Residence of Guests
at the Platte Valley House**

Platte Valley House

Number of Guests
1 - 5
6 - 25
26 - 50
51 - 150
> 150

Source: Guests per 12 weeks derived from
the Platte Valley House guest register
for 1870-1871.

100   0   100   200   300   Miles

8.3   The travel hinterland of the Platte Valley House, Plattsmouth, Nebraska, September 1870–April 1871. (GIS map by John C. Barney, University of New Mexico School of Architecture and Planning)

was regularly patronized by people from much larger cities. Forty-five percent of the guests at the Platte Valley House came from states farther east: Illinois accounted for 8 percent of all the hotel's guests, with the rest coming from New York, Ohio, Indiana, Massachusetts, Missouri, and other states located mostly in the Midwest, Northeast, and uppermost South. Of these travelers from farther afield, the great majority were urbanites from Chicago, New York, Boston, Philadelphia, Cincinnati, and other state metropolises. Fewer than 1 percent of guests came from places west of Plattsmouth. Overall, the hotel's clientele represented fewer than half of the thirty-seven states then in the Union.

A few additional features of the data are worthy of note. Employees of the Burlington and Missouri Railroad accounted for fully 11 percent of guests, indicating the importance of the rail network and the hotel's integration into a coordinated system of transportation and accommodation. On a related note, guests from farther away were far more likely to hail from the largest cities in their states, suggesting that long-distance travel occurred primarily within the urban system and indicating that because many of the Platte Valley House's overnight guests came from the many tiny towns that dotted Nebraska and Iowa, they, too, probably enjoyed at least some contact with the eastern urbanites who stopped at Plattsmouth. Finally, for comparative purposes it bears mentioning that of the 709 guests identifiable from the register, only two were foreigners: one from Canada West, the other from Bristol, England. The international presence at the hotel was thus existent but negligible.

The Exchange-Ballard Hotel in Richmond occupied an intermediate urban position. Richmond had been the largest city in the Old Dominion since the colonial period, and the organization of its first railway and the Tredegar Iron Works in the 1830s made it into a regional industrial powerhouse. The city continued to grow and served as the Confederate capital, and despite a serious wartime fire and major flooding five years later, by 1870 it had just over 51,000 inhabitants. In comparative terms, however, it ranked only in the upper-middle range of urban places: it was the nation's twenty-fourth-most-populous city, with about fifteen times as many residents as Plattsmouth yet only one-twenty-sixth as many as New York City. The Exchange-Ballard was formed from two hostelries: the Exchange Hotel, a four-story 1841 Greek Revival structure designed by Isaiah Rogers, and the Ballard House, a five-story Italianate building that opened in 1855. After several years as competitors, the two hotels merged, joined by a pedestrian bridge over the street between them. While the Exchange and Ballard had been leading hotels before the Civil War, in subsequent years the limitations of their older architecture kept them just short of the ranks of the city's premier houses.[10]

The distribution of guests at the Exchange-Ballard Hotel in 1870 and 1871 (fig. 8.4) indicates a national hinterland, yet with a very strong intraregional and in-state orientation. The hotel welcomed visitors from thirty-two of thirty-seven states, but this constituted a very uneven geographic profile. No fewer than 68 percent of the hotel's patrons came from the South, making it very much a regional institution. Moreover, fully 45 percent came from Virginia alone, a measure that would make the Exchange-Ballard seem more limited by subregion than the Platte Valley House but for the fact that Virginia was so much more populous than Nebraska. The hotel's nonsouthern clientele was heavily northeastern and even more heavily urbanized. New York, Pennsylvania, New Jersey, and the states of New England accounted for 87 percent of nonsouthern guests, with the largest cities disproportionately represented: 339 of 366 visitors from New York State were from Manhattan and Brooklyn, 105 of 146 Pennsylvanians were Philadelphians, and 39 of 53 guests from Massachusetts hailed from the Boston area. Finally, while the Exchange-Ballard hosted a few people from overseas, the 11 visitors from England, 1 from Scotland, 2 from Canada, and 2 from Cuba represented a puny proportion of the almost 2,700 guests who stayed at the hotel on the fifty-two days surveyed.

A rather different hotel hinterland was that of New York City's St. Nicholas Hotel, which a visiting Charles Dickens called "the lordliest caravanserai in the world" and a local newspaper referred to as "the *ne plus ultra* of expense, of richness, of luxury." Opened in 1853, the St. Nicholas was a five-story masonry structure that occupied an entire city block along Broadway, contained five hundred rooms, and had been the first hotel to cost more than one million dollars. The hotel served a city that had for decades been the unchallenged national metropolis of the United States, with a population, including Brooklyn, of

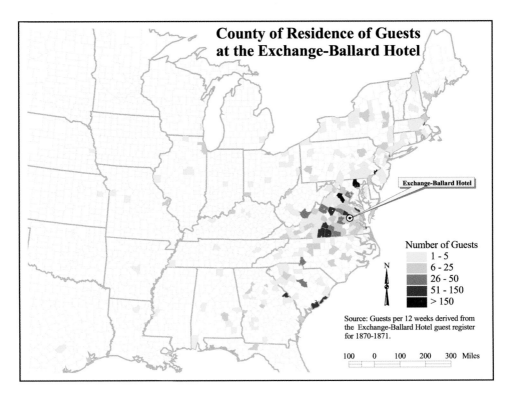

County of Residence of Guests at the Exchange-Ballard Hotel

Exchange-Ballard Hotel

Number of Guests
1 - 5
6 - 25
26 - 50
51 - 150
> 150

N

Source: Guests per 12 weeks derived from the Exchange-Ballard Hotel guest register for 1870-1871.

100   0   100   200   300 Miles

8.4   The travel hinterland of the Exchange-Ballard Hotel, Richmond, Virginia, March 1870–August 1871. (GIS map by John C. Barney, University of New Mexico School of Architecture and Planning)

about one million people. In terms of its position within American hoteldom, the colossal St. Nicholas overshadowed the Exchange-Ballard and was the polar opposite of the Platte Valley House.[11]

The distribution of more than 2,800 guests at the St. Nicholas (fig. 8.5), derived from four weeklong samples taken from the spring and summer of 1858, reveals an exceptionally extensive hinterland that drew mainly from cities within the United States but also had a significant overseas reach. During those twenty-eight days, the hotel received visitors from every one of the nation's then-thirty-two states. Moreover, state-by-state analysis indicates a geographically proportionate clientele. No single state predominated: 17 percent of guests were from New York (not an unexpectedly high number for a state with a quarter of the nation's twenty most-populous cities), 15 percent came from Massachusetts (with one-sixth of the forty largest cities), 9 percent called Pennsylvania home, and 8 percent hailed from Virginia, but after that no one state exceeded 5 percent of the total. The guests were heavily urbanized, with Bostonians accounting for more than three-quarters of those from Massachusetts, Philadelphians amounting to more than four-fifths of Pennsylvanians, and about 96 percent of Marylanders hailing from Baltimore. The characteristic that most distinguished the St. Nicholas from its smaller cousins, however, was its international

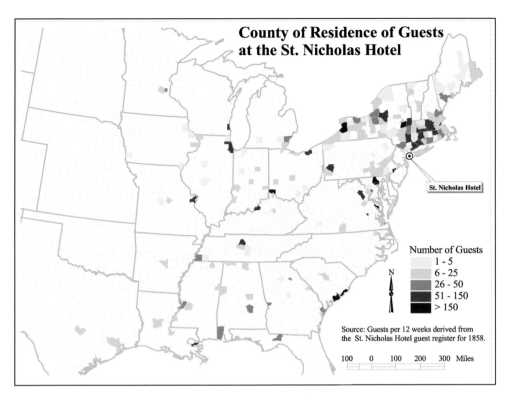

County of Residence of Guests at the St. Nicholas Hotel

St. Nicholas Hotel

Number of Guests
1 - 5
6 - 25
26 - 50
51 - 150
> 150

N

Source: Guests per 12 weeks derived from the St. Nicholas Hotel guest register for 1858.

100   0   100   200   300   Miles

8.5   The travel hinterland of the St. Nicholas Hotel, New York City, April–July 1858. (GIS map by John C. Barney, University of New Mexico School of Architecture and Planning)

clientele. Almost 5 percent of its guests came from foreign countries and territories, including England, Canada, Scotland, France, Spain, Germany, Mexico, Sweden, Puerto Rico, South Africa, Brazil, Venezuela, Cuba, Trinidad, and India.

The lived experience of being at the St. Nicholas must therefore have involved a constant stream of arrivals of people from far away. On any given day, an observer could have expected to see a dozen Bostonians checking in as guests, along with seven Philadelphians, four people from Albany, and three from Baltimore, these among the hundreds of people who passed through the hotel for other reasons. The scores of new daily arrivals would typically have included a traveler from overseas not just every day but about every two to three hours. At the St. Nicholas, guests who had traveled hundreds or even thousands of miles were not an occasional curiosity but a regular presence, and the hotel's managers would have been accustomed to constant interaction with visitors from many different places and cultures. In terms of human hinterlands and networks of influence, these guests represented a continuous flow of information and a source of contacts. Any sufficiently determined person could walk into the St. Nicholas on any given day and, using the guest register, gain access to people with firsthand knowledge of much of the United States; within a week or two, one could meet people from much of the Atlantic world. In effect, the St. Nicholas was a cosmopolitan crossroads, home to constantly revolving colonies of visitors from scores of other cities and a number of foreign countries.

Far more important than the differences among these three hotels, however, was the fact that all did the same kind of work: each welcomed travelers whose presence and activities helped determine its city's place within the urban hierarchy. These hotels represent just three out of the many thousands that operated in the nineteenth-century United States, each having its own hinterland, and all collectively forming an economy of human mobility that extended across the continent and overseas. Hotel hinterlands functioned in ways that were analogous to commodity and capital hinterlands. In the same way that cities became prosperous by making themselves markets for goods or entrepôts of capital, hotels depended for success upon their ability to simultaneously attract and accommodate flows of travelers—the human agents who actually operated and coordinated the kinds of economic activity that have more commonly attracted the attention of historians. Whatever a hotel's size, class, and drawing power, every one played the essential urbanistic role of tying its community into expanding networks of commerce, politics, and association.

COMMERCE, CONSUMPTION, AND MATERIAL CULTURE AT THE HOTEL

Nineteenth-century Americans traveled for many reasons, the most important of which was to make a living. It is easy to forget how personal business was in the nineteenth century. In a time before mail-order catalogues and when telegraphs were prohibitively expensive, trade necessarily involved direct interactions between people. At every level of commerce and in every line of business—wholesale and retail, durables and consumables, and especially personal services and entertainment—the work of buying and selling required people to go from place to place.

The nineteenth-century United States was abuzz with commercial travelers. Peddlers, for centuries a familiar sight on the roads of Europe and America, continued to move from town to town plying their wares. They were joined around 1810 by wholesale jobbers who purchased large shipments of goods and broke them into smaller lots for shopkeepers unable to buy in bulk. Because this new arrangement offered retailers a wider range of goods, they traveled more frequently to see jobbers in places like New York City, Philadelphia, and Baltimore. In the 1820s, big-city jobbers started sending their clerks on lengthy trips to visit store owners, and in the 1830s, many of these clerks began selling directly to householders, heralding the birth of the traveling salesman. These dunning clerks and drummers, as they were then called, formed a veritable army of commerce that set out from urban centers and trooped around hinterlands. For all these commercial travelers and many others, hotels were both temporary homes and places of business.[12]

Cleveland sources contain a wealth of detail on how itinerant salesmen made use of hotels. Because house-to-house soliciting was not yet common, commercial travelers eager to make the most efficient use of their time in town often published advance notices

8.6   The St. Louis Hotel in New Orleans housed one of the busiest slave markets in the United States. People were sold from atop the block at center. (Collection of the author)

in local newspapers informing the public of what they were selling and at which hotel they could be found. In the 1850s, for example, the Cleveland Hotel hosted agents for the *New York Albian* newspaper, the "celebrated Dodge Patent Coal Grates," and the latest volumes of *Benton's Abridgements of the Debates in Congress.* Agricultural devices were among the favorite wares of hotel-based vendors. "While passing the City Hotel," reported the *Cleveland Leader* in 1858, "our attention was called to a new agricultural implement called 'Piccincott's Corn Planter and Coverer.' The inventor claims one man can furrow, plant, and cover ten acres of corn per day." Other salesmen offered items like "Felton's Grist Mill" or a "portable flouring mill and dressing machine." Some goods were marketed specifically to women, as when in 1857 "the ladies of Cleveland [were] invited to the parlor of the Bennett House . . . to examine a system for cutting and making dresses invented by S. F. Taylor," editor of the New York–based *Le Bon Ton.* Among the other innovative devices offered for sale in Cleveland hotels were "an invention for trimming vessels," a "Patent Candle Mould to make your own candles out of cold tallow," and "newly invented pantoscopic glasses." Focusing on Cleveland excludes an essential category of nineteenth-century business, and it is important to remember that one of the nation's leading slave markets was also conducted in a hotel rotunda (fig. 8.6). So depending on where they were traveling, people passing through a hotel lobby might see the latest wonders from the world of technology; or they might witness men, women, and children being vended as merchandise.[13]

Goods were not the only things sold at hotels; services were also on offer. Traveling purveyors of services were involved in something rather more personal than trade in goods: they interacted more closely with their clients, typically promising to transform them in some way. Many itinerants were practitioners of the paranormal. Some who visited Cleveland worked under the rubric of spiritualism, such as the group that "heard and witnessed strange communications" at the American House in 1850, or the famous Foxes, a mother-daughter team billed as "the original rappers." Others offered their services individually, like "Mademoiselle Arabella Hunter, planet reader and doctress," "Miss Zan, the clairvoyant," and "Madam Williams, the Celebrated Astrologist."[14]

But it was medical services that were most regularly offered in Cleveland's hotels. Local physicians were complemented by numerous travelers, ranging from qualified practitioners to probable quacks. The city's hotels served as examination rooms for legitimate doctors and dentists like Dr. Newton of Cincinnati, who received patients at the Euclid Place Hotel, and Dr. M. Hart of Philadelphia, who "advertised to do dental work of all kinds . . . free of charge" in his office at the Cleveland Temperance House. Rather more questionable were the practices of figures like "Dr. Lawrence, of New York, skilled oculist and aurist," who in 1864 was reportedly "working 'miracles' in restoring lost and injured sight and hearing" at the American House, or the "great French 'electrotician'" who visited the City Hotel in 1867 with "a new mode of galvanic treatment . . . enabl[ing] the dumb to talk, the deaf to hear, and the lame to walk." Clevelanders' readiness to accept medical care from strangers was particularly indicative: dabbling in the occult with a traveling medium might have seemed a harmless bit of fun; but allowing access to one's body to a person who had just arrived in town and would shortly be leaving, perhaps never to be seen again, bespoke a profound embrace of outsiders.[15]

Entertainers were also regular attractions. From traveling lecturers to touring thespians to circus performers, hotels frequently hosted people whose livelihood exposed audiences to attitudes and behaviors not rooted in their own communities. Among the speakers seeking to enlighten and persuade Clevelanders were Professor O. S. Fowler of New York, who offered "Private lectures to men only" on "Manhood, its Decline and Restoration," and "To ladies only" on "Maternity and Female Reflection"; John Allen, a "well-known lecturer on social wrongs and their remedy"; and the French exile Théophile Guérin, who spoke on "The Destinies and Prospects of France." The city was also visited by various actors and other stage performers, including "the dramatic company of which the Webb Sisters are the principal attraction," who stayed at the Angier House in 1861; "Sam Shapley and his minstrels," guests at the American House in 1864; and "W. J. Florence, the comedian, accompanied by Mr. Charles Gayler, the popular dramatist," who came in 1874. Actors could be especially influential tutors in self-fashioning: not only did their work involve taking on different roles and reenacting scenes from faraway places, their famously countercultural ways were also on display offstage since their temporary quarters at the hotel might allow local people to meet them in person. Even spectacles like "L. B. Lent's mammoth national circus," which did three Cleveland shows in July 1858, played a part in propagating new ideas by filling children and adults alike with wonder at the mysterious and exotic cultures that lay beyond their horizons and perhaps tempting them to run away and join the proverbial circus.[16]

While these paths of influence mostly involved travelers from regional and national metropoles serving as emissaries to hinterlands, there were other sorts of commercial activity in which local people made their voices heard higher up the urban hierarchy. Producers, tradespeople, and entrepreneurs formed business groups at the state and regional level in order to advance their shared interests in centers of political and economic power. Such trade groups made regular use of hotels, particularly when their conventions welcomed members and associates from far away. In Cleveland the Cleveland Hotel and the Kennard House hosted Ohio railroad men in 1854, the Ohio Editorial Association in 1858, a "convention of threshing machine manufacturers . . . from various parts of the country" in 1863, the "national convention of U.S. assessors" in 1864, "Freight Agents of all the railroads in the country" in 1866, the American Pharmaceutical Association in 1872, the Telegraph Associations of Buffalo, Erie, Cleveland, and Toledo in 1875, and the Ohio State Dairymen's Association in 1876. By the beginning of the twentieth century, hotel-based business conventions had become so common as to make group portraits of conferees seated at tables in hotel ballrooms (fig. 8.7) into something of a visual subgenre, with groups as varied as the American Bankers Association, the National Boot and Shoe Manufacturers' Association, the Deep Waterway Association, the National Association of Agricultural Implement and Vehicle Manufacturers, and, inevitably, the Illinois State Hotel Clerks Association posing for photographs.[17]

8.7 Many local, regional, and national organizations held conventions and other events in hotels, often commemorating such occasions with formal photographic portraits. (Library of Congress)

The role of hotels in propagating culture through commerce also operated in the realms of design, décor, and consumption. Hotels could advance new standards of material culture because they made décor into a capital good. When a hotelkeeper spent money to furnish and decorate his establishment, he did so with the expectation that his expenses and more would be returned to him in the form of higher income in the future. In purely economic terms, a hotel proprietor's purchases of furniture, carpeting, mirrors, drapery, dishes, silverware, and the like were analogous to a factory owner's installation of new machinery or a planter's procurement of enslaved Africans; all three fully intended to increase profits through capital investments. This is not to deny that hotelkeepers' choices were made in the interest of beauty and comfort but rather to emphasize that a hotel's aesthetic was itself a moneymaking proposition. The competitiveness of the hotel industry produced a continual escalation of capital spending on ornamentation; this dynamic was not limited to luxury hotels, since commercial houses and other midrange hostelries advertised the quality of their amenities alongside their lower rates. There were other establishments in which décor was a capital good, including theaters, pleasure gardens, and museums. But these could not serve as models for household consumption because they did not contain everyday domestic spaces. That role fell to the hotel, whose basic institutional imperatives made it an unattainable, yet perhaps no less compelling, model for private households.

Hotels served as leading exemplars for household decoration, furniture, and technology. The public parlors of hotels proved especially influential. The parlor was a room that existed both in the hotel and in the refined family dwelling, and the experience of lounging in a hotel parlor could influence guests in at least two ways. At the basic level of visual and tactile perception, every respectable hotel parlor featured well-appointed furniture and ornamentation, making the idea of owning such refinements seem not only possible but real and even expected. There was also the performative aspect: when hotel patrons fraternized in public parlors, they were in effect rehearsing a set of genteel behaviors that required certain material objects and environments. It is hardly surprising that many of the furniture manufacturers that supplied hotels also did a brisk business producing for the private-household market. The hotel's influence in the realm of technology was even more pronounced. Hotelkeepers could justify installing expensive devices as capital expenditures, effectively spreading their cost among the many users who passed through hotel bedchambers and public rooms. As a result, hotels became pioneers of domestic conveniences. Many amenities that would later become standard household accessories, including internal plumbing, steam heating, gas and electric lighting, and private telephones, had their first extensive trials in hotels.[18]

Hotels' role as propagators of material culture was amplified by their guests, who carried new ideas and practices over any distance they traveled. The urban historian Timothy Mahoney has demonstrated that hotels were particularly influential in the broad band of settlement between St. Louis and Chicago. The people who built and populated the towns of this region traveled regularly, and the aesthetic influence of hotel décor can be mapped out along their itineraries. In antebellum Iowa and Illinois, for example, wealthy families began to furnish their parlors in a new and more elegant style, purchasing expensive carpets and carefully crafted furniture, marble ornaments and mantelpieces, mirrors, curtains, and even gaslit chandeliers. The inspiration for these purchases involved two hotels frequented by midwestern wayfarers. The first was the Planters Hotel in St. Louis, the décor of which was copied by hotels constructed in the towns of Galena, Davenport, Quincy, and Dubuque in the 1840s and 1850s. The second was New York City's St. Nicholas Hotel, whose opulent parlors were particularly popular among the first families of Dubuque. The parlors of private homes in the river towns of the Midwest were thus part of networks of metropolitan aspiration that extended across distances of more than a thousand miles. Other historians have suggested how travel experiences, including hotel stays, influenced people in the South and the mountain West.[19]

The aggregate effect of the hotel system—which combined an exuberant commercial culture with legions of mobile human participants—was to serve as a conduit for goods, services, behaviors, and styles in a developing and expanding market culture. While economic exchange itself was a simple, utilitarian transaction, it was surrounded by a rich accretion of accompanying activities and practices that brought people together, led them to associate in new ways, and allowed them to influence one another. Because this influence worked not just through commodities but by way of actual personal interactions and expressive experiences, it made even mannerisms into potential cultural imports or exports. With the full maturation of the transportation network and the hotel system by the late nineteenth century, fewer and fewer Americans could long remain untouched by the commonalities and contrasts between their lives and those of people in cities and towns elsewhere in the nation.

HOTELS AND NATIONAL POLITICS

Less quotidian but more conspicuous than the economic function of hotels was their political role. Like the taverns that preceded them, hotels served as places of public assembly and deliberation; but they operated on a far larger geographic scale, integrating thousands of distant communities into a single national polity. Hotels became centers of political hospitality, places where citizens welcomed seekers and holders of high office, from state lawmakers and governors to congressmen and presidents. In time hotels assumed a broader significance that went beyond organizing electoral activity and hosting officials. By the era of the Civil War, hotels had become important political symbols, and violent incidents in local hotels often captured the attention of the entire nation.

The vast extent of the United States presented problems for the traditional practice of politics. In early America political authority had been exercised mostly within small, self-governing communities. While the governments of colonies and states did wield a significant measure of power, it was usually mediated through local officials before being brought to bear on individuals or families. Politics was thus conducted on the basis of face-to-face interactions in familiar gathering places like taverns and town halls. A nation that extended over hundreds of miles and comprised millions of citizens could not be governed in this way, however. Theorists of democratic governance had long believed that no republic could grow too extensive without reverting to despotism, and most Americans were suspicious of a government that could exercise power over them out of sight and at a far remove from their communities. Indeed, the Founders debated precisely this point while framing the Constitution. In *The Federalist* no. 14, James Madison argued that a central government could justly administer the entire United States and specifically proposed that this would require more and better public houses. Madison predicted that "the intercourse throughout the Union will be facilitated by new improvements" and that along with roads and coastal navigation, "accommodations for travelers will be multiplied and meliorated."[20]

Madison's expectations were fulfilled several years later by the invention of the hotel, but it was only in the 1830s that hotels demonstrated their capacity for integrating the United States politically. The local political uses of hotels soon expanded to include the creation of grassroots groups that coordinated their efforts with national political campaigns. In Cleveland, for example, local Whig supporters of William Henry Harrison for president met at the Franklin House in 1840 to organize a "Tippecanoe Club," the first of many formed in the city to mobilize support for national candidates. That year's election, often considered the first modern presidential campaign, saw unprecedented efforts by candidates to display themselves to voters in person. Harrison arrived in Cleveland that June on the steamer *Sandusky* and, before giving a speech at the American House, "insisted on walking from the dock to the hotel in order to demonstrate his physical fitness for the presidency despite his advanced age." The next morning he breakfasted with a group of gentlemen at the Pearl Street House and was introduced to "a roomful of ladies who assembled at seven o'clock to pay homage to the distinguished visitor" at his hotel. Locally coordinated campaign stops like these became a commonplace in the decades that followed.[21]

Once elected, political figures continued to use travel as a way to reinforce connections with their constituents. Official visits often partook of a set choreography reminiscent of George Washington's presidential tours. The officeholder would be greeted upon arrival by a delegation of local officials, public expressions of esteem and enthusiasm would be exchanged, and the visitor would be escorted to the leading hotel; later, the hotel dining room would be the site of a ceremonial dinner, followed in turn by lengthy orations by guests and local notables. In 1827, for example, Ohio Governor Allen Trimble arrived in Cleveland to celebrate the opening of the Erie and Ohio Canal. According to a newspaper account, "The governor's party disembarked at the foot of Superior street, and marched to the Public Square. In the afternoon, a large number of the visitors dined at the Franklin House." When Ohio Senator Benjamin F. Wade and Governor Salmon P. Chase stayed at the Angier House in 1856, they drew a crowd of fifteen hundred Clevelanders, who waved banners and played music in their honor. On his western tour of 1866, President Andrew Johnson traveled with an entourage that included "General Grant, Admiral Farragut,

Secretary Seward, Secretary Wells, General Custer, [and] Postmaster General Randall." The party, reported the *Cleveland Leader,* "arrived on the Lake Shore railroad in the afternoon. They were met by committees of soldiers and citizens and escorted to the Kennard House, where an informal supper was served, attended by the city council and invited guests. Afterwards President Johnson was introduced by Mayor Pelton from the balcony of the hotel to the crowd that had gathered."[22]

This last item, the speech from the hotel balcony, was the most repeated element of political visits. The highlight of Harrison's 1840 campaign visit to Cleveland came when he "spoke to a crowd of not less than three thousand people from the hotel balcony." In 1848 the Democratic presidential candidate General Lewis Cass gave a campaign speech from the balcony of Cleveland's New England Hotel, and General Winfield Scott "spoke from the balcony of the [American House] hotel" when he sought the presidency four years later. In 1852 Texas Senator Sam Houston recounted his exploits at the Battle of San Jacinto to a crowd gathered around the balcony of the Cleveland Hotel. And when General William Tecumseh Sherman stayed at the Kennard House in 1866, "throughout the day crowds gathered at the hotel but the General kept close to his room. The leading citizens, however, arranged an informal reception. . . . While [a band] was playing patriotic airs the general appeared on the balcony." Hotel balcony speeches were by no means unique to Cleveland. Not only did newspapers and magazines nationwide report such orations constantly, they also published illustrations of them frequently enough to make them into something of a set piece in American visual culture (fig. 8.8).[23]

Political travel in the United States redefined a practice that was common in monarchical societies but had to be recast on the basis of civil equality in order to work in a democracy. The royal visits of early modern and modern Europe, in which unelected rulers enjoyed the private hospitality of local nobles in their manor houses, were political performances intended to reinforce authority and obedience within a hierarchical system. Beginning with Washington's presidential tours, Americans created a democratic version of these visits in which enfranchised citizens welcomed elected officials and accommodated them in the local "palace of the public." In place of the personal hospitality of the local lord, the hotel expressed the collective hospitality of the community. This demonstrated an important kind of political reciprocity: in a reinscription of the host-guest relationship, each visiting politician was figuratively made into a member of the community's household in the same building where they welcomed other outsiders. In a democratic system, when public figures visited cities or towns, they acknowledged that the people were politically sovereign and validated their hosts' civic importance by situating them within a constellation of significant places.[24]

Communities recognized the importance of official travel, and used the visits of presidents, generals, and foreign dignitaries as indexes of their importance. When city boosters produced celebratory municipal histories in the late nineteenth and early twentieth centuries, they often included accounts of visits by such figures as Abraham Lincoln, Ulysses S. Grant, the marquis de Lafayette, and the Hungarian revolutionary Lajos Kossuth. Some

8.8   Hotels were the sites of innumerable public speeches, from Daniel Webster's 1851 oration at Boston's Revere House (*above*) to Theodore Roosevelt's 1901 appearance in front of the Antlers Hotel in Colorado Springs (*below*). (Newberry Library and Denver Public Library)

municipalities realized that political hospitality could influence their position in the urban system. The small town of Corydon, which had been designated the capital of the Indiana Territory, built a large stone hotel in 1816, apparently with the objective of making itself suitable as a permanent state capital. In a similar vein, the town of Columbia, which had served as the capital of the Republic of Texas, lost that title to Houston in 1836 in part because the Texas Congress decided that it lacked the kind of accommodations needed by government officials. This precedent must have served as a powerful lesson to the citizens of Austin, who in 1839 constructed the Bullock House, the city's first hotel, after the state capital was moved there.[25]

Over time, the political role of hotels broadened. In addition to integrating local communities into a national polity by hosting political travelers, hotels took on new organizational, symbolic, and iconographic functions. By midcentury, hotels served simultaneously as places of meeting and discussion, locations for political celebrations, staging areas for military musters, residences for public officials, national political headquarters, and targets of symbolic violence. The best way to understand how all these roles fit together is to consider the various ways hotels became implicated in national politics in the era of the Civil War.

A hotel figured prominently in one of the most pivotal incidents on the road to disunion. After the Kansas-Nebraska Act of 1854 organized the two territories for eventual statehood and stipulated that their inhabitants would decide by popular vote whether to be admitted as free or slave states, pro- and antislavery groups rushed to sponsor colonization efforts in an attempt to control the territories and their future representatives in Congress. Antislavery settlers founded Lawrence, Kansas, in 1854, anchoring the new town with the Free State Hotel, the name of which made abundantly clear their plans for the territory. On 21 May 1856, amid rising tensions over a stolen territorial election, a force of several hundred proslavery men armed with rifles and field artillery marched on Lawrence. After smashing the printing presses of the town's antislavery newspapers, the invaders cannonaded the hotel and set it ablaze. The attack on Lawrence was primarily symbolic: its target was not the inhabitants—none were killed during the incident—but the town's most important antislavery institutions. News of the sacking of Lawrence soon spread nationwide, with newspaper reports followed by dramatic illustrations of the ruins of the hotel (fig. 8.9). Two related incidents soon followed. On 22 May, Massachusetts Senator Charles Sumner, who had just given a speech denouncing previous aggressions against the "beleaguered town of Lawrence," was beaten into unconsciousness on the Senate floor by a South Carolina congressman whose uncle Sumner had insulted during his oration. And on 24 May the radical abolitionist John Brown and a group of Free State volunteers, enraged by the latest assault on Lawrence, murdered and dismembered five proslavery settlers in the infamous massacre at Pottawatomie, Kansas. The attack on Lawrence had initiated the most violent phase of Bleeding Kansas and inflamed sectional antagonism nationwide.[26]

Sectional divisions and hotel accommodations were also prominent at the national

8.9   A proslavery militia's demolition of the Free State Hotel in the town of Lawrence was one of the events that precipitated a years-long series of armed clashes known collectively as Bleeding Kansas. (Kansas State Historical Society)

political conventions of 1860. The Democratic Party met at South Carolina's largest hostelry, the Charleston Hotel. When the party's southern wing bolted the convention over northerners' refusal to advocate a federal slave code for the territories, one newspaper illustrated the scene by picturing despairing delegates leaving the hotel (fig. 8.10). The Republicans, who made Chicago's Tremont House hotel their convention headquarters, were also initially divided, but soon united behind Abraham Lincoln.[27]

In the political maneuvering that followed the election, hotels became focal points of official activity and symbols of sectional division. In early February 1861, Washington's Willard Hotel was the site of a peace conference chaired by ex-president John Tyler and attended by representatives from twenty-one northern and southern states that made a desperate effort to prevent disunion. The following month, two of the nation's leading newspapers illustrated the crisis with images that personified the conflict between the Union and the Confederacy (fig. 8.11). Two days before Abraham Lincoln's inauguration in March 1861, *Harper's Weekly* devoted its front page to an image of the president-elect addressing a cheering crowd from atop the portico of the Astor House in New York City; two weeks later, *Frank Leslie's Illustrated Newspaper* used virtually identical iconography in its own front-page image of Jefferson Davis speaking from the balcony of the Exchange Hotel in Montgomery, Alabama, shortly before his inauguration as provisional president of the Confederacy. In the military mobilization that followed, hotels were sites of troop musters, officer staff meetings, and other preparations for war, and newspaper illustrations reaffirmed the place of hotels in the visual vocabulary of the period. *Harper's Weekly* showed Confederate General Samuel McGowan reviewing the Thirty-Fifth Abbeville Volunteers of South Carolina (fig. 8.12) in front of the same hotel where the Democrats had split the previous year, and various newspapers carried illustrations of Union Army troops marching past their commanders in front of hotels in the North.[28]

But it was in wartime Washington that the political importance of hotels was most clearly demonstrated. Elected officials, their appointees and staffs, and workers in the fast-growing civil service converged on the nation's capital and soon made the Willard Hotel, located on Pennsylvania Avenue not far from the White House, into something of a shadow headquarters for the federal government and armed forces. Lincoln's first stop in Washington was at the Willard, and key administration figures like Ulysses S. Grant also took rooms at the hotel. The Willard's lobby and public rooms grew crowded with officials, reporters, and observers, and newspapers printed images of Lincoln and other leaders amid the throngs of people there (fig. 8.13). Writing in 1862, Nathaniel Hawthorne described the Willard as the city's alternate center of power:

8.10   The Charleston Hotel was the site of the 1860 convention that split the Democratic Party. (University of New Mexico Center for Southwest Research)

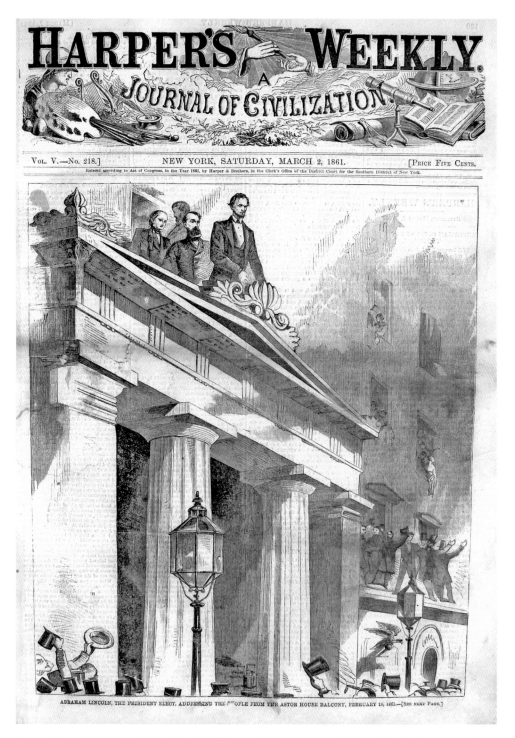

8.11 *Harper's Weekly* and *Frank Leslie's Illustrated Newspaper* used almost identical iconography in their coverage of the United States and Confederate presidents on the eves of their inaugurations. (University of New Mexico Center for Southwest Research and Library of Congress)

FRANK LESLIE'S
ILLUSTRATED

NEWSPAPER

Entered according to the Act of Congress, in the year 1861, by FRANK LESLIE, in the Clerk's Office of the District Court for the Southern District of New York.

No. 277—VOL. XI.]   NEW YORK, MARCH 16, 1861.   [PRICE 6 CENTS.

THE HON. JEFFERSON DAVIS, PRESIDENT-ELECT OF THE NEW SOUTHERN CONFEDERACY, ADDRESSING THE CITIZENS OF MONTGOMERY, ALA., FROM THE BALCONY OF THE EXCHANGE HOTEL, ON THE NIGHT OF FEBRUARY 16TH, 1861, AND PREVIOUS TO HIS INAUGURATION.—FROM A SKETCH BY OUR SPECIAL ARTIST.—SEE PAGE 258.

8.12   The year after the Democratic Party split there, the Charleston Hotel became a prime location for Confederate troop reviews. (Collection of the author)

It is the meeting-place of the true representatives of this country—not such as are chosen blindly and amiss by electors . . . but men who gravitate or are attracted hither by real business, or a native impulse to breathe the intensest atmosphere of the nation's life, or a genuine anxiety to see how this life-and-death struggle is going to deal with us. Nor these only, but all manner of loafers. Never, in any other spot, was there such a miscellany of people. You exchange nods with governors of sovereign states; you elbow illustrious men, and tread on the toes of generals; you hear statesmen and orators speaking in their familiar tones. You are mixed up with office-seekers, wire-pullers, inventors, artists, poets, prosers (including editors, army-correspondents, attachés of foreign journals, and long-winded talkers), clerks, diplomats, mail-contractors, railway directors, until your own identity is lost among them.

Another observer made the same point about the Willard some time later when he noted that "everybody called to Washington flocks to the halls of that great hotel if they desire to see anybody."[29]

Hotels were important symbolic sites throughout the war, with a constant drum-

8.13   An 1861 lithograph shows Abraham Lincoln at the Willard Hotel in Washington, where he stayed before moving into the White House. (Library of Congress)

beat of incidents confirming their political importance. The day after Virginia seceded, a Union colonel named Elmer E. Ellsworth entered the Marshall House in Alexandria to remove a rebel flag from its roof and was shot dead by the hotelkeeper, an ardent secessionist; Ellsworth was a friend of President Lincoln's and immediately became a martyr to the cause, his body lying in state at the White House and prints of his death selling briskly. Similar incidents involving California hotelkeepers flying Confederate flags were settled less violently but remained significant episodes in collective memory. In 1863 a Confederate force returned to Lawrence, Kansas, sacked and burned its rebuilt hotel and the rest of the town, and slaughtered more than a hundred of its inhabitants. And in 1864 an elaborate plot was hatched by suspected Confederate agents, who under cover of night simultaneously set fire to thirteen of the most important hotels in New York City. All the fires were quickly discovered and put out before they could spread, but the attempted arson received elaborate treatment in the press, with one newspaper running a full-page illustration of all of the establishments that had been attacked.[30]

The close association between politics and hotels turned out to be more or less permanent, taking on many different forms in later decades. Hotelkeepers parlayed visits by presidents, prime ministers, kings, and queens into advertisements for the high quality of their hospitality, publicizing and commemorating stays by important public figures with plaques, paintings, photographic portraits, and specially designated "presidential suites." Politicians continued to use hotels for party caucuses, campaign visits, constituent receptions, and national conventions. Indeed, a hotel provided one of the most evocative expressions in the American lexicon, an enduring shorthand for behind-the-scenes dealing among political insiders. When the Republican convention of 1920 deadlocked in open sessions at the Chicago Coliseum, a group of senators held a late-night meeting in a suite at the Blackstone Hotel and decided on Warren G. Harding as their candidate for president. The next day, the Associated Press reported that the nomination had been made in a "smoke-filled room."[31]

HOTELS AND NATIONAL ASSOCIATIONS

While it was in business and politics that hotels did the most to tie individual communities into national networks, they also served other associational purposes that had little to do with making money or exercising authority. The nation was, after all, held together by more than just commerce and elections—there were many other kinds of activity that contributed to civil society. "American political and industrial associations easily catch our eyes, but the others tend not to be noticed," Tocqueville remarked. "However, we should recognize that the latter are as necessary as the former to the American people; perhaps more so."[32]

Most social uses of hotels remained limited to particular towns or cities, but there were some cases in which locally based activities made the leap to being regionally or nationally organized. When that happened, hotels often provided the needed meeting space. Sometimes ventures of this kind began with a single episode that illustrated the usefulness of acting on a national scale. In 1859, for example, one Mr. Van Meter, a New York social worker, visited Cleveland "with forty homeless boys from the East, whom he wishes to place in responsible homes"; he made the Angier House his base for meeting potential adoptive parents. In subsequent decades, placing children in new homes became a national activity, one that often involved groups of orphans traveling on trains and being offered for adoption at local hotels. Recreational pursuits also occasionally took on a translocal character. In 1874 the *Cleveland Leader* reported the arrival of "James Wylie, champion draught or checker player," who was stopping at the Birch House to challenge local players. Tours of this kind were apparently not uncommon. "Since coming to this country some months ago," the newspaper explained, "he has had games with the best players of New York, Detroit, Boston, and the principal cities of Canada." Many other kinds of competitive activity came to be organized on a long-distance basis, with regional meets and national tournaments held yearly at hotels around the country.[33]

Other moves from local to national activity were more consequential because they involved the most influential noncommercial, nonstate organizations in the nation: churches. Large denominational conferences and missionary society meetings depended upon hotels for food, lodging, and meeting space. At the Episcopalian Centennial in Philadelphia in

1883, the 590 lay conferees and bishops met at Holy Trinity Church and lunched every day at the nearby Aldine Hotel. When more than five hundred delegates to the Presbyterian General Assembly converged upon Saratoga in 1890, the local paper noted that "sedate clergymen throng the corridors of hotels that one month later will be crowded with fashion's votaries." Along with the delegates, the city expected "an equal number of spectators from abroad" drawn by "the promise of a great debate." Two years later, the Christian Endeavor Society met in New York City, with 30,000 participants convening at Madison Square Garden and filling the city's hostelries: "They were suddenly present in great numbers in many of the quieter family hotels," reported the *New York Times*. The Lake Mohonk Conference for the Friends of the Indian, a nondenominational meeting at which clergy members, missionary society leaders, and writers from the religious press predominated, met at the Lake Mohonk Mountain House in New Paltz, New York, every year from 1883 to 1916.[34]

Even the kinds of social behavior that were usually most localized could be translated into regional or national affairs. Resort hotels that drew their guests from far afield made courting into a distinctly translocal activity, with anxious parents presenting their marriageable sons and daughters to society in a broad geographic context. These networks were less formally organized than other kinds of associational activity, but no less purposeful. Long before William Dean Howells and Edith Wharton set their novels at American resorts, other observers had come to understand the nature of romance at summer hotels. An 1853 editorial in the *New York Herald* explained that during the season, "the most desperate endeavors will be made to secure the great object in the life of a belle—a rich and good-natured husband." The English traveler George M. Towle viewed the entire scene as a sort of national marriage market, describing dress balls at Saratoga as "great matrimonial fairs, where the marriageable wares are shown off at their best," and explaining that "Newport and other American watering places" were "marriage bourses with their speculators and victims." Indeed, wrote Towle, this marketplace was not just national but international: "The best and the lowest types of exotic Europeans . . . spurious Italian counts and German music teachers with a spiritual air, if they strike the right social stratum—which they are bound to do—live in clover," eagerly sought out by an "American snobocracy" who "adore nothing so much as a title, or a foreign genius, and are only too glad to shower their money on such of this sort as they find willing to receive it." Hotelkeepers, keenly aware that these social networks were important to their profitability, took measures to guarantee the perfect environment for wooing. Some installed carefully positioned "proposal sofas" in secluded corners; Saratoga Springs had a "Courting Yard," and the grounds at White Sulphur Springs were imaginatively mapped with evocative names like "Lovers' Walk," "Courtship Maze," "Lovers' Rest," and "Acceptance Way to Paradise."[35]

Many more examples could be offered of social activities based in localities that subsequently attained a national scale. Whether nineteenth-century Americans wanted to congregate with coreligionists, meet fellow hobbyists, converse with chautauquans, socialize with other members of fraternal lodges, or compete with champion gamesmen, if they met on a regional or national basis, it was likely that they would be doing so at a hotel. The key point is that hotels provided essential infrastructure for the kinds of associations that could bring large numbers of people together over great distances. Hotels offered the physical locations that Americans needed in order to meet voluntarily, affiliate translocally, cooperate nationally, and collectively pursue happiness away from the pressures of the market and the attention of the state.

CONCLUSION: NETWORKED FORUMS

Civil society in nineteenth-century America comprised a tremendous variety of activities and institutions that allowed people to affiliate with one another and act in concert to sustain their democracy, deal collectively with economic challenges, and create rewarding social and associational lives for themselves. Civic participation by its very nature required physical spaces where people could meet, deliberate, and plan, and hotels hosted many activities that were crucial components of the nation's civil society. In some respects this was a distant echo of an earlier process in which people created a new and transformative institutional space: the seventeenth-century English coffeehouse, which became the center of an emergent bourgeois public sphere. Jürgen Habermas has famously argued that the political public sphere was born at a particular time and in specific urban spaces. In pursuit of the kind of reliable information necessary to their trading operations, seventeenth-century merchants established numerous headquarters in London coffeehouses. Every coffeehouse operated as a local gathering place and a nexus of commercial information from port cities at home and abroad, creating a thriving locus of both print and oral communication. Because regularly updated reports on government policies were essential to international trade, the actions of states became a topic of conversation and ultimately the subject of critiques. Habermas thus posits that political civil society owed its existence in large part to commercial capitalism because mercantile spaces and information flows were preconditions for ongoing public scrutiny of the state.[36]

There are some meaningful comparisons to be made here with hotels. Viewed schematically, coffeehouses transformed political life in England (as salons did in France and table societies in Germany) because they were key sites in the circulation of information in the form of news and opinion. Hotels facilitated circulation as well, but in a different medium: they allowed people to both gather locally and traverse distances regionally and nationally. Hotels' function as travel accommodations enabled citizens to integrate local public forums into larger networks, thereby bridging the divide between community activity and a national level of economy, politics, and associationalism. In a rapidly urbanizing nation, cities and towns were actively reaching out to make connections with other communities and thereby to secure their places in the developing urban system. Far from being isolated "island communities," American municipalities depended upon a constant flow of travelers to maintain the kinds of economic, political, and social linkages essential to urban prosperity and city life. While parallels like these must be made with care due to the very different times and places in which coffeehouses and hotels existed, such comparisons do indicate a pivotal role for social and architectural spaces in the larger story of the relationship between capitalism and civil society.[37]

This line of thinking suggests a particular historical narrative of civil society. According to Habermas, the ongoing development of capitalism eventually destroyed the public sphere: this most important aspect of civil society had emerged under specific economic conditions, and when these changed in the early nineteenth century, society did as well. Habermas's is thus a narrative of rise and fall. The history of the hotel, however, points toward a different trajectory, one in which hotels fostered the growth of a thriving American civil society in the nineteenth century and continued to function as preeminent gathering places well into the twentieth. This discrepancy has much to do with differing definitions of civil society. I have followed Mary Ryan and other scholars in defining civic engagement in very broad terms: the political public sphere extends beyond the realm of rational-critical discussion among relatively small groups of people, and also includes public protests, everyday sociability, theatrics, associational meetings, and other activities engaged in by a much larger proportion of the population. I therefore see the civil society born in coffeehouses as having continued to develop in public houses of a later vintage, the hotel prominent among them.

This conception of public life much more closely matches the lived experience of nineteenth-century Americans. Not everyone had the time, wherewithal, or inclination to read books, write letters, or publish pamphlets because leisure, wealth, and education were unevenly distributed. It was personal participation that was the most popular and vibrant aspect of civil society, and in many respects the most influential. While the circulation of textual information certainly could and did generate change, reading was something of a "thin" experience that lacked texture, tone, shape, and smell. Actual human contact, by contrast, was a literally fully fleshed-out, sensuous experience. As stimulating as reading could be, it was very different from seeing a huge throng gathered around a hotel balcony, hearing a speaker hold forth in a public parlor, catching the aroma of elaborate dishes as they were brought into a dining hall, or feeling a hotel ballroom shake as people clapped their hands and stamped their feet. Moreover, hotels created what might be called a multiplier effect: because people came to the same hotel spaces for many different reasons, there was constant crossing and commingling that exposed people to unexpected individuals and ideas. Someone who went to a hotel for a political caucus would also encounter travelers, their unfamiliar accents or foreign languages, and their styles of dress and comportment; by the same token, a person who ventured into a hotel for a shot of whiskey might thereby come into contact with antiliquor activists, itinerant physicians, society debutantes, or revivalist preachers. In short, hotels both focused and amplified the transformative power of human interaction.[38]

This is not to say that civil society in American hotels was an egalitarian affair. Hotels originated as elite, exclusionary institutions, and while they were democratized to some extent in the Jacksonian era, the rising economic inequality of the late nineteenth century served to attenuate earlier gains. Hotels were manifestly unequal in their accommodations and prestige, and allowed people with money and power to display their putatively superior taste and influence. For example, when a group of seven hundred extremely wealthy entrepreneurs, financiers, industrialists, and professionals and their wives dressed up as European royalty to attend a lavish ball at New York's Waldorf-Astoria Hotel—this in 1897, during the worst recession of the century, with millions of their fellow citizens unemployed—they were unmistakably exercising economic power and expressing social dominance. But the Waldorf was not the only hotel in town, and other denizens of the city were surely meeting at other hostelries to select precinct captains, enjoy a few rounds of drinks, hear lectures, or plan protests. It could be argued that grand hotels served hegemonic ends because they allowed the wealthiest Americans to inscribe their power on the built environment, but for every first-class establishment, there were dozens of middling and working-class hotels that served the economic, political, and social purposes of their much more numerous patrons and could not easily be captured by elites. Civil society at hotels was not egalitarian, but it was at least pluralistic, and could be so precisely because it was plural, supplanting unitary or dominant urban gathering places like the Greek agora, the Roman forum, or the Renaissance Italian piazza with a multicentered landscape of civic participation that included enough spaces to host a diverse and broadening civil society.[39]

Nine *Homes for a World of Strangers*

House, Hotel, Apartment Building

THE INFLUENCE OF HOTEL hospitality on everyday life also reached into the American home. The people of the United States had created in the hotel an extraordinarily versatile social technology and soon adapted it for yet another purpose. They began to make homes in hotels, and beginning in the middle of the nineteenth century the hotel became a key architectural and social model for a new type of residence, the apartment building. Apartment buildings emerged in a period when the American home was undergoing important transformations: people were changing the ways they built their homes, occupied the space within, and did the daily work of housekeeping. These changes often conflicted, however, with new domestic ideologies that defined the home as a private refuge that sheltered families from the competitive world outside. The result was a clash of theory and practice, one that pitted the cult of domesticity against new ways of dwelling and being in the city.[1]

American households were changing within the larger historical context of market transformation. The same capitalist imperatives that had transformed hospitality through increased travel were now influencing housing practices. In the case of the apartment building, it was the hotel's function of providing hospitality that made it a key point of articulation between the market and the household. But this process was also conditioned by many other factors, some of which were as much cultural as they were economic.

Hotel life and apartment living turned the space of many urban dwellings completely upside down. Before the hotel, hospitality was modeled on the individual household; but in the apartment building, Americans created a multifamily urban household often patterned on a new mode of hospitality. This account offers another example of how the hotel influenced American life and suggests that the genealogy of urban housing runs not only through residential spaces, as one might expect, but also through spaces of hospitality.

AMERICAN DOMESTICITY

The idea of home is among the most powerful symbols in the world. In most societies, people's relationship with their dwellings is more constant and permanent than with any other part of the built environment. As a result, homes are much more than just places of residence: they become expressions of self and community, repositories of individual identities and shared values. In North America, British colonists carried with them a set of residential preferences based on those that had long prevailed in England. The English domestic ideal generally involved a patriarchal household living in a freestanding structure sited on a substantial plot of land. This ideal had grown out of the manors of the landed gentry, but it was honored far from the countryside. In London those who had the means to choose their own living situation continued to opt for detached houses. Even as the city's population grew into the millions in the nineteenth century, its denizens made theirs a metropolis of individual, private homes; this contrasted sharply with their counterparts on the Continent, especially in Paris, where multistory, multifamily apartment buildings dominated the urban landscape by the 1840s.[2]

During the nineteenth century, Americans freighted the idea of home even more heavily by making domesticity into a bulwark against the dramatic socioeconomic changes of the age. The intensification of capitalism and the concomitant expansion of wage labor were transforming the nature of work and family relations. In the nation's fast-growing towns and cities, men increasingly worked away from home, venturing forth to sell their labor to the owners of workshops, firms, and factories or to compete as entrepreneurs in the rapidly developing commercial sector. Women of the middle and upper classes often remained at home, their time increasingly under their control because their customary roles in household production were being displaced by the goods manufactured and traded by their brothers, husbands, and fathers. This is not to say that the home lost its economic function. On the contrary, many women earned money at home by renting out rooms and selling domestic labor like cooking and cleaning to people who did not have households of their own.

Such disruptions of the traditional structures of everyday life left people grasping for ways to understand their place in this confusing new world. One of their responses was to redefine the home. The cultural representatives of a rising middle class increasingly portrayed the home in opposition to economic activity and public participation: if life outside the household involved men engaging in hardnosed capitalist competition and aggressively partisan politics, the home must become a place where women established a gentle, comfortable, and nurturing refuge in which men could recuperate from the stresses of the outside world and children could be prepared for it.[3]

While this domestic ideal bore little resemblance to most people's reality, it nonetheless did the ideological work of reinforcing Anglo-American residential preferences by providing another reason to valorize the individual household. If the purpose of the home was to insulate the family from the pressure and anxiety of capitalism, it made sense to design dwellings to accomplish this function. The ideal house should therefore be an independent structure that would separate family members from outsiders, protecting their privacy by giving them a space that was theirs exclusively.[4]

Yet the same socioeconomic changes that gave rise to the domestic ideal were making it ever harder to realize, for market transformation was not limited to workplace and gender relations—it also led to the commodification of land and living space in the form of real estate. Most people in the United States still lived in rural surroundings, but the fastest-growing segment of the population comprised the residents of towns and cities. The basic unit of urban space in early America was the independent household, ensconced in either a freestanding house or a row house. Beginning in the late eighteenth and early nineteenth centuries, however, the pursuit of profits through real estate speculation sent the price of land soaring, and the financial structure of the building trades meant that the supply of housing fell far short of the needs of the nation's city dwellers. As a result, fewer and fewer people could afford houses of their own. The families of workingmen and artisans bore the brunt of this shortage, but even the respectable middle class felt the pressure of the tight housing market. According to one estimate, between 1785 and 1815 the rate of home ownership in New York City fell from just under 30 percent to about 20 percent. There and in many other American cities, the first half of the nineteenth century was characterized by an almost continuous housing crisis.[5]

The emergent contradiction between ideal and reality in housing led some families to move away from urban centers to establish early suburbs; but it was urban concentration that was to characterize the American scene for more than a century to come. Rising land prices provided impetus for greater residential concentration, first through the expansion of individual households and later in the form of multifamily homes. In less affluent neighborhoods, landlords sought to maximize their rental income by building small houses in the rear of row-house lots, and the poorest families were compelled to rent out other people's attics and basements. Middle-class families struggled against the rising cost of real estate through the practice of boarding, whether by accepting paying lodgers into their own homes or by moving into other people's boardinghouses. Such arrangements were common, with some estimates suggesting that from a third to half of nineteenth-century urban households included boarders.[6]

The growth of multifamily living was soon expressed architecturally in the form of purpose-built structures containing a number of dwellings. Historians of architecture have traditionally described the process as one that began when poorly paid workers with few other options were packed into shared housing. In new manufacturing centers like Lowell, Massachusetts, factory owners constructed multiunit residences that put groups of six to twelve young mill hands and a landlady into a shared, quasi-familial household. A far more consequential innovation in congregate dwellings was the tenement house, which emerged in the 1830s alongside the nation's industrial working class. As land prices rose, urban landlords sought higher rental profits by converting warehouses into cheap housing for workers. They soon hit upon the idea of constructing a new type of building specifically intended to house a number of families. As Elizabeth Blackmar describes the process in New York City, "tenements—the first purposely built multifamily housing—rationalized three decades of tenants' ad hoc crowding into a new housing form." Within fifteen years, every major city in the United States had a high-density residential district. It thus seemed that multiple-tenant housing, usually on a rental basis, was to be the wave of the urban future.[7]

This did not sit well with the opinion makers of an American middle class that increasingly dominated public discourse. They were deeply invested in the cultural project of sacralizing private domesticity, and buildings that housed multiple families violated their notions of propriety by blurring the line between respectability and squalor. At a time when a changing economy was disrupting the accustomed stability of social relations, Americans were keenly aware of appearances and anxious not to be mistaken for their inferiors. Because tenements were associated primarily with the working class, people with social ambitions had good reason to avoid them. Why risk being linked, even symbolically, with a class of people whose very morality was constantly being called into doubt? Getting respectable Americans to accept multifamily dwellings was to be an uphill struggle because it required them to revise their beliefs about the meaning of home.[8]

HOTEL LIVING IN THE CITY

Hotels were an essential component of the urban trend toward multifamily residences, but their development as housing was different from that of boardinghouses and tenements. Chronologically, hotels were being used as homes well before the construction of the first purpose-built tenements. Economically, early hotel dwellers were not people driven by their financial circumstances to search for more affordable housing. Spatially, hotel habitations were not created as part of an effort to build dwellings; rather, they were an adaptation of the hotel's basic function of providing hospitality to travelers and other transients. This suggests not only that the hotel was influencing American housing practices long before it became a model for the apartment building but also that explaining how and why this happened requires us to understand the logic of hospitality along with that of capital.

Americans demonstrated enthusiasm for living in hotels from an early date in their development as a new building form. An 1809 description of the Exchange Coffee House in Boston noted its many "bed Chambers, occupied by travellers and resident boarders." In 1818 a British visitor to New York City wrote of his hotel: "Like the other hotels it is the residence of a good many permanent boarders, some of them men of considerable wealth, who sit down every day at the public table. The inn is with us, proverbially, the travelers' home, but here it is the home of a great many besides travelers." When it opened in 1829, Boston's Tremont House included a number of suites designed for long-term occupancy by families, and within two years, fourteen heads of household were listed in the city directory as permanent residents there. Four years later, a New York newspaper reported that the newly built Holt's Hotel "combine[d] all the advantages of a hotel and boarding house" and included numerous "apartments judiciously constructed for the use of families." And in 1836 Horace Greeley's *New Yorker* informed its readers that even before the Astor House was completed, half of the rooms at the hotel had already been reserved as family residences.[9]

It is important to emphasize at this juncture that hotels were the first practical purpose-built multiple dwellings in United States history. Other specifically designed multiple dwellings came later. The Lowell boardinghouses were constructed only in the 1820s, tenement houses in the 1830s, and the collective and cooperative dwellings of the communitarian socialists only in the 1840s.[10]

Hotel living began in luxury establishments, but as hotels diversified into a number of forms serving a broader clientele, hotel dwelling gradually spread into the urban middle class. Hotel advertisements and guidebook descriptions increasingly included room rates not only by the day or week but also by the year. In the upstart towns of the trans-Appalachian West, hotels often served as homes for recently arrived respectable families. In Chicago's city directory of 1844, for example, fully one listing in six was for an individual or family living in a hotel. This practice was not limited to developing cities: Walt Whitman stated in an 1856 newspaper article that nearly three-quarters of middle- and upper-class New Yorkers lived in hotels or boardinghouses. Indeed, by the time of his 1860 visit to the United States, the English novelist Anthony Trollope was so struck by this practice that he could say (with considerable exaggeration, to be sure) that long-term hotel residents were so numerous as to render travelers and other transient guests "not generally the mainstay of the house."[11]

How did hotels come to be adapted for residential use? Their mere existence did not, after all, dictate that they would become dwellings. Hotel living arose from the micro-economics of hotelkeeping, the residential needs of urbanites, rising real estate prices, and changing notions of gender and work. Understanding how and why hotels became increasingly popular as homes requires a close look at both the chronology and spatiality of hotel living, since these reveal not only why people decided to move into hotels but, equally important, how such an opportunity became available in the first place.

The supply side is the most easily understood. As we learned in Chapter 5, the hotel business was fiercely competitive, with hotelkeepers regularly forced to shutter their establishments when they could not keep up with payments. Because regular cash flow was indispensable to a hotel's operation and ongoing viability, hotelkeepers had good reason to seek out long-term tenants, since they could provide at least some level of guaranteed income. Hotel boarders were, in one sense, not the ideal occupants of a keeper's rooms, since their yearly rate was lower than for short-term guests—from 25 to almost 35 percent lower, if newspaper and guidebook notices reflected prevailing practice. But during the winter off-season or in the event of a slow week or month, a reliable contingent of boarders could mean the difference between survival and bankruptcy. As a result, most urban hotels contained a substantial proportion of boarders.[12]

But supply does not create demand, and before hotel residences could become popular, respectable people would have to choose to live in them despite their clear divergence from traditional standards of domesticity. The most commonly cited motivation was an economic one. Throughout the nineteenth century, whenever observers tried to explain why people went to live in hotels, they most often described the decision in terms of the cost of living. Horace Greeley, in his 1836 observations about the Astor House, explained that hotel dwellers were primarily "families who give up housekeeping on account of the present enormous rents in the city." In 1853 *Putnam's Monthly Magazine* proposed that hotel living could be accounted for by high rents, scarce servants, and the complications of home ownership. And in 1865 the *New York Times* noted that due to "the present high prices, men of moderate means and slim incomes find it an absolute impossibility to pay their debts, so that hundreds and thousands who four years since rented modest mansions, and indulged in the luxury of a house" instead went to live in hotels.[13]

Yet a closer look at the historical record indicates that economic duress was not, at least initially, the impetus for hotel living. The people who first moved into hotels were not forced to do so by the high cost of housing. The price of hotel housing relative to other residential options suggests that the decision to live in a hotel was an active, voluntary choice in the 1820s and 1830s, one that could have been made only by reasonably prosperous urbanites. New York City, the most expensive housing market in the nation, provides an instructive example. According to Blackmar, the rental cost of a newly built Manhattan row house in this period ranged from $275 to $500 per year. At this time, hotels cost about $2 per day, less the yearly discount of about 30 percent. Using these figures, we find that a single room at the heavily residential Astor House would have cost more than $500 per year, while boarding at the more affordable Holt's Hotel would still have come to just over $350 annually. What this suggests is that a person or family who could afford to live at a hotel could have lived less expensively (far less expensively in the case of a family, since they would need a suite of rooms) elsewhere in the city or the new suburbs. Moreover, such a household would have had to be fairly well-off, with an annual income of at least $1,000 to $2,000, a figure that would have put them solidly in the middle class. Indeed, the cost differential between hotels and houses in this period was probably even wider than these figures suggest, since hotels in Boston, Baltimore, and Philadelphia cost just as much as in New York even though housing costs were lower in the smaller cities.[14]

The cost of city living did become a factor in subsequent decades. The fast-rising real estate prices of the 1830s had fallen sharply after the Panic of 1837, but by the late 1840s and early 1850s, housing costs were climbing quickly once again. Soaring prices shut a growing proportion of people out of the market for single-family homes and, in combination with the emergence of nonluxury hotels, made hotel living a less expensive alternative to private homes.[15]

It must be remembered, however, that it was precisely the hospitality-driven spatial arrangement of hotels that determined their competitive economic advantages within urban housing markets. It was the efficient provision of hospitality, not domesticity, that guided the designers and builders of hotels. The process discussed in Chapter 5, in which hotel architects disaggregated the spaces and functions of the private household and re-configured them into a new kind of plan, was certainly a market response, but it was one that was shaped and mediated by the need to accommodate travelers. Hotels made efficient use of land in the sense that they could shelter more people than would be possible in houses built on an equivalent number of city lots precisely because they were multistory, multiple-occupant buildings with many shared spaces. In an environment of fast-rising real estate values, hotels were well positioned to realize savings on ground rents and pass them on to residents.

There were also other reasons why people chose hotel living. One set of incentives was based on gender and labor. As the architectural historians Dolores Hayden and Elizabeth Collins Cromley have pointed out, certain kinds of multiple dwellings offered women the possibility of freedom from the household work that was expected of them in the domestic ideology of the day. Some observers in the 1850s expressed this gendered dynamic when they suggested that wives had a particular affinity for hotel life. One male newspaper columnist groused on behalf of his sex that "if property rises in the neighborhood, we will yield to our wife's solicitations, sell it, and go to live in a hotel." In a short story published in *Harper's Weekly* in 1857, a narrator explained why he and his wife "went to live at the St. Thunder Hotel." Even though he had "wanted to keep house, having an eye to my own comfort," his wife "declared that her health was not equal to the task, and her mother asked me, in a fierce manner, if I wished to be the means of making her childless."[16]

It was precisely the imperatives of hotel hospitality that created the possibility of women's emancipation from domestic labor. The hotel's internal configuration corresponded to a new microgeography of labor that created a clear and systematic separation of work from living space. Hotel rooms were usually no more than bedchambers with an occasional attached sitting room. They contained no cooking facilities, the work of food preparation having been centralized in large-scale hotel pantries and kitchens (fig. 9.1).

9.1   Because hotels contained large-scale pantries and kitchens where a hired staff prepared meals
for guests, hotel residents were freed from the work of purchasing, storing, and cooking food.
(General Research Division, The New York Public Library, Astor, Lenox and Tilden Foundations)

The washing of clothes was likewise taken out of the hands of guests and relocated in
laundries that employed wage-working cleaners; the same went for tailoring and shoe
shining. Housecleaning could not be separated from the guest rooms, but it could be
contracted out to chambermaids who did their work while the guests were out, minimizing
the evidence of human labor in the upper floors of the hotel. Hotels thus made it difficult
or impossible for guests to perform any sort of traditional housework.[17]

    The upshot of this rearrangement of space and work was that in organizing them-
selves to serve travelers, hotels inverted the gendered order of labor within the household.
Wives had long been expected to perform unwaged work in the home, and the value of
their labor was the property of their husbands, who were not expected to pay for it. The
traditional household economy thus involved a constant transfer of value from wives to
husbands. But in a hotel wives did not need to cook, do laundry, or clean, because those
tasks were done by the hotel staff and paid for out of their husbands' wages. The gender
politics of hotel living did not go unnoticed. As we shall see, middle-class male commentators criticized hotel wives with great ferocity, suggesting just how radical a change this was,
and how much danger many men thought it posed to the patriarchal family. Meanwhile,
women's thinking about hotels gradually advanced from simple preference and escalated
into a full-scale critique of the structure of housework and the cult of domesticity.[18]

Hotel living generated public controversy. As the practice of dwelling in hotels became increasingly prevalent, America's middle-class guardians of domesticity began to fret about the danger that hotel life posed to the nation's families. They produced a barrage of criticisms of hotel dwellers, criticisms that would be repeated many times for decades thereafter. Some evinced a general unease about multifamily residences, paralleling similar suspicions about boardinghouses; others were specific to hotels. Underlying them were concerns about family, gender, sexuality, labor, and class. While they certainly did reveal the particular concerns and anxieties of the nineteenth-century middle class, they must not be taken to indicate a complete rejection of hotel living. They were, after all, just words, ephemeral utterances that were being hurled at something much more permanent and real: the masonry and wood of actual hotels and the choices of the people who lived in them.

There was general agreement among critics that hotels were not appropriate dwellings. An 1864 *New York Times* article headlined "Hotels versus Homes—What New-York Needs" was typical of an entire genre of screeds against hotel living. "Our greatest need," its author asserted, "is more private houses, and more families with the grace and good sense, and good taste to live in them." "The growing preference for hotel life," he declared, was "one of the curses of New-York, and [was] doing a serious injury to the whole community." Critics offered a number of reasons why hotel living was so problematic. The most general of these, and the one that informed all the others, was that hotels interfered with family life. One writer asserted that "the husband is but half a husband, the wife but half a wife, the child but half a child, when all three reside in some huge caravansera in common with some hundreds of other persons, separated from them by different tastes, feelings, opinions." Another was more specific in charging that hotel life drew family members away from each other and into extrafamilial social networks, with grave results: "The men find their pleasure and excitement in the reading-room, corridor, bar-room, billiard-room, and exchange; the ladies in the drawing-rooms; . . . the children become spoiled, petted, ruined; an utter upsetting of all home habits, an entire disregard of old-fashioned domesticity and comfort, are the normal sequences to this folly, extravagance, and fashion."[19]

On a related note, many critics expressed concern that hotel living would encourage sexual immorality. People were familiar with the frequency of illicit sexual behavior in hotels, and detractors of hotel living parlayed this knowledge into allegations that hotels' combination of publicity and opportunity would lead women astray. In one fictional account from the 1850s, a man named Bill Brown described the difficulties he faced after moving into a hotel with his wife. He felt compelled to keep her away from their window to prevent her from looking at a neighbor as he bathed; later, he found her misbehaving at a picnic of "four ladies, all married, and four gentlemen, all single. They had dined, and the Champagne had flowed freely." The author of an 1869 volume was even more explicit. "How many women," he moaned, "can trace their first infidelity to the necessarily demoralizing influence of public houses—to loneliness, leisure, need of society, interesting companions, abundance of opportunity, and potent temptation!" Notably, little or nothing was said in such accounts about men's sexual dalliances in hotels; it was threats to women's sexual purity that was the real peril at hand.[20]

Women's behavior was also at issue in another line of criticism in which family disruption was predicated upon the disposition of wives' labor. The basic idea was that because hotels provided families with so many domestic services usually presumed the rightful duties of married women—cooking, cleaning, child care, sewing, and the like— wives were thereby damaged. One particularly aggressive accuser held that "hotel life is in a large degree answerable" for the condition of American women, whom he believed to be "incapable, from physical and mental weakness, of extending parental care to their children, and womanly counsel and comfort to their husbands . . . they can not, as a general rule, discharge satisfactorily any one of the functions for which they were sent into the world." Another echoed similar themes in more detail, specifically implicating the hotel's tendency to free women from housework:

> There is a sanctity around a well-conducted household which lends an
> additional dignity and purity to the wife; that when in her own home the
> wife has aims in life which she can have in no other position; aims to accom-
> plish, duties to fulfill which give her a healthy occupation, and keep her
> morally as well as physically sound. But without a home, and occupying
> a suite of rooms at the Bunkum House, what is she? She has no occupation
> but that of dress; no aim but to assassinate to-day that she may get into to-
> morrow more quickly. Her husband all day at his business; all the evening
> in the smoking or bar-room, who will wonder if she forgets him? Idle and
> lazy, and dyspeptic from the want of exercise, she becomes such a mere
> puppet and machine that she loses all sense of individual responsibility,
> and—the atmosphere around her not being the most moral—soon loses
> also the sense of what she owes to the world.

Indeed, some critics were so thoroughly convinced of this basic thesis that they thought putting an end to hotel meal service could undo all the harm being done to families: "The main pillar of family hotel life was the table d'hôte," explained *Harper's Weekly;* "destroy that, and of necessity the women will have homes" (fig. 9.2).[21]

Hotel living was occasionally condemned on the basis of class, though not in the usual mode of denigrating the poor. On the contrary, to the extent that the opponents of hotel living raised issues of economic status, it was by way of denouncing the excessive luxury of hotels. The *Toronto Colonist* in 1857 accused New York City hotels of being "complete colleges for the teaching of extravagance" because their effect on women was to "inflame their strongest and least governable desires, namely, to possess those things which are rarest, and have the greatest attraction." Other critics expressed similar sentiments by emphasizing that hotels set a standard of luxury unattainable by individual householders. What this seems to suggest is that because it had been well-to-do families who had first moved into hotels, they were insulated from association with the tenement dwellings of the poor. This was an important indication of the way hotels established the cultural preconditions for apartment buildings: by certifying the respectability of at least this one kind of multiple dwelling.[22]

Public criticisms of hotel living were textual expressions of anxiety about structural changes in American urban life—a phalanx of words that moralists deployed in anger against tens or hundreds of thousands of people who were indifferent to their sensibilities. A truer understanding of how people felt about residential hotels and later kinds of multiple dwellings must depend less on textual evidence and more on people's actual behavior as demonstrated by the way they shaped the built environment.

HOTELS BECOME APARTMENTS

The widespread use of hotels as homes made them a frequent point of reference when city dwellers began around midcentury to call for new forms of residential architecture. As soaring prices shut a growing proportion of people out of the market for single-family homes, journalists and architects embarked upon a decades-long debate over how best to create a new building type for urban America. Some observers saw the hotel as a promising architectural model. In 1853 the author of the regular "New-York Daguerreotyped" feature in *Putnam's Monthly Magazine* noted, "Society is rapidly tending toward hotel life. . . . The advantages of a cluster of families living together under one roof, are everyday more apparent." A year later, the same column shifted its position slightly when it proposed applying hotel design to an entirely new kind of edifice:

> Splendors of architecture are not to be looked for here . . . until we shall
> have been educated to the point of discovering the superior advantages of
> a combination of interests in our private dwellings, to the present indepen-
> dent and isolated style of construction; when it shall be found that twenty
> or thirty families may live in a palace by combining their means, in the con-
> struction of one capacious dwelling, while they would be compelled to live
> in an inconvenient and plain house, if each one built separately. Our hotels
> are an indication of what might be done by the plan we have hinted at.[23]

While hotel architecture was a constant referent, it was not always by way of endorsement. When Calvert Vaux addressed city housing needs in a speech to the first meeting of the American Institute of Architects in 1857, he echoed critics of hotel living by noting that while "a family may live at a hotel or in a boarding-house, the ceaseless publicity that ensues, the constant change, and the entire absence of all individuality in the everyday domestic arrangements, will always render this method of living distasteful." Instead,

9.2   Two panels from a full-page illustration comparing life at home and in a hotel. Note that women do the work of serving in the home, whereas at the hotel, such tasks are performed by waiters. (University of New Mexico Center for Southwest Research)

Vaux advocated adapting European precedents. "In Europe," he noted, "extensive buildings, several stories high, are frequently arranged with all the rooms required for a family grouped together on one level. . . . This Continental plan, as it is called, seems to possess so many advantages, that it deserves more attention than has hitherto been accorded to it in America."[24]

   These divergent responses to the problem of middle-class urban housing represented two very different lines of development for multifamily dwellings in the United States. The one corresponding to Vaux's preferences generally involved taking household spaces and aggregating them—usually horizontally, but sometimes vertically—within a single architectural envelope. Vaux's speech was accompanied by preliminary drawings (fig. 9.3) for what he called "Parisian Buildings": eight units sharing a common entrance and stairway, each consisting of a parlor, dining room, kitchen, bedrooms, and bath distributed along a corridor running from front to back. A slightly different approach to the

HOME.

same idea was taken in Alexander Jackson Davis's House of Mansions (1859), an array of "eleven independent dwellings" of "twelve to eighteen rooms each" that were designed as a single, coordinated neo-Gothic block. The Stuyvesant Apartments of 1869, which architectural historians have frequently cited as the first American apartment building, also corresponded to this basic type: the five-story building contained sixteen units, each featuring a parlor, dining room, kitchen, servants' room, and three bedchambers (fig. 9.4). While the architects and builders of these structures often claimed novelty for their creations (Davis called his "altogether unique in its character and plan"), they undertook no spatial innovation more notable than establishing private households on a single- or split-level plan.[25]

It was the hotel-inspired approach to the apartment building that was truly path-breaking in its arrangement of domestic space. The prototype was Boston's Hotel Pelham (1857), the other most frequently mentioned candidate for America's first apartment house (fig. 9.5). While it was specifically designed as a residence and did not offer shelter to travelers or other transients, the Hotel Pelham's resemblance to an actual hotel went far beyond its name. Its apartments had no kitchens, so tenants ate together in a common dining room served by a centralized kitchen. The building also offered laundry services, housecleaning, and room service, and its ground floor contained stores and employed a concierge and porter. Indeed, given these features, it comes as no surprise that the Hotel Pelham's architect previously worked at a firm that had designed a number of transient hotels. Some of the same architectural ideas that went into the Hotel Pelham were replicated in subsequent Boston apartment buildings, including the similarly named Hotel Hamilton (1869), Hotel Kempton (1869), Hotel Boylston (1870), Hotel Agassiz (1872), and Hotel Cluny (1876). The frequent use of the term *hotel* in naming apartment buildings probably resulted from the fact that prominent Boston families had used transient hotels as residences for many years and continued to do so through the end of the century. What this suggests is that perhaps the top quarter or third of Bostonians had consciously embraced the hotel as a common and appropriate model and identifier for their other multiple dwellings.[26]

The hotel was adopted as the architectural and functional basis for the apartment building in other cities as well. In New York, the Haight House (1871) offered an architectural rejoinder to the Stuyvesant Apartments (which the *Real Estate Record and Builders'*

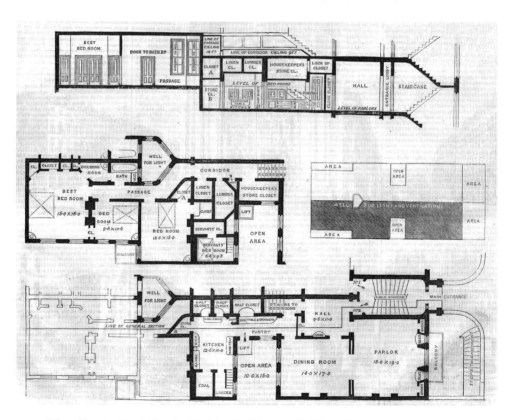

9.3 Calvert Vaux's 1857 design for "Parisian Buildings" called for self-contained single-family apartments, each with a private kitchen and servants' quarters. (University of New Mexico Center for Southwest Research)

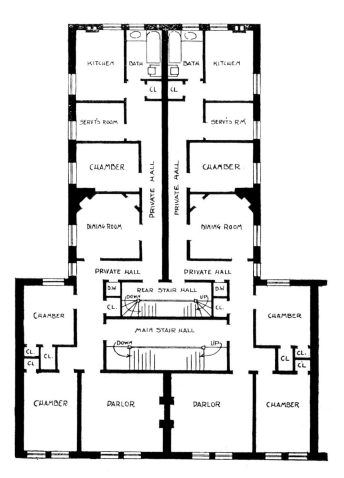

9.4 Units in New York City's Stuyvesant Apartments of 1869 were also fully privatized family homes with their own in-house kitchens and other work areas. (University of New Mexico Fine Arts Library)

Guide had criticized because "each family must of necessity keep a cook or do their own cooking") by putting in the basement a "general kitchen . . . where meals, prepared by a first-class cook" would be sent to each apartment; the Haight House also provided a shared steam laundry. The Stevens House, completed in New York in the same year, similarly divided the household by housing servants apart from their families. In Washington, D.C., the Portland Flats (1880) included a number of communal kitchens located throughout the building. The Cairo Apartments of 1894 were even more like a hotel, featuring a lobby, front desk, drugstore, lounge, and reading room; the building also housed a large public dining room, since only a few of the apartments had kitchens. Other buildings followed suit: "During the 1880s and early 1890s," notes the leading historian of the city's apartments, "few Washington apartment houses contained kitchens." In Chicago early apartment buildings like the Ontario Flats (1880), the Mentone (1882), and the Argyle (1886) were designed with, or were renovated to include, common dining rooms, central kitchens, public parlors, and other spaces modeled on hotels. Hotel-like elements continued to be built into apartment houses into the twentieth century.[27]

9.5   The Hotel Pelham (1857) was designed for permanent residence and did not accept transient guests, but tenants enjoyed many hotel-like features, including ground-level shops and a professionally staffed kitchen and dining room. (Bostonian Society/Old State House)

Indeed, hotel-like arrangements of space and labor in apartment buildings were so fundamental to the structural type that they became the key factor in how multiple dwellings were categorized. Similarity to hotels was in fact the pivotal issue in the first legal definition of the difference between tenement houses and apartment buildings. The apartment building emerged in the shadow of the tenement because middle-class families feared that their multiple dwellings might be mistaken for, or even become, working-class housing. In the early developmental years of the apartment building, however, the legal distinction between these building types depended not on income or occupation but on a division of labor and space modeled on hotels. The case of *Musgrave v. Sherwood* began in 1873, when John Sherwood sold Fannie Musgrave one of a row of houses he had built on Fifth Avenue in Manhattan. The title to all the houses specifically prohibited the construction of tenement houses on their lots. In 1875 Sherwood began to convert two of his houses into an apartment building, whereupon Musgrave accused him of violating their purchase agreement and filed for an injunction to halt construction. The ruling in the case, issued by the Supreme Court of New York and upheld by the state's Court of Appeals, stated that Sherwood's building was not a tenement house because it had shared facilities for cooking and washing. As the deciding judge put it: "The house is not . . . designed for the accommodation of transient guests or casual boarders. Rooms in suit[e]s or singly, on the different floors, are taken by families or individuals for some period. The cooking for all guests or residents of the hotel is done by the proprietor on the premises, the house having been provided with all the means and appliances for this purpose; no cooking or laundry work is allowed in the rooms of the guests." The judge's application of the word *hotel* to a building that he was ruling was an apartment house also bears upon the question of whether American hotels or European buildings were the preponderant influence on apartment buildings in the United States. While I have described apartment buildings as having followed either of two distinct lines of architectural development, it is telling that even in New York City, home to the French-inflected Stuyvesant Apartments, and less than ten years after their completion, the legal classification of multiple dwellings placed hotels and apartment buildings on one side, tenement houses and other self-contained residences on the other.[28]

The substantial degree of overlap between hotels and apartment buildings was by no means limited to the elite level of architects and judges; available evidence suggests it represented a broad-based popular understanding of the new building form. As the urban geographer and historian Paul Groth has noted, and as any further examination of advertising material and city directories will confirm, the word *hotel* was used constantly in describing early apartment buildings, making the line between the two forms indistinct. The heavy use of terms like *apartment hotel, family hotel,* and *hotel residence* indicates broad awareness of the influence of hotels on many apartment buildings. Moreover, these terms suggest that despite the protestations of middle-class foes of shared dwellings, builders themselves had little fear of the possible negative connotations of hotels in connection with residences: if middle-class Americans' antipathy toward hotel living had really been so widely held, it is hard to imagine that real estate developers would have spent hundreds of thousands of dollars to construct apartment buildings only to endanger their investments by calling them hotels. This was admittedly an ideological as well as an economic issue, but alongside bourgeois denunciations of hotel living, there emerged a very different set of understandings of multiple dwellings.[29]

NEW MEANINGS FOR HOTELS AND APARTMENTS

The nation's moralists and apostles of domesticity did not abandon their objections to hotel and apartment living as the decades passed. In 1886 a Brooklyn pastor published a collection of sermons, including one on the topic of "Hotels versus Homes" in which he called it "one of the great evils of this day" that "a large population of our towns and cities . . . have given up their homes" in favor of hotels, apartment buildings, and boarding-houses. In 1890 the author of an article in *American Architect and Building News* fretted that while house dwellers could "exclud[e] all strangers from the building, . . . in the apartment house there are always some portions of the interior . . . which are open, if not to all the world, at least to all the tenants of the building and their visitors." And in 1903 the *Architectural Record* could still editorialize that "the apartment hotel . . . is the most dangerous enemy American domesticity has yet had to encounter."[30]

Such denunciations appear to have had little effect. Urbanites flocked to residential hotels and apartment houses, spurring builders to erect ever more of them. In Boston in 1878 there were 108 apartment hotels; by 1890 there were more than 500. In a single year in the early 1880s, Chicago builders put up 1,142 apartment buildings. And in New York City the number of apartment buildings skyrocketed from 200 in 1876 to more than 10,000 by 1910.[31]

As more people moved into these congregate dwellings, the terms on which they were criticized began to shift. It was no longer the fact of living in an apartment house per se that posed the problem, but the class of people who lived in it. Architects, developers, and critics increasingly claimed that if an apartment house's tenants were properly screened, it might be exempt from charges of insufficient privacy. "An apartment house," asserted one architect in 1870, "must be built to accommodate a class of tenants who are in a nearly uniform social scale." The maintenance of such homogeneity distinguished respectable congregate dwellings from similar structures: tenements, with their impoverished occupants, and European apartments, with their mixed-class residents and questionable morality. Americans soon adopted this cultural logic, expressing heightened interest in the precise social profile of prospective apartment homes and scrutinizing the status of those who moved in after them. Rationalizations like these were essential to apartment buildings' emergence into the light of social acceptability.[32]

The increasing prevalence of hotel and apartment living involved more than just people adopting new and convenient dwelling practices or grudgingly accepting them. Some Americans, as Dolores Hayden has shown, consciously identified and embraced the socioeconomic possibilities of hotels and apartment buildings in explicitly political terms. They took the basic spatial and labor innovations that had made hotel hospitality a model for urban living—the disaggregation of household space and the application of wage labor to collectivized food preparation, cleaning, and other household work—and actively championed them.

Beginning in the 1860s a number of feminist philosophers and activists launched a pointed critique of the traditional household. The women's movement had long protested against women's subordination, inferior legal status, and inability to vote, but some thinkers came to believe that gender oppression also had roots in the structure of the home. As long as women were responsible for keeping house and raising children within single-family homes, these feminists charged, they would never have the time to develop their minds or participate in public life. Moreover, the fact that their work had to be done at home isolated them from human connections beyond the domestic realm. What was therefore needed was a way to rearrange the household so as to liberate women from both drudgery and isolation.[33]

When these feminist thinkers proposed solutions, they did so with constant reference to hotels and apartment buildings. Melusina Fay Peirce, who originated the term *cooperative housekeeping,* called for buildings with shared kitchens and laundry facilities and cited the Hotel Pelham as the way to organize residential space. The labor activist and communitarian Marie Stevens Howland helped plan a city composed of kitchenless houses and apartment hotels. The gender radical and free-love advocate Victoria Woodhull noted that "a thousand people can live in one hotel under one general system of superintendence at much less expense than two hundred and fifty families . . . can in as many houses" and thus advocated "the conversion of innumerable huts into immense hotels, as residences." And Charlotte Perkins Gilman, the most charismatic and original of her generation of feminist intellectuals, argued in *Women and Economics* (1898) that the "feminist apartment hotel" would be the logical product of the evolution of city life. In such apartment hotels, Gilman explained, "meals [from a common kitchen] could be served to the families in their rooms or in a common dining-room," and "cleaning . . . done by efficient workers, not hired separately by the families, but engaged by the manager of the establishment."[34]

Hotels and apartment buildings were also frequent points of reference for communitarians, socialists, and utopians who sought to reorganize society on a more equitable basis. American followers of the French radical Charles Fourier were behind a number of projects in New York: Stephen Pearl Andrews organized the "Unitary Household" (1858), a multifamily dwelling that combined private suites with shared parlors and dining rooms; in the 1880s and 1890s, the architect Philip G. Hubert designed and built at least eight cooperative apartment buildings that offered hotel-like services. Marie Howland and Albert Kimsey Owens described Pacific City (1889), their experimental community in Topolobampo, Mexico, as "hotel life on a grand and perfected scale." Families lived in "resident hotels," each with a "restaurant, dining-room, parlor, library, reading room, lecture hall, nursery, and play area, laundry, bath, and barber room common to all." Edward Bellamy, the most influential American utopian of the nineteenth century, described hotel-like operations in *Looking Backward* (1888), his tale of an ideal society in the year 2000. While families maintain private residences, one character explains, "our washing is all done at public laundries . . . and our cooking at public kitchens." Bellamy's narrator watches citizens eating their main meals in "a great pleasure-house and social rendezvous of the quarter," and learns that such establishments exist all over the city, "as well as country, mountain, and seaside houses for sport and rest in vacations." Bellamy's ideas inspired many architects, most notably John Pickering Putnam, a Bostonian who designed residential hotels with kitchenless apartments and collective cooking and housekeeping facilities (fig. 9.6) and proposed that they be built throughout the nation.[35]

When these and many other reformers and activists modeled their ideal dwellings

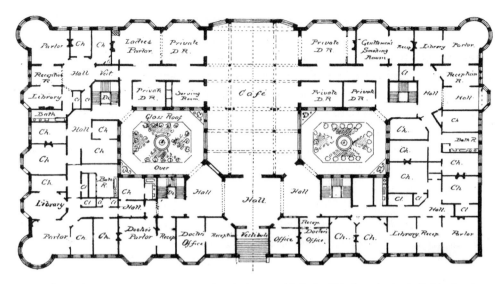

9.6   John Pickering Putnam's apartment hotel plan notably lacked kitchens in the individual units. (University of New Mexico Fine Arts Library)

on hotels and apartments, they demonstrated how important architectural precedents were to their thinking. They did not depend exclusively upon gender theory or political ideology but also drew upon spatial models that could be found on the streets of any substantial city. Years or decades before feminists and socialists adapted it to their use, the widespread practice of living in hotels and the consequent importance of the hotel in apartment building design had produced an institution that, quite unintentionally, demonstrated an alternative arrangement of work and space that could be enlisted in the cause of women's equality or universal brotherhood.

CONCLUSION: INFLUENTIAL SPACES

The hotel's influence on the American home was remarkable for both its transformative power and the breadth of its appeal. Hotels offered the nation's urbanites a new way to dwell by pioneering new architectural spaces, innovative labor practices, and novel business methods. Hotels also lent their cultural cachet to the development of new housing types: by putting well-to-do people in congregate housing from an early date, first-class hotels staved off social stigma by ensuring that tenements for the poor would not be the only kind of multiple dwelling on the cityscape. The result was that hotel and apartment living overcame middle-class cultural objections and became economically viable and hugely popular alternatives to the power relationships and work regimes of the private, patriarchal home. The people who adopted hotels as models for living showed tremendous professional and intellectual diversity. Hotels served as inspiration for architects seeking to design more affordable housing, builders and developers pursuing profits through real estate, feminists striving to release women from drudgery and isolation, and utopians hoping to remake society. It was a testament to the hotel's extraordinary originality and versatility that it could be embraced by capitalists and socialists, pragmatists and idealists.

It is essential to remember, however, that the reasons why Americans initially built hotels were not the same reasons why they subsequently adapted them into dwellings. Both were, to be sure, part of the larger process of market transformation; but they cannot be understood simply as products of some undifferentiated logic of capitalism. The most widely used and carefully theorized aspects of market-driven historical change—commodification, wage labor, and industrialization—did not by themselves produce residential hotels or apartment buildings. Hospitality had been bought and sold long before the creation of hotels, and waged domestic labor was employed in inns, taverns, and boardinghouses before and after the advent of the hotel form. In order to account for the rise of the hotel and its subsequent influence on housing, we must recognize that human geography and spatial practice were the key points of articulation. It was the rise of unprecedentedly large transient populations and the need to provide them with temporary shelter that drove the development of the hotel and in turn made it available as a model for new living arrangements and building types. These new architectures of urban living were thus in part architectures of hospitality: city people were dwelling in spaces that had originated not just as long-term residences but also as short-term homes for a world of strangers.

Ten

Accommodating Jim Crow

The Law of Hospitality and the Struggle for
Civil Rights

FREDERICK DOUGLASS WAS the most famous black person
in the world. But black he was, and so now, in 1851, a Cleveland
hotel clerk was telling him to get out. "Sir," said the clerk, "you
must leave this table."[1]

Douglass had been born into slavery in Maryland in 1818.
As he grew into adolescence, he chafed against the restrictions
placed upon him as a slave. He taught himself to read and write,
set up secret schools for other slaves, and attempted to organize
a mass escape to the North. At the age of twenty, he secured his
own liberation by disguising himself as a sailor, using borrowed
identity papers and buying passage to New York. Douglass settled
in Massachusetts, where he was drawn to antislavery meetings at
black churches. His powerful speeches about his life as a slave

soon drew the attention of the growing national antislavery movement, and he became a full-time orator, making hundreds of appearances in communities across the North. In 1845 he published *Narrative of the Life of Frederick Douglass, an American Slave,* which quickly sold tens of thousands of copies and was soon printed in French, Dutch, and German editions. The autobiography brought Douglass international fame and allowed him to start his own newspaper, embark upon further speaking tours, and involve himself in every aspect of the struggle against slavery.[2]

"And why must I leave this table?"

"I want no controversy with you. You must leave this table."

Douglass explained that he was a guest at the hotel. "I expected to pay the same charges imposed upon others; and I came to the table in obedience to the call of the bell; and if I left the table I must know the reason."

"We will serve you in your room. It is against our rules."

"You should have informed me of your rules earlier. Where are your rules? Let me see them."

"I don't want any altercation with you. You must leave this table."

"But have I not deported myself as a gentleman? What have I done? Is there any gentleman who objects to my being seated here?" None of the other people at the table said a word.

"Come, sir, come, sir, you must leave this table at once."

"Well, sir, I cannot leave it unless you will give me a better reason than you have done for my removal."

"Well, I'll give you a reason if you'll leave the table and go to another room."

"That, sir, I will not do. You have invidiously selected me out of all this company, to be dragged from this table, and have thereby reflected upon me as a man and a gentleman; and the reason for this treatment shall be as public as the insult you have offered."

Seeing that Douglass would not be moved, the clerk departed, promising to return with others who would remove him forcibly. He never did. Possibly he did not recognize Douglass, and once informed of his identity, he thought the better of trying to eject an international celebrity. Alternatively, he may have known who Douglass was but had decided nonetheless that the hotel's rule against black people in the dining room had to be enforced. Whatever the case, Douglass recalled that another employee soon appeared "to wait upon me with alacrity." The legendary abolitionist ordered a cup of coffee and, "assisting myself to some of the good things before me, I quietly and thankfully partook of my morning meal without further annoyance."[3]

While this incident ended to Douglass's satisfaction, it also laid bare a reality which he understood all too well: hotelkeepers presumed that they could exclude black people from their premises, the common law of innkeepers notwithstanding. The hotel's managers may have made an exception for him, but they did so at their discretion. If a different black person had been involved that day, the house staff could have ejected him, and done so feeling assured that no jury would convict them.

They had good reason to be confident. Racial segregation or outright exclusion was the norm in every part of the antebellum United States. A visitor to New York in the 1830s reported that when the son of a prominent Haitian general arrived in the city, "he ordered that his luggage be taken to the best hotel. But he found that they would not admit him because of his color. He went to another and another; but everywhere he met with the same result, until he found it necessary to take a room in the home of a black woman." On public transportation, white people's practice of taking their servants or slaves with them when they traveled made it impracticable to bar blacks entirely. Instead, the operators of steamboats, streetcars, and railroads established separate cabins and carriages for the use of black travelers. The proprietors of other kinds of establishments enforced similar rules and were upheld by courts of law. Even in Massachusetts, the most racially progressive jurisdiction in America in the 1850s, the state's highest court permitted theater owners to segregate black customers or, if they wished, to refuse to seat them at all. In these and other public places, the common law protected only those with fair skin.[4]

In the decades that followed, however, the law of innkeepers would become essential to black people's efforts to secure civil rights in public places. This process differed markedly from earlier changes in innkeeper law. The development of the common law in the antebellum period had consisted of numerous legal actions and rulings at the local and state levels; it proceeded in a quiet and gradual fashion, attracting little attention beyond courthouses and hotel offices. By contrast, the restructuring of citizenship and the coming of civil rights played out in the cataclysm of the Civil War and the smoldering ashes of Reconstruction, as millions of black people struggled to secure freedoms denied them under slavery. When southern whites resisted these efforts through evasion and violence, every local incident became a symbol of the meaning of the war and threatened to become a flashpoint in an ongoing political struggle. In this ideologically supercharged atmosphere, American blacks forced questions of equality and civil rights onto the national stage. By century's end, the law of hospitality would be debated in Congress, ruled upon by the Supreme Court, and written into statute books by nearly a score of state legislatures.

THE MEANING OF FREEDOM

The Civil War and Reconstruction led to a radical restructuring of American governance and a corresponding transformation in citizenship. These changes were not planned in advance, and did not take place in an orderly or systematic way. They were instead a series of reactions to the rapidly changing circumstances of the Civil War and its aftermath. The United States, once a nation in which centralized authority was relatively weak and most decisions were made by state governments, became one in which the federal government regularly exercised power within states, taking a direct role in people's lives at the local level. The first step in this transformation was the Emancipation Proclamation, which overruled the authority of the states by freeing most of the nearly four million enslaved Americans held as property under state slave laws. Emancipation crippled the Confederate war effort because it allowed black people to join in the work of crushing the rebellion by serving as scouts, laborers, and eventually soldiers in the Union Army.

The collapse of the Confederacy also raised complex issues of citizenship, the most difficult of which involved the freedpeople. What was to be the status of those liberated from slavery? Would they become full citizens with all the attendant privileges and protections, or would their liberation mean no more than what Congressman James A. Garfield called "the bare privilege of not being chained?" Resolving these questions was more than an exercise in political theory; it would have profound consequences, particularly since the former slaves made up almost one-eighth of the nation's population.[5]

In the wake of emancipation, black Americans sought to make their freedom meaningful by securing legal recognition of their rights. Long before Congress moved to guarantee these rights, black people convened their own representative bodies to convey their wishes to local and national authorities. The black convention held in Alexandria, Virginia, in 1865 demanded that "the laws of the Commonwealth shall give to all men equal protection; that each and every man may appeal to the law for his equal rights without regard to the color of his skin." A group of freedpeople in South Carolina offered a less formal statement to the same effect. "We have no master now," they said. "We is come to the law now."[6]

Southern whites had other ideas, however. Only eight years earlier, the Supreme Court had ruled in *Dred Scott v. Sandford* that blacks "had no rights which the white man was bound to respect," and many would not be convinced otherwise, even after the fall of the Confederacy. Beginning in the fall of 1865, a mere seven months after the surrender at Appomattox, numerous southern legislatures passed Black Codes, draconian laws that sharply curtailed the freedom of black people and explicitly did not apply to whites. Black Codes confined blacks to plantations by prohibiting them from renting land or doing nonagricultural work; imposed fines and imprisonment upon any black person without proof of employment; allowed black children to be "apprenticed" to white masters without their parents' consent; and prescribed heavy fines for a wide range of petty offenses (in Mississippi, these included "seditious speeches, insulting gestures, language or acts"). Black people unable to pay such fines in cash could be forced to work for any white person willing to pay the penalty in their stead. As one contemporary observer commented bitterly, the Black Codes were little more than "plans for getting things back as near to slavery as possible."[7]

The enactment of the Black Codes outraged voters in the North and West, who saw a just-defeated Confederacy attempting to continue the rebellion by other means. Many had already been angered by the outcome of the first postwar elections in the South, in which a white electorate returned much of the antebellum slaveholding elite to power, including many who had been rebel leaders: Georgia, for example, had sent Alexander Stephens, the vice president of the Confederate States of America, to represent it in the Senate. White southern intransigence and numerous episodes of organized violence against black people prepared the way for a series of enactments by Congress, including the Civil Rights Bill of 1866, the Fourteenth Amendment, the Reconstruction Acts of 1867, the Fifteenth Amendment, the Enforcement Acts of 1870–1871, and the Ku Klux Klan Act of 1871. These laws extended federal authority in the South in order to offer citizenship, guarantee equality, extend voting rights, and provide protection from violence to black people.

Of all these, it was the Fourteenth Amendment that had the most important legacy, and that most directly influenced battles over civil rights in public places. The Fourteenth Amendment for the first time in the nation's history provided a constitutional guarantee of equality to all citizens. It stipulated: "No State shall make or enforce any law which shall abridge the privileges or immunities of citizens of the United States; nor shall any State deprive any person of life, liberty, or property, without due process of law; nor deny to any person within its jurisdiction the equal protection of the laws." The provisions of the Fourteenth Amendment dramatically altered the balance between state and federal power by declaring that all citizens were federal citizens who would be protected by the federal government against unequal treatment by the states. In practice, this meant that state laws which explicitly discriminated against former slaves and other black people were declared null and void. For the first time, black people and all other U.S. citizens had recourse against state abuses by direct appeal to the federal government, which replaced the states as the primary protector of civil and other liberties.[8]

From the moment of its ratification in 1868, the Fourteenth Amendment was used as a legal basis for securing equal access to public accommodations. Black communities in cities like Louisville and Savannah staged nonviolent demonstrations in an effort to integrate public transportation, and black legislators in southern states introduced bills requiring equal rights on conveyances and in hotels. While such efforts initially met with defeat, the rising influence of black elected officials in the South translated into increasing success for civil rights statutes after 1870. Texas led the way in 1871 with a law prohibiting railroads from "making any distinction in the carrying of passengers," followed by Florida, Louisiana, Mississippi, South Carolina, and Arkansas, which in 1873 enacted statutes threatening the proprietors of public accommodations with fines, imprisonment, and revocation of licenses if they practiced "discrimination on account of race or color" or otherwise denied any customers "the same accommodations as are furnished other persons." Community pressure and state legislation did result in a few high-profile legal judgments and did in some cases improve black access to public places, particularly in the urban South. More commonly, however, local officials refused to enforce the antidiscrimination laws, and even when charges were filed, judges and juries declined to convict white proprietors. As a result, black plaintiffs were left without further legal recourse. The constant obstruction of antidiscrimination laws at the state level set the stage for federal civil rights legislation that would bring the power of the central government to bear where state and local officials feared or refused to tread.[9]

The federal civil rights bill was first introduced in the Senate in the spring of 1870. As initially drafted, the bill provided that "all citizens of the United States, without distinction of race, color, or previous condition of servitude," would be entitled to equal treatment in an exceptionally broad range of public places: conveyances, inns, theaters and other public amusements, public schools and other state-run educational institutions, churches, cemeteries, and benevolent associations. The fact that the bill outlawed discrimination in so many places and contexts conveyed a profound commitment to racial equality. At this juncture, the proposed act was far more than a public accommodations bill. It was an effort to use the power of the federal government to guarantee that black people and all other Americans would enjoy full civic equality in practically every area of life. While there was no formal statement on the source of congressional authority, the law's emphasis on equality and its reference to "citizens of the United States" both evoked the Fourteenth Amendment.[10]

The bill was the work of Senator Charles Sumner of Massachusetts. Sumner was one of the foremost Radical Republicans in Congress and a longtime supporter of equality for black Americans. He had been a determined foe of slavery, opposing its westward expansion and condemning compromises like the Fugitive Slave Act and the Kansas-Nebraska Bill with great intensity and often with colorful and inflammatory rhetoric. (It had been just such a speech that had so enraged the South Carolina congressman who beat Sumner into unconsciousness at his desk on the Senate floor, making him into an antislavery martyr and convincing people throughout the North of the essential brutality of slaveholders.) Sumner became a close confidant of President Lincoln's during the Civil War and helped persuade him to issue the Emancipation Proclamation. After the war, Sumner rallied support for legislation of importance to black Americans and became so closely associated with the cause of rights and equality that blacks throughout the country flooded his office with letters expressing their hopes and grievances and asking him to represent their interests in Washington.

Sumner's bill faced considerable resistance in Congress. This was in part because his provocative and hectoring style sometimes alienated potential allies and in part because he introduced the measure at a time when the northern public and politicians were beginning to lose interest in the plight of the freedpeople. But there were also legal reasons for congressional hesitance. The civil rights bill provided for direct federal jurisdiction whenever citizens faced discriminatory treatment in public places, allowing the national government to involve itself in local affairs within a state. This was by no means unprecedented, since the Fourteenth Amendment had provided a solid constitutional basis for Congress to prohibit the kind of active and official racial discrimination epitomized by the Black Codes. But the civil rights bill was designed to accomplish the much more ambitious goal of putting an end to virtually all forms of discrimination, including those that could be characterized as private or passive. This was a far more formidable task and presented a specific technical legal difficulty: the wording of the Fourteenth Amendment was that "No State" would be allowed to violate citizens' rights or deny them legal equality.

Congressional opponents of the proposed law seized upon this phrase, arguing that it rendered the entire civil rights bill unconstitutional because it applied to individuals and groups rather than state authorities. Invoking what later became known as the "state action" doctrine, they claimed that any activity not undertaken directly by a state government or its officers was immune to intervention by the federal government. The Ohio Democrat Allen Thurman, for example, attacked the bill as unconstitutional because it ignored the private status of proprietors and effectively made them part of the government: "It makes every tavern-keeper the State in which he lives; every manager of a theater the State in which he lives; every conductor of a railroad the State in which he lives." Similar objections were raised by a Connecticut Republican who protested against what he saw as an illegal usurpation of state sovereignty, a North Carolina Democrat who insisted that "Congress ha[d] no power under the Constitution to pass this bill," and a Georgia Democrat who invoked the threat of international communism and denounced the law as "the most dangerous precedent that has ever been set by this legislative body." These were, of course, political arguments made by people who often objected to the bill for other reasons, but regardless of the good or bad faith behind them, they did raise doubts in some legislators' minds.[11]

The sponsors of the bill thus had to convince their colleagues in Congress that public accommodations and other institutions to which the statute would apply were closely enough related to state governments that they could be regulated by federal authorities under the Fourteenth Amendment. It was in the process of that persuasion that the law of hospitality and related legal regimes became the pivot upon which the entire civil rights bill turned. Proponents of civil rights used hotels, inns, and taverns—all of which were public houses subject to the common law of innkeepers—to exemplify the close connection between states and proprietors. The bill's backers pointed out that innkeeper law required the owners of public houses to provide shelter and refreshment to all travelers. If state and local courts failed to uphold the common-law privileges of black people who wanted to stay at hotels or taverns, they were clearly violating the Fourteenth Amendment by "abridg[ing] the privileges or immunities of citizens" and denying them "the equal protection of the laws." And if this was true of hotels, taverns, and inns, it must also be true of steamboats, railroads, streetcars, and other common carriers, and by implication of theaters, associations, churches, and schools. The common law of innkeepers, in other words, served as the entering wedge of broader assertions about the federal government's authority to regulate a wide variety of institutions and categories of space.[12]

This line of legal reasoning was used time and again by supporters of the civil rights bill. Sumner repeatedly argued its merits on the basis of innkeeper and common-carrier law, which he then analogized to other kinds of institutions. Taking full advantage of his Harvard legal training and experience as a civil rights litigator, the Massachusetts senator asserted that "a legal institution, anything created or regulated by law . . . must be open equally to all without distinction of color." By way of example, he offered the following: "Notoriously, the hotel is a legal institution, originally established by the common law, subject to minute provisions and regulations; notoriously, public conveyances are in the nature of common carriers subject to law of their own; notoriously, schools are public institutions . . . " When another senator argued that some of these institutions were private property and thus beyond the reach of the Fourteenth Amendment, Sumner chided his colleague, replying that the "Senator knows well that the hotel is a legal institution. . . . A railroad corporation is also a legal institution. So is a theater." In a later speech, Sumner reiterated these points by speaking of inns, "which from the earliest days of our jurisprudence" were required to accept all comers, and public conveyances, "which the common law declares equally free to all alike," once more generalizing these points to schools, churches, and cemeteries. He then embarked upon a lengthy oration in which he documented the public status of inns and carriers by citing treatises and offering quotations from various legal authorities. In his summation, Sumner stated explicitly that "inns or public conveyances" were the legal "prototypes" for "theaters and other places of public amusement." He concluded: "As the inn cannot close its doors, or the public conveyance refuse a seat to any paying traveler, decent in condition, so must it be with the theater and other places of public amusement."[13]

The constant invocation of the common law of innkeepers and common carriers was not a tactic particular to Sumner. In the Senate, the New Jersey Republican Frederick Frelinghuysen used such formulations repeatedly in a single speech in an almost incantatory fashion, always using the law of innkeepers as the leading edge of his points by referring time and time again to "inns, places of public amusement, schools," "inns, places of amusement, and public conveyances" (three times), "inns, public conveyances, and places of amusement . . . institutions of learning and benevolence, and cemeteries," "inns or theaters . . . " Senator John Sherman of Ohio referred to the use of inns and carriers as rights that were "as innumerable as the sands of the sea" and explained: "You must go to the common law for them." The same tactic obtained in the House of Representatives, where Judiciary Committee Chairman Benjamin F. Butler opened debate with a speech on the rights shared by all: "Every man has a right to go into a public inn. Every man has a right to go into any place of public amusement . . . any line of stagecoaches, railroad, or other means of public carriage"; Butler then analogized to cemeteries, charitable institutions, and public schools. A Virginia Republican reminded his colleagues that a "hotel is a legal institution, originally established by common law and still subject to statutory regulations; railroads are legal institutions, chartered and vested with all their rights by legislative enactments." The repetition of these phrases and the consistent order in which inns and carriers were mentioned indicates that these legislators, who were familiar with the common law, were consciously using it as a wedge to provide expanded civil rights and remedies to black citizens.[14]

Hotels and other public accommodations were also referred to in ways that transcended narrowly technical argumentation. Many black people who had been denied

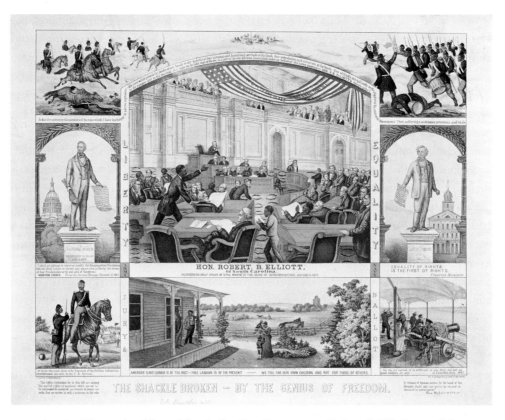

10.1   An 1874 lithograph celebrated South Carolina Congressman Robert B. Elliot's speech in favor of the Civil Rights Act of 1875, which was placed in the context of other major events in black Americans' struggle for freedom and equality. (Chicago History Museum)

accommodations wrote letters to Senator Sumner, who on several occasions read them aloud to his colleagues in the Senate chamber during debate. In the House of Representatives, the enfranchisement of ex-slaves had led to the election of a number of black congressmen, allowing aggrieved parties to speak for themselves from the floor. Robert B. Elliot, a lawyer representing South Carolina, emphasized personal and collective experience alongside legal argument when he declared (fig. 10.1) that "the evils of which we complain, our exclusion from the public inn, from the saloon and table of the steamboat, from the sleeping-coach on the railway, from the right of sepulture in the public burial-ground, are an exercise of the police power of the State." Another black South Carolinian, Representative Joseph H. Rainey, movingly described the treatment accorded his race in restaurants, hotels, conveyances, amusements, churches, and cemeteries. Congressman Richard H. Cain similarly protested that he and many of his associates were regularly refused service in hotels, on trains, and at restaurants.[15]

Opponents of the civil rights bill recognized that arguments based on innkeeper law put them in a difficult position. They were already a numerical minority in Congress and feared that undecided legislators would be swayed by displays of legal erudition and appeals for equality. It was thus critical that they formulate a coherent response, one that functioned at a comparable technical and ideological level. They developed a two-part strategy: first, they tried to reinterpret innkeeper law by counterposing the rights of hosts against those of guests; second, they argued that innkeeper law itself was a legal relic, an obsolete regulatory regime that should be superseded by the operation of free markets.

The common-law regimes governing innkeepers and carriers were so firmly established that they could not simply be dismissed. Instead, foes of the civil rights bill advanced an alternative reading of the common law. On this view, a hotel or an inn was not just a public facility operated by its keeper at the pleasure of the authorities; it must also be thought of as a private space that should be left under the control of its owner. What had previously been a straightforward assignment of duty to innkeepers was thus recast as a collision of competing rights—the guest's right to shelter and security versus the landlord's right to control his premises—that could be settled in favor of either without any contradiction in legal logic. The most aggressive formulation of this claim came from Congressman Milton Durham of Kentucky, who declared, "We have no more right or power to say who shall enter a theater or a hotel and be accommodated therein than to say who shall enter a man's private house or enter into any social amusement to pass away an evening's hour." This interpretation was not without precedent: something much like it had been on display in *Commonwealth v. Mitchel,* the 1850 case involving the keeper of the United States Hotel in Philadelphia. In the context of Reconstruction, it allowed critics of the civil rights bill to defend their position without risking the appearance of disregard for the law in a Congress that was, after all, full of lawyers.[16]

Some opponents of the proposed legislation took a different approach by calling for the outright abandonment of the law of hospitality. Senator William Hamilton, a Maryland Democrat, acknowledged the protective function of the common law but asserted that it was no longer necessary because in a competitive environment of numerous hotels and inns, the economic self-interest of hosts would compel them to admit all comers:

> So far as I am concerned, in reference to inns, I would brush away all the old common-law notions that attached to them hundreds of years ago. . . . The old common-law rights and responsibilities of innkeepers, while still in the law good and applicable, [are] being practically discarded every day; so that there is hardly a case known in the books at this day in which the responsibility of innkeepers has been involved in any suit for not receiving guests, except it may be under the kind of legislation now here attempted in this bill. It is a thing of the past; and if this bill is passed the States ought to change the common-law rule and put inns on the same footing with other common branches of business. Competition is the ruling spirit everywhere, and innkeepers and hotelkeepers now are only too anxious to get guests.

A similar position was staked out in the House of Representatives by William Phelps of New Jersey, who explicitly linked the abrogation of the common law of innkeepers with the laissez-faire imperatives of capitalism. Phelps denied that innkeeper law had been established to protect public safety by keeping travelers from harm. Instead, he claimed, it had been merely a side effect of a policy of official favoritism in which the state guaranteed the profitability of particular businesses: "Governments used to give especial privileges and monopolies to the inn-keeper, and then the government in proper reciprocity had a right to impose obligations and duties. . . . The reason of the law that used to govern them failing, the law itself fails. We no longer give to inn-keepers especial privileges—any monopoly in the business; we cannot therefore burden their business with any restrictions." Other enemies of the act went so far as to claim that it was not needed. Senator Lyman Trumbull of Illinois averred: "I know of no right to ride in a car, no right to stop at a hotel, no right to travel possessed by the white man that the colored man has not." Representative Q. C. Lamar of Mississippi implausibly insisted that *"throughout the length of the Southern section there does not exist in law* one single trace of privilege or discrimination against the black race. If there is, I know nothing of it." Indeed, continued Lamar, black people did in fact "travel precisely with the same facilities and with the same conveniences . . . [as] the white people of Mississippi."[17]

It is difficult to imagine that these politicians truly believed that the law of hospitality was unnecessary because capitalist competition ensured blacks equal treatment in public places. In fact, the operation of the free market yielded precisely the opposite result. Hotel-keeping was a highly competitive business, and keepers were indeed eager for customers. But the overwhelming majority of customers were white, and many of them would have been offended by the very idea of sleeping in a bedchamber on the same hall with a black man or sharing space at the dinner table with a black family. Under such conditions, even hoteliers who believed in equality could not have put their ideals into practice without destroying their livelihoods by losing their patrons to competitors who continued to discriminate. When it came to race and public accommodations, Adam Smith's "invisible hand" of the free market served to bar the door to black Americans.

But the real-life implications of the free market were really beside the point, since the actual reason that enemies of racial equality denigrated the common law and embraced the ideology of capitalism was as rhetorical cover for sheer racism. From the point of view of white supremacy, the benefit of laissez-faire arguments was precisely that they made it possible to defend discrimination with high-sounding theoretical language. In the political environment of Reconstruction, this was a useful stance. While southern whites and blacks nationwide were unlikely to alter their positions on the civil rights bill, the huge white electorate outside the South might yet be swayed. An explicitly racist opposition to the bill might offend their sense of equality and perhaps radicalize them into supporting it. But the softer, free-market basis for opposing the bill offered a way to keep blacks excluded from hotels and segregated on streetcars even as it purported to be racially neutral.

There was considerable irony here in terms of the development of Western political philosophy. The common law of innkeepers and carriers—a two thousand–year–old set of rules which had been codified in the despotism of the Roman Empire, sustained for centuries by a European ancien régime dedicated to the power of aristocrats and monarchs, and brought to America by English settlers who enslaved Africans and understood humanity as being divided between superiors and inferiors—became the key to racial equality in public places. Meanwhile, the ideology of the free market—a theory that had emerged in the age of the American Revolution and shared many of its intellectual assumptions, including the illegitimacy of arbitrary authority and the primacy and naturalness of human freedom—provided the surest defense of racial discrimination.[18]

It gradually became apparent that the common law marked the line between defeat and passage for the civil rights bill. Among undecided legislators, the proposed law's applicability to cemeteries and churches proved a sticking point. A Republican senator from Connecticut, for example, criticized Sumner's argument for the regulation of cemeteries as "a construction so extravagant that no one has followed him" and denounced efforts to include churches as "enter[ing] the sanctuary of God with unholy hand." He was echoed by an Indiana Republican who protested that churches, as "purely voluntary organizations," should not be subject to federal authority. Even Sumner's allies were wary of extending the bill beyond licensed commercial establishments. Fearing defections from among their ranks, they decided to strip the bill of its application to establishments other than inns, common carriers, and places of amusement (the last of these retained despite a concerted effort to strike it, as well). Sumner was furious, but his congressional cohorts were able to demonstrate that the law could not pass unamended. The federal civil rights law, in other words, could be made to reach only marginally farther than the common law.[19]

The changes to the bill persuaded wavering legislators not to oppose it, and the death of Senator Sumner galvanized support for its enactment as a tribute to the crusading elder statesman. The Civil Rights Act of 1875 became law by a vote of 35–18 in the Senate and 118–94 in the House of Representatives. In its final form, the law specified that "all persons within the jurisdiction of the United States shall be entitled to the full and equal enjoyment of the accommodations, advantages, facilities, and privileges of inns, public conveyances on land or water, theaters, and other places of public amusement; subject only to the conditions and limitations established by law, and applicable alike to citizens of every race and color, regardless of any previous condition of servitude." Any person who felt that he or she had been discriminated against could sue the offending proprietor in federal court, and in the event of a guilty verdict, would be entitled to collect five hundred dollars in statutory damages. In order to avoid the kind of obstructionism that had all but negated state public accommodations laws, the Civil Rights Act levied heavy fines upon any official who failed to take action on a legitimate complaint.[20]

The passage of the act wrote the law of hospitality into the federal statute books. The effort to make innkeeper and common-carrier law into a spearhead for equality in a far broader range of public places had mostly failed, though supporters felt that an important precedent had been set at the national level. But the true measure of the Civil Rights Act

CIVIL RIGHTS. (?)
Waiting for a Five-Hundred-Dollar Kick.

10.2 Echoing the views of racist hotelkeepers, a cartoonist for *Harper's Weekly* portrayed the Civil Rights Act of 1875 as driven by avarice rather than egalitarianism. (University of New Mexico Center for Southwest Research)

would be its effect in actual practice, and there was considerable uncertainty as to whether it would be enforced and how Americans would react to it.

CLAIMING CIVIL RIGHTS UNDER THE ACT

The debates in Congress had attracted a great deal of public attention, and the act's passage on the first day of March 1875 drew energetic responses from both supporters and opponents of the law (fig. 10.2). Southern whites were predictably hostile. Northern whites were more ambivalent: they still wished to see themselves as fair-minded and egalitarian, but were often indifferent to the problems of black Americans, particularly when protecting their rights required federal intervention in the South. This view was typified by a New York newspaper editorial that condescendingly predicted that black people in the North would "hardly deem it prudent to force themselves into first-class hotels or restaurants. . . . The negroes in this part of the country are quiet, inoffensive people who live for and to themselves, and have no desire to intrude where they are not welcome." The editors warned, however, that southern blacks could not be counted on to do the same. "In the South," they lamented, "there are many colored men and women who delight in 'scenes' and cheap notoriety."[21]

Southern hotelkeepers apparently shared this expectation, for many took immediate measures to avoid serving black people. Some closed their businesses outright. When the keeper of Baltimore's Park Hotel learned that the Civil Rights Act had passed, he shut his doors to the public, and on the same day, the managers of the two leading hotels in Alexandria, Virginia, surrendered their licenses and shuttered their premises. In other cases, proprietors took advantage of legal technicalities to foil the act. In Chattanooga, Tennessee, for example, two hotelkeepers handed back their licenses and reopened as private boardinghouses not subject to the new law. And throughout the state of Virginia, saloonkeepers set the price of a drink at five dollars—two or more days' wages for most American workers—but reserved the right to offer special discounts to their friends. "Presumably," notes the historian John Hope Franklin by way of explanation, "the proprietors had no Negro friends."[22]

Southern state governments also participated in efforts to evade the Civil Rights Act and intimidate its beneficiaries. The Tennessee state legislature abolished and the Delaware legislature modified the common law of innkeepers and carriers within state borders. This meant that black people could be barred from public accommodations without any violation of the Fourteenth Amendment's equal protection clause, since nobody, white or black, would be able to claim a legal right to stay at a hotel or ride in a first-class railway coach. The message was clear: Tennessee and Delaware lawmakers would rather leave white wayfarers unprotected by the common law than see it used to guarantee equal treatment to black people. An analogous bill introduced in the Virginia state legislature was explicitly intended "to punish parties creating disturbances in hotels, theaters, and other places of amusement." With such a law in place, proprietors could stage a prearranged ruckus whenever a black person ventured onto their premises. This would leave the "intruder" liable for state criminal penalties while protecting the owner from federal civil rights prosecution, since the commotion would prevent a formal request for service or an outright denial of it. The Virginia bill also required theater owners to mark their admission tickets "not transferable" in an effort to prevent black people from taking seats in the whites-only section bearing tickets bought for them by light-skinned blacks or sympathetic whites.[23]

Elaborate preparations like these made it clear that the defenders of white supremacy expected to be challenged on every street. They were right to be apprehensive. Black Americans moved quickly and decisively to claim their rights under the act, launching a wave of highly organized activism which, contrary to expectations that it would be limited to the South, also extended into the North and West. The day after the act's passage, several black citizens of Richmond methodically entered the bar room at the Exchange Hotel, a number of restaurants, and a barber shop and demanded service alongside other customers. In Philadelphia, a black minister asked for a room at the Bingham House. The hotel's managers initially turned him away on the grounds that the house was full. At that point, a white guest fortuitously appeared and offered to share his room with the reverend, which the proprietors refused to allow. The minister thereupon sat down in the hotel lobby, where he spent the entire night observing and taking notes as the desk clerk signed in and handed keys to white guests no fewer than eighteen times. The following day, he took his carefully collected evidence to the local U.S. attorney. Similarly sophisticated tactics were used in a New York case in which an agent for a black newspaper twice tried to enter the Grand Opera House, once with tickets bought by a light-skinned friend and a second time with tickets purchased by a white boy whom he paid ten cents for his assistance.[24]

Equally important were less coordinated but more numerous challenges to discrimination made by people across the nation in the months that followed. In Wilmington, North Carolina, a man demanded the arrest of a saloonkeeper who refused to serve him because he was black. In New Orleans a couple sought to take a stateroom on a Mississippi steamboat. In Galveston, Texas, two women tried to occupy seats in the Tremont Opera House. In Chicago two theatergoers insisted on seats in the dress circle of McVickers Theater. In New York a black man and his white friend tried to get into the parquet at Booth's Theater. And in San Francisco and Winona, Minnesota, complainants sought grand jury indictments of proprietors who denied them accommodations.[25]

It seems the only people unprepared for the popular uprising engendered by the Civil Rights Act were the federal officials responsible for enforcing it. The attorney general sent out no special instructions regarding the act despite having done so with much less important legislation, and Justice Department representatives in many districts had not even been supplied with official copies of the law. As a result, in March 1875 letters and telegrams requesting certified copies poured in from Tennessee, Ohio, Georgia, and other states, and from cities including Chicago, Savannah, New Orleans, and San Francisco. Black Americans' desire for equality in public places was unmistakable: by 1880 the United States Attorney General's office reported that despite their best efforts to clear their dockets, federal appeals courts still had a backlog of 158 cases.[26]

While resistance to equality in public accommodations was primarily a question of white discrimination against black people, there were signs that other varieties of prejudice could be involved as well. In June 1877 Joseph Seligman went with his family to the resort community of Saratoga, New York, where they planned to spend the season together. As they had for the previous ten summers, the Seligmans went to the Grand Union Hotel, an establishment owned by the New York City businessman Judge Henry Hilton. As they entered, Mrs. Seligman led the children into one of the public parlors while her husband went to the front desk to arrange for their rooms. The manager seemed confused. "Mr. Seligman," he announced after an uncomfortable silence, "I am required to inform you that Mr. Hilton has given instructions that no Israelites shall be permitted in future to stop at this hotel." "Do you mean to tell me," responded Seligman, "that you will not entertain Jewish people?" The manager had welcomed the Seligmans to the hotel in the past, and was embarrassed and apologetic. "Business at the hotel was not good last season," he explained, "and we had a large number of Jews here. Mr. Hilton came to the conclusion that Christians did not like their company, and for that reason shunned the hotel. He resolved to run the Union on a different principle this season, and gave us instructions to admit no Jew." Angry and disappointed, the Seligmans returned to their home in New York City.[27]

The incident quickly escalated into a national controversy. Seligman and Hilton exchanged barbs in open letters that ran in the New York dailies and were reprinted in newspapers nationwide, editorial boards and cartoonists provided running commentary, boycotts were launched, hotelkeepers and bankers issued statements pro and con, leading clergymen dedicated Sunday sermons to the issue, and people delivered themselves of public speeches. (One anti-Seligman oration offered in the middle of a play was met with a hail of handbags from ladies in the balcony.) Part of the reason the episode garnered so much attention was the novelty of publicly declared anti-Semitism: Jews had certainly been discriminated against before in America, but this was the first widely reported instance in which there was an open declaration, raising the subject for popular discussion. Even more relevant to the public's interest was the exclusion of such an eminent and influential citizen. The Seligman family included some of the most important bankers in the United States, and their recent deal with J. P. Morgan and the House of Rothschild to handle the sale of U.S. bonds in Europe had created the world's most powerful banking consortium. Joseph Seligman had been asked to run for mayor of New York City and had been nominated for secretary of the treasury during the Grant administration; he declined to enter politics but did aid Grant by organizing the clearance of the government's Civil War debt. The Saratoga incident gave the lie to claims that free-market economics was a panacea for discrimination. Capitalism had made Joseph Seligman wealthy, but even with his mastery of national and international financial markets, he was defenseless at the hotel check-in desk.[28]

Exclusion from hotels and other public places had become a full-scale cultural trend in American life. By far the most widespread and frequent manifestation remained discrimination against black people. The refusal of service to Jews was much less prevalent, but the practice had been on the rise since the end of the Civil War, and after the Seligman affair, numerous resort hotels barred Jewish patrons, a trend that intensified with the increased immigration from central and eastern Europe that began in the 1880s. This development was linked to another, somewhat different exclusionary tendency, one based on class. The rising prosperity of the second half of the nineteenth century had made vacations affordable for a greater proportion of Americans than ever before, and resorts that were once the exclusive province of a small, wealthy elite were increasingly patronized by a growing middle class. When hotelkeepers and resort owners barred Jews, they did so in part out of fear that their presence would democratize their establishments by driving away high-society patronage and turning them into haunts of the common people. While this kind of status anxiety and class snobbery was in many respects different from racial or religious discrimination, all these examples of exclusion indicated that public accommodations had become a barometer of acceptance and citizenship in the United States. They raised once again the question that had been at the forefront of national politics since Emancipation: what sort of civil rights protection could Americans expect from their federal government?

The constitutionality of the Civil Rights Act had been called into question since the debates over its passage, and some people, judges included, considered it an unwarranted and illegal arrogation of power by the federal government. A few months after the signing of the act, the editor of the *Galveston News* criticized a federal judge in Texas for a prosecution under it. A Tennessee circuit judge declared in the spring of 1875 that Congress had no right "to declare it a crime for any individuals to deny to negroes the full and equal enjoyment of accommodations," and a North Carolina jurist explicitly charged a jury to the effect that the act was unconstitutional and should not be enforced. Even some judges willing to support the law believed that the phrase "full and equal enjoyment" permitted segregation. In a before-the-fact elaboration of the "separate but equal" doctrine associated with the *Plessy v. Ferguson* case of 1896, judges in North Carolina and Texas suggested that while innkeepers were bound to maintain equal facilities for blacks and whites, they need not be the same facilities. Other jurists, like a U.S. district judge in Minnesota who stated that "the power of Congress can be exerted directly to put down all outrage or discrimination on the part of individuals when the motive originates only in race or color," clearly saw the act as an appropriate exercise of federal power. But such differences of opinion left many judges uncertain and desirous of a definitive statement on the constitutionality of the law.[29]

The statement was eight years in coming. The *Civil Rights Cases* consisted of five separate suits brought on the basis of the Civil Rights Act of 1875—two innkeeper cases, two theater cases, and a railroad case—that were bundled together for a single adjudication. A great deal was at stake in the *Civil Rights Cases.* The Supreme Court was faced with yet another dispute over the balance between federal and state power, one that, because it spoke directly to relations between white and black Americans, was freighted with tremendous emotional weight and practical consequences. Chief among these was the question of whether the national government would continue to play any role at all in protecting blacks from abuse, particularly in the states of the former Confederacy—this at a time when southern whites were intent on reestablishing themselves as a racial master class over a subservient caste of blacks.[30]

The Supreme Court shocked supporters of federally guaranteed civil rights and delighted opponents of the Civil Rights Act by declaring the law unconstitutional. An eight-judge majority ruled that the act unlawfully allowed the federal government to interfere with private action. In so doing, the Court adopted precisely the same logic of private property rights that had undergirded both Judge Parsons's decision in the 1850 *Commonwealth v. Mitchel* case and the objections to the act proffered during debates in Congress in the 1870s. According to the justices, while "state action of a particular character" was indeed prohibited by the Fourteenth Amendment, the "individual invasion of individual rights" was not. "The wrongful act of an individual," the majority wrote, "is simply a private wrong, or a crime of that individual." Such actions, they reasoned, must be provided with remedies at the state level. That many states consistently denied such remedies to people of color was, in the Court's view, simply beyond the purview of the federal government. Indeed, the justices went so far as to deny that it was even possible for an individual to deprive a fellow citizen of his or her rights because "civil rights, such as are guaranteed by the Constitution against State aggression, cannot be impaired by the wrongful acts of individuals, unsupported by state authority, *in the shape of laws, customs, or judicial or executive proceedings.*" The ruling thus accepted the private status of innkeepers, conveyances, and other accommodations, and declared that this status protected them from federal prosecution.[31]

Justice John Marshall Harlan's lone dissent in the *Civil Rights Cases* was a classic of the genre, the most significant objection to a majority ruling until his dissent in *Plessy v. Ferguson* thirteen years later. Harlan condemned the "narrow and artificial" grounds of the majority opinion, protesting fiercely against the way "the substance and spirit of the recent [Constitutional] amendments . . . have been sacrificed by a subtle and ingenious verbal criticism" that largely ignored the facts before the Court. He was angered by his fellow justices' willingness to rule on narrowly technical grounds when it was clear to all concerned what this would mean for black people throughout the South. As Harlan saw it, the intention of the Thirteenth and Fourteenth Amendments—to establish citizenship for almost four million freedpeople and protect their rights—was being ignored on the grounds of an unjust abstraction of legal theory. Against this privatistic interpretation that would leave black Americans defenseless before anything short of deliberate, state-sponsored discrimination, Harlan counterposed the common-law duty of hosts and other proprietors of traditionally regulated establishments to serve the public and protect travelers. He asserted that "innkeepers are a sort of public servants" and emphasized the "public nature of [their] employment"; he also cited case law defining a railroad as "established by public authority, intended for the public use and benefit," and noted that though a corporation might be private, "its work was public." But this common-law vision of the public good was no longer as important to American law as it once had been, and Harlan found himself in a minority of one.[32]

The ruling in the *Civil Rights Cases* had various meanings and implications. In the immediate legal sense, it invalidated the use of federal power to protect black citizens against "private" discrimination. States were given license to permit abuses against black people by doing nothing to prevent them. Hotels and other public accommodations would be governed by local, vernacular legal custom rather than operated according to a cosmopolitan ethic of national citizenship. People's use of public places would be a question of private right rather than public good. In a broader sense, a trend that had begun in the 1830s, that of extending the protections of the law of hospitality to a wider public, would founder on the shoals of American racism. And in the most general terms, Congress's effort to nationalize the law of hospitality, thereby making it into a protective regime that would apply to all citizens throughout the United States, would come to a halt.

Yet the Supreme Court's invalidation of the Civil Rights Act was by no means the end of the line for equal access to public accommodations. Within two years of the verdict in the *Civil Rights Cases,* states across the North and West enacted civil rights statutes modeled on the now-defunct federal act. Connecticut, Iowa, New Jersey, and Ohio legislated in 1884, followed by Colorado, Illinois, Indiana, Michigan, Minnesota, Nebraska, and Rhode Island in 1885. By century's end, counting Massachusetts, New York, and Kansas, which had enacted measures before the federal act, and with the addition of Pennsylvania (1887), Washington (1890), Wisconsin (1895), and California (1897), eighteen states had civil rights acts on the books.[33]

These state statutes conspicuously reproduced the same common-law formulations used in the federal act. In some cases, as with the New Jersey statute, the language was practically identical, prohibiting discrimination in "inns, public conveyances on land or water, theaters and other places of public amusement." Most other state statutes were considerably more detailed, and included many different kinds of space; this was done because in a number of earlier suits, the proprietors of bars, restaurants, barber shops, and other establishments not directly mentioned by the federal enactment had entered pleas that they were not covered by it. But while the state laws mentioned more kinds of establishments, these were usually grouped in such a way as to preserve the previous order of inns, carriers, and public amusements. This was done by grouping close legal analogues after the main establishment type, as in the Illinois statute, which prohibited discrimination in "inns, restaurants, eating-houses, barber shops, public conveyances on land and water, theatres, and all other places of public accommodation and amusement."[34]

In the South, the ruling in the *Civil Rights Cases* was greeted by whites in a very different spirit. The inauguration of the Hayes administration in 1877 had signaled the end of Reconstruction: even Republican politicos talked about leaving the South to put its own house in order, and there was a general troop withdrawal from southern states. As a result, white supremacists were left with little opposition to their plans to reestablish a racial hierarchy. Their first steps were to cut funding for public programs, increase poll taxes, and remove black people from offices and courtrooms. After the 1883 decision, they began to move more aggressively to repress black people in public places. Tennessee became the first state to pass a Jim Crow law on the railroads, a move soon seconded by Texas. Between 1888 and 1892 three more states passed segregation laws, followed by another five over the next decade.[35]

Black people did not passively accept the imposition of racial segregation and exclusion; they continued to protest and litigate against Jim Crow into the twentieth century. With the collapse of Reconstruction and the return of home rule to the South, however, there were few legal resources they could use to oppose discriminatory practices in public accommodations. After 1883 black people could no longer seek equal access on common-law grounds, the Supreme Court having declared "private" discrimination to be legally permissible. Within a few years, white supremacists became so politically powerful that state legislatures not only allowed racial segregation, they increasingly *required* it. It was in this legal and political environment that Homer Plessy mounted a challenge to Louisiana's segregation law by refusing to leave a first-class train compartment. In a ruling that has since become famous but was little noted at the time, the Supreme Court in *Plessy v. Ferguson* validated the state's argument that putatively "separate but equal" compartments did not violate the rights of black passengers. In the aftermath of this ruling, little stood in the way of total segregation in every aspect of southern life. For more than two generations hence, blacks were forced out of public accommodations or segregated within them with little hope of change.

CODA: INNKEEPER LAW AND CIVIL RIGHTS IN THE TWENTIETH CENTURY

When the long struggle against racial discrimination finally gained momentum in the mid-twentieth century, innkeeper law again played a crucial role. It was no accident that black activists and their allies focused so much attention on institutions that served travelers, since that focus allowed them once again to mobilize legal regimes of travel in order to translate demands for equality into judicial and legislative action.

Even as the shadows of Jim Crow spread across the South in the 1880s and 1890s, Americans' habit of moving from place to place was creating new possibilities for achieving racial equality. The sheer extent of the U.S. railroad system meant that some trains passed through a dozen states or more, making them subject to many different state statutes. The resultant jurisdictional conflicts threatened to hobble the smooth operation of interstate railroads that were vital to the national economy. Congress responded in 1887 by creating America's first modern administrative agency: the Interstate Commerce Commission. The ICC was granted plenary authority over the regulation of railroads and other means of interstate transportation, allowing it to override state law and create national standards for every aspect of commerce and travel.

Black Americans understood that white supremacist state legislatures would never willingly recognize their rights, but thought they saw an opportunity to enlist the federal government in their struggle. They demanded that the ICC use its authority to overrule state segregation laws. When this conflict of federal and state power came before the Supreme Court, however, it ruled in favor of states, deciding in 1890 that state segregation laws could be applied to travelers within a state without violating federal regulations regarding interstate commerce. Black litigants continued to appeal to the ICC, but with few exceptions, federal power over commerce proved no match for local enforcement of segregation. Whether sustained by custom, instituted by proprietors, or required by state law, discrimination against black people in public places was left unchecked by federal authority for three-quarters of a century.[36]

The twentieth century brought new possibilities for using federal authority in support of civil rights. The commerce power behind the ICC was redefined and augmented during the Progressive Era and the New Deal to address the problems of a national industrial economy and used to reduce food contamination, combat child labor, and regulate farms and factories. Beginning around midcentury, black Americans and their allies refashioned the commerce power into a new means by which traditional protections of travelers could be federalized and extended to all Americans in all categories of public space.[37]

Cases involving travel gave black litigants their first sustained victories against Jim Crow. In 1937 Congressman Arthur Mitchell of Illinois was ejected from a Pullman railroad car in Arkansas and filed a complaint with the ICC. Mitchell gained the support of the Roosevelt administration and in 1941 won a unanimous Supreme Court ruling that it was unconstitutional to deny blacks the use of such facilities as were available to other passengers in interstate travel. In 1945 the Court heard *Morgan v. Virginia,* the suit of a Maryland woman who had been arrested and fined for refusing to give up her seat on a Greyhound bus in Virginia. It ruled Virginia's segregation law unconstitutional when applied to interstate buses, stating that the United States must have "a single, uniform rule to promote and protect national travel." Similarly, in *Henderson v. United States* (1950), the Court ruled unanimously that racially segregated dining car facilities contravened federal laws governing interstate commerce.[38]

These verdicts were not based upon equal-protection arguments under the Fourteenth Amendment; no assertion was being made that the Constitution prohibited segregation. The rulings instead rested on the narrow grounds of federal powers that had been established to deal with interstate commerce: administration officials were permitted discretion over travel between states, and it was their choice whether and when to use it. The justices appointed to the Supreme Court by Franklin Delano Roosevelt had identified the rights of "discrete and insular minorities" as a pressing concern, but elected officials still considered it too politically risky to launch a frontal attack on Jim Crow.[39]

The pace of change quickened in the mid-1950s. The Supreme Court's ruling in *Brown v. Board of Education* signaled a newfound willingness to uphold direct and sweeping legal challenges to state-mandated segregation. The Court's decision did not put an immediate end to the practice. As recent histories of the civil rights movement have demonstrated, even the most authoritative verdicts were routinely ignored at the local level and usually required direct action by black activists to have any real effect. The *Brown* decision did, however, establish an important legal precedent against racial inequality in state-run institutions. Meanwhile, a bus boycott in Montgomery, Alabama, succeeded in desegregating public transit in the city and prompted the ICC to issue a general order prohibiting racial segregation in all modes of interstate transportation. The victory of the bus boycott heralded the activation of an existing grassroots movement that was ready to challenge Jim Crow not only in interstate travel but also in the local realm.[40]

These developments ushered in a new phase in the civil rights struggle. Litigation and demonstrations had led to important legal victories, but these had been possible only because they involved institutions over which the federal government had a solid claim to jurisdiction. *Brown* had depended upon the schools involved being clearly public, state-sponsored institutions subject to Fourteenth Amendment requirements of equal treatment. City-owned buses in Montgomery shared the same unquestionably public status. Buses and trains might escape federal regulation because they were privately owned, but if their routes took them across state lines, they instantly became subject to rules set by the ICC.

Yet many spaces were both private and local, complicating the effort to end discrimination. Segregationists recognized this and initiated a wave of privatization intended to shift the struggle onto more favorable legal terrain. Southern state legislatures passed bills permitting the abolition of public schools, providing for the lease or sale of school buildings to private parties, and permitting tax money to be turned over to all-white private academies. Meanwhile, counties and municipalities hastily transferred public facilities like buses, parks, and swimming pools to private hands that would conveniently reopen them on a whites-only basis. In so doing, the white South hoped to hide behind the state action doctrine established in the *Civil Rights Cases* of 1883 and preserve segregation by way of privatization. Only a few years after it had been resurrected as a force for equality, the Fourteenth Amendment seemed to have reached its limits.[41]

These new circumstances required a new legal strategy, and in working one out, civil rights lawyers once again turned to common-law protections of travelers. In 1959 Jack Greenberg, who would soon be appointed lead attorney of the NAACP Legal Defense Fund, published a book in which he described the state of American civil rights law and suggested future approaches to desegregation. Greenberg turned first to public accommodations, observing that most discrimination in such places was private and noting the difficulties presented by the state action doctrine. Yet there were other legal possibilities, he wrote, since "some common law doctrines deserve attention in connection with public accommodations," particularly the duties of innkeepers and common carriers. Greenberg paid special attention to the law of innkeepers in a detailed analysis of a century's worth of English and American cases and treatises. The relationship between the law of hospitality and contemporary civil rights was explicit: Greenberg explained that innkeeper law had been "developed to protect the traveler in a day when the solitary inn between cities was a necessity on long, dangerous journeys" and observed that "in states where Negroes may expect to be turned away from all places reserved for whites, their position rather closely approximates that of the old English traveler: food, shelter, and protection are hard to come by." The distant past was clearly in play in the mid-twentieth century.[42]

Greenberg was not alone in seeing the common law as crucial to the struggle for equality: many southern states had already reached the same conclusion. Recognizing that the traditional duty to offer hospitality could be used to require equal treatment of black people in public accommodations, segregationist legislators statutorily altered the common law. In 1953 Delaware exempted proprietors of inns, restaurants, and similar establishments from the duty to serve anyone whom they thought would be offensive to other customers. Louisiana in 1954 repealed an earlier law requiring innkeepers to serve all members of the public. Tennessee in 1955 reaffirmed its earlier abrogation of the common-law obligation to accept all comers. The following year, Mississippi granted any person operating a "public business" the right to select patrons. In 1958 Florida decreed that all public lodging and food establishments were private, giving their owners the right to turn away customers. In 1959 Alabama repealed the state code's incorporation of innkeeper law. That same year, Arkansas effectively trumped the common law by threatening with fines and imprisonment "any person who shall enter [a] public business and create disturbance or breach of peace in any way whatsoever."[43]

The state action doctrine of the *Civil Rights Cases* and the rush to privatize space in the South made it clear that real equality would require federal intervention, as it had in the 1870s. But the Eisenhower White House was ideologically resistant to expanding federal authority over the states, and the Kennedy administration was also reluctant to undertake any major civil rights initiative due to its electoral dependence upon white southern votes.

The impetus for further progress on civil rights came from black activists and their allies (fig. 10.3). The growing involvement of students in the civil rights movement fostered new, more assertive acts of civil disobedience and direct action, most notably sit-ins and freedom rides. The responses of southern whites ranged from humiliation to attempted mass murder: sit-in demonstrators were taunted, smeared with food, and punched from behind by crowds of jeering whites; when freedom riders stopped in Anniston, Alabama, a mob firebombed their bus. Incidents like these, combined with that year's multiple bombings and murders of civil rights activists and their children, forced the Kennedy White House to pursue a national public accommodations bill in hopes of averting more demonstrations, riots, and killings. It was indicative that in his "I Have a Dream" speech to the March on Washington in the summer of 1963, Martin Luther King specifically noted that black Americans could "never be satisfied as long as our bodies, heavy with the fatigue of travel, cannot gain lodging in the motels of the highways and the hotels of the cities."[44]

The civil rights struggle also had an important international component involving incidents in which African diplomats and other foreign dignitaries were turned away from hotels and restaurants. Since the beginning of the Cold War, episodes of racial discrimination against foreign visitors had been exposing U.S. consular officials to intense embarrassment. From a Mississippi hotel's refusal to accommodate Haiti's agriculture minister in 1947 to a Maryland restaurant's denial of service to the ambassador from Chad in 1961, repeated incidents had made Jim Crow into a major geopolitical liability. State Department officials repeatedly warned of the resultant damage to American prestige, emphasizing that such episodes were being reported globally and causing deep offense in precisely those nations in Africa, Asia, and Latin America where the United States was struggling to win allies. More than a century and a half after Immanuel Kant proposed that hospitality was a necessary condition for world peace, events were proving him right.[45]

The response from the White House and Congress was an omnibus civil rights bill of which the main innovation and primary importance consisted in Title II, the section on public accommodations. In phrasing that closely resembled the Civil Rights Act of 1875,

10.3   During a 1962 NAACP protest against hotel segregation in Atlanta, a civil rights worker
is confronted by a Klansman. (Atlanta Journal-Constitution Archives)

Title II proposed to outlaw discrimination in "any inn, hotel, motel . . . any restaurant, cafeteria, lunchroom, lunch counter, soda fountain . . . any motion picture house, theater, concert hall, sports arena, stadium or other place of exhibition or entertainment."[46]

In hearings on the civil rights bill, legislators heard testimony regarding the difficulties, indignities, and perils facing black travelers.[47] NAACP Executive Secretary Roy Wilkins reminded the Senate Judiciary Committee that "while we talk here today, while we talked last week, and while the Congress will be debating in the next weeks, Negro Americans throughout our country will be bruised in nearly every waking hour by differential treatment in, or exclusion from, public accommodations of every description. From the time they leave their homes in the morning, en route to school or to work, to shopping or to visiting, until they return home at night, humiliation stalks them." His sentiments were echoed by James Farmer, the national head of the Congress of Racial Equality, who explained to the House Judiciary Committee that "the humiliation and degradation every Negro faces when trying to just find accommodations is a day by day lifelong horror." After weeks of hearings that ran to thousands of pages of recorded testimony, Minnesota Senator Hubert H. Humphrey summarized Congress's findings by describing his realization that black wayfarers were forced to "draw up travel plans much as a general advancing across hostile territory."[48]

After months of debate, careful parliamentary maneuvering, and the first-ever breaking of a southern filibuster on a civil rights bill, the Civil Rights Act was passed by Congress and signed into law by President Johnson in an evening ceremony on 2 July 1964. Within two hours, Moreton Rolleston, an attorney and part-owner of the Heart of Atlanta Motel, filed a lawsuit challenging the act's constitutionality. Rolleston asserted that the Civil Rights Act of 1964 must be declared unconstitutional for the same reason the act of 1875 had been: the Fourteenth Amendment required state action to trigger federal enforcement, and the motel was a privately owned business. In making his case, he reached for the same property-rights arguments that had been used against federal civil rights legislation nearly a century earlier. Rolleston maintained that the "fundamental question . . . is whether or not Congress has the power to take away the liberty of an individual to run his business as he sees fit in the selection and choice of his customers." He also made two secondary constitutional arguments. The act was, he said, an unlawful contravention of the Fifth Amendment's prohibition against depriving a person of life, liberty, or property without due process of law. Rolleston also asserted that the civil rights law violated the Thirteenth Amendment because requiring the motel's managers to serve black customers was the same as making the former into slaves.[49]

The task facing the Department of Justice was to show why the Supreme Court should uphold the act of 1964 despite its being nearly identical to the act of 1875. In briefs filed by the Justice Department and state solicitors general in *Heart of Atlanta Motel v. United States,* the need to protect black travelers was the key justification offered for the act. The technical argument was based on the Constitution's commerce clause, but the line of reasoning rested more upon the need to protect actual travelers than it did upon an economistic notion of disrupted trade. Solicitor General Archibald Cox's brief pointed out that the act had been motivated by "overwhelming evidence that discrimination by hotels and motels impedes interstate travel by Negroes, and interstate travel is, of course, a form of interstate commerce. The plain truth is that in many places lodging is simply not available to Negro travelers."[50] State *amicus* briefs were even more focused on the protection of travelers. California's brief expressed concern for "the rights of California's citizens in their interstate travels" and noted that "commerce in people binds our nation together in a way that commerce in products alone could never do." The New York brief declared that while black people were "protected under the laws of this State . . . their ability to move freely in certain other parts of the country for pleasure or business has been impeded by discrimination." The Massachusetts brief noted that it was "obvious that many persons of the discriminated-against minority will avoid traveling in areas where they expect to be humiliated and degraded." While the means of travel and the modes of governance had certainly changed, the special attention to the needs of travelers would have been familiar to the American jurists of one hundred or two hundred years earlier.[51]

The law of hospitality was specifically invoked in support of the Civil Rights Act. The Justice Department's brief leaned heavily upon defining hotels, motels, and inns as places which were definitively public, a point it buttressed by emphasizing the long history of the innkeeper's duties: "A public inn is, of course, one of the most ancient and plainest examples of a business affected with a public interest." Since innkeepers had "conventionally been subject, since long before the Bill of Rights was adopted, to the common-law duty to serve all travellers equally," it was implausible to suggest that the Founders had intended for the Constitution to "include freedom to discriminate against a traveler." They made a similar point with regard to the Thirteenth Amendment. Pointing out that the effect of state and federal public accommodations statutes was simply to "codify and extend the common-law innkeeper rule, which of course long predated the ratification of the Thirteenth Amendment," they openly chided the Atlanta motel owners: "Certainly, appellant cannot believe that the Amendment was intended to abrogate this common-law principle."[52]

As the *Heart of Atlanta* case moved into the courtroom, the need to protect travelers and the law of innkeepers were raised repeatedly in oral arguments. In the initial hearing before a three-judge panel of the District Court in Georgia, U.S. Assistant Attorney General Burke Marshall defended the act not simply on the basis of interstate commerce but on the fact of travel itself. He explained that it applied to all of the Heart of Atlanta Motel's guests regardless of whether they moved from state to state. "It means people that are moving," he explained. "It means that . . . the hotel caters to transients. . . . It takes in people that usually come from some other place, but the some other place does not . . . have to be shown to have been another state." In explaining the basis for the act under the commerce power, he specified that a key justification was "simply the burden on Negro travelers."[53] Oral arguments before the Supreme Court also made clear that the case turned on whether the protection of travelers was sufficient to trigger the federal government's commerce power. Solicitor General Cox stated explicitly that "the fact that the particular establishment affects transient guests tends to link it more closely than it would be otherwise linked to commerce, and therefore to bring it farther within the ambit of Federal regulation."[54]

In its ruling on *Heart of Atlanta Motel v. United States,* the Supreme Court unanimously affirmed the constitutionality of the Civil Rights Act of 1964, doing so substantially on the basis of the need to protect travelers' access to hospitality. While the technical grounds of the ruling primarily involved the Constitution's commerce clause, it is essential to recognize that in the view of the justices, it was the effect of segregation on actual travelers that served as the trigger for the commerce power. Their discussion of "The Basis of Congressional Action" dealt almost exclusively with the plight of black wayfarers, and they even set aside the importance of commerce itself. "Commerce among the states," they stated, "consists of intercourse and traffic between their citizens, and includes the transportation of persons and property. . . . Nor does it make any difference whether the transportation is commercial in character."[55]

The character of travel also arose in the all-important matter of distinguishing *Heart of Atlanta* from the *Civil Rights Cases* ruling that had doomed the earlier civil rights bill. The conditions under which the 1875 act operated, the justices reasoned, had not been the same as in 1964: "Our populace had not reached its present mobility. . . . The sheer increase in volume of interstate traffic alone would give discriminatory practices which inhibit travel a far greater impact upon the Nation's commerce than such practices had upon the economy of another day." The justices also invoked the common law, confirming that "innkeepers, by the laws of all the States, so far as we are aware, are bound, to the extent of their facilities, to furnish proper accommodation to all unobjectionable persons who in good faith apply for them." They observed furthermore that many states had enacted public accommodations laws that "but codify the common law innkeeper rule" and were thus persuaded to dismiss Fifth and Thirteenth Amendment objections to the new law. The fact of travel and the protection of travelers were, in sum, as close to twentieth-century jurists' understanding of civil rights law as they had been to that of their nineteenth-century counterparts.[56]

CONCLUSION: HOSPITALITY AND EQUALITY

Understanding the importance of the law of hospitality and similar legal regimes in the African-American struggle for equality necessitates a reconsideration of the causes which underlay the movement. Civil rights were based on more than classical liberal notions of personal autonomy and formal equality; they were also predicated on much older ideas about hosts and guests, ideas that assumed personal vulnerability and unequal relations of dependence and duty. When black Americans and their allies protested against racial injustice, they invoked Enlightenment-inspired ideals of freedom and equality, making their claims all the more compelling for being in the familiar national tongue of liberty and natural rights. But when these ideals had to be put into practice—when the time came to draft civil rights legislation, move it through Congress, and defend it against legal challenge—the law of hospitality and its special protections for travelers became an indispensable legal basis for federal enforcement of equal rights for all Americans.

This interpretation also calls attention to the importance of the built environment in two of the most important periods in American history. From Reconstruction through to the civil rights movement, equality in public places stood alongside voting rights, school integration, and equal opportunity in employment and housing as conditions which black people claimed as necessary attributes of a just society. Public accommodations thus became a sort of index of the progress of American society, a set of physical locations where people could find out whether the national ideals of freedom, equality, and pluralism were actually being practiced. This was especially important in the twentieth century, when the ongoing rise in human mobility and the presence of an international press made Americans' treatment of visitors from abroad into a major diplomatic concern. Under these circumstances, the relation of host and guest became a global drama that was played out before the eyes of the entire world.

To assert that the realization of black America's dream of equality depended in part upon centuries-old legal regimes is to run the risk of being misunderstood. This is not to suggest that the struggle, suffering, and sacrifices of the 1950s and 1960s were in any sense unequal to the task, or, worse, that they were somehow not even necessary; they unmistakably were. Nor is it to say that the ancient Roman or Anglo-American law of hospitality was somehow dormant or implicit in the nation's law, and that it could, in its original form, have been played as some sort of trump card that would guarantee racial equality in public places: far from it, since the classical, medieval, and early modern worlds that created and re-created common-law protections of travelers made no commitment to human equality, and the creators of those laws in no wise intended for them to be used in this way.

We must nevertheless recognize that the history of civil rights in public places shows how human societies reinterpret and revise the rules they live by, mixing progress and precedent in unexpected ways. However much modern notions of equal access to public space owe to the eighteenth-century intellectual legacy of the Enlightenment, they also rest upon a definitively premodern vision of protection and public good rooted in an ethic of hospitality that is at least two millennia old.

Conclusion

HOSPITALITY IS THE idea which more than any other encapsulates this book's subject matter and conceptual approach. The idea of hospitality has provided narrative continuity to this history's pivotal episodes, from the invention of the hotel to developments in the business of hotelkeeping to the struggle for equality in public places. More important, hospitality has served as a cultural indicator, an empirical measure of changes in the way Americans welcomed strangers, populated the national territory, and organized their political and social affairs. In the most general sense, thinking in terms of hospitality offers a new perspective on the human condition not only in the national past but also in the globalizing present and future (fig. 4).

Any inquiry into the importance of hospitality in the modern world must begin with Immanuel Kant. As we have seen, in *Toward Perpetual Peace* (1795), Kant declared three "Definitive Articles for Perpetual Peace." The first two required that a federation of states be formed and that only nations with a republican form of government be allowed to participate. The third stated: "Cosmopolitan right shall be limited to conditions of universal *hospitality*." Kant specified that every person must possess a *"right to visit . . . to present oneself for society."* This right to hospitality would allow new arrivals in a land "to *seek* commerce with the old inhabitants." "In this way," he explained, "distant parts of the world can enter peaceably into relations with one another . . . and so finally bring the human race ever closer to a cosmopolitan constitution." Kant's vision of a peaceful world was dependent upon travelers as agents of communication among nations, and for this reason the safety and proper reception of wayfarers had to be guaranteed as a precondition. In a very real sense, Kant's state of perpetual peace would make hosts and guests into its ambassadors, and hospitality into one of its defining ethics.[1]

Kant's theory was both brilliant and visionary, and his influence has been felt in the fields of international relations and human rights for more than two centuries. His thinking anticipated the

Hotel La Salle

CHICAGO'S FINEST HOTEL

HOSPITALITY

WITH wordless gesture the friendly Red Man welcomed the stranger to his camp. ℂ In Chicago today the Indian is only a memory but at HOTEL LA SALLE you will find that spirit of helpful service and genuine welcome which has ever been the essence of real hospitality. ℂ No other hotel is better equipped to minister to the personal needs, comfort, and contentment of the traveler.

HOTEL LA SALLE
La Salle at Madison Street
ERNEST J. STEVENS
Vice-President · Manager

4   One of several 1920s advertisements for Chicago's Hotel La Salle that emphasized its hospitality using historical and cultural references. Other ads in the series used the imagery of the Holy Land, Vikings, Puritans, Hawaiians, and Versailles. (National Museum of American History)

shape of European diplomacy throughout the long nineteenth century, and his concepts were key points of reference in the creation of the League of Nations and the United Nations. In the 1950s and 1960s, the U.S. Department of State's attempt to end racial discrimination against foreign dignitaries in places of public accommodation demonstrated the importance of hospitality to global diplomacy. In the 1990s, as public intellectuals struggled to theorize a new basis for international governance after the collapse of the Soviet Union, Kant's ideas were cited repeatedly in their debates. And in the new millennium, scholars in a variety of disciplines continue to make reference to Kant's cosmopolitan ideal and the concept of hospitality.[2]

Yet it is the *theory* of hospitality that has received all the intellectual attention; the actual *practice* of hospitality has been largely ignored. The conditions that Kant theorized were not yet in place during his lifetime. He specified that each nation must be a republic, but there was precious little representative governance among European states. He presumed that nations would permit their citizens to travel, yet most still imposed restrictions on people's mobility. Finally, he supposed that governments would supervise hospitality, but apart from diplomatic visitors who received official welcomes and state-sponsored accommodation, the day-to-day work of receiving wayfarers was still done by the citizenry, and at a fairly rudimentary level. Thus while Kant was one of the foremost figures declaring a theoretical freedom to travel throughout the world, there remained a great deal of material work to be done before this ideal could be put into practice.

The creators of the first American hotels were doing precisely this material work, and it makes sense to see Kant's theoretical efforts and hotel builders' architectural endeavors as manifestations of the same cosmopolitan impulse. The built environment expresses the values of the people who created it, and a community's public houses spoke volumes about its attitude toward outsiders. As late as the 1780s the people of the United States were still accommodating travelers and strangers in undistinguished structures that had not been built for the purpose and were better suited to selling liquor than welcoming wayfarers; as George Washington's presidential tours revealed, even the most revered guests could not expect much in the way of commercial hospitality. Beginning in the 1790s, however, Americans radically transformed the architecture of hospitality, and for more than a century thereafter, they devoted ever-increasing amounts of creativity, labor, and money to edifices specifically designed to welcome outsiders. This national enthusiasm for hotel building is best thought of as a sort of material cosmopolitanism.[3]

Hotels were part of a larger project that created a new American space. This involved a number of overlapping efforts, all of which were intended to remove barriers to mobility, freeing people to move about the national territory in pursuit of arable land, commercial opportunities, and new forms of social and political association. One part of this project was infrastructural, comprising the building of hotels, turnpikes, bridges, canals, steamboats, railroads, and the like. Another was legal and regulatory and included the end of land entail, the abrogation of limits on people's comings and goings, and eventually the creation of a federally protected right to hospitality.[4]

This project was driven primarily by economic imperatives. Hotel builders were entrepreneurs who established a new transportation and accommodation infrastructure in hopes of ensuring that the United States could participate and prosper in an emergent capitalist world system. Unlike Kant, they had little apparent interest in the loftier issues of peace, amity, and reciprocity; on the contrary, in their immediate historical context, they were apostles of privilege and exclusion. Yet in creating and developing the hotel form, they helped unleash the transformative power of people in motion, setting the stage for a series of sometimes unanticipated historical changes that led to essentially emancipatory outcomes. Kant's humanitarian mission and the hotel builders' economic project shared key assumptions about what the future would look like: both were predicated upon democratic governance and commercial economies that would bring people from many different nations into contact with one another in pursuit of trade. Kantian intellectual cosmopolitanism and American material cosmopolitanism were thus both responses to the very modern question of what to do with strangers in a world where economic change was making people increasingly mobile.

This book is not, however, a simple story of modernization in which an undifferentiated logic of capitalism manifests itself in similar ways across different times and places. The imperatives of the market existed in constant tension with the demands of many different value systems. While the rise of the hotel and the emergence of a new American space were undeniably occasioned by broader economic transformations, they were also shaped by culture and politics. Workingmen and artisans denounced the aristocratic social pretensions of early hotels, which by the 1830s had to be culturally repositioned to conform to the aggressively democratic political culture of the age. Many hotel guests, unused to institutional hospitality and discomfited by the behavior of hotel workers, vented their frustrations by creating a folklore of arrogant clerks and unclean chambermaids. And as hotels became homes, middle-class moralists warned darkly of wifely infidelity and family disintegration in their effort to prevent prospective tenants from abandoning the cult of domesticity.

But it was the ethic of hospitality that most clearly displayed the tensions between capitalism, cosmopolitanism, and other systems of value. In theory, hotels were functionally cosmopolitan because they were places where outsiders were welcomed into local communities. In practice, hotelkeepers regularly excluded entire groups of people on the basis of class, religion, and especially race. Capitalism alone could not produce a hospitality that was open to all comers: in both the nineteenth and twentieth centuries, it was segregationists who most avidly embraced market-based legal reasoning because it provided the surest defense of racial discrimination. Equality depended instead upon a much older, pre-Enlightenment, nonmarket commitment to the morality of offering shelter to strangers. Hospitality was a foundational cultural norm, one with powerful ethical and religious resonances that put the onus on hosts not to reject guests. Civil rights protesters understood this better than anyone; when they demonstrated against racial discrimination in hotels, some invoked the nativity story by carrying signs that read: "Room at the inn for weary (white) travelers." As Kant implied, what seemed like minor violations of the law of host and guest could have far greater consequences, and indeed, hospitality's discontents dramatically raised the stakes of the conflict. What began with local lawsuits in the 1830s moved onto the national political agenda during Reconstruction, and in the twentieth century it escalated into an issue that was covered by newspapers around the world and threatened to tip the balance of power in the global struggle of the Cold War.[5]

While I have in this book focused on the United States, the hotel was part of a broader epochal transformation, and there is much more to be learned about hospitality in other places and times. I have argued that the American hotel was architecturally, socially, and politically distinct from travel accommodations elsewhere in the modern world, and that it set the standard for Europe. Historical study of commercial hospitality in other parts of the world is relatively new, however, and future findings may well challenge this part of my argument. I have also proposed that Americans' high degree of mobility led them to organize geographic and architectural space in particular ways. That said, there clearly was something analogous going on in Europe, and it is to be hoped that scholars will continue to investigate other iterations of what appears to have been an internationally manifested aspect of modernity.[6]

Understanding the history of the host-guest relationship may also be useful as we look toward a future in which hospitality is likely to grow in importance. The ongoing process of globalization will continue to set people in motion, since the same economic imperatives that drive the movement of goods, capital, and information also propel human beings over distances and across borders. Trade will continue to depend upon hotels to serve as outposts for the mobile professionals and migrant laborers who move around the globe coordinating and maintaining the world economy. The most privileged of these workers will also patronize hotels as they seek out scenic or exotic locations at which to spend their leisure time. Other people may react very differently to globalization by turning inward, embracing local identities, and developing a mistrust of those from far away. For them, hotels may symbolize corrupting outside influences; notably, in the past decade hotels have been the sites of numerous terrorist attacks, acts easily interpretable as xenophobic efforts to discourage visits by foreigners or to drive away outsiders who have already arrived.[7] Whatever the direction of things to come, the essential questions of hospitality will remain. Because in a modern world that is becoming ever more mobile and internationalized, we all, sooner or later, find ourselves in the position of the stranger.

Introduction

1. Consider, for example, widely viewed soap operas like *La Venganza* and *Amantes de Luna Llena,* Thomas Mann's novella *Death in Venice* or Vicki Baum's *Menschen im Hotel,* Amitabh Bachchan's films like *Naseeb* and especially *Namak Halal,* the 1970s BBC comedy series *Fawlty Towers,* Haruki Murakami's *A Wild Sheep Chase* and *After Dark,* and such songs as Rodgers and Hart's "There's a Small Hotel," Elvis Presley's "Heartbreak Hotel," and the Eagles' "Hotel California."

2. Scholars in a number of academic disciplines have implicitly or explicitly cited geographic immobility as a common characteristic of precapitalist societies. See, for example, Karl Polanyi, *The Great Transformation: The Political and Economic Origins of Our Time* (New York, 1944), 81–82, 87, 90–93; C. B. Macpherson, *The Political Theory of Possessive Individualism: Hobbes to Locke* (Oxford, 1962), 49–51; Benedict Anderson, *Imagined Communities: Reflections on the Origin and Spread of Nationalism* (New York, 1980), 114–115; John R. Stilgoe, *Common Landscape of America, 1580 to 1845* (New Haven, 1982), 19–24; James E. Vance, *Capturing the Horizon: The Historical Geography of Transportation Since the Transportation Revolution of the Sixteenth Century* (New York, 1986), 3–7, 25–26; William Leach, *Country of Exiles: The Destruction of Place in American Life* (New York, 1999), 9–11. Note also the literal meaning of the frequently used scholarly term "social dislocation."

3. George W. Pierson, "The M-Factor in American History," *American Quarterly* 14 (1962), 275–289.

4. Max Weber, "The Nature of the City," in Richard Sennett, ed., *Classic Essays on the Culture of Cities* (New York, 1969), 23; Georg Simmel, "The Stranger," from "Der Fremde," in *Soziologie* (Munich, 1980), trans. Donald N. Levine, 685–691; Robert Park, "The City: Suggestions for the Investigation of Human Behavior," *American Journal of Sociology* 20 (1915), 155; Louis Wirth, "Urbanism as a Way of Life," *American Journal of Sociology* 44 (1938), 1–24. See also S. Dale McLemore, "Simmel's 'Stranger': A Critique of the Concept," *Pacific Sociological Review* 13 (1970), 86–94; Zygmunt Bauman, "Strangers: The Social Construction of Universality and Particularity," *Telos* 88 (Winter 1988–1989), 7–42. A careful defining of terms is in order here to clarify distinctions among different categories of human mobility. I use the term *transience* to indicate a state of regular coming and going in which people travel to different places but stay only briefly, for a few days or weeks. Transience is closely related to and subsumes *sojourning,* which involves a more prolonged yet still temporary presence at a location. Transience and sojourning are thus different from *migration,* which generally denotes a permanent or at least long-term relocation to a new place of residence. Hotels were designed primarily for transients, frequently patronized by sojourners, and occasionally used on a temporary basis by migrants.

5. Karl Marx, *The Communist Manifesto* (1848); Ferdinand Tönnies, *Gemeinschaft und Gesellschaft* (1887); Emile Durkheim, *The Division of Labor in Society* (1893); Max Weber, *The Protestant Ethic and the Spirit of Capitalism* (1904); Michel Foucault, *Discipline and Punish: The Birth of the Prison,* trans. Alan Sheridan (New York, 1977); Marshall Berman, *All That Is Solid Melts into Air: The Experience of Modernity* (New York, 1982); Anderson, *Imagined Communities;* David Harvey, *The Condition of Postmodernity: An Enquiry into the Origins of Cultural Change* (Cambridge, 1989); James C. Scott, *Seeing Like a State: How Certain Schemes to Improve the Human Condition Have Failed* (New Haven, 1998).

6.   Immanuel Kant, *Toward Perpetual Peace*, in *Immanuel Kant: Practical Philosophy*, ed. and trans. Mary J. Gregor (Cambridge, 1996), 313, 328–331. All emphases in original.

7.   I seek to situate my argument within a decades-long debate in which the foundational works are Karl Polanyi's *The Great Transformation*, C. B. Macpherson's *The Political Theory of Possessive Individualism*, and Fernand Braudel's *Civilization and Capitalism*. While each of these volumes offers a different definition, chronology, and teleology of markets and capitalism, all agree that economic relations constituted the major engine of large-scale social change in the early modern and modern periods. Fernand Braudel, *Civilization and Capitalism*, vols. 1–3 (1967–1979). Later scholars refined and in many cases disputed the political economy and anthropology behind these theories, but the basic assumptions of the early theoretical works remain in place. See John Dunn, *The Political Thought of John Locke* (Cambridge, 1969); Alan MacFarlane, *The Origins of English Individualism* (New York, 1978) and *The Culture of Capitalism* (Oxford, 1987); William M. Reddy, *The Rise of Market Culture: The Textile Trade and French Society, 1750–1900* (Cambridge, 1984); Jean-Christophe Agnew, *Worlds Apart: The Market and the Theater in Anglo-American Thought, 1550–1750* (Cambridge, 1986).

8.   The analytical approaches developed in these works were derived mainly from European history, but they have also been taken up by historians of the United States, who have reinterpreted major events and periods of the nation's history in light of the dynamics and imperatives of the market and capitalism. See, for example, William E. Nelson, *The Americanization of the Common Law* (New York, 1976); Joyce Appleby, *Capitalism and a New Social Order: The Republican Vision of the 1790s* (New York, 1984) and *Liberalism and Republicanism in the Historical Imagination* (Cambridge, Mass., 1992); Christopher Clark, *The Roots of Rural Capitalism: Western Massachusetts, 1780–1860* (Ithaca, 1990); James A. Henretta, *The Origins of American Capitalism: Collected Essays* (Boston, 1991); Charles Sellers, *The Market Revolution: Jacksonian America, 1815–1846* (New York, 1991); Winifred Barr Rothenberg, *From Market-Places to a Market Economy: The Transformation of Rural Massachusetts, 1750–1850* (Chicago, 1992); William Cronon, *Nature's Metropolis: Chicago and the Great West* (New York, 1994); Amy Stanley, *From Bondage to Contract: Wage Labor, Marriage, and the Market in the Age of Slave Emancipation* (New York, 1998); Lizabeth Cohen, *A Consumers' Republic: The Politics of Mass Consumption in Postwar America* (New York, 2003); T. H. Breen, *Marketplace of Revolution: How Consumer Politics Shaped American Independence* (New York, 2004). For a historiographic summary of key parts of this larger discussion, see Naomi R. Lamoreaux, "Rethinking the Transition to Capitalism in the Early American Northeast," *Journal of American History* 90 (2003), 437–461.

9.   Sam Bass Warner, *The Private City: Philadelphia in Three Periods of Its Growth* (Philadelphia, 1968); Kenneth T. Jackson, *Crabgrass Frontier: The Suburbanization of the United States* (New York, 1986); Sean Wilentz, *Chants Democratic: New York City and the Rise of the American Working Class, 1788–1850* (New York, 1984); Amy Bridges, *A City in the Republic: Antebellum New York and the Origins of Machine Politics* (Cambridge, 1984); Christine Stansell, *City of Women: Sex and Class in New York, 1789–1860* (Urbana, 1987); Elliott Gorn, *The Manly Art: Bare-Knuckle Prize Fighting in America* (Ithaca, 1986); Roy Rosenzweig, *Eight Hours for What We Will: Workers and Leisure in an Industrial City, 1870–1920* (Cambridge, 1983); John Bodnar, *The Transplanted: A History of Immigrants in Urban America* (Bloomington, Ind., 1985); Olivier Zunz, *The Changing Face of Inequality: Urbanization, Industrial Development, and Workers in Detroit, 1880–1920* (Chicago, 1982); James R. Grossman, *Land of Hope: Chicago, Black Southerners, and the Great Migration* (Chicago, 1989); Thomas Sugrue, *The Origins of the Urban Crisis: Race and Inequality in Postwar Detroit* (Princeton, 1996).

10.   On home and family, see Barbara Welter, "The Cult of True Womanhood, 1820–1860," *American Quarterly* 18 (1966), 155–174; Gerda Lerner, "The Lady and the Mill Girl: Changes in the Status of

Women in the Age of Jackson," *Midcontinent American Studies Journal* 10 (1969), 5–15; Nancy Cott, *The Bonds of Womanhood: "Woman's Sphere" in New England, 1780–1835* (New Haven, 1977); Tamara K. Hareven and Maris Vinovskis, eds., *Family and Population in Nineteenth-Century America* (Princeton, 1978); Thomas Dublin, *Women at Work: The Transformation of Work and Community in Lowell, Massachusetts, 1820–1860* (New York, 1979); Mary Ryan, *Cradle of the Middle Class* (New York, 1980); Elizabeth Blackmar, *Manhattan for Rent, 1785–1850* (Ithaca, 1989). On the middle class, see Paul E. Johnson, *A Shopkeeper's Millennium: Society and Revivals in Rochester, New York, 1815–1837* (New York, 1978); Ryan, *Cradle of the Middle Class;* Stuart M. Blumin, *The Emergence of the Middle Class: Social Experience in the American City, 1760–1900* (New York, 1989). On consumer culture, see Kathy Peiss, *Cheap Amusements: Working Women and Leisure in Turn-of-the-Century New York* (Philadelphia, 1986); Simon J. Bronner, ed., *Consuming Visions: Accumulation and Display of Goods in America, 1880–1920* (New York, 1989); William Leach, *Land of Desire: Merchants, Power, and the Rise of a New American Culture* (New York, 1993); Lizabeth Cohen, *Making a New Deal: Industrial Workers in Chicago, 1919–1939* (Chicago, 1990) and *A Consumers' Republic;* Breen, *Marketplace of Revolution.*

11. The claims here are modest; I do not mean to suggest that this approach is as broadly applicable as the historical syntheses just mentioned. But close attention to the movement of people through space does explain key features of American life, particularly in cities and towns, in a way that the earlier works do not.

12. This is in large part a legacy of the scholarly study of urbanism, which has long been attentive to the spatiality of the city. Urban historians, sociologists, and geographers have devoted a great deal of attention to the ways in which the physical layout of cities reflects the vitality and generativity of urban life, as well as how the built environment conditions behavior by structuring interactions among city dwellers. It is no accident that many of the most influential scholarly works on urbanism deal explicitly with the physical structure of cities and metropolitan areas. See, for example, Jane Jacobs, *The Death and Life of Great American Cities* (New York, 1961); Herbert J. Gans, *The Urban Villagers: Group and Class in the Life of Italian-Americans* (New York, 1962); Sam Bass Warner, *Streetcar Suburbs: The Process of Growth in Boston, 1870–1900* (New York, 1962); Richard Sennett, *The Fall of Public Man* (New York, 1976); Dolores Hayden, *The Grand Domestic Revolution: A History of Feminist Designs for American Homes, Neighborhoods, and Cities* (Cambridge, Mass., 1981); Claude S. Fischer, *To Dwell Among Friends: Personal Networks in Town and City* (Chicago, 1982); Arnold R. Hirsch, *Making the Second Ghetto: Race and Housing in Chicago, 1940–1960* (Cambridge, 1983); Jackson, *Crabgrass Frontier.*

13. This book also represents an effort to engage the work of theorists like Henri Lefebvre, David Harvey, and Edward Soja, who have urged us to take space more seriously in our efforts to understand past and present human societies. I deal throughout with the production of space and the spatiality of capitalism, and this book may be useful to theorists studying how the organization of space conceals or resolves problems within local and global economies. At the same time, however, I try to treat spatiality as an independent variable in historical change by demonstrating how particular configurations of space led to distinctive historical outcomes. See Henri Lefebvre, *The Production of Space* (Cambridge, 1991); Harvey, *The Condition of Postmodernity;* Edward J. Soja, *Postmodern Geographies: The Reassertion of Space in Critical Social Theory* (New York, 1989). See also Miles Ogborn, *Spaces of Modernity: London's Geographies, 1680–1780* (New York, 1998), and Michael J. Dear and Steven Flusty, *Spaces of Postmodernity: Readings in Human Geography* (Oxford, 2002).

14. This methodology and epistemology follow the work of J. B. Jackson and his associates and students. For an introduction, see J. B. Jackson, *Discovering the Vernacular Landscape* (New Haven, 1986); Michael P. Conzen, ed., *The Making of the American Landscape* (New York, 1990); Paul Groth and Todd Bressi, eds., *Understanding Ordinary Landscapes* (New Haven, 1997); J. B.

Jackson, *Landscape in Sight: Looking at America,* ed. Helen Horowitz (New Haven, 2000); Chris Wilson and Paul Groth, eds., *Everyday America: Cultural Landscape Studies after J. B. Jackson* (Berkeley, 2003).

15. The *Oxford English Dictionary,* 2nd ed. (Oxford, 1989), 7: 427, puts the first usage of the term in English in 1766. Paul Robert, *Dictionnaire alphabétique et analogique de la langue française,* 2nd ed. (Paris, 1985), 5: 261–262: the town-hall variant was usually rendered as *hôtel de ville.* The word could also be used in referring to a hospital, *hôtel-dieu.* See also E. Littré, *Dictionnaire de la langue française* (Paris, 1878), 2: 2053; John Trusler, *Modern Times, or the Adventures of Gabriel Outcast* (London, 1785), 3: 76; Thomas Vaughan, *The Hotel; or, The Double Valet* (London, 1776), 21.

16. Rufus King, *Life and Correspondence* (Boston, 1894), 1: 20; *Pennsylvania Gazette,* 19 April 1794; American Antiquarian Society, Early American Imprints Collection, first series, broadsides, 1792. The Quinn Hotel Collection at the New-York Historical Society has clippings folders for every year between 1780 and 1810; these contain numerous examples of the described phenomenon which can be cross-checked with the Society's comprehensive collection of New York city directories.

17. F. H. W. Sheppard, ed., *Survey of London,* vol.36, *The Parish of St. Paul [and] Covent Garden* (London, 1970), 1–9.

18. Paul Langford, *A Polite and Commercial People* (Oxford, 1989), 61–71, 101–108; Peter Borsay, *The English Urban Renaissance* (Oxford, 1983); Peter Clark, *The English Alehouse: A Social History, 1200–1650* (London, 1943); Walter William Ison, *The Georgian Buildings of Bath* (London, 1948), 92–98; "Hotels," in Elain Harwood and Andrew Saint, *London* (London, 1991). See also Aytoun Ellis, *The Penny Universities: A History of the Coffee-Houses* (London, 1956).

19. Nikolaus Pevsner, *A History of Building Types* (Princeton, 1976), 172; Moritz Hoffmann, *Geschichte des deutschen Hotels: Vom Mittelalter bis zur Gegenwart* (Heidelberg, 1961); Maria Wenzel, *Palast-hotels in Deutschland: Untersuchungen zu einer Bauaufgabe im 19. und frühen 20. Jahrhundert* (New York, 1991).

Part One. BUILDINGS AND SYSTEMS

1. David J. Rothman, *Discovery of the Asylum: Social Order and Disorder in the New Republic* (Boston, 1990), 19–25, 46–48; Josiah Henry Benton, *Warning Out in New England* (Boston, 1911).

2. Rothman, *Discovery of the Asylum,* 19–25, 46–48; Edward Johnson, *Wonder-Working Providence of Sions Saviour in New-England* (London, 1654), 71, 35.

3. Rothman, *Discovery of the Asylum,* 21–25; "The Diary of Robert Love," P-363 of the Pre-Revolutionary War Diaries at the Massachusetts Historical Society.

4. Bernard Bailyn, *New England Merchants in the Seventeenth Century* (New York, 1964), especially 105–111, 139–142; Benton, *Warning Out in New England.* It is worth noting that in American English as of the late eighteenth and early nineteenth centuries, the terms *foreign* and *foreigner* referred to things and people not of other nations but of other states within the United States. See, for example, the Eleventh Amendment (1798).

1. A Public House for a New Republic

1. Don Jackson and Dorothy Twohig, eds., *The Diaries of George Washington* (Charlottesville, 1979), 5: 460–462.

2. T. H. Breen, "The Bumpy Path to a New Republic," *New York Times,* 14 February 1999; Jackson and Twohig, *Diaries,* 5: 453; Gordon Wood, *The Creation of the American Republic, 1776–1787* (Chapel Hill, 1969), 463–467; Jack Rakove, *Original Meanings: Politics and Ideas in the Making of*

the Constitution (New York, 1996), chapters 4, 5; Roger H. Brown, *The Republic in Peril* (New York, 1964), chapter 1.

3. David Waldstreicher, *In the Midst of Perpetual Fetes: The Making of American Nationalism, 1776–1820* (Chapel Hill, 1997), 117–141.

4. GW to John Hancock, 22 October 1789, in W. W. Abbott and Dorothy Twohig, eds., *The Papers of George Washington* (Charlottesville, 1993), 4: 212–214; GW to William Washington, 8 January 1791, ibid., 7: 211; Jackson and Twohig, *Diaries*, 5: 491, 497.

5. Jackson and Twohig, *Diaries*, 5: 493–497, 6: 98–169, especially 113–121, 134, 147, 158–160.

6. Waldstreicher, *In the Midst of Perpetual Fetes*, 117–126.

7. Peter Thompson, *Rum Punch and Revolution: Taverngoing and Public Life in Eighteenth-Century Philadelphia* (Philadelphia, 1999), 149–153. While an argument could be made for New York's City Tavern or Boston's Royal Exchange Tavern rather than the City Tavern in Philadelphia as the nation's finest public house, these establishments did not differ materially from each other in size, cost, or architecture; *Columbian Centinel* (Boston), 7 November 1818.

8. On taverns, see David W. Conroy, *In Public Houses: Drink and the Revolution of Authority in Colonial Massachusetts* (Chapel Hill, 1992); Thompson, *Rum Punch and Revolution;* and Sharon V. Salinger, *Taverns and Drinking in Early America* (Baltimore, 2002). Also useful are Kym S. Rice, *Early American Taverns: For the Entertainment of Friends and Strangers* (Chicago, 1983); Donna-Belle Garvin and James L. Garvin, *On the Road North of Boston: New Hampshire Taverns and Turnpikes, 1700–1900* (Lebanon, N.H., 1988). Jackson and Twohig, *Diaries*, 5: 461. In England, however, public houses were carefully categorized with fixed designations and statuses: see Peter Clark, *The English Alehouse: A Social History, 1200–1650* (London, 1943). Note that boardinghouses were not public houses at all: while they did provide shelter to travelers, it was on a purely private basis, without a license and therefore without the privilege of selling alcohol.

9. See, for example, John Davis, *Travels of Four Years and a Half in the United States of North America* (London, 1803), 127–130; Rice, *Early American Taverns*, 74; Jackson and Twohig, *Diaries*, 5: 494; Barbara G. Carson, "Early American Tourists and the Commercialization of Leisure," in *Of Consuming Interests: The Style of Life in the Eighteenth Century*, ed. Cary Carson et al. (Charlottesville, 1994), 374, 382–395. The City Tavern, for example, was said to have been modeled on the country home of one of its subscribers; Thompson, *Rum Punch and Revolution*, 148–150; Rice, *Early American Taverns*, chapter 9.

10. *The Direct Tax of 1798* (volume held at the Massachusetts Historical Society); James Grant Wilson, *The Memorial History of the City of New York* (New York, 1892–1893), 3: 150–151; Samuel Adams Drake, *Old Boston Taverns and Tavern Clubs* (Boston, 1917), appendix.

11. Colonial Williamsburg Foundation, *A Study of Taverns of Virginia in the Eighteenth Century* (Williamsburg, 1973), 8; Conroy, *In Public Houses*, 47–48; Thompson, *Rum Punch and Revolution*, 56–60; Rice, *Early American Taverns*, 102–106.

12. Rice, *Early American Taverns*, 102–106; marquis de Chastellux, *Travels in North America in the Years 1780, 1781, and 1782* (Paris, 1786; ed. Howard C. Rice, Jr., 1963), 2: 374; Davis, *Travels*, 327; Henry Wansey, *Journal of an Excursion to the United States of North America* (London, 1794), 196; Conroy, *In Public Houses*, 88, 149; Thompson, *Rum Punch and Revolution*, 57–60; "Biographical Sketch of Waightstill Avery," *North Carolina University Magazine* 4 (1855), 249; Herman Melville, *Moby-Dick* (Boston, 1851), chapter 3.

13. Robert Hunter, Jr., *Quebec to Carolina in 1785–1786* (San Marino, Calif., 1943), 200, 274–286; Wansey, *Journal*, 40, 51–54, 100–110; Francis Baily, *Journal of a Tour in Unsettled Parts of North America in 1796 and 1797* (London, 1856), 129–130; Charles William Janson, *The Stranger in America* (London, 1807), 85; Davis, *Travels*, 2. See also Salinger, *Taverns and Drinking*, 211–216; Charles H. Sherrill, *French Memories of Eighteenth-Century America* (New York, 1915), 227; Rice, *Early*

American Taverns, 41–42; Garvin and Garvin, *On the Road North of Boston,* 19–20; "The Journal of Colonel John May, of Boston, 1789," *Pennsylvania Magazine of History and Biography* 45 (1921), 120.

14. Salinger, *Taverns and Drinking,* 210–216.

15. Rice, *Early American Taverns,* chapter 9; Colonial Williamsburg Foundation, *Taverns of Virginia;* Thompson, *Rum Punch and Revolution,* 149–150.

16. Kenneth Hafertepe, "Samuel Blodget, Jr.," *American National Biography,* ed. John A. Garraty and Mark C. Carnes (New York, 1999), 3: 38–40; Irving Atkins, "Blodget's Hotel, Federal City, 1793–1836," unpublished 1981 ms. held at Massachusetts Historical Society, 5–14; *Samuel Blodget Papers, 1758–1813,* at Massachusetts Historical Society; Joseph Jackson, *Encyclopedia of Philadelphia* (Harrisburg, 1931), 301–303.

17. Atkins, "Blodget's Hotel," 3–10; *Gazette of the United States,* 19 January 1793; *Newport Mercury,* 1 April 1793; *Columbian Centinel* (Boston), 6 March 1793.

18. *Gazette of the United States,* 17 July 1793; Atkins, "Blodget's Hotel," 5, 7–10.

19. Bob Arnebeck, *Through a Fiery Trial: Building Washington, 1790–1800* (Lanham, Md., 1991), 393.

20. James Sterling Young, *The Washington Community, 1800–1828* (New York, 1966), 13–23, 97–106; Atkins, "Blodget's Hotel," 9–15; Richard R. John, *Spreading the News: The American Postal System from Franklin to Morse* (Cambridge, Mass., 1995), 51.

21. W. B. Bryan, "Hotels of Washington Prior to 1814," *Records of the Columbia Historical Society* 7 (1904), 71–106.

22. William L. Stone, *History of New York City* (New York, 1872), 320.

23. W. Harrison Bayles, *Old Taverns of New York* (New York, 1915), 314, 326, 331, 337, 353, 371; City Hotel board members list from Bayles cross-referenced with person catalogue at New-York Historical Society.

24. Meryle R. Evans, "Knickerbocker Hotels and Restaurants, 1800–1850," *New-York Historical Society Quarterly* 36 (1952), 382–384; Wilson, *Memorial History,* 3:150–151.

25. Folder for 1794, W. Johnson Quinn Collection, New-York Historical Society; *New York Journal,* 25 February 1797; Evans, "Knickerbocker Hotels and Restaurants," 377.

26. *Acts of the General Assembly of Rhode Island,* 1795; "Newport Long-Wharf, Hotel, and Public School Lottery. By authority of the legislature," in the American Antiquarian Society's Early American Imprints, first series broadsides, 1795. Most lotteries in Rhode Island in the 1790s were for no more than twenty thousand dollars or so, and the next-largest lottery previously advertised in the *Newport Mercury,* where both the Federal City and Newport hotel lotteries were publicized, totaled only forty thousand dollars; *Newport Mercury,* 1 April 1793, 27 January, 24 March, and 15 September 1795, 5 May 1796; "Meetings of the Proprietors of Long Wharf, 1800–1863" (Newport Historical Society Manuscript No. 2020); Antoinette F. Dowling and Vincent J. Scully, Jr., *The Architectural Heritage of Newport, Rhode Island, 1640–1915* (New York, 1967); Richard Bayles, *History of Newport County* (New York, 1891), 481–482.

27. Harold Kirker, *The Architecture of Charles Bulfinch* (Cambridge, Mass., 1969), 6–16.

28. *Columbian Centinel* (Boston), 14 September 1796.

29. Talbot Hamlin, *Benjamin Henry Latrobe* (New York, 1955), 56–58, 117–120.

30. Benjamin Henry Latrobe, "Architectural Drawings for a Theatre and Hotel Building" (Richmond, 1797), held at the Library of Congress.

31. Harold Kirker, "The Boston Exchange Coffee House," *Old-Time New England* 52 (1961), 11 ; Petition to apply to the Massachusetts legislature for an act of incorporation for the Massachusetts Fire Insurance Company, dated Boston 1785, held at Massachusetts Historical Society; George P. Wetmore Papers, microfilm P521, reel 7, 7th series, vols. ix–x, also at MHS; Records of the Department of State, American Letters, vol. 3, no. 120, 4 November 1786–1789 October 1788, at the National

Archives; Mary Caroline Crawford, *Famous Families of Massachusetts* (Boston, 1930), 2: 146–147; *Memorial History of Boston, Including Suffolk County, Massachusetts, 1630–1880,* ed. Justin Winsor (Boston, 1880–1881), 4: 208, 212.

32. Charles Shaw, *A Topographical and Historical Description of Boston* (Boston, 1817), 229–233; "Description of the Boston Exchange Coffee-House," *Omnium Gatherum* 1 (1809), 4–9; Kirker, "Boston Exchange Coffee House," 11–13. See also Jack Quinan, "The Boston Exchange Coffee House," *Journal of the Society of Architectural Historians* 38 (1979), 256–262; Jane Kamensky, *The Exchange Artist: A Story of Paper, Bricks, and Ash in Early National America* (New York, forthcoming).

33. Shaw, *A Topographical and Historical Description of Boston,* 229–233; *Port Folio* (Boston) 1 (1809), 452–453; *Columbian Centinel* (Boston), 7 November 1818; *Independent Chronicle* (Boston), 11 November 1818.

34. Edwin G. Burrows and Mike Wallace, *Gotham: A History of New York City to 1898* (New York, 1999), 415, 424–426.

35. George Waldo Browne, *Hon. Samuel Blodget: The Pioneer of Progress in the Merrimack Valley* (Manchester, N.H., 1907), 15–16, 31–50; canal and bridge stock certificates in the Samuel Blodget Papers, Massachusetts Historical Society; Pamela Scott, "Benjamin Henry Latrobe," in Garraty and Carnes, *American National Biography* 13: 241–245; John, *Spreading the News,* 51; Pliny Miles, "History of the Post Office," *Bankers' Magazine* 7 (November 1857), 363.

36. Conroy, *In Public Houses,* 88; Charles Wright and Charles Ernest Fayle, *A History of Lloyd's* (London, 1928), 9–12.

37. Elizabeth Blackmar, *Manhattan for Rent, 1785–1850* (Ithaca, 1981), 35–38, 186; Atkins, "Blodget's Hotel," 5; City Hotel board members list from Bayles, *Old Taverns of New York,* cross-referenced with card catalogue at New-York Historical Society; Jackson, *Encyclopedia of Philadelphia,* 303.

38. Drew R. McCoy, *The Elusive Republic* (New York, 1980), 76–104.

39. Hafertepe, "Samuel Blodget, Jr.," 3: 38–40; *Acts of the General Assembly of Rhode Island,* January 1795, 8; *Boston Independent Chronicle,* 6 July 1809.

40. Paul Langford, *A Polite and Commercial People: England, 1727–1783* (New York, 1989), chapter 3; Richard Bushman, *The Refinement of America: Persons, Houses, Cities* (New York, 1992); Peter Clark, *The English Alehouse: A Social History, 1200–1650* (London, 1943); Aytoun Ellis, *The Penny Universities: A History of the Coffee-Houses* (London, 1956); Jürgen Habermas, *The Structural Transformation of the Public Sphere* (Darmstadt, 1962; trans. Thomas Burger and Frederick Lawrence, Cambridge, Mass., 1989); F. H. W. Sheppard, ed., *Survey of London,* vol. 36, *The Parish of St. Paul [and] Covent Garden* (London, 1970), 1–11. See also Peter Borsay, *The English Urban Renaissance* (Oxford, 1983).

41. *Port Folio* (Boston) 1 (1809), 452–453; Quinn Collection folders, 1790–1810.

42. Thompson, *Rum Punch and Revolution,* 40–41, 46, 89–90, 98–99; Rice, *Early American Taverns,* 49–56, 21, 75, 105–106. See also Eve Kosofsky Sedgwick, *Between Men: English Literature and Male Homosocial Desire* (New York, 1985); Conroy, *In Public Houses,* 319–320; Waldstreicher, *In the Midst of Perpetual Fetes,* 82.

43. Thompson, *Rum Punch and Revolution,* chapters 3, 4.

44. Conroy, *In Public Houses,* chapters 4–6; Carl Bridenbaugh, *Cities in Revolt: Urban Life in America, 1743–1776* (New York, 1955), 358; Folders for 1780–1790, Quinn Collection.

45. David S. Shields, *Civil Tongues and Polite Letters in British America* (Chapel Hill, 1997), 311–314 and chapter 6; Thompson, *Rum Punch and Revolution,* chapters 3, 4; Waldstreicher, *In the Midst of Perpetual Fetes,* 80, 136; Burrows and Wallace, *Gotham,* 315–323.

46. Burrows and Wallace, *Gotham,* 315–323.

47. Ibid.

48. *Port Folio* (Boston) 1 (1809), 452–453.

49. *New York Journal,* 25 February 1797; *New York Gazette,* 19 May 1796; duc de la Rouchefoucauld-Liancourt, *Voyage dans les États-Unis d'Amérique* (Paris, 1798), 2: 326; Janson, *Stranger in America,* 203; *Washington Gazette,* 28 September 1796; Samuel Blodget, Jr., *Economica: A Statistical Manual for the United States of America* (Washington, 1806), i–iii; Winsor, *Memorial History of Boston,* 4: 55; *Independent Chronicle* (Boston), 11 November 1818. For colonial-era house assault, see Peter Orlando Hutchinson, *The Diary and Letters of Thomas Hutchinson* (Boston, 1884), 67, 72. For later examples, see Chapter 8.

50. Burrows and Wallace, *Gotham,* 294–296; Jackson and Twohig, *Diaries,* 5: 474; Massachusetts Historical Society, Broadsides, 1789, 1791; Richard Gerry Durnin, "Presidential Visits to Salem," in *Essex Institute Historical Collections,* July 1964, 345; Transcripts of addresses to George Washington from his visit in 1790, in manuscript box "George Washington," Newport Historical Society; Douglas Southall Freeman, *George Washington* (New York, 1954), 6: 314–315.

51. Burrows and Wallace, *Gotham,* 296; Jackson and Twohig, *Diaries,* 5: 493–497, 6: 98, 99–169, especially 113–121, 134, 147, 158, 160; Bayles, *History of Newport County,* 514.

52. Bayles, *History of Newport County,* 514; George Woodbridge, "George Washington at Newport," *Newport History* 220, no. 64 (1991), 128; Transcripts of addresses to George Washington; Abbott and Twohig, *Papers,* 6: 284; Exeter *Gazetteer,* 7 November 1789; Jackson and Twohig, *Diaries,* 6: 127; Richard Wortman, *Scenarios of Power: Myth and Ceremony in Russian Monarchy* (Princeton, 2000); Daniel Unowsky, *The Pomp and Politics of Patriotism: Imperial Celebrations in Habsburg Austria, 1848–1916* (West Lafayette, Ind., 2005).

53. See Tontine Coffee House Papers, 1789–1823, New-York Historical Society; Damie Stillman, "City Living, Federal Style," in *Everyday Life in the Early Republic,* ed. Catherine E. Hutchins (Winterthur, 1999), 143–144.

54. Wansey, *Journal,* 226. Analogous dynamics in the process of nation building are explored in John, *Spreading the News,* Waldstreicher, *In the Midst of Perpetual Fetes,* and Shields, *Civil Tongues,* especially 321–322.

55. Bryan, "Hotels of Washington," 71–106; J. Thomas Scharf and Thompson Westcott, *History of Philadelphia, 1609–1884* (Philadelphia, 1884), 980–998; I. N. Phelps Stokes, *Iconography of Manhattan Island, 1498–1909* (New York, 1967), 6: 456–464; *Newport Mercury,* 20 July 1805; Davis, *Travels,* 39; *New York Evening Post* clipping, "Hotels" folder, exhibition notes for "The Larder Invaded," Library Company of Philadelphia; Folders for 1790–1810, Quinn Collection.

56. *Independent Chronicle* (Boston), 6 July 1809; Burrows and Wallace, *Gotham,* 415, 424.

2. Palaces of the Public

1. Donald B. Dodd, ed., *Historical Statistics of the States of the United States: Two Centuries of the Census, 1790–1990* (Westport, Conn., 1993), 183.

2. D. W. Meinig, *The Shaping of America,* vol. 2, *Continental America, 1800–1867* (New Haven, 1993), 4, 223. For additional detail, see Peter Onuf, *Statehood and Union: A History of the Northwest Ordinance* (Bloomington, Ind., 1987); Colin G. Calloway, *The American Revolution in Indian Country: Crisis and Diversity in Native American Communities* (New York, 1995). The nation's northeastern extent was also established with the admission of Maine (1820).

3. Douglass C. North, *The Economic Growth of the United States, 1790–1860* (New York, 1966), 46–58; Jeremy Atack and Peter Passell, *A New Economic View of American History,* 2nd ed. (New York, 1994), 13–14, 143–173. See also Stuart Bruchey, *The Roots of American Economic Growth, 1607–1861: An Essay in Social Causation* (New York, 1965).

4. George Rogers Taylor, *The Transportation Revolution, 1815–1860* (New York, 1951), 15–103. For more current reconceptualizations of antebellum transportation improvements and developmental investment, see John Majewski, *A House Dividing: Economic Development in Pennsylvania and Virginia Before the Civil War* (Cambridge, Mass., 2000), and John Lauritz Larson, *Internal Improvement: National Public Works and the Promise of Popular Government in the Early United States* (Chapel Hill, 2001).

5. The illustrations of taverns and hotels carried no accompanying comment. See Taylor, *Transportation Revolution,* following pages 14, 78, 110.

6. Bryan Clark Green, Calder Loth, and William M. S. Rasmussen, *Lost Virginia: Vanished Architecture of the Old Dominion* (Charlottesville, 2001), 169; J. Thomas Scharf, *History of St. Louis City and County* (Philadelphia, 1883), 1441; *Connecticut Courant,* 27 April 1819, 2; Daniel Boorstin, *The Americans: The National Experience* (New York, 1965), 142–143.

7. W. B. Bryan, "Hotels of Washington Prior to 1814," *Records of the Columbia Historical Society* 7 (1904), 71–106; J. Thomas Scharf, *History of Baltimore City and County* (Baltimore, 1971), 514; *National Advocate,* 12 November 1819; Stephen Jenkins, *The Greatest Street in the World: The Story of Broadway, Old and New, from the Bowling Green to Albany* (New York, 1911), 177; Library Company of Philadelphia, exhibit notes for The Larder Invaded.

8. Samuel Blodget, Jr., *Economica: A Statistical Manual for the United States of America* (Washington, D.C., 1806), i–iii; "Proposals for Making Sale of the Exchange Coffee House" (Boston, January 1810), in Broadsides, Massachusetts Historical Society; William Havard Eliot, *A Description of the Tremont House* (Boston, 1830), 1; Barry N. Poulson, *Economic History of the United States* (New York, 1981), 185–189; North, *Economic Growth,* chapter 6; George Dangerfield, *The Era of Good Feelings* (New York, 1952), 179–189.

9. Hiram Hitchcock, "The Hotels of America," in *One Hundred Years of American Commerce,* ed. Chauncey Depew (New York, 1895), 1: 149–156.

10. Edwin G. Burrows and Mike Wallace, *Gotham: A History of New York City to 1898* (New York, 1999), 429–430; Meinig, *Shaping of America,* 2: 319–323.

11. James Weston Livingood, *The Philadelphia-Baltimore Trade Rivalry, 1780–1860* (New York, 1947); Carter Goodrich, *Government Promotion of Canals and Railroads, 1800–1890* (New York, 1960); Harry N. Scheiber, *Ohio Canal Era: A Case Study of Government and the Economy, 1820–1861* (Athens, Ohio, 1969); Diane Lindstrom, *Economic Development in the Philadelphia Region, 1810–1850* (New York, 1978).

12. Doris Elizabeth King, "Hotels of the Old South, 1793–1860: A Study of the Origin and Development of the First-Class Hotels," Ph.D. diss., Duke University, 1952, 41–49; James D. Dilts, *The Great Road: The Building of the Baltimore and Ohio, the Nation's First Railroad, 1828–1853* (Stanford, 1993), chapters 3, 4.

13. Doris Elizabeth King, "The First-Class Hotel and the Age of the Common Man," *Journal of Southern History* 23 (1957), 181–183; John F. Stover, *History of the Baltimore and Ohio Railroad* (West Lafayette, Ind., 1987), 13–16; Doris Elizabeth King, "Early Hotel Entrepreneurs and Promoters, 1793–1860," *Explorations in Entrepreneurial History* 8 (1956), 153–155; Scharf, *History of Baltimore,* 515–516; *Baltimore Gazette and Daily Advertiser,* 25 October 1826.

14. Nikolaus Pevsner, *A History of Building Types* (Princeton, 1976), 176; King, "First-Class Hotel," 184; "Our Public Hotels," *National Intelligencer,* 18 June 1827.

15. Joseph Jackson, *Encyclopedia of Philadelphia* (Harrisburg, 1931), 2: 774; James Weston Livingood, *Philadelphia-Baltimore Trade Rivalry,* 1–24; Ellis Paxson Oberholtzer, *Philadelphia: A History of the City and Its People* (Philadelphia, 1912), 2: 255. Other continuities, however, may have limited the hotel's claim to be competitive with Baltimore's City Hotel. Oberholtzer's sources claim that the

United States Hotel was in part a conversion rather than a purely purpose-built hotel, though the regularity of its fenestration and chimneys suggests otherwise.

16. Various claims have been made regarding the importance of the Tremont House in the development of the American hotel: Jefferson Williamson, *The American Hotel: An Anecdotal History* (New York, 1930), 13–15; Molly W. Berger, "The Modern Hotel in America, 1829–1929," Ph.D. diss., Case Western Reserve University, 1997, chapter 2; J. Anthony Lukas, *Big Trouble: A Murder in a Small Western Town Sets Off a Struggle for the Soul of America* (New York, 1997), 512. In most respects, however, it reflected continuity with preexisting trends. The Tremont was no larger or more expensive than earlier hotels, its dimensions, number of guest rooms, extent of public areas, and cost of construction all falling close to or below its immediate predecessors in Baltimore and Washington. Indeed, it was less impressive even than its Boston predecessor of twenty years before, since the Exchange Coffee House far surpassed the newer edifice in terms of size, cost, and capacity. The Tremont House was undoubtedly quite luxurious, though again there is reason to suspect that it was not more so than other hotels: when the first keeper of the Tremont composed advertisements for the hotel, he made no mention of singular amenities or new technologies; moreover, many travelers evidenced considerably more enthusiasm for their accommodations at the City Hotel in Baltimore. The Tremont House was also architecturally unrepresentative of the nation's luxury hotels. Its irregular polygonal floor plan and projecting wing of guest rooms was very much at variance with the far more common rectangular city block configuration, and thus it cannot properly be interpreted as the primary model for later hotels. The Tremont's aesthetic styling was excellent, but ultimately it was more representative of the Greek Revival than of the American hotel.

17. King, "Early Hotel Entrepreneurs," 155; Berger, "Modern Hotel," 46–47, 50–52; Pevsner, *History of Building Types,* 175; Neil Harris, *Building Lives: Constructing Rites and Passages* (New Haven, 1999), 64.

18. An excellent review of central-place theory in theory and practice can be found in William Cronon, *Nature's Metropolis: Chicago and the Great West* (New York, 1991), 31–41. For a contemporary expression, see *The Western Monthly Magazine, and Literary Journal* (March 1836), 152.

19. James E. Vance, Jr., *Capturing the Horizon: The Historical Geography of Transportation* (New York, 1986); George Rogers Taylor, *The Transportation Revolution* (New York, 1951), 60, 138.

20. The sources for the first hotels in twenty-four of the cities on the map are listed in the notes of this and the previous chapter. The sources for the remaining cities, in descending size order, are: Brooklyn: Henry R. Stiles, *The Civil, Political, Professional and Ecclesiastical History . . . [of] the City of Brooklyn* (New York, 1884), 2: 1359, cross-referenced with William Perris, *Maps of the City of Brooklyn* (New York, 1855), showing the earlier Clinton House as a row-house conversion; Newark: *Newark Daily Advertiser,* 30 July 1863 and notes in "Newark—Hotels" file at the Newark Public Library; Portland: Joyce K. Bibber, "Charles Q. Clapp," from *A Biographical Dictionary of Architects in Maine,* Maine Historic Preservation Commission publications, vol. 5, no. 5 (1988), 2; Salem: Bryant F. Tolles, Jr., *Salem: An Illustrated Guide* (Lebanon, N.H., 2004), 92; Mobile: King, "Hotels of the Old South," 106; New Bedford: Kingston Wm. Heath, *The Patina of Place: The Cultural Weathering of a New England Industrial Landscape* (Knoxville, 2001), 61–65, and consultation with the author; Savannah: Malcolm Bell, Jr., "Ease and Elegance, Madeira and Murder: The Social Life of Savannah's City Hotel," *Georgia Historical Quarterly* 76 (1992), 554; Petersburg: Green, Loth, and Rasmussen, *Lost Virginia,* 172; Springfield: Moses King, *King's Handbook of Springfield, Massachusetts* (Springfield, 1884), 100–101; Lynn: L.H. 3, Neg B-72, Lynn Museum, Lynn, Mass.; Nantucket: Clay Lancaster, *Holiday Island: The Pageant of Nantucket's Hostelries and Summer Life, from Its Beginnings to the Mid-Twentieth Century* (Nantucket, 1993), 34; Lancaster: H. Ray Woermer, "The Taverns of Lancaster and the Later-Day Hotels," *Journal of the Lancaster Historical Society* 73 (1969), 60; Reading: George M. Meiser and Gloria Meiser, *The Passing Scene* (Reading,

1983), 2: 200, 5: 15, 32–35, 6: 46, 131, 7: 21, 41, 124, 8: 208, 9: 89, 125, 10: 108, 11: 6–9, 208; Wilmington: Irene Long, "The Queen of Market Street," *Delaware History* 24 (1991), 187–194; Newport: Antoinette F. Dowling and Vincent J. Scully, Jr., *The Architectural Heritage of Newport, Rhode Island, 1640–1915* (New York, 1967), Plate 155; Portsmouth: James L. Garvin, "Academic Architecture and the Building Trades in the Piscataqua Region of New Hampshire and Maine," Ph.D. diss., Boston University, 1983, 501–502.

21. Richard M. Bayles, *History of Providence County, Rhode Island* (New York, 1891), 1: 310; Rollin G. Osterweis, *Three Centuries of New Haven, 1638–1938* (New Haven, 1953), 260–261; Paul Mange, *Our Inns from 1718 to 1918* (Worcester, 1918), 25; Arthur L. Eno, Jr., ed., *Cotton Was King: A History of Lowell, Massachusetts* (Lowell, 1976), 243.

22. Williamson, *American Hotel,* 282–283; Arthur J. Weise, *History of the City of Troy* (Troy, 1876), 135; Arthur J. Weise, *Troy's One Hundred Years, 1789–1889* (Troy, 1891), 121; Rutherford Hayner, *Troy and Rensselaer County: A History* (New York, 1925), 1: 147; Mary Ryan, *Cradle of the Middle Class: The Family in Oneida County, New York, 1790–1865* (Cambridge, 1981), 24, 92; John J. Walsh, *From Frontier Outpost to Modern City: A History of Utica, 1784–1920* (Utica, 1978), 20–21; G. M. Davison, *The Traveller's Guide Through the Middle and Northern States* (New York, 1837), 206; Blake McKelvey, *Rochester, the Water-Power City, 1812–1854* (Cambridge, Mass., 1945), 96–97; John Devoy, *Rochester and the Post Express: A History of the City of Rochester* (Rochester, 1895), 29.

23. Green, Loth, and Rasmussen, *Lost Virginia,* 172, 175; Pevsner, *History of Building Types,* 176–177; Boorstin, *The Americans: The National Experience,* 136; Williamson, *American Hotel,* 97–99; Amy Waters Yarsinske, *Norfolk, Virginia: The Sunrise City by the Sea* (Virginia Beach, 1994), 69; Mary Louise Christovich, Roulhac Toledano, Betsy Swanson, and Pat Holden, eds., *New Orleans Architecture,* vol. 2, *The American Sector* (Gretna, La., 1972), 47.

24. Blanche M. G. Linden, "Inns to Hotels in Cincinnati," *Cincinnati Historical Society Bulletin* 39 (1981), 134–135; Clara Longworth de Chambrun, *Cincinnati: Story of the Queen City* (New York, 1939), 142; John E. Kleber, ed., *The Encyclopedia of Louisville* (Lexington, Ky., 2001), 404–406; George H. Thurston, *Allegheny County's Hundred Years* (Pittsburgh, 1888), 53; J. Cutler Andrews, *Pittsburgh's Post-Gazette* (Boston, 1936), 114; Blue Cross of Western Pennsylvania, *No. 1 Smithfield Street* (Pittsburgh, 1962), 6; Scharf, *History of St. Louis,* 1440–1448; John W. Reps, *St. Louis Illustrated: Nineteenth-Century Engravings and Lithographs of a Mississippi River Metropolis* (Columbia, Mo., 1989), 26–28.

25. *Daily Chicago American,* 27 May 1837 and 29 April 1839, quoted in Bessie Louise Pierce, *A History of Chicago* (New York, 1937), 1: 213; Frank H. Severance, *The Picture Book of Earlier Buffalo* (Buffalo, 1912), 164; Samuel P. Orth, *A History of Cleveland, Ohio* (Chicago, 1910), 1: 430; David D. Van Tassel and John J. Grabowski, eds., *Encyclopedia of Cleveland History* (Bloomington, Ind., 1987), 524; C. M. Burton, *The City of Detroit, Michigan, 1701–1922* (Detroit, 1922), 1537; *Detroit Free Press,* 23 March 1836, quoted in Wilma Wood Henrickson, *Detroit Perspectives: Crossroads and Turning Points* (Detroit, 1991), 30–31.

26. Green, Loth, and Rasmussen, *Lost Virginia,* 170; *The American Magazine of Useful and Entertaining Knowledge* 3 (1839), 437; Donna-Belle Garvin and James L. Garvin, *On the Road North of Boston: New Hampshire Taverns and Turnpikes, 1700–1900* (Lebanon, N.H., 1988), 5.

27. Boston directory held at Massachusetts Historical Society; Philadelphia directory at Library Company of Philadelphia; Twichel map of St. Louis at Missouri Historical Society; Boynton map of Boston at Massachusetts Historical Society. The New-York Historical Society's holdings include six binders of hotel ephemera in the Bella Landauer Collection that illustrate the richness of the material culture of antebellum hotels in the city.

28. *National Intelligencer,* 18 June 1827. The same imagery was still in use a quarter-century later. In 1852 one observer remarked that the hotel was "devoted to the accommodation of the public [yet]

equal to a European palace." Another wrote that because "the people of the United States are sovereigns . . . their public houses begin to rival the residences of European kings." See *Gleason's Pictorial Drawing-Room Companion,* 21 February 1852, 113, and *New York Post,* 21 August 1852, cited in Carolyn R. Brucken, "Consuming Luxury: Luxury Hotels in Antebellum America, 1825–1860," Ph.D. diss., George Washington University, 1997, 87. For other scholars' readings of this article, see Boorstin, *The Americans: The National Experience,* 135; King, "Hotels of the Old South," 54–55; Berger, "Modern Hotel," 5, 17, 23.

29. *New York Journal,* 25 February 1797; *New York Gazette,* 19 May 1796; Duc de la Rouchefoucauld-Liancourt, *Voyage dans les États-Unis d'Amérique* (Paris, 1798), 2: 326; Charles William Janson, *The Stranger in America* (London, 1807), 203; *Washington Gazette,* 28 September 1796; Winsor, *Memorial History of Boston,* 4: 55; *Independent Chronicle* (Boston), 11 November 1818.

30. On Jacksonian America, see Arthur M. Schlesinger, Jr., *The Age of Jackson* (Boston, 1945); John Ashworth, *Agrarians and Aristocrats: Party Political Ideology in the United States, 1837–1846* (Cambridge, 1983); Harry L. Watson, *Liberty and Power: The Politics of Jacksonian America* (New York, 1990); Daniel Feller, *The Jacksonian Promise: America, 1815–1840* (Baltimore, 1995).

31. I. N. Phelps Stokes, *The Iconography of Manhattan Island* (New York, 1915–1928), 3: 528; *Baltimore Sun,* 17 May 1837; King, "Hotels of the Old South," 208*n*93; Williamson, *American Hotel,* 28–29; James Logan, *Notes of a Journey Through Canada, the United States of America, and the West Indies* (Edinburgh, 1838), 67, 180; Linden, "Inns to Hotels," 135.

32. Robert A. Margo and Georgia C. Villaflor, "The Growth of Wages in Antebellum America," *Journal of Economic History* 47 (1987), 893–894. Proprietary farmers' earnings were not included due to high variability, the prevalence of noncash transactions, and the scarcity of data, but one would not expect them to differ markedly from those of other manual laborers. See also Sean Wilentz, *Chants Democratic: New York City and the Rise of the American Working Class, 1788–1850* (New York, 1984), 117–118, 419; Christine Stansell, *City of Women: Sex and Class in New York, 1789–1860* (Urbana, 1987), 111.

33. Stuart M. Blumin, *The Emergence of the Middle Class: Social Experience in the American City, 1760–1900* (New York, 1989), 112–115.

34. Edward Pessen, "The Egalitarian Myth and the American Social Reality: Wealth, Mobility, and Equality in the 'Age of the Common Man,'" *American Historical Review* 76 (1971), 989–1034, and *Riches, Class, and Power Before the Civil War* (Lexington, Mass., 1973); Frederic Cople Jaher, *The Urban Establishment: Upper Strata in Boston, New York, Charleston, Chicago, and Los Angeles* (Urbana, 1982).

35. William L. Barney, *The Passage of the Republic* (Lexington, Mass., 1987), 89.

36. Francis J. Grund, *The Americans in Their Moral, Social, and Political Relations* (London, 1837), 2: 235; Frederic Marryat, *Second Series of a Diary in America* (Philadelphia, 1840), 38; *Cleveland Herald and Gazette,* 25 July 1838, 4 December 1838; *Cleveland Herald,* 29 July 1835, 7 June 1837.

37. James Boardman, *America, and the Americans* (London, 1833), 177; Matilda Charlotte Houstoun, *Hesperos; or, Travels in the West* (London, 1850), 1: 212; Boorstin, *The Americans: The National Experience,* 146. See also Paul E. Groth, *Living Downtown: The History of Residential Hotels in the United States* (Berkeley, 2004), 28–30; Catherine Cocks, *Doing the Town: The Rise of Urban Tourism in the United States, 1850–1915* (Berkeley, 2001), 74.

38. *New York Mirror,* 25 June 1836, quoted in Brucken, "Consuming Luxury," 173.

39. *Workingman's Advocate,* 9 January 1830, 22 May 1830, 29 May 1830, 28 August 1830, 11 September 1830, 23 October 1830, 28 October 1830, 30 October 1830, 25 December 1830, 15 October 1831, 3 March 1832, 18 August 1832, 31 October 1833, 7 May 1834, 8 November 1834, 14 November 1835; see, e.g. Resolutions, 23rd Congress, 1st Session, 12 March 1834, no. 168, and 24 June 1834, no. 473.

40. *Workingman's Advocate,* 6 April 1833, 18 May 1833; J. W. Smith, *Report of the Debates and Proceedings of the Convention for the Revision of the Constitution of the State of Ohio, 1850–1851* (Columbus, 1851), 2: 264–265, quoted in Jane Boyle Knowles, "Luxury Hotels in American Cities, 1810–1860," Ph.D. diss., University of Pennsylvania, 1972, 291.

41. John Majewski, "Toward a Social History of the Corporation: Shareholding in Pennsylvania Banking and Transportation Companies, 1800 to 1840," in *The Past and Future of Early American Economic History: Needs and Opportunities,* ed. Cathy Matson (forthcoming).

42. *Laws of the State of New York* (Albany, 1825–1840); *Laws of the General Assembly of the Commonwealth of Pennsylvania* (Harrisburg, 1825–1840); *Acts of a Local Nature . . . of the State of Ohio* (Columbus, 1825–1840); *Acts of the General Assembly of Virginia* (Richmond, 1825–1840); *Acts . . . of the State of Louisiana* (New Orleans, 1825–1840); Naomi R. Lamoreaux, "Partnerships, Corporations, and the Theory of the Firm," *American Economic Review* 88 (1998), 66–71.

43. On the historiography of government involvement in nineteenth-century economic development, see John Lauritz Larson, "'Bind the Republic Together': The National Union and the Struggle for a System of Internal Improvements," *Journal of American History* 74 (1987), 364; Berger, "Modern Hotel," 50–52.

44. *Acts of Louisiana* (1831), 16–18; (1835), 22–23; (1836), 167–168; (1837), 35–36, 75–76; *Acts of Virginia* (1838), 183–187; (1839), 145; (1840), 115–117; *Acts of Ohio* (1834), 48–49; (1835), 210–211; (1836), 606–607; (1837), 219–220.

45. City Hotel ledgers held at Maryland Historical Society.

46. Berger, "Modern Hotel," 51–55.

47. Susan G. Davis, *Parades and Power: Street Theatre in Nineteenth-Century Philadelphia* (Philadelphia, 1986); Knowles, "Luxury Hotels in American Cities," 148–155.

48. Reginald Charles McGrane, *The Panic of 1837: Some Financial Problems of the Jacksonian Era* (Chicago, 1924); William G. Shade, *Banks or No Banks: The Money Question in the Western States, 1832–1865* (Detroit, 1972), 20–111; Marie Elizabeth Sushka, "The Antebellum Money Market and the Economic Impact of the Bank War," *Journal of Economic History* 36 (1976), 809–835.

3. The Hotel System

1. Domingo Faustino Sarmiento, *Viajes por Europa, África i América, 1845–1847,* trans. Michael Aaron Rockland (Princeton, 1970), 6–24, 67–69, 284.

2. The best overviews of this emergent geography are D. W. Meinig, *The Shaping of America,* vol. 3, *Transcontinental America, 1850–1915* (New Haven, 1998), and James E. Vance, Jr., *Capturing the Horizon: The Historical Geography of Transportation* (New York, 1986), chapter 4.

3. George Rogers Taylor, *The Transportation Revolution, 1815–1860* (New York, 1951), 79; Vance, *Capturing the Horizon,* 276; Meinig, *Shaping of America,* 3: 5.

4. William L. Barney, *The Passage of the Republic* (Lexington, Mass., 1987), 163.

5. Meinig, *Shaping of America,* vol. 3, chapter 1.

6. Jno. Dalley, "A Map of the Road from Trenton to Amboy" (n.p., c. 1745); Christopher Colles, *A Survey of the Roads of the United States of America* (New York, 1789); S. S. Moore and T. W. Jones for Mathew Carey, *The Traveller's Directory; or, A Pocket Companion* (Philadelphia, 1802, 1804).

7. Taylor, *Transportation Revolution,* 139–145.

8. Carol Sheriff, *The Artificial River: The Erie Canal and the Paradox of Progress* (New York, 1996), 82–85, 119, 147; *Radcliffe's Executors v. Mayor of Brooklyn,* 4 Comst. 195 (N.Y., 1850), 206–207.

9. *Baltimore and Ohio Railroad Timetable* (Baltimore, 1859), 23; *Thurston's Route Book, Philadelphia to Chicago* (Pittsburgh, 1863), 34. For travel distances and times around 1850 and 1870, see *Burke's*

Traveller's Guide Through the United States and Canada (Buffalo, 1851) and *Travelers Official Railway Guide to the United States and Canada* (New York, 1871).

10. *Seventh Census,* vol. 1 (Washington, D.C., 1853), table I, "Population of the United States Decennially from 1798 to 1850," table L, "Professions, Occupations, and Trades of the Male Population in the United States over Fifteen Years of Age"; *The Population of the United States in 1860* (Washington, D.C., 1864), table 6, "Occupations"; *Ninth Census,* vol. 1, *The Statistics of the Population of the United States* (Washington, D.C., 1872), "Table of the Population," table 29, "Number of Persons in the United States Engaged in Each Special Occupation"; *Statistics of the Population of the United States at the Tenth Census* (Washington, D.C., 1883), table 16, "The Elements of the Population," table 22, "Number of Persons in the United States Engaged in Each Special Occupation"; *Report on the Population of the United States at the Eleventh Census, 1890,* part 2 (Washington, D.C., 1897), table 1, "Table of Population of the States and Territories at Each Census, 1790–1890," tables 78 and 79, "Total Males and Females Ten Years of Age and Over Engaged in Selected Occupations"; *Occupations at the Twelfth Census* (Washington, D.C., 1904), table 32, "Total Persons Ten Years of Age and Over Engaged in Each of 503 Specified Occupations"; *Thirteenth Census of the United States Taken in the Year 1910,* vol. 1, *Population* (Washington, D.C., 1904), table 10, "Population of the United States by Divisions and States, 1790–1910"; vol. 4, table 2, "Total Persons Ten Years of Age and Over Engaged in Each Special Occupation Classified by Sex, by States: 1910."

11. Russell Duncan, *Freedom's Shore: Tunis Campbell and the Georgia Freedmen* (Athens, Ga., 1986); Tunis G. Campbell, *Hotel Keepers, Head Waiters, and Housekeepers' Guide* (Boston, 1848), 42, 44, 49, 56.

12. Philip Kelland, *Transatlantic Sketches* (Edinburgh, 1858), 20–21; Isabella L. Bird, *The Englishwoman in America* (London, 1856), 125. Some people who spoke of the "hotel system" meant its national geography; others used the term to describe its internal workings. See also Molly W. Berger, "The Modern Hotel in America, 1829–1929," Ph.D. diss., Case Western Reserve University, 1997, 97.

13. My seven-part nomenclature coincides at three points with Paul Groth's four-part division as set forth in *Living Downtown: The History of Residential Hotels in the United States* (Berkeley, 1994), chapters 2–5.

14. Jefferson Williamson, *The American Hotel: An Anecdotal History* (New York, 1930); Doris E. King, "Hotels of the Old South, 1793–1860: A Study of the Origin and Development of the First-Class Hotels," Ph.D. diss., Duke University, 1952; Arthur S. White, *Palaces of the People: A Social History of Commercial Hospitality* (London, 1968); Jane Boyle Knowles, "Luxury Hotels in American Cities, 1810–1860," Ph.D. diss., University of Pennsylvania, 1972; Berger, "Modern Hotel," except chapter 7; Carolyn R. Brucken, "Consuming Luxury: Luxury Hotels in Antebellum America, 1825–1860," Ph.D. diss., George Washington University, 1997. The principal exception to this rule is Groth's *Living Downtown.*

15. Williamson, *American Hotel,* 123; Timothy B. Spears, *100 Years on the Road: The Traveling Salesman in American Culture* (New Haven, 1995), 95. See also "The Merchant's Hotel, S. W. Cor. 12th and Olive," advertisement clipping in author's possession.

16. Williamson, *American Hotel,* 123–125; Spears, *100 Years on the Road,* 91, 95.

17. John A. Kouwenhoven, *The Columbia Historical Portrait of New York* (New York, 1953), 138.

18. Spears, *100 Years on the Road,* 26–35. See also Lewis E. Atherton, *The Pioneer Merchant in Mid-America* (New York, 1969). See 1840s or 1850s city directories for New York, Boston, Philadelphia, Baltimore, Louisville, Chicago, or St. Louis; "Commercial Hotel," Landauer Collection, New-York Historical Society, box 74; "Commercial Hotel," Warshaw Collection, National Museum of American History, Hotels, box 4, folder 30.

19. Groth, *Living Downtown,* chapter 3; Occidental Hotel trade card, Landauer Collection, New-York Historical Society, Hotel scrapbook no. 2.

20. American Exchange trade card, Warshaw Collection, National Museum of American History, Hotels, box 1, folder 28; Broadway Hotel advertisement, Landauer Collection, New-York Historical Society, Hotel scrapbook no. 3.

21. Groth, *Living Downtown,* 25 and chapter 5.

22. Ibid., chapters 4, 5.

23. Kenneth T. Jackson, ed., *The Encyclopedia of New York City* (New Haven, 1995), 984–985; "Los Dos Amigos" and "U.S. Hotel," both in Watkins photo collection, nos. 58.372, 188.514, Huntington Library; William H. Jackson, postcard of the "Snowflake Hotel," Utah, in author's possession; Sharon E. Wood, *The Freedom of the Streets: Work, Citizenship, and Sexuality in a Gilded Age City* (Chapel Hill, 2005), 172–178.

24. Groth, *Living Downtown,* chapter 5; Jacob Riis, *How the Other Half Lives* (New York, 1890; Dover ed., 1971), 69.

25. Alf Evers, Elizabeth Cromley, Elizabeth Blackmar, Neil Harris, and John Margolies, *Resorts of the Catskills* (New York, 1979), 2–4, 72–75; Theodore Corbett, *The Making of American Resorts: Saratoga Springs, Ballston Spa, Lake George* (Piscataway, N.J., 2001), 15–17, 27–30; Nancy Goyne Evans, "The Sans Souci, a Fashionable Resort Hotel in Ballston Spa," *Winterthur Portfolio* 6 (1970), 111–126; Charlene M. Boyer Lewis, *Ladies and Gentlemen on Display: Planter Society at the Virginia Springs, 1790–1860* (Charlottesville, 2001), 18; John Sterngass, *First Resorts: Pursuing Pleasure at Saratoga Springs, Newport & Coney Island* (Baltimore, 2001), 7–9.

26. Thomas Jefferson, *Notes on the State of Virginia* (1781), query V; Sterngass, *First Resorts,* 17; Evers et al., *Resorts of the Catskills,* 2–4, 72–75; Corbett, *Making of American Resorts,* 41–47; Dona Brown, *Inventing New England: Regional Tourism in American Culture* (Washington, D.C., 1995), 15–40.

27. Barbara Carson, "Early American Tourists and the Commercialization of Leisure," in *Of Consuming Interests: The Style of Life in the Eighteenth Century,* ed. Cary Carson, Ronald Hoffman, and Peter J. Albert (Charlottesville, 1995), 390–396; Evans, "The Sans Souci," 117; Brown, *Inventing New England,* 15–16, 23–28, 48–50; Roland Van Zandt, *The Catskill Mountain House* (Cornwallville, N.Y., 1982), 19. See also Earl Pomeroy, *In Search of the Golden West: The Tourist in Western America* (New York, 1957), 20, 26–27, 164.

28. William Dean Howells, *The Rise of Silas Lapham* (Boston, 1885), chapter 2. Other literary treatments of resort hotels include Howells's *A Hazard of New Fortunes* (1890), *A Traveller from Altruria* (1894), and *The Landlord at Lions Head* (1897); Wharton's *The Age of Innocence* (1920) and *The Buccaneers* (1938); and Chopin's *The Awakening* (1899).

29. For an extensive array of exterior views of resort hotels, see the New-York Historical Society's Bella Landauer Collection under "Hotels"; Jeffrey Limerick, Nancy Ferguson, and Richard Oliver, *America's Grand Resort Hotels* (New York, 1979), 64–161.

30. *American Architect and Building News,* 2 June 1877, 25 January 1879; Christine Barnes, *Great Lodges of the National Parks* (Bend, Ore., 2002).

31. William Prescott Smith, *The Book of the Great Railway Celebrations of 1857* (New York, 1858), chapter 15; Edward C. Hungerford, *The Story of the Baltimore and Ohio Railroad* (New York, 1928), 1. 295–296; Allen W. Trelease, *The North Carolina Railroad, 1849–1871, and the Modernization of North Carolina* (Chapel Hill, 1991), 39, 85–86, 226–227.

32. Brantz Mayer, "A June Jaunt," *Harper's New Monthly Magazine* 14 (1856–1857), 593–594; *The Great West Illustrated in a Series of Photographic Views Across the Continent; Taken Along the Line of the Union Pacific Railroad, West from Omaha, Nebraska* (New York, 1869), plate 15; see also Jim Porterfield, "Introduction" to *Dining on Rails* (New York, 1990). Notably, there were very few

large terminal hotels in the European style built in the United States. See Christopher Monkhouse, "Railway Hotels," in *Railway Architecture,* ed. Marcus Binney and David Pearce (London, 1979).

33. *Hotel World,* 22 October 1881.

34. Donna-Belle Garvin and James L. Garvin, *On the Road North of Boston: New Hampshire Taverns and Turnpikes, 1700–1900* (Lebanon, N.H., 1988), 1, 36, 82. Images of settlement hotels in the West: Joseph Armstrong Baird, *California's Illustrated Letter Sheets, 1849–1869* (San Francisco, 1967), plates 60, 54, 95; C. E. Watkins "Grand Central Hotel, Tahoe City, August 1874" and "Mammoth Tree Grove Hotel, Calaveras City, California," both in Watkins photo collection, 74.284, 74.312, Huntington Library. See also "Silver Dollar City of the Ozarks," postcard with 1881 settlement hotel photograph, in author's possession.

35. John Kobler, *Ardent Spirits: The Rise and Fall of Prohibition* (New York, 1973), 108–109; Eliza Daniel Stewart, *Memories of the Crusade: A Thrilling Account of the Great Uprising of the Women of Ohio in 1873 Against the Liquor Crime* (Ohio, 1889; rpt. New York, 1972), 167–169, 335–336; C. C. Pearson and J. Edwin Hendricks, *Liquor and Anti-Liquor in Virginia, 1619–1919* (Durham, 1967), 113n4; Raymond Calkins, *Substitutes for the Saloon* (New York, 1971), 306, 329; W. J. Rorabaugh, "Edward C. Delavan," in *American National Biography,* ed. John A. Garraty and Mark C. Carnes (New York, 1999), 6: 384–385. The *Journal of the American Temperance Union* carried numerous temperance hotel advertisements and articles in the 1840s and 1850s. See also Ohio Historical Records Survey Project, Works Projects Administration, *Historic Sites of Cleveland: Hotels and Taverns* (Columbus, 1942), 15, 156.

36. Kathleen Neils Conzen, *Immigrant Milwaukee, 1836–1860: Accommodation and Community in a Frontier City* (Cambridge, 1976), 44–45; *New Yorker Staats-Zeitung,* 5 May 1857 (trans. Kathleen N. Conzen); see, for example, the Hotel Française trade card, Landauer Collection II, New-York Historical Society, box 61; Hotel Disch trade card, Warshaw Collection, National Museum of American History, Hotels, box 5, folder 35.

37. Myra B. Young Armstead, "Revisiting Hotels and Other Lodgings: American Tourist Spaces Through the Lens of Black Pleasure-Travelers, 1880–1950," *Journal of Decorative and Propaganda Arts* 25 (2005), 137–159.

38. Stephen Birmingham, *Our Crowd: The Great Jewish Families of New York* (New York, 1967), 139–150; Evers et al., *Resorts of the Catskills,* 82–88; Hasia R. Diner, *A Time for Gathering: The Second Migration, 1820–1880* (Baltimore, 1992), 191–193.

39. Anne C. Rose, *Victorian America and the Civil War* (New York, 1992), 141–143, 190–191; Ohio Historical Records Survey Project, WPA, *Historic Sites of Cleveland,* 49.

40. For differing views on the Civil War and the postbellum economy, see Edward Chase Kirkland, *Dream and Thought in the Business Community, 1860–1900* (Ithaca, 1956); Alfred D. Chandler, Jr., *The Visible Hand: The Managerial Revolution in American Business* (Cambridge, Mass., 1977), 213, 259, 290; Mark R. Wilson, *The Business of Civil War: Military Mobilization and the State, 1861–1865* (Baltimore, 2006), especially chapter 6.

41. Thomas C. Cochran, *Railroad Leaders, 1845–1890: The Business Mind in Action* (Cambridge, Mass., 1953); Alfred L. Thimm, *Business Ideologies in the Reform-Progressive Era, 1880–1914* (University, Ala., 1976); James A. Ward, "Image and Reality: The Railway Corporate-State Metaphor," *Business History Review* 55 (1981), 491–516; John Lauritz Larson, "'Bind the Republic Together': The National Union and the Struggle for a System of Internal Improvements," *Journal of American History* 74 (1987), 363–387.

42. John F. Ropes, *The New-York Traveler, and United States Hotel Directory* (New York, 1858); J. T. Boyd, *Boyd's Hotel Directory and Tourists' Guide* (New York, 1872); W. E. Statia, *Statia's Hotel List Guide* (Portland, Maine, 1874); David M. Gazlay, *Gazlay's United States Hotel Guide for 1875* (New

York, 1875); James B. Bradford, *Bradford's Hotel Guide to the United States and Canada* (Chicago, 1875).

43. Boyd, *Boyd's Hotel Directory*, 18–19, 29–33, 46–48.

44. Some contemporary railroad guides include *The Travelers' Official Railway Guide to the United States and Canada* (New York, 1868); *The Middle States: A Handbook for Travellers* (Boston, 1874); *The Pacific Tourist: Adams and Bishop's Illustrated Trans-Continental Guide of Travel, from the Atlantic to the Pacific Ocean* (New York, 1884).

45. These included the *United States Official Hotel Red Book* (New York, 1886–) and the *Hotel Blue Book: The Standard Hotel Directory for the United States and Canada* (New York, 1891–). See also J. R. Watts, *Southern Travelers' Official Railway Guide and Hotel Directory for the Southern States* (Baltimore, 1879); *United States Official Hotel Directory and Railroad Indicator* (New York, 1886); W. M. Peterson, *The Hotel Guide: A Pacific Coast Hotel Directory* (San Francisco, 1889).

46. See sources cited in note 10.

47. Data from same tables as previous note.

48. D. R. Hundley, *Social Relations in Our Southern States* (New York, 1860), 56.

49. Robert W. Rydell, *All the World's a Fair: Visions of Empire at American International Expositions, 1876–1916* (Chicago, 1984), 17–19.

50. Bruno Giberti, *Designing the Centennial: A History of the 1876 International Exhibition in Philadelphia* (Lexington, Ky., 2002), 33–45; Free Library of Philadelphia Centennial Exhibition Digital Collection, http://libwww.library.phila.gov/CenCol/exh-org2.htm (accessed July 2006).

51. Rydell, *All the World's a Fair,* 11; Giberti, *Designing the Centennial,* chapter 2.

52. Hotels listed alphabetically in albums and by place in vertical files, Landauer Collection, New-York Historical Society, boxes 75, 76, 81, 82.

53. Free Library of Philadelphia Centennial Exhibition Digital Collection on attendance figures, http://libwww.library.phila.gov/CenCol/exh-attend.htm (accessed July 2006); Rydell, *All the World's a Fair,* 19, 32–34.

54. Images and statistics from Free Library of Philadelphia Centennial Exhibition Digital Collection. For numerous images of women and children at the Centennial Exhibition, see Lally Weymouth and Milton Glaser, *America in 1876: The Way We Were* (New York, 1976), 18–44, and the many prints published in *Harper's Weekly* during the centennial summer.

4. Imperial Hotels and Hotel Empires

1. Neil Harris, "On Vacation," in Alf Evers, Elizabeth Cromley, Elizabeth Blackmar, Neil Harris, and John Margolies, *Resorts of the Catskills* (New York, 1979), 102–104; Cindy S. Aron, *Working at Play: A History of Vacations in the United States* (New York, 1999), 128, 140–147; Catherine Cocks, *Doing the Town: The Rise of Urban Tourism in the United States, 1850–1915* (Berkeley, 2001), 106–110. For essential theoretical background, see Dean MacCannell, *The Tourist: A New Theory of the Leisure Class* (New York, 1976).

2. Aron, *Working at Play,* 127–155; Harris, "On Vacation," 102–104; Hugh DeSantis, "The Democratization of Travel: The Travel Agent in American History," *Journal of American Culture* 1 (1978), 1–19.

3. Earl Pomeroy, *In Search of the Golden West: The Tourist in Western America* (New York, 1957); Anne Farrar Hyde, *An American Vision: Far Western Landscape and National Culture, 1820–1920* (New York, 1990), 107–146; Marguerite S. Shaffer, *See America First: Tourism and National Identity, 1880–1940* (Washington, D.C., 2001), 1–26. See also Mary Louise Pratt, *Imperial Eyes: Travel Writing and Transculturation* (New York, 1992).

4. Shaffer, *See America First,* 283; Hyde, *American Vision,* 161–174; Pomeroy, *Golden West,* 19–23.

5. Marta Weigle and Barbara Babcock, eds., *The Great Southwest of the Fred Harvey Company and the Santa Fe Railway* (Phoenix, 1996), 11–35; Lesley Poling-Kempes, *The Harvey Girls: Women Who Opened the West* (New York, 1989), 55–56; Chris Wilson, *The Myth of Santa Fe: Creating a Modern Regional Tradition* (Albuquerque, 1997), 80–95 and generally; Sandra D. Lynn, *Windows on the Past: Historic Lodgings of New Mexico* (Albuquerque, 1999), chapter 5. Harvey died in 1901, leaving his sons to run the company.

6. Richard C. Wade, *The Urban Frontier: The Rise of Western Cities, 1790–1830* (Cambridge, 1959), 1.

7. Kathleen A. Brosnan, *Uniting Mountain and Plain: Cities, Law, and Environmental Change Along the Front Range* (Albuquerque, 2002), 92–115; Hyde, *American Vision,* 174–183, 187–190.

8. D. W. Meinig, *The Shaping of America,* vol. 3, *Transcontinental America, 1850–1915* (New Haven, 1998), 55–69; Pomeroy, *Golden West,* 25–27, 58; Hyde, *American Vision,* 183–187.

9. David Leon Chandler, *Henry Flagler: The Astonishing Life and Times of the Visionary Robber Baron Who Founded Florida* (New York, 1986), 51–52, 85–88. See also Sidney Walter Martin, *Florida's Flagler* (Athens, Ga., 1949), 90–95; Susan R. Braden, *The Architecture of Leisure: The Florida Resort Hotels of Henry Flagler and Henry Plant* (Gainesville, Fla., 2002), 20–23; Edward N. Akin, *Flagler: Rockefeller Partner and Florida Baron* (Kent, Ohio, 1988), 26, 107.

10. Chandler, *Henry Flagler,* 95–104, 123–141, 169, 176; Braden, *Architecture of Leisure,* 5–8; Akin, *Flagler,* 118–123, 145–147, 163–164. See also Martin, *Florida's Flagler,* 114–122, 145–148, 162–163.

11. Braden, *Architecture of Leisure,* 105–132.

12. Brosnan, *Uniting Mountain and Plain,* 100; Mark David Spence, *Dispossessing the Wilderness: Indian Removal and the Making of the National Parks* (Oxford, 1999), 56–60.

13. Matilda McQuaid with Karen Barlett, "Building an Image of the Southwest: Mary Colter, Fred Harvey Company Architect," in Weigle and Babcock, *The Great Southwest,* 24–35; Diane F. Pardue, "Marketing Ethnography: The Fred Harvey Indian Department and George A. Dorsey," ibid., 102–109; Spence, *Dispossessing the Wilderness,* 83–86, 117; Hyde, *American Vision,* 255–262. See also Christine Barnes, *Great Lodges of the National Parks* (Bend, Ore., 2002).

14. Colonial Hotel, Nassau, box 4, folder 31, Warshaw Collection of Business Americana—Hotels, Archives Center, National Museum of American History; John O. Collins, *The Panama Guide,* ICC Press, Quartermaster Division, Mt. Hope, C.Z., 1912; for example, the Copper Queen Hotel (1902) in Bisbee, Arizona. For European analogues, see Annabel Jane Wharton, *Building the Cold War: Hilton International Hotels and Modern Architecture* (Chicago, 2001), 41–47.

15. Nikolaus Pevsner, *A History of Building Types* (Princeton, 1976), 177–178.

16. Daniel Boorstin, *The Americans: The National Experience* (New York, 1965), 138; Pevsner, *History of Building Types,* 177; George Augustus Sala, "American Hotels and American Food," *Temple Bar Magazine* 2 (1861), 345.

17. Pevsner, *History of Building Types,* 188–191.

18. *Ninth Census,* vol. 1, *The Statistics of the Population of the United States* (Washington, D.C., 1872), 674; *Tenth Census,* vol. 1 (Washington, D.C., 1883), 744; United States House of Representatives, *Special Census Report on the Occupations of the Population of the United States at the Eleventh Census, 1890* (Washington, D.C., 1896), 11; *Twelfth Census,* vol. 2, part 2 (Washington, D.C., 1903), 505; *Thirteenth Census,* vol. 4 (Washington, D.C., 1912), 94. Note that boardinghouse and lodging house keepers were enumerated separately. Chicago city directory, 1880 and 1910; Paul Groth, *Living Downtown: The History of Residential Hotels in the United States* (Berkeley, 1994), 181, 188–189. Note that the counting methods were different in each city, since the Chicago count is fewer than in San Francisco, a smaller city; but within each municipality, the increases are nonetheless significant. On tall hotels in small cities, see hotel postcards in the Landauer Collection, New-York Historical Society.

19. Ward Morehouse III, *The Waldorf-Astoria: America's Gilded Dream* (New York, 1991), 20–21; Curtis Gathje, *At the Plaza: An Illustrated History of the World's Most Famous Hotel* (New York, 2000), 11–17.

20. Rufus Jarman, *A Bed for the Night: The Story of the Wheeling Bellboy E. M. Statler and His Remarkable Hotels* (New York, 1950), 18–23, 66–70, 98–106; Floyd Miller, *Statler: America's Extraordinary Hotelman* (New York, 1968), 33–55, 61–102. These are celebratory works, but are largely accurate on biographical details.

21. Jarman, *Bed for the Night,* 67–70, 98–102; Miller, *Statler,* 56–64, 67, 71–73, 80. There were almost certainly other influences on Statler's management practices: standardization and interchangeability from manufacturing, scientific management, and especially the methods of the Fred Harvey Company. See David A. Hounshell, *From the American System to Mass Production: The Development of Manufacturing Technology in the United States* (Baltimore, 1984); Daniel Nelson, *Frederick W. Taylor and the Rise of Scientific Management* (Madison, Wis., 1980); Weigle and Babcock, *The Great Southwest.* Statler's biographers make no mention of these other influences, perhaps because it would conflict with their portrayal of Statler as a homegrown innovator and self-educated prophet of new business practices rather than an exceptionally successful product of his times. The leading work on modern business management remains Alfred D. Chandler, *The Visible Hand: The Managerial Revolution in American Business* (Cambridge, Mass., 1977).

22. Jarman, *Bed for the Night,* 130–132; Miller, *Statler,* 91–96.

23. Miller, *Statler,* 87–102, 114–117, 130–133, 166–187, 218–219; Molly W. Berger, "The Modern Hotel in America, 1829–1929," Ph.D. diss., Case Western Reserve University, 1997, 316–317.

24. Lisa Pfueller Davidson, "Early Twentieth-Century Hotel Architects and the Origins of Standardization," *Journal of Decorative and Propaganda Arts* 25 (2005), 82–87; Jarman, *Bed for the Night,* 131–136; W. Sidney Wagner in *Architectural Forum* 27 (1917), 115–118, 166–170; 28 (1918), 15–18. The *Avery Index to Architectural Periodicals* includes more than three dozen Statler-related articles.

25. Miller, *Statler,* 84–85, 132–134, 138–150.

26. Ibid., 132–134; Jarman, *Bed for the Night,* 2–3.

27. Miller, *Statler,* 47; Jarman, *Bed for the Night,* 1.

28. Daniel Levinson Wilk, "Cliff Dwellers: Modern Service in New York City, 1800–1945," Ph.D. diss., Duke University, 2005, 67–77; Weigle and Babcock, *The Great Southwest,* 11–35; hotel chain stationery in hotel albums, Landauer Collection, New-York Historical Society, and Warshaw Collection, National Museum of American History, Hotels, box 13, folder 63, box 15, folders 4 and 14, box 20, folder 14; Miller, *Statler,* 92–96, 133–134, 140–144, 188–198; Berger, "Modern Hotel," 309–328; Paul L. Ingram, *The Rise of Hotel Chains in the United States, 1896–1980* (New York, 1996), 3–6 and generally.

29. Virginia Scharff, *Taking the Wheel: Women and the Coming of the Motor Age* (New York, 1991), 7–12. See also James J. Flink, *America Adopts the Automobile, 1895–1910* (Cambridge, Mass., 1970).

30. Clay McShane, *Down the Asphalt Path: The Automobile and the American City* (New York, 1994), 103–109; Miller, *Statler,* 117–119; James J. Flink, "Henry Ford," in *American National Biography,* ed. John A. Garraty and Mark C. Carnes (New York, 1999), 8: 226–235.

31. Bruce E. Seely, *Building the American Highway System: Engineers as Policy Makers* (Philadelphia, 1987); Mark H. Rose, *Interstate: Express Highway Politics, 1939–1989* (Knoxville, 1990), 1–14.

32. Warren James Belasco, *Americans on the Road: From Autocamp to Motel, 1910–1945* (Baltimore, 1979), 41–74; John A. Jakle, Keith A. Sculle, and Jefferson S. Rogers, *The Motel in America* (Baltimore, 1996), 20. The growing enthusiasm for inns and taverns is suggested by books like W. Harrison Bayles, *Old Taverns of New York* (New York, 1915), Samuel Adams Drake, *Old Boston Taverns and Tavern Clubs* (Boston, 1917), Mary Harrod Northend, *We Visit Old Inns* (Boston, 1925).

33. United States Bureau of the Census, *1930 Census of Hotels*, 2, 5. The bureau's standard for a substantial hotel was one having at least twenty-five guest rooms, meaning that many smaller establishments went uncounted.

Part Two. HOSPITALITY

1. Julian Pitt-Rivers, "The Law of Hospitality," in *The Fate of Shechem; or, The Politics of Sex: Essays in the Anthropology of the Mediterranean* (Cambridge, 1977), 94–97. It should be noted here that this definition excludes the provision of hospitality to locals and acquaintances. A more complete definition might recognize that a "stranger" might be an outsider to the household, not only an outsider to the community.
2. Ibid., 94–99.
3. *Oxford English Dictionary*, 2nd ed. (Oxford, 1989), 6: 925, 7: 414–418, 427; *Webster's Ninth New Collegiate Dictionary* (Springfield, Mass., 1986), 541, 583.
4. Nineteenth-century representations of the crowd are brilliantly analyzed in Walter Benjamin's "On Some Motifs in Baudelaire" (1939). Also representative of European literary interest in the crowd and the stranger are Balzac's "The Girl with the Golden Eyes," Hugo's various descriptions of Paris crowds, and Kierkegaard's *Diary of a Seducer* (1843). Author's translation.
5. Paul Boyer, *Urban Masses and Moral Order in America, 1820–1920* (Cambridge, Mass., 1978), 5, 73–74; Karen Halttunen, *Confidence Men and Painted Women: A Study of Middle-Class Culture in America, 1830–1870* (New Haven, 1982), 36; Herman Melville, *The Confidence-Man: His Masquerade* (Boston, 1857). This story of Poe's was set in London despite his not having lived there in many years.
6. Paul Langford, *A Polite and Commercial People* (Oxford, 1989), 61–71, 101–108, 391–417; George Rogers Taylor, *The Transportation Revolution, 1815–1860* (New York, 1951).
7. William Blackstone, *Commentaries on the Laws of England* (Oxford, 1765–1769), book 1, chapter 1, "Of the Absolute Rights of Individuals" (though it is worth noting that Blackstone was primarily writing about the right not to be imprisoned); John Torpey, *The Invention of the Passport: Surveillance, Citizenship, and the State* (Cambridge, 2000), 21–32.
8. Julian Ursyn Niemcewicz, *Under Their Vine and Fig Tree: Travels Through America in 1797–1799, 1805, with Some Further Account of Life in New Jersey*, trans. Metchie J. E. Budka (Elizabeth, N.J., 1965), 161.
9. Torpey, *Invention of the Passport*, chapter 3.
10. In the terms of critical geographers like Henri Lefebvre and David Harvey, this was part of the emergence of a new kind of spatiality, one that was dialectically related to the advent of modernity. See Lyn Lofland, *A World of Strangers: Order and Action in Urban Public Space* (Ithaca, 1973); Halttunen, *Confidence Men and Painted Women;* Henri Lefebvre, *The Production of Space*, trans. Donald Nicholson-Smith (Oxford, 1991); David Harvey, *The Condition of Postmodernity* (Oxford, 1990).

5. The House of Strangers

1. Henry Glassie, *Vernacular Architecture* (Bloomington, Ind., 1999), 79–90, 116–131; Gabrielle M. Lanier and Bernard L. Herman, *Everyday Architecture of the Mid-Atlantic: Looking at Buildings and Landscapes* (Baltimore, 1997), 31–33.
2. Richard Longstreth, "Architecture and the City," in *American Urbanism: A Historiographical Review*, ed. Howard Gillette, Jr., and Zane L. Miller (Westport, Conn., 1987), 165.

3. Dell Upton, "Another City: The Urban Cultural Landscape in the Early Republic," in *Everyday Life in the Early Republic,* ed. Catherine E. Hutchins (Winterthur, Del., 1999), 65–95.

4. Ibid., 61–63, 85–95.

5. The experiential distinction is marked nicely by the modern-day contrast between the impersonality of hotel accommodations and the distinctly personalistic, face-to-face host-guest experience of the bed and breakfast.

6. The strangers list, which at an average of only 220 visitors per day to a city of about a quarter-million people (exclusive of Brooklyn) probably represented a substantial undercount, is cited in Meryle R. Evans, "Knickerbocker Hotels and Restaurants, 1800–1850," *New-York Historical Society Quarterly* 36 (1952), 377–378; *American Railroad Journal* 1, no. 24 (12 June 1845), 373: since the figures excluded way and through passengers, they were probably fairly good estimates of actual arrivals in the two cities combined; *American Railroad Journal* 1, no. 45 (6 November 1845), 707. All population figures taken from the United States Census Bureau.

7. Ohio Historical Records Survey Project, Works Projects Administration, *Historic Sites of Cleveland: Hotels and Taverns* (Columbus, 1942), 23, 43, 388; Diary of Mr. and Mrs. James Drew (1845), 74, manuscript held at the New-York Historical Society; "The St. Nicholas Hotel," 1856 booklet held at the New York Public Library, 3; weekly samplings taken from 1858 St. Nicholas Hotel register held at the New-York Historical Society.

8. Tontine Hotel Corporation Minutes, 20 March 1826, ms. B-22, item IV-D, New Haven Colony Historical Society; R. G. Dun ledgers, Baker Library, Harvard University: W. H. Chapman, Conn. v. 40, p. 566, Gage & Bros., Ill. v. 27, p. 46, Potter Palmer, Ill. v. 28, p. 6; Albert Bigelow Paine, "The Workings of a Modern Hotel," *World's Work* 5 (March 1903), 3171–3187; L. F. Byington and Oscar Lewis, *The History of San Francisco* (Chicago, 1931), 168; Doris Elizabeth King, "Hotels of the Old South, 1793-1860: A Study of the Origin and Development of the First-Class Hotels," Ph.D. diss., Duke University, 1952, 230–234; Thomas L. Nichols, *Forty Years of American Life* (London, 1864), 2: 12; William Chambers, *Things as They Are in America* (London, 1854), 180.

9. *Baltimore Sun,* 17 May 1837; *Atkinson's Sunday Evening Post,* 19 September 1835; *The Hotel Folly* (Philadelphia, 1857); for a sense of the rapidity of turnover, see the complete collection of New York city directories at the New-York Historical Society; John B. Jegli's *Louisville Directory* (Louisville, 1848 and 1851); R. G. Dun ledgers, Baker Library, Harvard University, for example, Sidney Sea (Chicago, 1860–1871), Jas Barker (New Haven, 1870–1877), and Norman W. Rood (New Haven, 1878–1881); Daniel Levinson Wilk, "Cliff Dwellers: Modern Service in New York City, 1800–1945," Ph.D. diss., Duke University, 2005, 65; *Hotel Red Book* (Chicago, 1887): see New York City; Chicago; St. Louis; Omaha; Charleston, South Carolina; and Columbus, Ohio. On the general rate of business failure, see Stuart M. Blumin, *The Emergence of the Middle Class: Social Experience in the American City, 1760–1900* (Cambridge, 1989), 115.

10. J. Richard Beste, *The Wabash; or, Adventures of an English Gentleman's Family in the Interior of America* (London, 1855), 1: 73–74, 164, 173; Isabella Lucy Bird, *The Englishwoman in America* (London, 1856), 94; Archibald W. Finlayson, *A Trip to America* (Glasgow, 1879), 31; Alfred Falk, *Trans-Pacific Sketches* (Melbourne, 1877), 20–21; Historical Records Survey Project, WPA, *Historic Sites of Cleveland,* 13.

11. Evans, "Knickerbocker Hotels and Restaurants," 377; Fold-out maps in *Historic Sites of Cleveland;* Nichols, *Forty Years,* 1: 183–184.

12. Max O'Rell, *A Frenchman in America* (New York, 1891), 25–26; Chambers, *Things as They Are,* 181; Henry A. Murray, *Lands of the Slave and the Free* (London, 1857), 11; Frank W. Green, *Notes on New York, San Francisco, and Old Mexico* (Wakefield, England, 1886), 26–27; Thomas Hamilton, *Men and Manners in America* (Edinburgh, 1834), 2: 11; William Hancock, *An Emigrant's Five Years in the Free States of America* (London, 1860), 142.

13. Williamson, *American Hotel*, 64–66; Paul Groth, *Living Downtown: The History of Residential Hotels in the United States* (Berkeley, 1994), 183. See also Henry Latham, *Black and White: A Journal of a Three Months' Tour in the United States* (London, 1867), 10–11.

14. Bird, *Englishwoman in America*, 102–103; Emily Faithfull, *Three Visits to America* (Edinburgh, 1884), 206–208; Esor, *Eighty-Eight Days in America* (London, 1884), 85; Grantley F. Berkeley, *The English Sportsman in the Western Prairies* (London, 1861), 366; Hancock, *Emigrant's Five Years*, 143; O'Rell, *Frenchman in America*, 25; Chambers, *Things as They Are*, 180–181; Molly W. Berger, "The Modern Hotel in America, 1829–1929," Ph.D. diss., Case Western Reserve University, 1997, 67.

15. Faithfull, *Three Visits*, 206–208. For the transition to tipping, see, for example, William N. Blane, *An Excursion Through the United States and Canada* (London, 1824), 17–18; James Boardman, *America, and the Americans* (London, 1833), 121; James Stuart, *Three Years in North America* (Edinburgh, 1833), 1: 120–121; Beste, *The Wabash*, 1: 174; John Chester Grenville, *Transatlantic Sketches in the West Indies, South America, Canada, and the United States* (London, 1869), 352–353; Green, *Notes*, 32–33; Henry Pearson Grattan, *As a Chinaman Saw Us* (New York, 1904), 58–60.

16. Frederick Law Olmsted, *A Journey in the Seaboard Slave States* (New York, 1856), 1–2; O'Rell, *Frenchman in America*, 27.

17. Sala quoted in Groth, *Living Downtown*, 40. A cheval glass is a mirror in a tilting frame; a pier glass is a high, wall-mounted mirror.

18. Plans of Exchange Coffee House, Principal Story and Fourth Gallery; Plans of Tremont House, part II, neg. 1618, both at Bostonian Society Library and Special Collections; the Cosmopolitan Hotel's rooms remain in their nineteenth-century configuration; *American Architect and Building News* 1, no. 290 (18 November 1876), 2, no. 174 (2 June 1877), 2, no. 188 (16 June 1877), 3, no. 29 (25 January 1879); Groth, *Living Downtown*, 71, 77, 79, 98, 101, 145; Elizabeth Collins Cromley, *Alone Together: A History of New York's Early Apartments* (Ithaca, 1990), 197. See also plans in the Warshaw Collection, National Museum of American History, Hotels, box 11, folder 40, box 14, folder 47.

19. Grenville, *Transatlantic Sketches*, 352; Stuart, *Three Years*, 2: 2–3, 215; Matilda Charlotte Houston, *Hesperos; or, Travels in the West* (London, 1850), 1: 266; O'Rell, *Frenchman in America*, 27–28; Bird, *Englishwoman in America*, 148.

20. Berger, "Modern Hotel," 66, 99, 101–103; Bird, *Englishwoman in America*, 98, 101; Thomas Fitzpatrick, *A Transatlantic Holiday* (London, 1891), 23; Chambers, *Things as They Are*, 182, 185; Murray, *Lands of the Slave and Free*, 13.

21. Williamson, *American Hotel*, 24, 33, 55–62; Berger, "Modern Hotel," 65–66, 99–100; J. F. Campbell, *A Short American Tramp in the Fall of 1864* (Edinburgh, 1865), 305; Berkeley, *English Sportsman*, 366–367. See also Catherine Cocks, *Doing the Town: The Rise of Urban Tourism in the United States, 1850–1915* (Berkeley, 2001), 76.

22. Groth, *Living Downtown*, 59–61, 78. The only partial exception to this tendency was in residential hotels, on which more in Chapter 9.

23. Karen Halttunen, *Confidence Men and Painted Women: A Study of Middle-Class Culture in America, 1830–1870* (New Haven, 1982); John F. Kasson, *Rudeness and Civility: Manners in Nineteenth-Century Urban America* (Chapel Hill, 1990).

24. Charles Richard Weld, *A Vacation Tour in the United States and Canada* (London, 1855), 32; John Benwell, *An Englishman's Travels in America* (London, 1857), 122; Chambers, *Things as They Are*, 180–181, 186–187; Hancock, *Emigrant's Five Years*, 144; Horton Rhys, *A Theatrical Trip for a Wager!* (London, 1861), 29; J.P., *A Chat About America* (Manchester, 1885), 16; Bird, *Englishwoman in America*, 99–101; Carolyn R. Brucken, "Consuming Luxury: Luxury Hotels in Antebellum America, 1825–1860," Ph.D. diss., George Washington University, 1997, 107, 144.

25. Anthony Trollope, *North America* (New York, 1863), 2: 287; Murray, *Lands of the Slave and the Free,* 11.

26. Platte Valley House Register, Nebraska Historical Society; Theodore Dreiser, *Sister Carrie* (1900; ed. Donald Pizer, New York, 1991), 252.

27. Bird, *Englishwoman in America,* 100; James Horatio Booty, *Three Months in Canada and the United States* (London, 1862), 88; O'Rell, *Frenchman in America,* 25; J.P., *Chat,* 16; Brucken, "Consuming Luxury," 202–203. This division of space paralleled that on most forms of transportation in the United States. See Barbara Young Welke, *Recasting American Liberty: Gender, Race, Law, and the Railroad Revolution, 1865–1920* (New York, 2001), 253–255, 326–329, the source for my conceptualization of the gendered space of the hotel.

28. Bird, *Englishwoman in America,* 100; E. T. Coke, *A Subaltern's Furlough* (New York, 1833), 1: 33–34; Weld, *Vacation Tour,* 379–380; J.P., *Chat,* 19–20; Latham, *Black and White,* 79–80.

29. Bird, *Englishwoman in America,* 100–101, 149–151; Finlayson, *Trip to America,* 17; Latham, *Black and White,* 16–17; J. S. Buckingham, *America, Historical, Statistic, and Descriptive* (New York, 1841), 1: 348–350; Booty, *Three Months,* 90; Grenville, *Transatlantic Sketches,* 352–353; O'Rell, *Frenchman in America,* 25–34; Chambers, *Things as They Are,* 185, 189; Green, *Notes,* 30–33; J. H. Grandpierre, *A Parisian Pastor's Glance at America* (Boston, 1854), 98. I am in general agreement with Paul Groth here.

30. Daniel Boorstin, *The Americans: The National Experience* (New York, 1965), 147; Murray, *Lands of the Slave and Free,* 13; Beste, *The Wabash,* 1: 91–92; Chambers, *Things as They Are,* 185; Coke, *Subaltern's Furlough,* 1: 31–33; Hancock, *Emigrant's Five Years,* 141; O'Rell, *Frenchman in America,* 25–26; M. H. Dunlop, *Sixty Miles from Contentment: Traveling the Nineteenth-Century American Interior* (New York, 1995), chapter 6.

31. Nichols, *Forty Years,* 12; Coke, *Subaltern's Furlough,* 1: 34; Houston, *Hesperos,* 1: 75.

32. Tunis G. Campbell, *Hotel Keepers, Head Waiters, and Housekeepers' Guide* (Boston, 1848), 23–26, 34–35.

33. Williamson, *American Hotel,* 197–198; Grandpierre, *Parisian Pastor's Glance,* 98; Chambers, *Things as They Are,* 189.

34. Weld, *Vacation Tour,* 31; Chambers, *Things as They Are,* 183; J. J. Aubertin, *A Fight with Distances* (London, 1888), 234; Beste, *The Wabash,* 1: 182–183; O'Rell, *Frenchman in America,* 35; Houston, *Hesperos,* 1: 75–76; John Finch, *Travels in the United States of America and Canada* (London, 1833), 13; Coke, *Subaltern's Furlough,* 1: 32–33; Murray, *Lands of the Slave and Free,* 13; Green, *Notes,* 31–32. See also Dunlop, *Sixty Miles from Contentment,* 135–137; sea turtles: William Faux, *Faux's Memorable Days in America* (London, 1823), 66; *Oxford Mirror* (Oxford Junction, Iowa), 2 July 1891; *Marion Daily Start* (Marion, Ohio), 19 January 1886.

35. J.C. and Jun, *The United States and Canada* (London, 1862), 122; Houston, *Hesperos,* 1: 76–77; Brucken, "Consuming Luxury," 203. See also Booty, *Three Months,* 88; Trollope, *North America,* 2: 288; Weld, *Vacation Tour,* 33; Chambers, *Things as They Are,* 179–182; Dunlop, *Sixty Miles from Contentment,* chapter 7.

36. Hugh Seymour Tremenheere, *Notes on Public Subjects Made During a Tour in the United States and in Canada* (London, 1852), 126–127; Beste, *The Wabash,* 1: 88; Chambers, *Things as They Are,* 184; Murray, *Lands of the Slave and the Free,* 11; Finlayson, *Trip to America,* 16–17; Booty, *Three Months,* 88, 90; Frederick Marryat, *Second Series of a Diary in America* (Philadelphia, 1840), 33; Brucken, "Consuming Luxury," 144.

37. Boorstin, *The Americans: The National Experience,* 146; Price Collier, *America and the Americans from a French Point of View* (New York, 1897), 177–178; Beste, *The Wabash,* 1: 88; Francis J. Grund, *The Americans in Their Moral, Social, and Political Relations* (London, 1837), 2: 234; Domingo

Faustino Sarmiento, *Viajes por Europa, África i América, 1845–1847,* trans. Michael Aaron Rockland (Princeton, 1970), 148–149.

38. Berger, "Modern Hotel," 65, 100, 102; Arwen P. Mohun, *Steam Laundries: Gender, Technology, and Work in the United States and Great Britain* (Baltimore, 1999); Faithfull, *Three Visits,* 208–209; William Hepworth Dixon, *White Conquest* (London, 1876), 2: 236–237; Bird, *Englishwoman in America,* 102–103.

39. J.P., *Chat,* 18, 22; Bird, *Englishwoman in America,* 102–103; Finlayson, *Trip to America,* 19; Latham, *Black and White,* 16–17; Serjeant Ballantine, *The Old World and the New* (London, 1884), 172.

40. Hamilton, *Men and Manners,* 1: 19; Arthur Giles, *Across Western Waves and Home in a Royal Capital* (London, 1898), 85–86; J.P., *Chat,* 19.

41. Murray, *Lands of the Slave and the Free,* 105; Stuart, *Three Years,* 1: 125; Chambers, *Things as They Are,* 186–187; Green, *Notes,* 27.

42. Chambers, *Things as They Are,* 186; J.P., *Chat,* 19; Green, *Notes,* 27.

43. Levinson Wilk, "Cliff Dwellers," 100–101; *Frank Leslie's Popular Monthly,* June 1877, 721–727, quoted ibid.

44. See job announcements in any issue of *Hotel Monthly* or *Hotel World;* Anonymous, *Abuses; or, About Hotels* (Chicago, 1879), 4–5, 9–10; Anonymous, *Horrors of Hotel Life. By a Reformed Landlord* (Washington, D.C., 1884), 8–9, 16; on wages, see Stephan Thernstrom, *Poverty and Progress: Social Mobility in a Nineteenth-Century City* (Cambridge, Mass., 1964), 94. See also Nichols, *Forty Years,* 2: 72; Dixon, *White Conquest,* 2: 236–237; Faithfull, *Three Visits,* 278.

45. Levinson Wilk, "Cliff Dwellers," 87–88, 95–104, 454. See also Cocks, *Doing the Town,* 89–94.

46. Henry Hooper, *The Lost Model* (Philadelphia, 1874), 381; Williamson, *American Hotel,* 173–175; Mark Twain, *Roughing It* (Hartford, 1872), 268; *Harper's Weekly,* 18 April 1857, 242.

47. *Harper's New Monthly Magazine* 71, no. 426 (November 1885), 969; William Dean Howells, *Their Wedding Journey* (Boston, 1872), 98. See also L. A. Abbott, *Seven Wives and Seven Prisons; or, Experiences in the Life of a Matrimonial Monomaniac* (New York, 1870), 14–17, 203; Mary Clemmer, *His Two Wives* (Cambridge, Mass., 1875), 317; Lillie Devereux, *Fettered for Life; or, Lord and Master* (New York, 1874), 35.

48. Eliza Leslie, *The Behavior Book: A Guide for Ladies by Miss Leslie* (Philadelphia, 1855), 106; Anonymous, *Horrors of Hotel Life,* 5 and generally.

49. *Harper's Weekly,* 18 April 1857, 242.

50. For a longer version of this argument with additional evidence, see A. K. Sandoval-Strausz and Daniel Levinson Wilk, "Princes and Maids of the City Hotel: The Cultural Politics of Commercial Hospitality in America," *Journal of Decorative and Propaganda Arts* 25 (2005), 160–185.

51. Comparisons made using the relative value calculator for the unskilled wage at Economic History Resources, online at http://www.measuringworth.com/calculators/compare/. The two-dollar and four-dollar figures represent prices at hotels just below the most expensive in each period. For sources on prices, see notes to Chapter 2 and the first *Hotel Red Book* (New York, 1886).

52. Beste, *The Wabash,* 1: 177; Hancock, *Emigrant's Five Years,* 140–141.

53. Hiram Fuller, *Grand Transformation Scenes in the United States* (New York, 1875), 28; Green, *Notes,* 26. See also Nicholas Augustus Woods, *The Prince of Wales in Canada and the United States* (London, 1861), 385; J.C. and Jun., *United States and Canada,* 17; O'Rell, *Frenchman in America,* 36; Rush C. Hawkins and W. J. Fanning, "The American Hotel of Today," *North American Review* 157 (1893), 197.

6. The Law of Hospitality

1. Peter Clark, *The English Alehouse: A Social History, 1200–1650* (London, 1943); Gallus Thomann, *Colonial Liquor Laws* (New York, 1887); William J. Novak, *The People's Welfare: Law and Regulation in Nineteenth-Century America* (Chapel Hill, 1996), 87, 92, 156–160, 172–189. A similar licensing regime was applied to victuallers. See Henry Davenport, *The Publican's Lawyer* (London, 1797).

2. Thomann, *Colonial Liquor Laws*, 76, 140; *Laws of New York* (New York, 1800), Twenty-second Session, 424.

3. On the common law, see Oliver Wendell Holmes, Jr., *The Common Law* (Boston, 1881), part 3; Morton J. Horwitz, "The Conservative Tradition in the Writing of American Legal History," *American Journal of Legal History* 17 (1973), 275, and *The Transformation of American Law, 1780–1860* (Cambridge, Mass., 1977), 1–30. On specific common-law regimes, see Horwitz, *Transformation*, chapter 6; *Pierson v. Post*, 3 Cai. R. 175, 2 Am. Dec. 264 (NY, 1805); *The Century Edition of the American Digest* (St. Paul, 1900), 8: 1681–1752, 16: 1367–1877; Lea S. VanderVelde, "The Legal Ways of Seduction," 48 *Stanford Law Review* 817 (1996); R. H. Helmholz, "Bastardy Litigation in Medieval England," *American Journal of Legal History* 13 (1969).

4. *General Laws of Massachusetts to 1822* (Boston, 1823), 299. Some states referred to the duties of the innkeeper and provided public penalties for their contravention without naming them specifically, as in *The Public Statute Laws of the State of Connecticut* (Hartford, 1808), 642; *Public Acts of the General Assembly of North Carolina* (Newbern, 1804), 122; *Marbury and Crawford's Digest of Laws of Georgia* (Philadelphia, 1800), 445.

5. Joseph Story, *Commentaries on the Law of Bailments* (Boston, 1834), ch. vi, art. vii, §§470–477. For additional details, see A. K. Sandoval-Strausz, "Travelers, Strangers, and Jim Crow: Law, Public Accommodations, and Civil Rights in America," *Law and History Review* 23 (2005), 64n16.

6. *The Laws of Vermont to 1824* (Windsor, 1825), 483; *Delaware Statutes* (Wilmington, 1824), 253; Massachusetts act of 1793, vol. 2, digest 1184, prosecuted in *Commonwealth v. Shortridge* (1830), 6 Marsh. 638; Novak, *People's Welfare*, 92; North Carolina act of 1798, ch. 501, prosecuted in *State v. Wynne* (1821), 8 N.C. 451.

7. *Laws of the State of New-Hampshire* (Exeter, 1815), 346; *Laws of the State of Maine* (Portland, 1834), 75. See also *General Laws of Massachusetts to 1822*, 407; *Laws of Georgia*, 481.

8. James Kent, *Commentaries on American Law* (New York, 1827), 2: 592–597, with some phrases apparently taken from the leading English treatise by William Jones; Story, *Bailments*, ch. vi, art. vii, §464. Note that this aspect of innkeeper law also provided hosts with a measure of protection: they had a lien on the baggage of any guest who tried to leave without paying.

9. Novak, *People's Welfare*.

10. *General Laws of Massachusetts to 1822*, 298; *The Public Statute Laws of the State of Connecticut*, 640; see also *General Laws of Pennsylvania, 1700–1849* (Philadelphia, 1849), 598, and *New York Laws, 1785–1888*, 710; Kent, *Commentaries*, 2: 460.

11. *General Laws of Pennsylvania, 1700–1849*, 600; Novak, *People's Welfare*, 161–162. See also *The Laws of Maryland* (Baltimore, 1811), 396.

12. Steve Reece, *The Stranger's Welcome: Oral Theory and the Aesthetics of the Homeric Hospitality Scene* (Ann Arbor, 1993); Harry Levy, "The Odyssean Suitors and the Host-Guest Relationship," *Transactions and Proceedings of the American Philological Association* 94 (1963), 145–153.

13. Julian L. Greifer, "Attitudes to the Stranger: A Study of the Attitudes of Primitive Society and Early Hebrew Culture," *American Sociological Review* 10 (1945), 741–745. Note also the *lamed vavnik*, a persistent figure in Jewish folklore of whom thirty-six wander the earth as strangers in need. Thanks to Thane Rosenbaum for this item.

14. Luke 2:7 and 10:33–35, Romans 12:13, 1 Timothy 3:2, Titus 1:8, 1 Peter 4:9.

15. David S. Bogen, "Ignoring History: The Liability of Ships' Masters, Innkeepers, and Stablekeepers Under Roman Law," *American Journal of Legal History* 36 (1992), 326–360, and "The Innkeeper's Tale: The Legal Development of a Public Calling," *Utah Law Review* 51 (1996), 51–92; Bernhard Bischoff and Michael Lapidge, eds., *Biblical Commentaries from the Canterbury School of Theodore and Hadrian* (Cambridge, 1994), 415; Story, *Bailments,* ch. vi, art. vii, §467; Nicolas Delamare, *Traité de la Police* (Paris, 1722), cited in Thomas E. Brennan, *Public Drinking and Popular Culture in Eighteenth-Century Paris* (Princeton, 1988), 277; William Blackstone, *Commentaries on the Laws of England* (Oxford, 1765–1769), 1: 13.402, 1: 417–418, 2: 30.451, 3: 9.164, 4: 13.168.

16. Horwitz, *Transformation;* Novak, *People's Welfare.*

17. *Calye's Case,* 8 Coke 32. In the strictest legal sense, the case dealt with the loss of goods by a guest at an inn rather than the right of entry; but later rulings in both English and American courts cite this dictum on travelers in support of all manner of claims against innkeepers.

18. *Fell v. Knight* (1841), 8 M. and W. (Exchequer Reports) 269; *Hawthorn v. Hammond* (1844), 1 C. and K. (Oxford Spring Circuit) 404.

19. *Rex v. Ivens* (1835), 7 C. and P. (Oxford Circuit) 220–221.

20. *Hawthorn v. Hammond,* 407–408.

21. *The Queen v. Rymer* (1877), 2 Q.B.D. (Queen's Bench Division) 138, 140.

22. *Lamond v. Richard and the Gordon Hotels, Limited* (1897), 1 Q.B. (Queen's Bench) 543–544, 548.

23. This trend was also evidenced in *Holder v. Soulby* (1860), 8 C.B. 254; *Allen v. Smith* (1862), 12 C.B. 638 was a contradictory outlier.

24. *Markham v. Brown* (1837), 8 N.H. 526, 529.

25. *Commonwealth v. Mitchel* (1850), 1 Phila. (Pa.), 433–437. Emphasis in original. See also *State v. Steele* (1890), 106 N.C. 766.

26. *State v. Whitby* (1854), 51 Har. (Del.) 495.

27. *Atwater v. Sawyer* (1884), 76 Me. 538. See also *Wintermute v. Clarke* (1851), 5 Sandf. (N.Y.) 246.

28. See, for example, *Adams v. Freeman* (1816), 12 Johnson (N.Y.) 408, an apparent outlier on the restriction of privileges to travelers; *Mason v. Thompson* (1830), 9 Pick. (Mass.) 280–284; *Markham v. Brown,* 527; *State v. Whitby,* 496; *Walling v. Potter* (1868), 35 Conn. 185; *Atwater v. Sawyer,* 538–539.

29. Doris Elizabeth King, "The First-Class Hotel and the Age of the Common Man," *Journal of Southern History* 23 (1957), 173–188; Karl B. Raitz and John Paul Jones III, "The City Hotel as Landscape Artifact and Community Symbol," *Journal of Cultural Geography* 9 (1988), 23–28; Daniel Boorstin, *The Americans: The National Experience* (New York, 1965), 135–141.

30. Horwitz, *Transformation;* Novak, *People's Welfare.*

31. On Jacksonian Democracy, see Arthur M. Schlesinger, Jr., *The Age of Jackson* (Boston, 1945); Lee Benson, *The Concept of Jacksonian Democracy: New York as a Test Case* (Princeton, 1961); John Ashworth, *"Agrarians" and "Aristocrats": Party Political Ideology in the United States, 1837–1846* (London, 1983); Harry L. Watson, *Liberty and Power: The Politics of Jacksonian America* (New York, 1990). See also King, "First-Class Hotel."

32. Oscar Handlin and Mary Flug Handlin, *Commonwealth, a Study of the Role of Government in the American Economy: Massachusetts, 1774–1861* (New York, 1947); Novak, *People's Welfare.*

33. On the quality of tavern fare, see Chapter 1. Suits involving the second duty of innkeepers typically involved access to a hotel restaurant or bar. Specific pleadings on the responsibility to provide refreshment were in pursuit of this right rather than of food or drink itself. See, for example, *Atwater v. Sawyer* or *The Queen v. Rymer.* On the importance of income from refreshment, see Donna-Belle Garvin and James L. Garvin, *On the Road North of Boston: New Hampshire Taverns and Turnpikes, 1700–1900* (Lebanon, N.H., 1988), 170.

34. *State v. Wynne,* 455; *Commonwealth v. Shortridge,* 638, 641.

35. *Century Digest, Cases to 1896,* vol. 2, under "Innkeepers" (New York, 1911).

36. *Berkshire Woollen Co. v. Proctor* (1851), 7 Cush. (Mass.) 419; *Pinkerton v. Woodward* (1867), 33 Cal. 561–562; *Hall v. Pike* (1868), 100 Mass. 496; *Shoecraft v. Bailey* (1868), 25 Iowa 553; *Jailey v. Cardinal* (1874), 35 Wisc. 118. See also contrary holding in *Horner v. Harvey* (1885), 3 N.M. 197.

37. *Carter v. Hobbs* (1863), 6 Nor. (Mich.) 52; *Pinkerton v. Woodward* (1867), 33 Cal. 557. See also *Carpenter v. Taylor* (1856), 1 Hilt. (N.Y.) 193; *Commonwealth v. Weatherbee* (1869), 101 Mass. 214.

38. *Berkshire Woollen Co. v. Proctor* (1851), 7 Cush. (Mass.) 417; *McDaniels v. Robinson* (1854), 26 Vt. 316; *Pinkerton v. Woodward* (1867), 33 Cal. 557.

39. *Pinkerton v. Woodward* (1867), 33 Cal. 574.

40. In addition to the cases noted above, see the following. On guests versus boarders: a dozen cases are cited in *Century Edition of the American Digest* (St. Paul, 1901), 27: 2407–2408; *Hall v. Pike* (1868), 100 Mass. 495. Parts of a hotel: *Epps v. Hinds* (1854), 41 Ala. 657–658; *Krohn v. Sweeny* (1867), 2 Daly (N.Y.) 200. Servants' standing: *Berkshire Woollen Co. v. Proctor* (1851), 7 Cush. (Mass.) 420; *Coykendall v. Eaton* (1869), 55 Barb. (N.Y.) 188; *Kellogg v. Sweeney* (1870), 1 Lans. (N.Y.) 397–398. Drunkenness: *Rubenstein v. Cruikshanks* (1884), 54 Mich. 199, but see also *Walsh v. Porterfield* (1878), 87 Pa. 376. Porters: *Century Edition of the American Digest,* 27: 2414–2416, 2424, 2426. Other excuses: *Norcross v. Norcross* (1865), 53 Me. 163; *Lanier v. Youngblood* (1883), 73 Ala. 587; but see also *Fitch v. Casler* (1879), 17 Hun. (N.Y.) 126.

41. *Century Edition of the American Digest,* 27: 2421–2422; *Noble v. Milliken* (1885), 77 Me. 359.

42. *Century Edition of the American Digest,* 27: 2430–2434; *Stanton v. Leland* (1855), 4 E. D. Smith (N.Y.) 88; *Johnson v. Richardson* (1855), 7 Peck (Ill.) 302; *Pinkerton v. Woodward.*

43. *Century Edition of the American Digest,* 27: 2412–2414, 2435–2436, 2440.

44. *Century Edition of the American Digest,* 27: 2423–2424, 2427–2430; *Fowler v. Dorlon* (1856), 24 Barb. (N.Y.) 384; *Packard v. Northcraft's Administrator* (1859), 2 Metc. (Ky.) 439; *Hulett v. Swift* (1865), 33 N.Y. 571; *Baker v. Dessauer* (1874), 49 Ind. 28; *Jalie v. Cardinal* (1874), 35 Wis. 118; *Coskery v. Nagle* (1889), 83 Ga. 696.

45. *Gastenhofer v. Clair* (1881), 10 Daly (N.Y.) 265; *Fitch v. Casler* (1881), 17 Hun. (N.Y.) 126; *Carter v. Hobbs* (1863), 12 Mich. 52. See also *Arcade Hotel Co. v. Wiatt* (1886), 44 Ohio St. 32.

46. *Quinton v. Courtney* (1794), 36 N.C. 1; *Towson v. Havre de Grace Bank* (1823), 6 Harris and Johnson (Md.) 47 (the plaintiff in the case was a traveler, making it difficult to say whether this status was the point upon which the case turned); *Mason v. Thompson,* 284. This broadening trend was also extant in English common law, and so did not represent the same kind of clear departure as with the right of entry to an inn. *McDonald v. Edgerton* (1849), 5 Barb. (N.Y.) 560; *Read v. Amidon* (1868), 41 Vt. 15. See also *Washburn v. Jones* (1851), 14 Barb. (N.Y.) 193; *Korn v. Schedler* (1882), 11 Daly (N.Y.) 234; *Russell v. Fagan* (1886), 7 Houst. (Del.) 389. The nation's courts were not unanimous on this point: see *Healey v. Gray* (1878), 68 Me. 489; *Toub v. Schmidt* (1891), 60 Hun. (N.Y.) 409. See also *Carter v. Hobbs.*

7. Unruly Guests and Anxious Hosts

1. In addition to the cases cited in this chapter, a sense of the frequency of articles of this kind can be gleaned from searches in the American Periodicals Series; between 1845 and 1906, for example, the *National Police Gazette* alone published dozens of accounts of hotel sex.

2. *New York Times,* 1 July 1858. For further details on the case, see ibid., 31 October 1857, 3 November 1857, 4 November 1857, 5 November 1857, 6 November 1857, 9 November 1857, 11 November 1857, 14 November 1857, 18 November 1857, 20 November 1857, 4 August 1858.

3. Ibid., 1 July 1858.

4. Ibid.

5. *Washington Post,* 11 May 1888; *New York Times,* 12 September 1899. See also *Reno Evening Gazette,* 2 October 1879; *Marshfield Times* (Wis.), 11 May 1894; *The Republican* (Hamilton, Ohio), 31 August 1894.

6. Lea S. VanderVelde, "The Legal Ways of Seduction," 48 *Stanford Law Review* 817 (1996); Pamela Haag, *Consent: Sexual Rights and the Transformation of American Liberalism* (Ithaca, 1999).

7. Timothy B. Spears, *100 Years on the Road: The Traveling Salesman in American Culture* (New Haven, 1995), 136–138; Davenport, Iowa, *Democrat,* 8 June 1884. Thanks to Sharon Wood for the citation.

8. *New York Times,* 13 April 1869; *Cleveland Leader,* 17 and 18 February 1871; *Washington Post,* 23 March 1896. The citations to Cleveland newspapers in this chapter come from Ohio Historical Records Survey Project, Work Projects Administration, *Historic Sites of Cleveland: Hotels and Taverns* (Columbus, 1942). See also *New York Daily Times,* 18 January 1855; *Davenport Daily Gazette,* 16 January 1880; *Fort Wayne Weekly Gazette,* 12 August 1897.

9. Sharon E. Wood, *The Freedom of the Streets: Work, Citizenship, and Sexuality in a Gilded Age City* (Chapel Hill, 2005), chapter 8.

10. Timothy J. Gilfoyle, *City of Eros: New York City, Prostitution, and the Commercialization of Sex, 1790–1920* (New York, 1992), 18, 47, 89, 122. See also Paul Groth, *Living Downtown: The History of Residential Hotels in the United States* (Berkeley, 1994), 120–121, 217–218.

11. Wood, *Freedom of the Streets,* 172–178.

12. Allan Pinkerton, *Thirty Years a Detective* (New York, 1884), 82–84; Frank Morn, "Allan Pinkerton," in *American National Biography,* ed. John A. Garraty and Mark C. Carnes (New York, 1999), 17: 544–546; Frank Morn, *The Eye That Never Sleeps: A History of the Pinkerton National Detective Agency* (Bloomington, Ind., 1982), x. Pinkerton was also widely reviled by working-class Americans for his agency's tireless and frequently brutal suppression of labor organizers, a role reflected in the workers' folk tune "My Father Was Killed by a Pinkerton Man."

13. *Washington Post,* 16 March 1896; *New York Times,* 2 February 1854. See also *Daily Northwestern* (Oshkosh, Wis.), 21 March 1899; *Daily Nebraska State Journal* (Lincoln), 3 November 1886; *Galveston Daily News,* 28 April 1868; *Saint Joseph Herald* (Mich.), 30 January 1886; *Galveston Daily News,* 5 January 1885; *Fort Wayne Morning Journal,* 16 July 1897; *Indiana Weekly Messenger* (Pa.), 24 February 1886; *Evening Gazette* (Cedar Rapids, Iowa), 21 November 1893; *Janesville Gazette* (Wis.), 4 October 1878.

14. The great exception to this rule was, of course, that in most places in nineteenth-century America, a poor white and especially any black person was automatically considered suspicious. *New York Times,* 29 January 1871.

15. Ibid., 11 June 1852, 18 July 1858.

16. Ibid., 2 October 1851, 16 June 1857, 21 September 1869.

17. Ibid., 22 September 1852; *Washington Post,* 16 December 1885.

18. *Washington Post,* 22 April 1881; *Pinkerton v. Woodward* (1867), 33 Cal. 557.

19. *Washington Post,* 16 March 1896.

20. *New York Times,* 15 April 1864, 13 October 1865, 10 February 1872, 7 December 1862, 2 February 1854; *Cleveland Plain Dealer,* 27 January 1865; *Cleveland Leader,* 23 November 1865. For a rare possible case of hotel pickpocketing, see *Cleveland Leader,* 8 December 1866.

21. *New York Times,* 20 December 1862; *Cleveland Leader,* 2 April 1857.

22. *Cleveland Leader,* 21 April 1856, 17 June 1874; *New York Times,* 7 December 1862, 23 July 1865, 11 October 1852, 16 December 1876, 22 August 1857.

23. *Cleveland Leader,* 29 January 1864, 17 March 1854; *New York Times,* 7 December 1862, 6 June 1859; *Cleveland Plain Dealer,* 21 March 1866. See also *Cleveland Leader,* 3 December 1873; *Daily Nevada*

State Journal (Reno), 21 November 1895. On deadbeat-guest statutes, see *Century Edition of the American Digest* (St. Paul, 1901), 27: 2447.

24. On nineteenth-century urban law enforcement, see Eric H. Monkkonen, *The Dangerous Class: Crime and Poverty in Columbus, Ohio, 1865–1880* (Cambridge, Mass., 1975), and *Police in Urban America, 1860–1920* (Cambridge, Mass., 1981).

25. *Cleveland Leader,* 20 July 1875, 1 August 1866, 11 and 12 November 1861; *New York Times,* 3 December 1853, 16 June 1858, 11 December 1869, 27 and 29 May 1858; *Cleveland Daily True Democrat,* 21 November 1849; *Cleveland Plain-Dealer,* 5 February 1863.

26. *Washington Post,* 10 September 1896; *New York Times,* 24 and 25 October 1860, 17 December 1876; *Cleveland Leader,* 22 November 1861, 5 May 1856.

27. *New York Times,* 25 February 1858.

28. Ibid., 15 March 1858, 20 August 1878; *Washington Post,* 16 February 1889; *Cleveland Leader,* 24 November 1868; *Indiana Progress* (Pa.), 21 September 1876.

29. *Cleveland Daily True Democrat,* 31 March 1852, 22 November 1855, 26 April 1858. For additional examples, see *New York Times,* 1 December 1853, 7 November 1854, 24 September 1869, 17 October 1886; *Burlington Hawk-Eye* (Iowa), 31 January 1850; *Bangor Daily Whig and Courier,* 29 April 1891.

30. *New York Times,* 28 November 1878, 22 March 1854. On the use of violence in defense of sexual purity, see Hendrik Hartog, "Lawyering, Husbands' Rights, and 'The Unwritten Law' in Nineteenth-Century America," *Journal of American History* 84 (1997), 67–96. On the Boston murder see the *National Police Gazette,* 4 April 1846.

31. *New York Times,* 13 April 1869; *Cleveland Leader,* 17 and 18 February 1871; *Washington Post,* 23 March 1896; Mark Twain and Charles Dudley Warner, *The Gilded Age: A Tale of Today* (1873), chapter 46. The most sensational hotel murders were reported in newspapers nationwide: see, for example, the New York murder reported in the *Galveston Daily News,* 17 August 1898; *Evening Democrat* (Warren, Pa.), 18 August 1898; *Naugatuck Daily News* (Conn.), 26 August 1898. The so-called Southern Hotel Trunk Murder was covered in the *New York Times,* 16 April 1885; *Marion Daily Star* (Ohio), 17 April 1885; *Daily Gazette* (Colorado Springs), 19 April 1885; *Galveston Daily News,* 7 May 1885; *Newark Daily Advocate* (Ohio), 8 May 1885; *Daily Gazette* (Fort Wayne), 11 May 1885; *Bismarck Daily Tribune,* 11 August 1885; *Daily Review* (Decatur, Iowa), 21 May 1886; *Mitchell Daily Republican* (S.D.), 6 June 1886.

32. This discussion of suicide is included in a section on crime only because it was categorized as such in nineteenth-century American law. *Niles' Weekly Register,* 3 August 1833, 15 October 1836; Jefferson Williamson, *The American Hotel: An Anecdotal History* (New York, 1930), 25; *New York Times* computer index searched for " 'suicide' and 'hotel' " for 1851–1900. See also *Oakland Daily Evening Tribune,* 4 February 1890; *Oakland Tribune,* 26 December 1895, 23 November 1897; *Evening Times* (Trenton, N.J.), 19 May 1896; *Middletown Daily Argus* (N.Y.), 20 May 1896, 1 September 1897; *Evening Herald* (Syracuse), 25 May 1897; *Dubuque Herald,* 28 August 1900.

33. *American Journal of Insanity* 1 (January 1845), 243–244, cited in Howard I. Kushner, *Self-Destruction in the Promised Land: A Psychocultural Biology of American Suicide* (New Brunswick, N.J., 1989), 35; Christopher J. Castañeda, *Invisible Fuel: Manufactured and Natural Gas in America, 1800–2000* (New York, 1999), 13–36; Theodore Dreiser, *Sister Carrie* (1900; ed. Donald Pizer, New York, 1991), 367.

34. Simeon Ford, *A Few Remarks* (New York, 1903), quoted in Williamson, *American Hotel,* 26; Palmer Cox, *Squibs of California; or, Every-Day Life Illustrated* (San Francisco, 1874), 457.

35. Anthony Trollope, *North America* (New York, 1863), 2: 287; William and Ellen Craft, *Running a Thousand Miles for Freedom* (London, 1860), 34.

36. Garland Mower, *Reminiscences of a Hotel Man of Forty Years* (New York, 1912), 56–59, 129–130; Pinkerton, *Thirty Years a Detective,* 82, 84, facing 96.

37. Jane Jacobs, *The Death and Life of Great American Cities* (New York, 1964); Michel Foucault, *Discipline and Punish: The Birth of the Prison,* trans. Alan Sheridan (New York, 1977).

38. Karen Halttunen, *Confidence Men and Painted Women: A Study of Middle-Class Culture in America, 1830–1870* (New Haven, 1982); John F. Kasson, *Rudeness and Civility: Manners in Nineteenth-Century Urban America* (Chapel Hill, 1990).

39. Eliza Leslie, *The Behavior Book: A Guide for Ladies by Miss Leslie* (Philadelphia, 1853), 101.

40. Leslie, *Behavior Book,* 101; S. A. Frost, *The Laws and By-Laws of American Society* (New York, 1869), 118.

41. Leslie, *Behavior Book,* 115.

42. Ibid., 130–131; M. Hoeffner, "Young Men's Polka, Dedicated to the Belle of the Anniversary Ball at the St. Louis Hotel the 8th of January 1850 by the Managers" (New Orleans, 1850); "Southern Hotel Polka," University of Arkansas Mary Dengler Hudgins Collection, rec. 83; Van der Weyde, "Prescott House Polka" (New York, 1853), Bella Landauer Collection, New-York Historical Society, Greenbox, Hotels and Restaurants, P (the Landauer Collection contains numerous other examples); *Oxford English Dictionary,* 2nd ed. (Oxford, 1989), 12: 7–8.

43. Cecil B. Hartley, *The Gentleman's Book of Etiquette and Manual of Politeness* (Boston, 1860), 176–178, 299; George Winfred Hervey, *Principles of Courtesy* (New York, 1852), xiii, 203. For a visual representation of a man guiding a woman to a hotel, see Kasson, *Rudeness and Civility,* 135.

44. Frost, *Laws and By-Laws,* 118–119.

45. Anonymous, *The Handbook of the Man of Fashion* (Philadelphia, 1845), 77–78.

8. American Forum

1. Alexis de Tocqueville, *Democracy in America* (1835; trans. George Lawrence, ed. J. P. Mayer, New York, 1966), 520. On civil society, see Jean L. Cohen and Andrew Arato, *Civil Society and Political Theory* (Cambridge, Mass., 1997); Craig Calhoun, ed., *Habermas and the Public Sphere* (Cambridge, Mass., 1997). My own thinking has been influenced in particular by Mary P. Ryan, *Civic Wars: Democracy and Public Life in the American City During the Nineteenth Century* (Berkeley, 1997); David M. Henkin, *City Reading: Written Words and Public Spaces in Antebellum New York* (New York, 1998). In this chapter I am deliberately using the term *civil society* in a nineteenth-century Tocquevillian sense that combines political, economic, and associative activity. Many modern theorists of civil society define it more narrowly, especially by separating it from economy and politics; this is done to give the concept of civil society a more critical edge for application to modern capitalist democracies. While there are good reasons to use this latter definition to analyze the present, the former lends itself more readily to historical inquiry of the kind undertaken in this book. See Cohen and Arato, *Civil Society and Political Theory,* Introduction, 253, 477–480.

2. On the importance of embodied citizenship, successive public spaces, and the continuities between them, see Richard Sennett, *Flesh and Stone: The Body and the City in Western Civilization* (New York, 1994). See also Sennett, *The Fall of Public Man* (New York, 1977).

3. Ohio Historical Records Survey Project, Work Projects Administration, *Historic Sites of Cleveland: Hotels and Taverns* (Columbus, 1942).

4. Ibid., 7, 9, 11, 13, 15, 24, 29, 33–38, 44–47, 56 (individual businesses); 13–14, 27, 32–33, 108–109, 622, 625 (specific meetings); 35, 69, 105, 111, 128–129, 160, 415, 714–715 (trade groups).

5. Ibid., 22, 31, 109–111, 116–118, 372, 537, 555, 623. See also 33, 156, 209, 281–282, 310, 365, 517, 523.

6. Ibid., 10–19, 22–27, 32–35.

7. Archives and indexes documenting everyday uses of hotels include the Quinn Hotel Collection of the New-York Historical Society, the New Haven Hotels Collection at the New Haven Historical

Society, and the online *New York Times* and *Washington Post.* Examples of municipal histories with hotel sections include J. Thomas Scharf, *History of Baltimore City and County* (Baltimore, 1881), chapter 32; Richard M. Bayles, *History of Providence County, Rhode Island* (New York, 1891), 303–312; Alfred Sorensen, *The Story of Omaha from the Pioneer Days to the Present Time* (Omaha, 1923), 224–239. Hotels figure in scholarly monographs including Mary P. Ryan, *Cradle of the Middle Class: The Family in Oneida County, New York, 1790–1865* (Cambridge, 1981); Timothy R. Mahoney, *River Towns in the Great West: The Structure of Provincial Urbanization in the American Midwest, 1820–1870* (Cambridge, 1990), and *Provincial Lives: Middle Class Experience in the Antebellum Middle West* (Cambridge, 1999); George Chauncey, *Gay New York: Gender, Urban Culture, and the Making of the Gay Male World, 1890–1940* (New York, 1994); and Anthony J. Lukas, *Big Trouble: A Murder in a Small Western Town Sets Off a Struggle for the Soul of America* (New York, 1997).

8. Michael P. Conzen, "The Maturing Urban System in the United States, 1840–1910," *Annals of the Association of American Geographers* 67 (1977), 88–108, and see also Conzen, "Capital Flows and the Developing Urban Hierarchy: State Bank Capital in Wisconsin, 1854–1895," *Economic Geography* 51 (1975), 321–338; William Cronon, *Nature's Metropolis: Chicago and the Great West* (New York, 1991), especially chapters 6, 7.

9. A. T. Andreas, *History of the State of Nebraska* (Chicago, 1882), Cass County, part III; *Nebraska Herald,* 18 August 1870, 4. The Platte Valley House register is held at the Nebraska State Historical Society. Register sample comprises 17–23 September, 22–28 October, 12–19 November, and 3–9 December 1870, and 7–13 January, 18–24 February, 4–10 March, and 15–18 April 1871.

10. Jefferson Williamson, *The American Hotel: An Anecdotal History* (New York, 1930), 283–284. The Exchange-Ballard registers from which the sample was taken are held at the Virginia Historical Society. Register sample comprises 7–13 March, 11–17 April, 9–15 May, 10–16 October, 7–13 November, and 5–11 December 1870 and 12–18 June, 10–16 July, and 7–13 August 1871.

11. Williamson, *American Hotel,* 51–53. The St. Nicholas Hotel register is held at the New-York Historical Society. Register sample comprises 26 April–2 May, 24–30 May, 21–27 June, and 12–18 July 1858. I attempted to find a register from closer to 1870 for a first-class hotel in a large city, but none could be located.

12. Alfred D. Chandler, *The Visible Hand: The Managerial Revolution in American Business* (Cambridge, Mass., 1977), 25–28; Timothy B. Spears, *100 Years on the Road: The Traveling Salesman in American Culture* (New Haven, 1995), 25–27, 32–33. See also T. J. Jackson Lears, *Fables of Abundance: A Cultural History of Advertising in America* (New York, 1995), part 1; Walter A. Friedman, *Birth of a Salesman: The Transformation of Selling in America* (Cambridge, 2004).

13. Ohio Historical Records Survey Project, WPA, *Historic Sites of Cleveland,* 160, 172, 182; 121, 169, 234; 171; 19, 33, 211.

14. Ibid., 19, 27, 127, 168, 173, 213.

15. Ibid., 43, 128, 156, 241. See also 29, 41, 44, 133, 160, 174–175, 231.

16. Ibid.: lecturers, 41, 159, 374; actors: 44, 391, 423; circuses: 34, 291, 341.

17. Ibid., 177–178, 371, 376, 397, 402, 413, 421; Library of Congress Prints and Photographs Division, Washington, D.C., Digital ID numbers pan 6a24958, pan 6a24977, pan 6a27022, pan 6a25200, pan 6a25002.

18. Katherine C. Grier, *Culture and Comfort: People, Parlors, and Upholstery, 1850–1930* (Rochester, N.Y., 1988), 19–21, 29–38; Carolyn R. Brucken, "Consuming Luxury: Luxury Hotels in Antebellum America, 1825–1860," Ph.D. diss., George Washington University, 1997, 146–158; Daniel Boorstin, *The Americans: The National Experience* (New York, 1965), 137–138; Dolores Hayden, *The Grand Domestic Revolution: A History of Feminist Designs for American Homes, Neighborhoods, and Cities* (Cambridge, Mass., 1981), 19, 73; Molly W. Berger, "The Modern Hotel in America, 1829–1929," Ph.D. diss., Case Western Reserve University, 1997.

19. Mahoney, *River Towns,* 256–262; Mahoney, *Provincial Lives,* 89–90, 133, 138–140, 147, 153; Daniel Kilbride, "The Cosmopolitan South: Privileged Southerners, Philadelphia, and the Fashionable Tour in the Antebellum Era," *Journal of Urban History* 26 (2000), 563–590; Sandra Dallas, *No More Than Five in a Bed: Colorado Hotels in the Old Days* (Norman, Okla., 1967), 36–40, 47, 55–87, 91–114. See also Richard A. Van Orman, *A Room for the Night: Hotels of the Old West* (New York, 1966).

20. Quoted in Gordon S. Wood, *The Creation of the American Republic, 1776–1782* (New York, 1969), 500–501, 527.

21. Ohio Historical Records Survey Project, WPA, *Historic Sites of Cleveland,* 9, 278, 280; further examples on 80, 164, 382, 495.

22. Ibid., 291, 375, 413; see also 25, 33, 49, 386.

23. Ibid., 9, 24, 164, 412. See also 22, 178, 331, 373, 375, 382, 401, 415, 495. For illustrations of hotel balcony speeches, see *Gleason's Pictorial Drawing Room Companion,* 7 June and 27 December 1851; *Illustrated News* (New York), 30 July 1853; *Frank Leslie's Illustrated Newspaper,* 10 May 1856, 19 October 1860, 2 March 1861. See also Arthur James Weise, *History of the City of Troy* (Troy, N.Y., 1876), 139–141, 227.

24. On political travels in nondemocratic societies, see Richard Wortman, *Scenarios of Power: Myth and Ceremony in Russian Monarchy* (Princeton, 2000); Daniel Unowsky, *The Pomp and Politics of Patriotism: Imperial Celebrations in Habsburg Austria, 1848–1916* (West Lafayette, Ind., 2005).

25. Boorstin, *The Americans: The National Experience,* 142; Louis Wiltz Kemp, "The Capitol at Columbia," *Southwestern Historical Quarterly* 48 (1945); Alexander W. Terrell, "The City of Austin from 1839 to 1865," *Southwestern Historical Quarterly* 14 (1911).

26. David M. Potter, *The Impending Crisis, 1848–1861* (New York, 1976), 208–211; "Memorial of the New England Emigrant Company, Paying Indemnification for the Destruction of Property at Lawrence, Kansas, May 21, 1856," mis. doc. no. 29, 37th Congress, 3rd Session.

27. William E. Gienapp, *Abraham Lincoln and Civil War America* (New York, 2002), 68–70.

28. *Frank Leslie's Illustrated Newspaper,* 16 and 23 February 1861. On troop reviews, see 26 June 1858, 27 September 1862, 30 January 1864.

29. Garnett Laidlaw Eskew, *Willard's of Washington: The Epic of a Capital Caravansary* (New York, 1954), 45–60, illustrations following 64; Nathaniel Hawthorne, "Chiefly About War Matters," *The Atlantic,* July 1862; *National Republican,* 1867, quoted in Eskew, *Willard's of Washington,* xii.

30. *Frank Leslie's Illustrated Newspaper,* 1 June 1861, cover and 40–41; John W. Robinson, *Los Angeles in Civil War Days* (Los Angeles, 1977), 58; Van Orman, *Room for the Night,* 29–30; James M. McPherson, *Battle Cry of Freedom* (New York, 1988), 786; *Frank Leslie's Illustrated Newspaper,* 12 December 1864, 200.

31. James R. Grossman, Ann Durkin Keating, and Janice L. Reiff, eds., *Encyclopedia of Chicago History* (Chicago, 2004), 759.

32. Tocqueville, *Democracy in America,* 517.

33. *Historic Sites of Cleveland,* 70, 378. See also Linda Gordon, *The Great Arizona Orphan Abduction* (Cambridge, 1999), 73, 109–113.

34. *New York Times,* 15 May 1890, 10 July 1892, 2 October 1883, 10 August 1886. On the Lake Mohonk Conference see Cathleen D. Cahill, "'Only the Home Can Found a State': Gender, Labor and the United States Indian Service, 1869–1928," Ph.D. diss., University of Chicago, 2004, 29–38. See also *New York Times,* 25 February 1896, 19 May 1888, 7 December 1870, 4 May 1892, 19 March 1898; *Wheeling Register,* 26 July 1882.

35. Williamson, *American Hotel,* 225–228.

36. Jürgen Habermas, *The Structural Transformation of the Public Sphere* (Darmstadt, 1962; trans. Thomas Burger and Frederick Lawrence, Cambridge, Mass., 1989). Some doubts about Haber-

mas's formulation are raised in Steve Pincus, "'Coffee Politicians Does Create': Coffeehouses and Restoration Political Culture," *Journal of Modern History* 67 (1995), 807–834.

37. Two works on public space and civil society that have strongly influenced my thinking are David W. Conroy, *In Public Houses: Drink and the Revolution of Authority in Colonial Massachusetts* (Chapel Hill, 1994), and David Waldstreicher, *In the Midst of Perpetual Fetes: The Making of American Nationalism, 1776–1820* (Chapel Hill, 1997). The idea of "island communities" comes from Robert Wiebe's influential synthesis *The Search for Order* (New York, 1966). The notion that small towns and cities in the United States were isolated into the late nineteenth and early twentieth centuries is difficult to sustain in light of the findings in this book.

38. This definition of reading is of the private sort emphasized by Habermas and is used in response to earlier scholarly work; but as David Henkin has rightfully pointed out in *City Reading,* people also interacted with texts in ways that were definitively public and popular. For an analysis that places the decline of civil society in the United States in the second half of the twentieth century, see Robert D. Putnam, *Bowling Alone: The Collapse and Revival of American Community* (New York, 2000).

39. The party at the Waldorf is recounted in Sven Beckert, *The Monied Metropolis: New York City and the Consolidation of the American Bourgeoisie, 1850–1896* (New York, 2001), 1.

9. Homes for a World of Strangers

1. This chapter draws heavily upon an existing debate among a number of scholars, most notably Dolores Hayden, Elizabeth Collins Cromley, and Paul Groth. See Hayden, *The Grand Domestic Revolution: A History of Feminist Designs for American Homes, Neighborhoods, and Cities* (Cambridge, Mass., 1981); Cromley, *Alone Together: A History of New York's Early Apartments* (Ithaca, 1990); and Groth, *Living Downtown: The History of Residential Hotels in the United States* (Berkeley, 1994).

2. Gwendolyn Wright, *Building the Dream: A Social History of Housing in America* (Cambridge, Mass., 1981), xv–xix; Kenneth T. Jackson, *Crabgrass Frontier: The Suburbanization of America* (New York, 1986), chapter 3; Robert Fishman, *Bourgeois Utopias: The Rise and Fall of Suburbia* (New York, 1987), chapter 2; Sharon Marcus, *Apartment Stories: City and Home in Nineteenth-Century Paris and London* (Berkeley, 1999), 17, 83–101.

3. Barbara Welter, "The Cult of True Womanhood: 1820–1860," *American Quarterly* 18 (1966), 151–174; Gerda Lerner, "The Lady and the Mill Girl: Changes in the Status of Women in the Age of Jackson," *Midcontinent American Studies Journal* 10 (1969), 5–15; Nancy F. Cott, *The Bonds of Womanhood: "Woman's Sphere" in New England, 1780–1835* (New Haven, 1977); Elizabeth Blackmar, *Manhattan for Rent, 1785–1850* (Ithaca, 1989), especially 10–13, 51–71, 109–126; Jeanne Boydston, *Home and Work: Housework, Wages, and the Ideology of Labor in the Early Republic* (New York, 1990).

4. Blackmar, *Manhattan for Rent,* chapter 4; Cromley, *Alone Together,* chapters 1, 2.

5. Blackmar, *Manhattan for Rent,* chapter 2.

6. Ibid., 60–63, 88, 134–135; Wendy Gamber, "Away from Home: Middle-Class Boarders in the Nineteenth-Century City," *Journal of Urban History* 31 (2005), 289–305, and *The Boardinghouse in Nineteenth-Century America* (Baltimore, 2007), 3, citing John Modell and Tamara K. Hareven, "Urbanization and the Malleable Household: An Examination of Boarding and Lodging in American Families," *Journal of Marriage and the Family* 35 (1973), 467–479; Michael B. Katz, *The People of Hamilton, Canada West: Family and Class in a Mid-Nineteenth-Century City* (Cambridge, Mass., 1975), 36, 222–236, 264–270; Mark Peel, "On the Margins: Lodgers and Boarders in Boston, 1860–1900," *Journal of American History* 72 (1986), 816–817; and Groth, *Living Downtown,* 92.

7. John Coolidge, *Mill and Mansion: A Study of Architecture and Society in Lowell, Massachusetts, 1820–1865* (New York, 1942), 9–57; Wright, *Building the Dream,* 117–118; Blackmar, *Manhattan for Rent,* 185. See also James Ford, *Slums and Housing* (Cambridge, Mass., 1936), 95; Roy Lubove, *The Progressives and the Slums: Tenement House Reform in New York City, 1890–1917* (Pittsburgh, 1962), 1–4; Lee Philpott, *The Slum and the Ghetto: Neighborhood Deterioration and Middle-Class Reform, Chicago, 1880–1930* (New York, 1978). Note that the Lowell workers' housing was occupied by individual mill hands rather than multiple families.

8. Cromley, *Alone Together,* 20–26.

9. "A Description of the Boston Exchange Coffee-House, written in 1809," 1818 rpt. held at Massachusetts Historical Society; John M. Duncan, *Travels Through Part of the United States and Canada in 1818 and 1819* (Glasgow, 1823), 2: 247; Groth, *Living Downtown,* 38; Molly W. Berger, "The Modern Hotel in America, 1829–1929," Ph.D. diss., Case Western Reserve University, 1997, 81; *Mechanics' Magazine, and Journal of the Mechanics' Institute,* January 1833, 1; Jefferson Williamson, *The American Hotel: An Anecdotal History* (New York, 1930), 116. For more detail on the Boston Exchange Coffee House, see Jane Kamensky, *The Exchange Artist: A Story of Paper, Bricks, and Ash in Early National America* (forthcoming).

10. Admittedly the huge complex at Chaco Canyon and the *Gemeinhauser* of German Pennsylvania were constructed earlier, but neither became a durable building type. On the timing of multiple residences in the United States, see Coolidge, *Mill and Mansion,* 9–57; Wright, *Building the Dream,* 117–118 and chapter 4; Blackmar, *Manhattan for Rent,* 185; Ford, *Slums and Housing,* 95; Hayden, *Grand Domestic Revolution,* 33–37.

11. *Picture of New York* (New York, 1828), transcription at Quinn Hotel Collection, 1828 folder, New-York Historical Society; Daniel Boorstin, *The Americans: The National Experience* (New York, 1965), 145; Groth, *Living Downtown,* 56–57; Anthony Trollope, *North America* (New York, 1863), 2: 174. For other sources on hotel residence, see Carolyn R. Brucken, "Consuming Luxury: Luxury Hotels in Antebellum America, 1825–1860," Ph.D. diss., George Washington University, 1997, 300–302; Stuart M. Blumin, *The Emergence of the Middle Class: Social Experience in the American City, 1760–1900* (New York, 1989), 168.

12. See also Groth, *Living Downtown,* 19–20.

13. Williamson, *American Hotel,* 116; Cromley, *Alone Together,* 67; *New York Times,* 21 November 1865.

14. Blackmar, *Manhattan for Rent,* 194. On the cost of hotels, see I. N. Phelps Stokes, *The Iconography of Manhattan Island* (New York, 1915–1928), 3: 528; *Baltimore Sun,* 17 May 1837; Doris Elizabeth King, "Hotels of the Old South, 1793–1860: A Study of the Origin and Development of the First-Class Hotels," Ph.D. diss., Duke University, 1952, 208*n*93; Williamson, *American Hotel,* 28; James Logan, *Notes of a Journey Through Canada, the United States of America, and the West Indies* (Edinburgh, 1838), 67; *Picture of New York.*

15. Robert A. Margo, "The Rental Price of Housing in New York City, 1830–1860," *Journal of Economic History* 56 (1996), 612–615.

16. Hayden, *Grand Domestic Revolution;* Cromley, *Alone Together; Harper's Weekly,* 5 September 1857, 563, and 26 December 1857, 824.

17. Groth, *Living Downtown,* 62–63.

18. Blackmar, *Manhattan for Rent,* 53–59, 112, 122–125; Cromley, *Alone Together,* 20–24; Groth, *Living Downtown,* 208–211.

19. *New York Times,* 15 March 1864, 21 November 1865; *Harper's Weekly,* 5 September 1857, 563.

20. *Harper's Weekly,* 26 December 1857, 824–826; Junius Henri Browne, *The Great Metropolis: A Mirror of New York* (Hartford, 1869), 398, quoted in Cromley, *Alone Together,* 24. See also *Harper's Weekly,* 5 September 1857, 563; Groth, *Living Downtown,* 216.

21. *Harper's Weekly,* 2 May 1857, 274, and 5 September 1857, 563; Cromley, *Alone Together,* 22–24.

22. Quoted in the *New York Times*, 10 June 1857. See also *Harper's Weekly*, 7 March 1857, 146, and 30 May 1857, 338; *New York Times*, 21 November 1865; Cromley, *Alone Together*, 25–26; Groth, *Living Downtown*, 208–209.

23. Margo, "Rental Price of Housing," 617; *Putnam's Monthly Magazine*, April 1853, 367, March 1854, 1.

24. Vaux's speech was reprinted in *Harper's Weekly*, 19 December 1857, 809–810.

25. Cromley, *Alone Together*, 28–31; "For Sale on Moderate Terms: The Block of Dwelling Houses upon Murray Hill," advertisement, Alexander Jackson Davis Collection II, item 43-1, Avery Architectural Library, Columbia University; Cromley, *Alone Together*, 82–83.

26. Jean Follett, "The Hotel Pelham: A New Building Type for America," *American Art Journal* 15 (1983), 58–73; Douglas Shand-Tucci, *Built in Boston: City and Suburb, 1800–2000* (Boston, 2000), 101–106; Hayden, *Grand Domestic Revolution*, 75. *American Architect and Building News* 1 (1876), 290 (shared laundry), 2 (1877), 188 (kitchenless rooms). See also Groth, *Living Downtown*, 51–52 and 321*n*61.

27. Amy Kallman Epstein, "Multifamily Dwellings and the Search for Respectability: Origins of the New York Apartment House," *Urbanism Past and Present* 10 (1980), 37–39; James M. Goode, *Best Addresses: Apartments in Washington* (Washington, D.C., 1988), 5–7, 29, 536–540; C. W. Westfall, "From Homes to Towers: A Century of Chicago's Best Hotels and Tall Apartment Buildings," in *Chicago Architecture, 1872–1922*, ed. John Zukowsky (Munich, 1987), 269–273. See also Neil Harris, *Chicago Apartments* (Chicago, 2004). On the hybrid of the apartment hotel see Groth, *Living Downtown*, 84–86, and Andrew S. Dolkart, "Millionaires' Elysiums: The Luxury Apartment Hotels of Schultze and Weaver," *Journal of Decorative and Propaganda Arts* 25 (2005), 15–17.

28. *Musgrave v. Sherwood*, 53 How. Pr. 311, N.Y. Sup., 1877 (granting Musgrave a temporary injunction); *Musgrave v. Sherwood*, 23 Hun. 674, 54 How. Pr. 338, N.Y. Sup., 1878 (lifting the injunction and dismissing Musgrave's suit); *Musgrave v. Sherwood*, 76 N.Y. 194, 1879 WL 10612, N.Y., 1879 (affirming the previous ruling). Note that in New York, the Court of Appeals rather than the Supreme Court is the highest court in the state. The relevant tenement house law is found in *Laws of the State of New York, Passed at the Ninetieth Session of the Legislature* (New York, 1867), vol. II, ch. 908, p. 2273. The lawsuit was remarked on in *American Architect and Building News* 2, no. 89 (8 September 1877), 290, and 3, no. 111 (9 February 1878), 45. The latter *AABN* article is cited in Cromley, *Alone Together*, 6.

29. Groth, *Living Downtown*, especially 52.

30. T. DeWitt Talmadge, *The Wedding Ring, A Series of Sermons . . .* (New York, 1886), 119; Cromley, *Alone Together*, 110; Hayden, *Grand Domestic Revolution*, 194.

31. Shand-Tucci, *Built in Boston*, 103; Wright, *Building the Dream*, 138; Cromley, *Alone Together*, 4.

32. Cromley, *Alone Together*, chapter 4, especially 125.

33. Hayden, *Grand Domestic Revolution*, Introduction.

34. Cited ibid., 68–73, 91, 102, 188–189.

35. Ibid., 95, 106–108, 135, 147, 189–192.

10. Accommodating Jim Crow

1. David W. Blight, Introduction to Frederick Douglass, *Narrative of the Life of Frederick Douglass, An American Slave* (Boston, 1993; orig. pub. 1845), 16. For a more legally technical variant of the argument made in this chapter, see A. K. Sandoval-Strausz, "Travelers, Strangers, and Jim Crow: Law, Public Accommodations, and Civil Rights in America," *Law and History Review* 23 (2005), 53–94.

2. Roy E. Finkenbine, "Frederick Douglass," in *American National Biography*, ed. John A. Garraty and Mark Carnes (New York, 1999), 6: 816–819. See also Benjamin Quarles, *Frederick Douglass* (Washington, D.C., 1948), and William S. McFeely, *Frederick Douglass* (New York, 1991).

3. Julia Griffiths, ed., *Autographs for Freedom* (Cleveland, 1853), 160–161.

4. Leon Litwack, *North of Slavery: The Negro in the Free States, 1790–1860* (Chicago, 1961), chapters 3, 4; Richard C. Wade, *Slavery in the Cities: The South, 1820–1860* (New York, 1964), chapter 9; Lorenzo de Zavala, *Viaje a los Estados Unidos del Norte de América* (1834; trans. Wallace Woolsey, Austin, 1980), 110; *McCrea v. Marsh*, 78 Mass. 211 (1858); *Burton v. Scherpf*, 83 Mass. 133 (1861). While there were a few antebellum efforts at securing equal treatment in public accommodations, these were local movements as opposed to the subsequent national political struggle.

5. Eric Foner, *Reconstruction: America's Unfinished Revolution, 1863–1877* (New York, 1988), xxv–xxvii, 77–123; Barbara J. Fields, *Slavery and Freedom on the Middle Ground: Maryland During the Nineteenth Century* (New Haven, 1985), chapters 5, 6; Garfield quoted in Eric Foner, *The Story of American Freedom* (New York, 1998), 100.

6. Freedmen quoted in Julie Saville, *The Work of Reconstruction: From Slave to Wage Laborer in South Carolina, 1860–1870* (New York, 1994), 92.

7. *Dred Scott v. Sandford*, 19 How. (60 U.S.) 393 (1857); Foner, *Reconstruction*, 199.

8. Foner, *Story of American Freedom*, 105; Alfred H. Kelly, Winfred A. Harbison, and Herman Belz, *The American Constitution: Its Origins and Development* (New York, 1991), 332–361. See also Herman Belz, *Reconstructing the Union: Theory and Policy During the Civil War* (New York, 1969); William E. Nelson, *The Fourteenth Amendment: From Political Principle to Judicial Doctrine* (New York, 1988); Robert J. Kaczorowski, *The Politics of Judicial Interpretation: The Federal Courts, Department of Justice, and Civil Rights, 1866–1876* (New York, 1985); Bruce Ackerman, *We the People*, vol. 2, *Transformations* (Cambridge, Mass., 2000); Akhil Reed Amar, *The Bill of Rights: Creation and Reconstruction* (New Haven, 2000).

9. Foner, *Reconstruction*, 368–372; Charles Vincent, *Black Legislators in Louisiana During Reconstruction* (Baton Rouge, 1976), 92–97; C. Vann Woodward, *The Strange Career of Jim Crow* (New York, 1955), 27–28; *The Revised Statute Laws of the State of Louisiana* (New Orleans, 1876), 128–129, 441–443; *A Digest of the Statutes of Arkansas* (Little Rock, 1874), 257–260.

10. *Congressional Globe*, 41st Congress, 2nd Session, 13 May 1870, 3434; *Congressional Globe*, 42nd Congress, 1st Session, 9 March 1871, 21; *Congressional Globe*, 42nd Congress, 2nd Session, 20 December 1871, 244. Alfred Avins's "The Civil Rights Act of 1875: Some Reflected Light on the Fourteenth Amendment and Public Accommodations," *Columbia Law Review* 66 (1964), 873–915, provides a useful overview of the congressional debates over the act, though a caveat must be included that Avins was writing in opposition to the Civil Rights Act of 1964.

11. *Congressional Globe*, 42nd Congress, 2nd Session, 21 December 1871, 279–280; *Congressional Globe*, 42nd Congress, 2nd Session, 8 February 1872, 892–893; *Appendix to the Congressional Record*, 43rd Congress, 1st Session, vol. 2, part 6, 22 May 1874, 318; *Congressional Globe*, 42nd Congress, 2nd Session, 9 February 1872, 928.

12. This is not to suggest that inns preceded carriers every time they were mentioned. In some cases this order was reversed, including in the first draft of the proposed act. Once the debate began in earnest, however, the wording of the act was changed on 18 January 1872 to mention inns before carriers (the form in which it was finally enacted), and Sumner and other supporters of the bill gave precedence to the law of innkeepers. *Congressional Globe*, 42nd Congress, 2nd Session, 22 January 1872, 487. For additional detail, see Sandoval-Strausz, "Travelers, Strangers, and Jim Crow," 61.

13. *Congressional Globe*, 42nd Congress, 2nd Session, 20 December 1871, 242; 21 December 1871, 280; 15 January 1872, 381–383.

14. *Congressional Record,* 43rd Congress, 1st Session, 29 April 1874, 3452–3453; *Congressional Globe,* 42nd Congress, 2nd Session, 6 February 1872, 843; *Congressional Record,* 43rd Congress, 1st Session, vol. 2, part 1, 19 December 1873, 340; 6 January 1874, 427.

15. For letters to Sumner, see *Congressional Globe,* 42nd Congress, 1st Session, 20 December 1871, 244–245, and 2nd Session, 17 January 1872, 429–435, and 31 January 1872, 726–730; *Congressional Record,* 43rd Congress, 1st Session, vol. 2, part 1, 6 January 1874, 408, 19 December 1873, 343–344, and 7 January 1874, 565–567.

16. *Congressional Record,* 43rd Congress, 1st Session, vol. 2, part 1, 6 January 1874, 405. See also, for example, *Congressional Record,* 43rd Congress, 1st Session, 22 May 1874, 4144; *Congressional Globe,* 42nd Congress, 2nd Session, appendix part 6, 25 January 1872, 4 and 6 February 1872, 28–29; On the common law, see chapter 6, note 3. See also Joseph William Singer, "No Right to Exclude: Public Accommodations and Private Property," *Northwestern University Law Review* 90 (1996), 1283–1497, especially 1446, and my response in "Travelers, Strangers, and Jim Crow," 63*n*15.

17. *Appendix to the Congressional Record,* 43rd Congress, 1st Session, vol. 2, part 6, 22 May 1874, 363; *Congressional Record,* 43rd Congress, 2nd Session, 4 February 1875, 1001–1002; *Congressional Globe,* 42nd Congress, 2nd Session, 8 May 1872, 3191; *Congressional Record,* 43rd Congress, 2nd Session, 4 February 1875, 980.

18. For a fuller elaboration of this claim, see Sandoval-Strausz, "Travelers, Strangers, and Jim Crow," especially 54–56, 66–69, 92–94.

19. *Congressional Globe,* 42nd Congress, 2nd Session, 8 February 1872, 893–899, and 21 May 1872, 3729–3740.

20. 18 Stat. 335 (1875).

21. *New York Times,* 2 and 6 March 1875, quoted in John Hope Franklin, "The Enforcement of the Civil Rights Act of 1875," *Prologue,* Winter 1974, 226.

22. Franklin, "Enforcement," 227.

23. *Acts of the 39th Tennessee General Assembly,* 1st Session (1875), 216–217; *Revised Statutes of the State of Delaware* (Wilmington, 1893), 440 (ch. 194, vol. 15, passed 25 March 1875); Franklin, "Enforcement," 227.

24. Franklin, "Enforcement," 226–228, 230.

25. Ibid., 226–227.

26. Ibid., 228–232; Stephen J. Riegel, "The Persistent Career of Jim Crow: Lower Federal Courts and the 'Separate but Equal' Doctrine, 1865–1896," *American Journal of Legal History* 28 (1984), 23.

27. *New York Times,* 19 June 1877; Judge Henry Hilton was no relation to Conrad Hilton.

28. Stephen Birmingham, *Our Crowd: The Great Jewish Families of New York* (New York, 1967), 139–150. Seligman might have used the Civil Rights Act of 1875 to gain access but was probably wary of associating his cause too closely with that of black people, who were increasingly unpopular in white America.

29. Franklin, "Enforcement," 229–233.

30. Kelly, Harbison, and Belz, *American Constitution,* 352–361; Foner, *Reconstruction,* 587.

31. *Civil Rights Cases* (1883), 109 U.S. 3, 11, 17.

32. Ibid., 109 U.S. 3, 26, 38, 41.

33. See Milton R. Konvitz and Theodore Leskes, *A Century of Civil Rights* (New York, 1962), 155–159.

34. *Compiled Statutes of New Jersey* (Newark, 1911), 1442; *Annotated Statutes of the State of Illinois* (Chicago, 1896), ch. 38, ¶84; *Revised Statutes of the State of Indiana* (Chicago, 1888), §1291a. See also *Revised Statutes of Colorado* (Denver, 1908), §609; *Annotated Code of the State of Iowa* (Des Moines, 1897), §5008; *Compiled Laws of the State of Michigan* (Lansing, 1899), §11759; *Annotated Revised Statutes of the State of Ohio* (Cincinnati, 1898), §4426-1. See also Elizabeth Dale, "Social

Equality Does Not Exist Among Themselves, nor Among Us: *Baylies v. Curry* and Civil Rights in Chicago," *American Historical Review* 102 (April 1997), 311–339.

35. Foner, *Reconstruction,* 587–601; Charles Lofgren, *The Plessy Case* (New York, 1986), 20–23. See also Patricia Hagler Minter, "The Failure of Freedom: Class, Gender, and the Evolution of Segregated Transit Law in the Nineteenth-Century South," *Chicago-Kent Law Review* 70 (1995), 993–1009; Kenneth W. Mack, "Law, Society, Identity, and the Making of the Jim Crow South," *Law and Social Inquiry* 24 (1999), 377–409; Edward L. Ayers, *The Promise of the New South: Life After Reconstruction* (Oxford, 1992), 136–146, and on efforts specifically to control black mobility, 150–152.

36. Barbara Young Welke, *Recasting American Liberty: Gender, Race, Law, and the Railroad Revolution, 1865–1920* (New York, 2001), chapter 9, especially 343–348, 358–364, 374; Foner, *Reconstruction,* 587–598; C. Vann Woodward, *Origins of the New South, 1877–1913* (Baton Rouge, 1951), 210–212; Lofgren, *The Plessy Case,* 20–27; Howard N. Rabinowitz, *Race Relations in the Urban South, 1865–1890* (New York, 1978), 182–197. See also Michael Perman, *The Road to Redemption: Southern Politics, 1869–1879* (Chapel Hill, 1984); Ayers, *Promise of the New South.*

37. On the expansion of federal regulatory authority, see Robert Wiebe, *The Search for Order, 1877–1920* (New York, 1967); Stephen Skowronek, *Building a New American State: The Expansion of National Administrative Capacities, 1877–1920* (Cambridge, 1982); Thomas K. McCraw, *Prophets of Regulation* (Cambridge, Mass., 1984); Morton Keller, *Regulating a New Economy: Public Policy and Economic Change in America, 1900–1933* (Cambridge, Mass., 1990), and *Regulating a New Society: Public Policy and Social Change in America, 1900–1933* (Cambridge, Mass., 1994); William J. Novak, "The Legal Origins of the Modern American State," American Bar Foundation Working Paper 9925 (1999).

38. *Mitchell v. United States* (1941), 313 U.S. 80; *Morgan v. Virginia* (1946), 328 U.S. 373; *Henderson v. United States* (1950), 339 U.S. 816. For additional detail, see Sandoval-Strausz, "Travelers, Strangers, and Jim Crow," 81*n*40.

39. *U.S. v. Carolene Products Co.,* 304 U.S. 144 (1938), footnote 4.

40. *Brown v. Board of Education of Topeka, Kansas,* 349 U.S. 294 (1954). For an excellent review of the historiography of the effect of *Brown,* see Michael J. Klarman, "How *Brown* Changed Race Relations: The Backlash Thesis," *Journal of American History* 81 (June 1994), 81–118; John Dittmer, *Local People: The Struggle for Civil Rights in Mississippi* (Urbana, 1994), 41–69; J. Mills Thornton III, *Dividing Lines: Municipal Politics and the Struggle for Civil Rights in Montgomery, Birmingham, and Selma* (Tuscaloosa, 2002), 20–140, especially 47 on the relationship between the boycott and the *Brown* decision.

41. Many efforts at segregation through privatization were recognized for what they were by the courts and disallowed, but establishments that had not been public previously seemed impervious to further federal action. Woodward, *Strange Career,* 158, 162, 167; Catherine A. Barnes, *Journey from Jim Crow: The Desegregation of Southern Transit* (New York, 1983), 101–156; William H. Chafe, *Civilities and Civil Rights: Greensboro, North Carolina, and the Black Struggle for Freedom* (New York, 1980), 65–82; Thornton, *Dividing Lines,* 101–109, 222–225, 254–259; Dittmer, *Local People,* 43, 59.

42. Jack Greenberg, *Race Relations and American Law* (New York, 1959), 82–87, 96–101.

43. Delaware Code Ann. Tit. 24, §1501; Louisiana Acts 1954, no. 194, §1; Tennessee Code Ann. §62-710; Mississippi Code Ann. §2046.5 (1956 Supp.); Florida Statutes Ann. §509.092 (1958 Supp.); Arkansas Act no. 226, §1. Cited in Greenberg, *Race Relations and American Law,* 97, 419. On Alabama, see Senate Commerce Committee Report no. 872, 88th Congress, 2nd Session (1964), 10.

44. Chafe, *Civilities and Civil Rights,* 98–214; Taylor Branch, *Parting the Waters: America in the King Years, 1954–1963* (New York, 1988), chapters 10–22; Taylor Branch, *Pillar of Fire: America in the*

King Years, 1963–65 (New York, 1998), parts 1, 2; Thornton, *Dividing Lines,* 227–230, 239–253; Dittmer, *Local People,* 90–99, 153–157, 165–169, 193–199.

45. Mary L. Dudziak, *Cold War Civil Rights: Race and the Image of American Democracy* (Princeton, 2000), 39–40, 152–248.

46. *Civil Rights Act of 1964,* 78 Stat. 241. The act did not mention modes of transportation because these had already been officially desegregated by ICC order.

47. 88th Congress, Senate Committee on Judiciary Published Hearing, CIS no. 88 S1592 (three parts); 88th Congress, House Committee on Judiciary Published Hearing, CIS no. 88 H2036 (four parts); 88th Congress, Senate Committee on Commerce, *Civil Rights—Public Accommodations,* CIS no. 88 S1580-0, especially 9–10, 22. On the Civil Rights Act more generally, see Charles Whalen and Barbara Whalen, *The Longest Debate: A Legislative History of the 1964 Civil Rights Act* (Washington, D.C., 1985); Robert D. Loevy, *To End All Segregation: The Politics of the Passage of the Civil Rights Act of 1964* (Lanham, Md., 1990); Robert D. Loevy, ed., *The Civil Rights Act of 1964: The Passage of the Law that Ended Segregation* (Albany, 1997).

48. Senate Commerce Committee Hearings, 656–657; House Judiciary Hearings, 2223; Brief of Appellees in *Heart of Atlanta v. U.S.,* 42–43.

49. It is not clear whether Rolleston had direct knowledge of *Commonwealth v. Mitchel;* my point here involves shared logic rather than necessarily direct textual borrowing. Richard C. Cortner, *Civil Rights and Public Accommodations: The Heart of Atlanta and McClung Cases* (Lawrence, Kan., 2001), 35–37; Brief of Appellant in *Heart of Atlanta Motel v. United States,* 16, 32, 40–45, 51–58. For a detailed account of litigation against the act, see Cortner, *Civil Rights and Public Accommodations,* especially 90–96, 106–114.

50. Brief of Appellees in *Heart of Atlanta v. U.S.,* 8–13, 38–39, 42–43, 48–56.

51. Brief of the State of California as *Amicus Curiae,* 1, 4–8, 6–7; Brief of the Attorney General of the State of New York as *Amicus Curiae* in Support of Affirmance, 1, 3–10; *Amicus Curiae* Brief on Behalf of the Commonwealth of Massachusetts, 1, 16.

52. Brief of Appellees, 56–59, 61. See also State of New York as *Amicus Curiae,* 9–10: "The Civil Rights Act of 1964 only deprives operators of public places catering to transients of the freedom to deny their accommodations to a segment of the public, a so-called freedom that innkeepers never had under the common law."

53. Transcript of oral arguments, *In the United States District Court for the Northern District of Georgia,* 52, 62–66.

54. Oral argument transcript from Philip B. Kurland et al., eds., *Landmark Briefs and Arguments of the Supreme Court of the United States: Constitutional Law* (Washington, D.C., 1975–), 60: 15–16, 21–25, 44–53. Cox also pointed out that Rolleston's claims implied "that the Anglo-American common law for centuries has subjected to slavery innkeepers, hackmen, carriers, wharfage men, ferriers, and all kinds of other people holding themselves out to serve the public." Kurland, *Landmark Briefs,* 60: 42.

55. *Heart of Atlanta Motel v. United States* (1964), 379 U.S. 241, 252–253, 256, 260–261.

56. Ibid., 379 U.S. 241, 251–253, 256, 258–261. It is worth noting that travel was also a key issue in *Katzenbach v. McClung,* the companion case to *Heart of Atlanta Motel,* which dealt with the Civil Rights Act's applicability to a local barbecue restaurant far from any interstate thoroughfares and serving a local clientele. See *Katzenbach v. McClung* (1964), 379 U.S. 300.

Conclusion

1. Immanuel Kant, *Toward Perpetual Peace*, in *Immanuel Kant: Practical Philosophy*, ed. and trans. Mary J. Gregor (Cambridge, 1996), 313, 328–331. All emphases in original.

2. Martha C. Nussbaum et al., *For Love of Country: Debating the Limits of Patriotism*, ed. Joshua Cohen (Boston, 1996), which reprints parts of an exchange between Nussbaum and a number of respondents that began in the *Boston Review* (October–November 1994); Pheng Cheah and Bruce Robbins, eds., *Cosmopolitics: Thinking and Feeling Beyond the Nation* (Minneapolis, 1998); Carol Appadurai Breckenridge, Homi K. Bhabha, and Dipesh Chakrabarty, eds., *Cosmopolitanism* (Durham, N.C., 2002); Steven Vertovec and Robin Cohen, eds., *Conceiving Cosmopolitanism: Theory, Context, and Practice* (New York, 2002); Daniele Archibugi, ed., *Debating Cosmopolitics* (New York, 2003); David A. Hollinger, *Cosmopolitanism and Solidarity: Studies in Ethnoracial, Religious, and Professional Affiliation in the United States* (Madison, Wisc., 2006). Hollinger's essay in Vertovec and Cohen, *Conceiving Cosmopolitanism*, provides the best summary of the extent of the cosmopolitanism debate. See also Stephen Toulmin, *Cosmopolis: The Hidden Agenda of Modernity* (New York, 1990); Daniele Archibugi and David Held, eds., *Cosmopolitan Democracy: An Agenda for a New World Order* (Cambridge, 1995); Timothy Brennan, *At Home in the World: Cosmopolitanism Now* (Cambridge, Mass., 1997); John Rawls, *The Law of Peoples* (Cambridge, Mass., 1999); Pico Iyer, *The Global Soul: Jet Lag, Shopping Malls, and the Search for Home* (New York, 2000); Bonnie Honig, *Democracy and the Foreigner* (Princeton, 2003); Jacques Derrida and Anne Dufourmantelle, *Of Hospitality* (Stanford, 2000); Mireille Rossello, *Postcolonial Hospitality: The Immigrant as Guest* (Stanford, 2001).

3. The phrase *material cosmopolitanism* parallels Dolores Hayden's term *material feminism* as used in her influential study *The Grand Domestic Revolution: A History of Feminist Designs for American Homes, Neighborhoods, and Cities* (Cambridge, Mass., 1981).

4. See J. B. Jackson, *American Space* (New York, 1977).

5. "16 Firms Face NAACP Picketing," *Atlanta Journal*, 3 July 1962, echoing Luke 2:7.

6. See Olivia Remie Constable, *Housing the Stranger in the Mediterranean World: Lodging, Trade, and Travel in Late Antiquity and the Middle Ages* (Cambridge, 2003); Felicity Heal, *Hospitality in Early Modern England* (Cambridge, 1991); Rebecca Spang, *The Invention of the Restaurant: Paris and Modern Gastronomic Culture* (Cambridge, Mass., 2000); John Torpey, *The Invention of the Passport: Surveillance, Citizenship, and the State* (Cambridge, 2000); Ciro Caraballo Perichi, *Hoteleria y Turismo en la Venezuela Gomecista* (Caracas, 1993). See also Daryl W. Palmer, *Hospitable Performances: Dramatic Genre and Cultural Practices in Early Modern England* (West Lafayette, Ind., 1992); James William Brodman, *Charity and Welfare: Hospitals and the Poor in Medieval Catalonia* (Philadelphia, 1998); Katharine Brophy Dubois, "Strangers and Sojourners: Pilgrims, Penance, and Urban Geography in Late Medieval Rome," Ph.D. diss., University of Michigan, 2001.

7. A number of examples are recorded on the Web site of the U.S. Department of State at http://www.state.gov/r/pa/ho/pubs/fs/5902.htm.

ACKNOWLEDGMENTS

The idea for this book first came to me as I sat in the lobby of the Palmer House in Chicago in the spring of 1996, but its true origins date back to more than a quarter-century earlier.

My parents, to whom this book is dedicated, provided wonderful homes for me and made my childhood and adolescence almost impossibly happy. Together, the old-school European intellectual and the new-style Latin American woman of letters taught me the joy of learning and, later, of teaching. I only wish that my dear mother had lived long enough to read this book, and to be vexed by my grammar when she heard me say, "*¡Este e' para tí, Mamita!*"

My teachers in elementary and high school were fabulously dedicated, endlessly creative, and absolutely indispensable to anything I might have achieved after leaving their classrooms. My sincerest thanks to Mr. Ofori-Mankata at the United Nations International School, Mrs. Browne at Siwanoy School, and the faculty and staff at Rye Country Day School, especially Mr. Angus-Smith, Mrs. Black, Coach Effinger, Mr. Godfrey, Mrs. Jones and Mr. Jones, Mr. Koskores, Dr. Lipnick, Miss Marks, Mr. Moore, Mr. Paige, Mr. Pike, Ms. Reichhardt, Mr. Robertson, and Miss Schlotter.

Imitation is the sincerest form of flattery, and my college history professors at Columbia made me want to become one myself. I am grateful to my undergraduate mentor Kenneth T. Jackson, who sparked my interest in urban history and persuaded me that the best New Yorkers often come from somewhere else, and to Mark Carnes, István Deák, Eric Foner, and James Shenton.

The University of Chicago Department of History was a marvelous place to learn the historian's craft. Kathleen Conzen inspired absolute trust, offered trenchant and constructive criticism of my archival research, conceptualization, organization, and writing style, mobilized institutional support, explained scholarly protocols, displayed great patience, and invariably pointed me in the right direction. Neil Harris imparted skills without which I could never have undertaken this project. He proposed that I seek out architectural and visual evidence as avidly as textual sources, and taught me how to interpret them. Bill Novak's distinctive combination of broad historiographic vision and unparalleled intellectual exuberance meant that I always left his office excited about my work and eager to get back to it. Amy Stanley provided amazingly detailed critiques and professional encouragement when I needed them most. For further instruction and advice, thanks to George Chauncey, Tom Holt, Mae Ngai, and Julie Saville.

My time at the University of Chicago was also the most fun I've ever had. It was my distinct honor and great pleasure to have studied and socialized with Gabriela Arredondo,

Kathleen Brosnan, Cathleen Cahill, Tom Chappelear, David Churchill, Andrew Cohen, Eduardo Contreras, Drew Digby, Sean Forner, Daniel Greene, John Hankey (to whom thanks for countless conversations, citations, and chapter edits, locutional coaching, field trips nationwide, and his and Frances Hankey's extraordinary hospitality), Karrin Hanshew, Marc Jolin, Geoff Klingsporn, Scott Lien, Matthew Lindsay, Gretchen Long, Donn MacMinn, Ian McGiver, Ajay Mehrotra, Rebekah Mergenthal, Megan Miller, Andrew Oppenheimer, Kim Reilly, Greta Rensenbrink, Laurel Spindel, David Tanenhaus, Tiffany Trotter, Neda Ulaby, Kyle Volk, Mike Wakeford, Amber Wilke, Michael Willrich, and Mark Wilson. Contrary to popular folklore about graduate school in general and Chicago in particular, the people in history and allied fields created a supportive, sociable, festive, and even romantic milieu. Seriously—check our rate of endogamy.

At the University of New Mexico, colleagues past and present have provided intellectual fellowship, good advice, and constant help with my work. I want to express my appreciation to all, especially Beth Bailey, John Barney, Judy Bieber, Cathleen Cahill, David Farber, Dan Feller, Miguel Gandert, Tim Moy, Noel Pugach, Patricia Risso, Rob Robbins, Jay Rubenstein, Enrique Sanabria, Virginia Scharff, Jane Slaughter, Jason Scott Smith, Frank Szasz, Sam Truett, Chris Wilson, and Mel Yazawa. Thanks also to Heather Hawkins for intrepid research assistance, and for that disco ball.

The archival research that went into this book would not have been possible without financial assistance, and I offer my sincerest thanks for the support of the University of Chicago Division of the Social Sciences, the Andrew W. Mellon Foundation, Harvard Business School, the New-York Historical Society, the Library Company of Philadelphia, the Massachusetts Historical Society, the Huntington Library and Art Collections, and the University of New Mexico Research Allocation Committee. For subvention assistance, I thank the Historical Society of New Mexico, and at the University of New Mexico, University College, the College of Arts and Sciences, the Department of History, and the Feminist Research Institute.

In the process of research and writing, I have benefited from the intellectual acumen and tremendous generosity of colleagues, friends, and family who have listened to preliminary ideas, read drafts, identified flaws in my arguments, proposed alternate formulations, passed along archival finds, suggested relevant readings, offered encouragement, saved me from factual and interpretive errors, and generally speaking made this a better book than it would have been without their help. I am deeply grateful to Elizabeth Blackmar, Cathleen Cahill, Wendy Gamber, Paul Groth, John Hankey, Ellen Levine, Dan Levinson Wilk, Virginia Scharff, Jason Scott Smith, Ivan Strausz, and Chris Wilson for having read and critiqued the entire manuscript, and to Molly Berger, Carolyn Brucken, Chris Capozzola, Tom Carter, Jeff Cohen, Lizabeth Cohen, Michael Conzen, Seth Cotlar, Elizabeth Collins Cromley, Lisa Pfueller Davidson, Bill Deverell, Jim Grossman, Dolores Hayden, Kim Hoagland, Tom Hubka, Alison Isenberg, Richard John, Jane Kamensky, Linda Kerber, William Leach, John Majewski, Martha McNamara, Cecilia Miller, Eric Morser, Mary Ryan, Sharon Salinger, David Scobey, Pam Simpson, Ellen Stroud, Chris Tomlins, Dell

Upton, Barbara Welke, Annabel Wharton, and Sharon Wood (to whom thanks also for professional advice, timely introductions, and superb cocktail recipes) for helping with various chapters, articles, conference papers, and thoughts-in-progress. I could not have completed this project without the invaluable assistance of the people at dozens of state and local historical societies and state historic preservation offices, or without the incredible online collections of the Library of Congress, the National Museum of American History, and the New York Public Library. I also want to thank the many panelists and participants at the annual meetings of the Vernacular Architecture Forum, the Urban History Association, the Organization of American Historians, and the Business History Conference.

When the time came to find a publisher, Ellen Levine, my longtime friend and literary agent nonpareil, shaped and shepherded the book proposal, advised me on my prose style, and brought me together with the perfect press for this project, for which she has my heartfelt thanks. At Yale University Press, Chris Rogers showed unmatched editorial vision and was positively heroic in arranging for the illustrations needed for my scholarly arguments while simultaneously making this book accessible and available to a broader audience. Assistant editor Laura Davulis guided me through the production process with skill and flair, manuscript editor Dan Heaton excised errors, repaired infelicitous phrasings, and made me laugh out loud with his witty marginalia, and designer Sonia Shannon made the book into an objet d'art.

Over the years, friends and family from beyond the academy have sustained me with their emotional warmth, lively conversation, wild parties, wise counsel, holiday observances, celebrations of happy news, and sympathy for sad tidings. For all this and much more, my appreciation and affection to Rungson Samroengraja, Andi Jones, Michael Parker, Alisha Tonsic, Jennifer English, Ezra Kenigsberg, Juliet DeMasi, Abraham Waya, and Fredrik Wallenberg; and to the Nathensons, Bea and Sam Levine, Dennis and Pam Cahill, Kevin Cahill, and Christine and Bill Disbrow.

Finally, I want to acknowledge the person who perfectly combines sweetness and mischief, who encourages my modest virtues and restrains my manifest faults, who makes the rhythms and routines of everyday life into a pageant of wonder and delight: my friend, my love, my bride, my companion, accomplice, and confidante, Cathleen.

Frontispiece "St. Nicholas Hotel, Broadway, New York, Uriah Welch, Proprietor," PR020, Geographic File (Flat), Prints, Hotels N–Z, negative number 43370. **1** © Robert Reck **2** Image from *Town and Country,* 1912, box 14, folder 24, Warshaw Collection of Business Americana—Hotels, Archives Center **3** T. Sinclairs Lith., *Eagle Hotel, No. 139 North 3rd Street, Philadelphia,* c. 1855, *W102[P.2040] **1.1** Print from Isaac Weld, *Travel Through the States of North America* (London, 1798) **1.2** John Johnson, *Green Dragon Tavern,* watercolor, 1773 **1.3** John Lewis Krimmel, *Village Tavern,* 1813–14, Florence Scott Libbey Bequest in Memory of Maurice A. Scott, 1954.13 **1.4** William Birch, detail from *Bank of Pennsylvania,* Sn 27b/P.8717 **1.5** J. Banton, *Watercolor of Blodget's Hotel* (1818) **1.6** G. Hayward, "City Hotel, Trinity & Grace Churches, Broadway 1831 . . . for Valentine's Manual 1854" **1.7** *Theatre, Assembly Rooms and an Hotel,* Richmond, Virginia, ADE-UNIT 2885, no. 10, Benjamin Henry Latrobe Archive **1.8** Frontispiece from *Omnium Gatherum* (Boston) 1 (1809) **1.9** *Theatre, Assembly Rooms and an Hotel,* Richmond, Virginia, ADE-UNIT 2885, no. 6, Benjamin Henry Latrobe Archive **1.10** N. Currier, *Washington's Reception by the Ladies, on Passing the Bridge at Trenton, N.J., April, 1789* (New York, 1845) **2.1** City Hotel, color plate in John H. B. Latrobe, *Picture of Baltimore* (1842) **2.2** National Hotel, Washington City, Bella Landauer Collection of Business and Advertising Ephemera, PR-031, box 63, folder "East Coast Region" **2.3** D. S. Quintin, "United States Hotel, Chestnut Street, Philadelphia," in *Nature on Stone* (Philadelphia, c. 1842), *W417[P.2228] **2.4** Samuel Walker, pub., *View of Tremont House, Boston* (n.d.) **2.5** Map by author, rendered by Natalie Hanemann **2.6** From the LHS Archive **2.7** Box 16, folder 39, Warshaw Collection of Business Americana—Hotels, Archives Center **2.8** *St. Charles Hotel in Flames,* 1992.156 **2.9** First Galt House, Subject Photos, HOT-24 **2.10** J. W. Orr, *The First American Hotel,* in Frank H. Severance, *Picture Book of Earlier Buffalo* (Buffalo, 1912), 164 **2.11** Society Photo Archive **2.12** John W. Barber, Main Street, Cleveland **2.13** Franklin House, 195 Broadway, Hayes and Treadwell, Bella Landauer Collection of Business and Advertising Ephemera, PR-031, box 61, folder "NYC Hotels, Misc. D-F" **2.14** Stock certificate lost from Pratt Library, Baltimore, but reproduced in Doris E. King, "Hotels of the Old South" (Ph.D. diss., Duke University, 1952), following 47 **2.15** Revere House at Bowdoin Square, Bostonian Society Library and Special Collections #000224 **3.1** Christopher Colles, *A survey of the roads of the United States of America* (New York, 1789), "New York to Stratford," Am 1789 Col, 60691.0 **3.2** *Harper's Weekly,* 28 April 1883 **3.3** Pearl Street House and Ohio Hotel, delineator and engraver M. Osborne, MCNY #44.126.9 **3.4** Box 4, folder 51, Warshaw Collection of Business Americana—Hotels, Archives Center **3.5** Wurts Brothers, "Manhattan: Greenwich Street–Cedar Street," 1914, *Photographic Views of New York City,* Milstein Division of United States History, Local History, and Genealogy **3.6** Glass negative DN-0062007, Chicago, 1914, Photographer—Chicago Daily News **3.7** J. R. Smith, *Catskill Mountain-House* (Philadelphia, 1830) **3.8** Edward Beyer, *Album of Virginia* (Richmond, 1858) **3.9** *Frank Leslie's Illustrated Newspaper,* 2 September 1876 **3.10** Unknown photographer and printer, postcard #4411 **3.11** Plate 15 from Andrew J. Russell, *The Great West Illustrated in a Series of Photographic Views Across the Continent,* Yale Collection of Western Americana **3.12** Linda Beierle Bullen/Pullman State Historic Site **3.13** New Hampshire Central House, Goffstown, New Hampshire, c. 1865, NHHS Collections **3.14** National Hotel, Forbestown, Butte County, California, Bancroft Library #BANC PIC 1905.10710-CASE **3.15** Champion Temperance Hotel business card, Bella Landauer Collection of Business and Advertising Ephemera, PR-031, box 63, folder "NY State, Misc." **3.16** Union Hotel, Chattanooga, Tennessee, c. 1899, Prints and Photographs Division #LOT 11306 **3.17** *Gazlay's United States Hotel Guide* (1875), title page **3.18** Centennial Exposition, Park View Hotel, Bella Landauer Collection of Business and

Advertising Ephemera, box 63, folder "Hotels, PA" **3.19** *Harper's Weekly,* 27 May 1876 **3.20** *Harper's Weekly,* 25 November 1876 **4.1** Clipping from the *City Argus,* San Francisco, 1893 **4.2** Produced by the Krebs Lithographing Company of Cincinnati, c. 1900 **4.3** *Harper's Weekly,* 20 November 1886 **4.4** Detroit Publishing Company, postcard #13555 **4.5** Keystone View Company, "Hotel del Coronado, San Diego, Calif.," c. 1928, Prints and Photographs Division, Stereo U.S. Geog. File—California—San Diego—Hotels **4.6** Harris Co., "Alcázar, Córdova & Ponce de León, St. Augustine, Florida," 1910, Prints and Photographs Division #PAN U.S. Geog.—Florida no. 6 **4.7** Colonial Hotel, Nassau, box 4, folder 31, Warshaw Collection of Business Americana—Hotels, Archives Center **4.8** I.C.C. Hotel Tivoli, 1910, Prints and Photographs Division, Foreign Geog. File—Panama **4.9** Eric de Mare, Queen's Hotel, The Promenade, Cheltenham, Gloucestershire, NMR Reference #AA98/04301 **4.10** Detroit Publishing Company #16546, "Victoria Hotel, Unter den Linden, Berlin, Germany," 1905, Prints and Photographs Division #LOT 13411, no. 0340 **4.11** "Raffles Hotel in early 1900 with verandah," from Raffles picture stock **4.12** Glass negative, DN-0006911, Chicago, 1909, Photographer—*Chicago Daily News* **4.13** A. Loeffler, Waldorf-Astoria, New York, c. 1901, Prints and Photographs Division #LOT 5941-1 **4.14** Wurts Brothers, "The Hotel Plaza, New York," Photography Collection, Miriam and Ira D. Wallach Division of Art, Prints, and Photographs **4.15** R. J. Waters and Co., San Francisco, Fairmont Hotel, San Francisco, California, c. 1920, Prints and Photographs Division, U.S. Geog. File—California—San Francisco—Buildings **4.16** Detroit Publishing Company, postcard #70423, c. 1912 **4.17** Lisa Pfueller Davidson **4.18** F. Graham Cootes, "Prince Geo. Hotel," Art and Architecture Collection, Miriam and Ira D. Wallach Division of Art, Prints and Photographs **5.1** Hotel Astor, sectional drawing, 1915, The Byron Collection, MCNY #93.1.1.5403 **5.2** Henry Glassie, *Vernacular Architecture* (Bloomington, Ind., 2000), 119 **5.3** Gabrielle M. Lanier and Bernard L. Herman, *Everyday Architecture of the Mid-Atlantic* (Baltimore, 1997), 33 **5.4** Old Stone Tavern, Main Street, Greenwich, Cumberland County, New Jersey, HABS NJ, 6-GREWI **5.5** Plans of Exchange Coffee House, Principal Story and Fourth Gallery, Bostonian Society Library and Special Collections **5.6** Plans of Tremont House, part II, Bostonian Society Library and Special Collections Neg. 1618 **5.7** John Haviland, Philadelphia Arcade, Burd Papers, Am. 0364 **5.8** Robert Mills, *Guide to the National Executive Offices* (Washington, 1841), 14 **5.9** Box 109, folder 5, Warshaw Collection of Business Americana—Hotels, Archives Center **5.10** *Hotel Monthly,* January 1913, 61 **5.11** Ground Plan of Asylum Building, *Annual Report* (Philadelphia, 1855–1861), front matter, (7)1322.F.485b **5.12** Box 13, folder 66, box 14, folder 49, box 1, folder 28, box 14, folder 23, Warshaw Collection of Business Americana—Hotels, Archives Center **5.13** L. C. McClure, "Lobby of the Brown Palace," Western History Collection, MCC-2401 **5.14** H. S. Poley, "Victor Hotel Lobby," Western History Collection, P-2021 **5.15** Hotel Register, Manuscripts, BV St. Nicholas Hotel **5.16** George C. Boldt, "Royal Suite, Waldorf-Astoria Hotel" (1902), Prints and Photographs Division # LOT 3247 (H) **5.17** *Harper's Weekly,* 13 April 1878 **5.18** T. de Thustrup, Lobby of a Chicago Hotel in Winter, *Harper's Weekly,* 25 March 1893 **5.19** Print from *A Traveler's Sketch* (Philadelphia, 1861) **5.20** *Harper's Weekly,* 1 October 1859 **5.21** New Haven Hotel, Menu, Bella Landauer Collection of Business and Advertising Ephemera, PR-031, box 63, folder "East Coast Region" **5.22** *Harper's Weekly,* 1 October 1859 **5.23** Cullen, after Cary, *The reading-room of the Fifth Avenue Hotel, discussing the news from Chicago,* 1871, Picture Collection, The Branch Libraries **5.24** Print from *A Traveler's Sketch* (Philadelphia, 1861) **5.25** Box 11, folder 70, Warshaw Collection of Business Americana—Hotels, Archives Center **5.26** *Harper's Weekly,* 21 February 1874 **6.1** H. T. Anthony and Co., "Burnet House," stereoscopic view #7578 from *Views in and Around Cincinnati, Ohio* (n.d.) **6.2** *Frank Leslie's Illustrated Newspaper,* 26 June 1858 **7.1** Strobridge Litho. Company, "Hotel Topsy Turvy," POS-TH-1899.H68, no. 1, Theatrical Poster Collection **7.2** *National Police Gazette,* 20 January 1894 **7.3** *National Police Gazette,* 26 July 1879 **7.4** Allan Pinkerton, *Thirty Years a Detective* (New York, 1884), facing 96 **7.5** *National Police Gazette,* 12 March 1904 **7.6** *National Police Gazette,* 13 December 1845 **8.1** Anonymous, "Manhattan: Nassau Street–Washington Street," *Photographic Views of New York City,* Milstein Division of United States History, Local History, and Genealogy **8.2** © 2006 Board of Trustees, National Gallery of Art **8.3, 8.4, 8.5** A. K. Sandoval-Strausz and

John C. Barney **8.6** Detroit Publishing Company, postcard #10295 **8.7** Geo. R. Lawrence Co., "Twenty-seventh Annual Banquet of the Hotel Association of New York City, Waldorf-Astoria," 1906, Prints and Photographs Division, Pan Subject—Groups no. 280 **8.8** *Gleason's Pictorial Drawing-Room Companion,* 17 May 1851, and H. S. Poley, "President Roosevelt in front of the Antlers Hotel, Colo. Springs," c. 1901–1903, Western History/Genealogy Department, #P-536 **8.9** From Sara T. L. Robinson, *Kansas: Its Interior and Exterior Life* (1856), KSHS Item No. 100051 **8.10** *Harper's Weekly,* 28 April 1860 **8.11** *Harper's Weekly,* 2 March 1861, and *Frank Leslie's Illustrated Newspaper,* 16 March 1861 **8.12** *Harper's Weekly,* 23 February 1861 **8.13** Thomas Nast, "Abraham Lincoln in Willard's Hotel in Washington," March 1861, Prints and Photographs Division # E457.R74 **9.1** *Frank Leslie's Illustrated Newspaper,* 15 December 1860 **9.2** *Harper's Weekly,* 12 August 1871 **9.3** *Harper's Weekly,* 19 December 1857 **9.4** *Architectural Record,* July 1901, 479 **9.5** Hotel Pelham, Boylston Street, Bostonian Society Library and Special Collections #002202 **9.6** *American Architect and Building News* 27 (January 1890), 3 **10.1** Lithographer unknown, Lithograph ICHi-22125, "The Shackle Broken—By the Genius of Freedom" (n.p., 1874) **10.2** *Harper's Weekly,* 17 April 1875 **10.3** Bill Young/*Atlanta Journal-Constitution* **4** Box 10, folder 53, Warshaw Collection of Business Americana—Hotels, Archives Center.

Details from the following illustrations appear on part- and chapter-opening pages: **2** page 228; **3** page 136; **1.3** page 13; **2.15** page 45; **3.9** page 10; **3.16** page 75; **4.3** page 110; **5.13** page 142; **6.1** page 186; **7.1** page 203; **8.2** page 231; **9.5** page 263; **10.3** page 284.

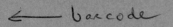